In *All I Need*, Mary Suggs delivers a collection of insightfully written, spiritually enriching, and personally challenging meditations that are eminently readable. Like a warm cup of coffee in the morning, these devotional thoughts will help you come to life each day; more importantly, they will help you come to God. I am grateful for Mary's thoughtful contribution to this often simplistic genre. I plan to use *All I Need* myself as well as recommend it to the pastors and leaders I serve.

Dr. Samuel D. Rima
Executive Minister, Columbia Baptist Conference

The fuel empowering the church is great thoughts of God with great love for God. *All I Need*, brings together a potent blend of both. This book will help us lift our eyes above this world and aspire after things above. Nothing could be more purifying and energizing.

Raymond C. Ortlund Jr.
First Presbyterian Church, Augusta, Georgia

Mary Suggs offers us the best of gifts—a daily invitation to worship through the whisper of the Word itself. This is a book to be treasured.

Nancy Groom
Author of *Risking Intimacy*

In the face of all the demands of life, practicing the presence of God remains supremely important. This practice centers on daily devotion, and this book is a tool from a seasoned Christian that can add a dimension of delight. This devotional is unique in that it includes Scripture, doctrine, teaching, application, and challenge. Even more than that, it touches the human spirit. Thank God for this vehicle of transportation into the presence of God.

Pastor Joey Johnson
Senior Pastor, the House of the Lord

This devotional focuses on the beauty and power of Scripture, adds related thoughts from outstanding Christian writers, and completes the reading with a sensitive but penetrating thought from the author. The sentences from the Bible beginning each devotional are woven together in a wonderfully creative way, allowing Scripture to reinforce and interpret Scripture. On nearly every page, I found the biblical passages reminding me of the words of hymns and worship choruses, a connection that adds yet another Spirit-led dimension to the devotional.

Ronald G. Johnson
President, Malone College

Frequently I remind college students, "If you think you don't need anyone, you just haven't lived long enough." Sooner or later, life teaches us what our pride does not want to admit. We need help, most importantly from the Lord. *All I Need* is a treasure trove of wisdom celebrating the character, promises, and provision of the Sovereign Creator God. As the author puts it, "He Seeks Us," "Look Only to Him." You can't read this book without uttering praise.

Rex M. Rogers
President, Cornerstone University

ALL I NEED

Meditations on the Master

Compiled by Mary Morrison Suggs

Fleming H. Revell

A Division of Baker Book House Co
Grand Rapids, Michigan 49516

Published by Fleming H. Revell
a division of Baker Book House Company
P.O. Box 6287, Grand Rapids, MI 49516-6287

Printed in the United States of America

Library of Congress Cataloging-in-Publication Data

All I need / compiled by Mary Morrison Suggs.
    p.   cm.
Includes bibliographical references and index.
ISBN 0-8007-1791-0
1. Devotional calendars. I. Suggs, Mary Morrison.

BV4810 .A45 2001
242´.2—dc21   2001041797

To Bob

Together we have learned that God is all we need

GOD OF ALL

David expressed his praises to the Lord: . . . Riches and honor come from you alone, and you are the Ruler of all mankind; your hand controls power and might, and it is at your discretion that men are made great and given strength. ❖ Even heaven and the highest heaven cannot contain you. ❖ God that made the world and all things therein, seeing that he is Lord of heaven and earth, dwelleth not in temples made with hands. ❖ For by Him all things were created that are in heaven and that are on earth, visible and invisible, whether thrones or dominions or principalities or powers. All things were created through Him and for Him. ❖ Therefore You are great, O Lord GOD. For there is none like You, nor is there any God besides You. ❖ Who is like you, O LORD, among the gods? Who is like you, majestic in holiness, awesome in splendor, doing wonders? ❖ To him be glory now and for all eternity!

1 CHRON. 29:10, 12 TLB; 1 KINGS 8:27 NRSV; ACTS 17:24; COL. 1:16 NKJV;
2 SAM. 7:22 NKJV; EXOD. 15:11 NRSV; 2 PETER 3:18 NEB

From Him and through Him and to Him are all things; to Him be the glory forever (Rom. 11:36). This is the design, the inner logic, and the intention of all reality.

RAYMOND C. ORTLUND

Because He is "spirit" He fills heaven and earth.

ARTHUR W. PINK

The Psalmist . . . cried: "My soul, wait thou only upon God, for my expectation is from him. He only is my rock and my salvation: he is my defense; I shall not be moved. In God is my salvation and my glory: the rock of my strength and my refuge is in God."

At last God was everything to him; and then he found that God was enough.

HANNAH WHITALL SMITH

It was said of Moses that he spent forty years in the wilderness learning to be nothing so that he might spend the next forty years proving God to be everything.

JAMES MONTGOMERY BOICE

God of power and majesty, help me find my everything in you.
God of the universe, you are all I need.

HE IS OVER ALL

I am the Alpha and Omega, the first and the last, the beginning and the end. ❖ From eternity to eternity I am God. No one can oppose what I do. ❖ Consider the work of God; for who can make straight what He has made crooked? ❖ For You are great, and do wondrous things; You alone are God. ❖ The LORD gave, and the LORD hath taken away; blessed be the name of the LORD. ❖ Let the name of God be blessed forever and ever, for wisdom and power belong to Him. And it is He who changes the times and the epochs; He removes kings and establishes kings; He gives wisdom to wise men, and knowledge to men of understanding. ❖ Let them know that you alone, whose name is the LORD, are the Most High over all the earth. ❖ For of him, and through him, and to him, are all things: to whom be glory for ever. Amen.

REV. 22:13 NEB; ISA. 43:13 TLB; ECCLES. 7:13 NKJV; PS. 86:10 NKJV; JOB 1:21; DAN. 2:20–21 NASB; PS. 83:18 NRSV; ROM. 11:36

God's sovereignty is the attribute by which He rules His entire creation and to be sovereign God must be all-knowing, all-powerful, and absolutely free.

A. W. TOZER

You will feel that He must rule and control each day. All of life and conversation must be in the Spirit. My prayer, my faith, my fellowship with the Father, and all my work in God's service, must be completely under His sway. As the Spirit of Holiness, He is the Spirit of my sanctification.

ANDREW MURRAY

If God is sovereign, and he is on our side, then nothing can stop him from his determination to keep us secure.

R. C. SPROUL

How do I respond to God's sovereignty? With worship and obedience or with indifference or fear?
What parts of my life are still not under his control?

GOD IS UNCHANGING

The LORD God of their fathers, the God of Abraham, the God of Isaac, and the God of Jacob, has appeared to you. ❖ The Glory of Israel will not lie or change His mind. ❖ He is mighty in strength and wisdom. ❖ The counsel of the LORD stands forever, the plans of His heart from generation to generation. ❖ But you are the same, and your years have no end. ❖ The Creator . . . shines forever without change or shadow. ❖ When all things began, the Word already was. The Word dwelt with God, and what God was, the Word was. The Word, then, was with God at the beginning. ❖ Jesus Christ never changes! He is the same yesterday, today, and forever.

EXOD. 4:5 NKJV; 1 SAM. 15:29 NASB; JOB 36:5; PS. 33:11 NASB; PS. 102:27 NRSV; JAMES 1:17 TLB; JOHN 1:1–2 NEB; HEB. 13:8 CEV

All God's reasons come from within His uncreated being. Nothing has entered the being of God from eternity, nothing has been removed, and nothing has been changed.

A. W. TOZER

His words are as true as his own existence. He is unchangeable. He has never had to alter one saying or call back a single sentence.

CHARLES HADDON SPURGEON

You, O Lord, never change. Just as you loved Adam, you love me. You knew Adam's need and provided a companion for him. And you meet my needs. Just as you loved and protected Noah, telling him how to make a boat that would keep him safe, you protect me. Just as you loved and led Abraham to the place you wanted him to go, you lead me. You counsel me with your eye upon me (Ps. 32:8). Just as you loved and disciplined David, drawing him back to your way, you discipline me. Just as you loved and spoke truth to Elijah, you speak truth to my heart through your Holy Spirit. You are eternal. You never change.

MMS

If God is always the same and has always been the same, what does that mean to me?
He's not like me. He doesn't change his mind or have second thoughts.

FOREVER GOD

From everlasting to everlasting you are God. ❖ Your throne is established from of old; You are from everlasting. ❖ Your kingdom is an everlasting kingdom, and your dominion endures throughout all generations. ❖ His kingdom will never end. ❖ The LORD will be king over all the earth. ❖ The eternal God is thy refuge, and underneath are the everlasting arms. ❖ The LORD shall reign for ever and ever. ❖ Alleluia: for the Lord God omnipotent reigneth. ❖ The LORD is the everlasting God. ❖ For a child will be born to us, a son will be given to us . . . and His name will be called . . . Eternal Father. ❖ But to the Son He says: "Your throne, O God, is forever and ever." ❖ The kingdoms of this world are become the kingdoms of our Lord, and of his Christ; and he shall reign for ever and ever. ❖ "I am the Alpha and the Omega," says the Lord God, "who is and who was and who is to come, the Almighty." ❖ I am the First and the Last. ❖ Now unto the King eternal, immortal, invisible, the only wise God, be honour and glory for ever and ever. Amen.

PS. 90:2 NRSV; PS. 93:2 NKJV; PS. 145:13 NRSV; LUKE 1:33 CEV; ZECH. 14:9 NASB; DEUT. 33:27; EXOD. 15:18; REV. 19:6; ISA. 40:28 NRSV; ISA. 9:6 NASB; HEB. 1:8 NKJV; REV. 11:15; REV. 1:8 NASB; REV. 1:17 NKJV; 1 TIM. 1:17

All that God does agrees with all that God is, and being and doing are one in Him.
A. W. TOZER

You are forever God, forever my Redeemer.
MMS

I bow before you, eternal God of the universe.
The true God has no beginning and no end.

THE AWESOME GOD

Your throne, O God, endures forever. ❖ The LORD All-Powerful will rule. ❖ By those who come near Me I must be regarded as holy; and before all the people I must be glorified. ❖ Tremble before him, all the earth. ❖ Whatever the LORD pleases, He does, in heaven and in earth, in the seas and in all deeps. ❖ No one can restrain His hand or say to Him, "What have You done?" ❖ The LORD reigns; let the peoples tremble! ❖ My flesh trembles for fear of You. ❖ The LORD reigneth; let the earth rejoice. ❖ O come, let us worship and bow down: let us kneel before the LORD our maker. For he is our God; and we are the people of his pasture, and the sheep of his hand.

Ps. 45:6 TLB; Isa. 24:23 CEV; Lev. 10:3 NKJV; Ps. 96:9 NIV; Ps. 135:6 NASB; Dan. 4:35 NKJV; Ps. 99:1 RSV; Ps. 119:120 NKJV; Ps. 97:1; Ps. 95:6–7

Christ reigns in his church as a shepherd-king. He has supremacy, but it is the superiority of a wise and tender shepherd over his needy and loving flock. He commands and receives obedience, but it is the willing obedience of well-cared-for-sheep, offered joyfully to their beloved Shepherd, whose voice they know so well. He rules by the force of love and the energy of goodness.

CHARLES HADDON SPURGEON

Every believer may be brought to understand that the only object of his life is to help to make Christ King on the earth.

ANDREW MURRAY

God is the awesome Ruler of the universe but he is also my Savior and my Friend. Praise him!
Is he the ruling King of my life or just a figurehead?

ALMIGHTY GOD

Tremble, O earth, at the presence of the LORD. ❖ I am Almighty God; walk before Me and be blameless. ❖ Holy, holy, holy, Lord God Almighty, Who was and is and is to come! ❖ I will sanctify my great name. ❖ He will reign on David's throne and over his kingdom, establishing and upholding it with justice and righteousness from that time on and forever. ❖ With righteousness he shall judge the poor, and decide with equity for the meek of the earth. ❖ Surely in the LORD I have righteousness and strength. ❖ O Lord, you are righteous. ❖ Enter into his gates with thanksgiving, and into his courts with praise.

Ps. 114:7 RSV; GEN. 17:1 NKJV; REV. 4:8 NKJV; EZEK. 36:23; ISA. 9:7 NIV; ISA. 11:4 RSV; ISA. 45:24 NKJV; DAN. 9:7 TLB; PS. 100:4

If we do not tremble before God, the world's system seems wonderful to us and pleasantly consumes us.

JAMES MONTGOMERY BOICE

Until we understand how holy God is, we will never understand how gracious he has been in his longsuffering attitude toward sin.

R. C. SPROUL

As a good Christian should consider every place holy because God is there, so he should look upon every part of his life as a matter of holiness because it is to be offered unto God.

WILLIAM A. LAW

Do I tremble before him?
Have I meditated on his holiness and pondered his wonders?

HE IS RIGHTEOUS AND HOLY

O LORD God of Israel, You are righteous. ❖ This is the name by which he will be called: "The LORD is our righteousness." ❖ The LORD is upright; he is my rock, and there is no unrighteousness in him. ❖ You answer us with awesome deeds of righteousness, O God our Savior. ❖ Great and marvelous are Your works, Lord God Almighty! Just and true are Your ways, O King of the saints! Who shall not fear You, O Lord, and glorify Your name? For You alone are holy. For all nations shall come and worship before You, for Your judgments have been manifested. ❖ The LORD of hosts shall be exalted in judgment, and God that is holy shall be sanctified in righteousness. ❖ They will . . . stand in awe of the God of Israel. ❖ Righteousness and justice are the foundation of Your throne; mercy and truth go before Your face. Blessed are the people who know the joyful sound! They walk, O LORD, in the light of Your countenance.

EZRA 9:15 NKJV; JER. 23:6 RSV; PS. 92:15 RSV; PS. 65:5 NIV; REV. 15:3–4 NKJV; ISA. 5:16; ISA. 29:23 NRSV; PS. 89:14–15 NKJV

There is something about the holiness of God that attracts us, but there is also something about the holiness of God that frightens us. It fascinates us, but it also terrifies us.

R. C. SPROUL

God's compassion flows out of His goodness, and goodness without justice is not goodness.

A. W. TOZER

My God is holy; all that he does is right and good.
Though he is holy and righteous, he has made a way for me, so unholy and
unrighteous, to approach him. Jesus is the way.

MAKER OF HEAVEN AND EARTH

The LORD is the everlasting God, the Creator of the ends of the earth. ❖ By the word of the LORD were the heavens made; and all the host of them by the breath of his mouth. ❖ God, who made the world and everything in it, since He is Lord of heaven and earth, does not dwell in temples made with hands. ❖ Lord GOD! Behold, You have made the heavens and the earth by Your great power and outstretched arm. There is nothing too hard for You. ❖ You are robed with honor and with majesty and light! You stretched out the starry curtain of the heavens. ❖ Worship him that made heaven, and earth, and the sea, and the fountains of waters. ❖ O great and powerful God, whose name is the LORD Almighty, great are your purposes and mighty are your deeds. ❖ You are worthy, O Lord, to receive glory and honor and power; for You created all things, and by Your will they exist and were created.

ISA. 40:28 RSV; PS. 33:6; ACTS 17:24 NKJV; JER. 32:17 NKJV; PS. 104:1 TLB; REV. 14:7; JER. 32:18–19 NIV; REV. 4:11 NKJV

The universe operates as an orderly system, not by impersonal laws but by the creative voice of the immanent and universal Presence, the Logos.

A. W. TOZER

This world, after all our science and sciences, is still a miracle; wonderful, inscrutable, magical and more, to whosoever will think of it.

THOMAS CARLYLE

He is the maker of heaven and earth; how amazing it is to think that he cares about me!
Does his creation speak to me of his power, wisdom, and love?

THE GOOD CREATION

O LORD God of Israel, the One who dwells between the cherubim, You are God, You alone, of all the kingdoms of the earth. ❖ It is he who made the earth by his power, who established the world by his wisdom, and by his understanding stretched out the heavens. ❖ For by him were all things created, that are in heaven, and that are in earth, visible and invisible, whether they be thrones, or dominions, or principalities, or powers: all things were created by him, and for him. ❖ O LORD, how many are Your works! In wisdom You have made them all. ❖ And God saw every thing that he had made, and, behold, it was very good. ❖ Everything God created is good. ❖ O give thanks unto the LORD; for he is good: for his mercy endureth for ever. . . . To him that by wisdom made the heavens. . . . To him that stretched out the earth above the waters. . . . To him that made great lights. . . . The sun to rule by day. . . . The moon and stars to rule by night: for his mercy endureth for ever. ❖ He is the Creator of all. . . . The Lord Almighty is his name.

2 KINGS 19:15 NKJV; JER. 10:12 RSV; COL. 1:16; PS. 104:24 NASB; GEN. 1:31; 1 TIM. 4:4 CEV; PS. 136:1, 5–9; JER. 10:16 TLB

He created all things, and that "for Himself" (Col. 1:16), yet it was not in order to supply a lack, but that He might communicate life and happiness to angels and men, and admit them to the vision of His glory.

ARTHUR W. PINK

O Lord and Maker of all things, from whose creative power the first light came forth, who dost look upon the world's first morning and see that it was good, I praise Thee for this light that now streams through my windows to rouse me to the life of another day.

JOHN BAILLIE

Am I thankful for all that God has created?
Do I see in his creation the evidence of his love for me?

MY CREATOR

Remember now your Creator. ❖ Is not God your Father? Has he not created you? ❖ I made the earth, and created humankind upon it. ❖ As the clay is in the potter's hand, so are ye in mine hand. ❖ The rich and poor meet together: the LORD is the maker of them all. ❖ It is written that at the beginning God created man and woman. ❖ Your hands have made me and fashioned me. ❖ For you created my inmost being; you knit me together in my mother's womb. I praise you because I am fearfully and wonderfully made. ❖ The LORD he is God: it is he that hath made us, and not we ourselves; we are his people, and the sheep of his pasture. ❖ You have granted me life and favor, and Your care has preserved my spirit. ❖ O LORD, You are our Father; we are the clay, and You our potter; and all we are the work of Your hand. ❖ O come, let us worship and bow down: let us kneel before the LORD our maker. ❖ Trust yourself to God who made you.

ECCLES. 12:1 NKJV; DEUT. 32:6 TLB; ISA. 45:12 NRSV; JER. 18:6; PROV. 22:2; MATT. 19:4 TLB; PS. 119:73 NKJV; PS. 139:13–14 NIV; PS. 100:3; JOB 10:12 NKJV; ISA. 64:8 NKJV; PS. 95:6; 1 PETER 4:19 NLT

What would creation have been without his design? . . . every bone, joint, muscle, sinew, gland, and blood vessel demonstrates the presence of God working everything according to his wise design.

CHARLES HADDON SPURGEON

Now God designed the human machine to run on Himself. . . . God cannot give us happiness and peace apart from Himself, because it is not there. There is no such thing.

C. S. LEWIS

We are God's own; therefore let every part of our existence be directed towards him as our only legitimate goal.

JOHN CALVIN

He is my Maker, Father, Potter. I believe this and yet I still try to be my own creator.
Teach me who I am; make me what you want me to be.

A NEW CREATION

Therefore, if anyone is in Christ, he is a new creation; old things have passed away; behold, all things have become new. ❖ All that matters is that you are a new person. ❖ As many as received Him, to them He gave the right to become children of God, to those who believe in His name. ❖ Whoever believes that Jesus is the Christ is born of God. ❖ For you have been born again not of seed which is perishable but imperishable, that is, through the living and abiding word of God. ❖ Like as Christ was raised up from the dead by the glory of the Father, even so we also should walk in newness of life. ❖ God washed us by the power of the Holy Spirit. He gave us new birth and a fresh beginning. ❖ We serve not under the old written code but in the new life of the Spirit. ❖ Everything . . . connected with that old way of life has to go. It's rotten through and through. Get rid of it! And then take on an entirely new way of life—a God-fashioned life, a life renewed from the inside and working itself into your conduct as God accurately reproduces his character in you. ❖ Every child of God can defeat the world. ❖ And he that sat upon the throne said, Behold, I make all things new.

2 COR. 5:17 NKJV; GAL. 6:15 CEV; JOHN 1:12 NKJV; 1 JOHN 5:1 NKJV; 1 PETER 1:23 NASB; ROM. 6:4; TITUS 3:5 CEV; ROM. 7:6 RSV; EPH. 4:22–24 THE MESSAGE; 1 JOHN 5:4 CEV; REV. 21:5

It is I who have made you and I alone can teach you what you are.
BLAISE PASCAL

In the first creation He gave me myself; but in His new creation He gave me Himself, and by that gift restored to me the self that I had lost. Created first and then restored, I owe Him myself twice over in return for myself.
ST. BERNARD OF CLAIRVAUX

Am I willing to be made new? Am I willing to get rid of the old?
O God who made me, shape me, make me entirely new.

GOD KNOWS ME

As for you, my son Solomon, know the God of your father, and serve Him with a whole heart and a willing mind; for the LORD searches all hearts, and understands every intent of the thoughts. ❖ For the LORD is a God of knowledge, and by him actions are weighed. ❖ I am he who searches mind and heart. ❖ Man looks at the outward appearance, but the LORD looks at the heart. ❖ He knows the secrets of the heart. ❖ You know every thought. ❖ Everything about us is bare and wide open to the all-seeing eyes of our living God. ❖ O LORD, You have searched me and known me. . . . And are acquainted with all my ways. ❖ Lord, you know all things. ❖ For You, Lord GOD, know Your servant.

1 CHRON. 28:9 NASB; 1 SAM. 2:3; REV. 2:23 RSV; 1 SAM. 16:7 NKJV; PS. 44:21 NRSV; JER. 11:20 CEV; HEB. 4:13 TLB; PS. 139:1, 3 NKJV; JOHN 21:17 NIV; 2 SAM. 7:20 NKJV

The Holy Spirit knows a heart that will be tender toward the things of God. It is that heart that he urges to respond to the Savior. Praise you, Lord, for knowing my heart.

MMS

For God himself works in our souls, in their deepest depths, taking increasing control as we are progressively willing to be prepared for his wonder.

THOMAS KELLY

Not according to what I try to be when praying, but what I am when not praying, is my prayer dealt with by God.

ANDREW MURRAY

He knows me. I cannot hide from him.
The things I hide from myself, he knows.

HE IS OUR PROTECTION

Blessed are all they that put their trust in him. ❖ He guards the paths of justice, and preserves the way of His saints. ❖ But let all those rejoice who put their trust in You; let them ever shout for joy, because You defend them; let those also who love Your name be joyful in You. ❖ He is a shield to those who take refuge in him. ❖ I will say of the LORD, He is my refuge and my fortress: my God; in him will I trust. ❖ Let Your lovingkindness and Your truth continually preserve me. ❖ The LORD is good, a stronghold in the day of trouble; he knows those who take refuge in him. ❖ Keep them safe by the power of the name that you have given me. ❖ Keep them safe from Satan's power. ❖ The Lord is faithful, and he will strengthen and protect you from the evil one. ❖ "I am with you," declares the LORD.

Ps. 2:12; PROV. 2:8 NKJV; Ps. 5:11 NKJV; PROV. 30:5 NRSV; Ps. 91:2; Ps. 40:11 NKJV; NAHUM 1:7 RSV; JOHN 17:11 CEV; JOHN 17:15 TLB; 2 THESS 3:3 NIV; HAG. 1:13 NIV

He is always thinking about us. We are before his eyes. The Lord's eye never sleeps, but is always watching out for our welfare. We are continually on his heart.
CHARLES HADDON SPURGEON

We "make him our habitation" by faith.
HANNAH WHITALL SMITH

It is an act of the will to allow God to be our refuge. Otherwise we live outside of his love and protection, wondering why we feel alone and afraid.
MMS

Jesus asks, "Do you love me? Do you trust me?"
Am I dwelling within the refuge he provides?

GOD IS WITH US

They shall call His name Immanuel, which translated means, "God with us." ❖ God is our refuge and strength, a very present help in trouble. ❖ The LORD of hosts is with us; the God of Jacob is our refuge. ❖ The LORD is on my side; I will not fear. What can man do to me? ❖ Be still, and know that I am God; I will be exalted among the nations, I will be exalted in the earth! ❖ I am the LORD, I have called you in righteousness, I have taken you by the hand and kept you. ❖ It is the LORD who goes before you. ❖ When you go through deep waters and great trouble, I will be with you. ❖ If God be for us, who can be against us? ❖ I will never leave you nor forsake you. ❖ I know for certain that you are with me. ❖ In my integrity you uphold me and set me in your presence forever.

MATT. 1:23 NASB; PS. 46:1; PS. 46:7; PS. 118:6 NKJV; PS. 46:10 NKJV;
ISA. 42:6 RSV; DEUT. 31:8 NRSV; ISA. 43:2 TLB; ROM. 8:31; HEB. 13:5 NKJV;
PS. 56:9 CEV; PS. 41:12 NIV

They [Israel] had attempted to live with the Lord of the Universe visibly present in their midst; but, in the end, only two survived God's Presence. If you can barely endure candlelight, how can you gaze at the sun?

"Who of us can dwell with the consuming fire?" asked the prophet Isaiah. Is it possible that we should be grateful for God's hiddenness, rather than disappointed?

PHILIP YANCEY

God is over all things; under all things; outside all; within but not enclosed; without but not excluded; above but not raised up; below but not depressed; wholly above, presiding; wholly beneath, sustaining; wholly within, filling.

HILDEBERT OF LARARDIN

Our God contracted to a span;
Incomprehensibly made man.
CHARLES WESLEY

God has promised to be with me no matter where I am, no matter what I'm going through.
The God of the universe wants to be here with me.

HE SURROUNDS ME

For You, O LORD, will bless the righteous; with favor You will surround him as with a shield. ❖ You are my hiding place; You shall preserve me from trouble; You shall surround me with songs of deliverance. ❖ For the LORD will go before you, and the God of Israel will be your rear guard. ❖ The LORD himself will guide you. ❖ The sheep know their shepherd's voice. He calls each of them by name and leads them out. ❖ You both precede and follow me and place your hand of blessing on my head. ❖ Do you not know that you are God's temple and that God's Spirit dwells in you? ❖ Be filled with the Spirit. ❖ As the mountains are round about Jerusalem, so the LORD is round about his people from henceforth even for ever.

Ps. 5:12 NKJV; Ps. 32:7 NKJV; Isa. 52:12 NASB; Micah 2:13 NLT; John 10:3 CEV; Ps. 139:5 TLB; 1 Cor. 3:16 RSV; Eph. 5:18; Ps. 125:2

He is within and without. His Spirit dwells within me. His armor protects me. He goes before me and is behind me.

MMS

He pitches his test in our humble hearts, so that he may communicate with us constantly.

CHARLES HADDON SPURGEON

Not just your presence with me but your Spirit within me, in my body, always, richly!
Lord, help me to never lose the sense of your presence with me.

FULFILLMENT IN HIM

O fear the LORD, you his saints, for those who fear him have no want!
❖ The LORD will guide you continually, and satisfy your desire with
good things. ❖ But whoever drinks of the water that I shall give him
will never thirst. ❖ Let him that is athirst come. And whosoever will,
let him take the water of life freely. ❖ I am the bread that gives life! No
one who comes to me will ever be hungry. No one who has faith in me
will ever be thirsty. ❖ For He satisfies the longing soul, and fills the
hungry soul with goodness. ❖ I say to the LORD, "You are my Lord; I
have no good apart from you." ❖ The LORD is my shepherd; I shall not
want. ❖ From the fullness of his grace we have all received one blessing
after another. ❖ O Lord of the armies of heaven, blessed are those who
trust in you.

Ps. 34:9 RSV; ISA. 58:11 RSV; JOHN 4:14 NKJV; REV. 22:17; JOHN 6:35 CEV;
Ps. 107:9 NKJV; PS. 16:2 NRSV; PS. 23:1; JOHN 1:16 NIV; PS. 84:12 TLB

Focusing on Christ, keeping his all-sufficiency and his love in view rather than
my needs, desires, or weaknesses is the answer to victorious living. If I believe
that God is who he is, then even wondering if he knows my need and will meet
it is blasphemous. Let all that he is fill my spirit. I must stop crowding him out
with my self-reliance, self-interest, and fears.

MMS

God is, must be our answer to every question and every cry of need.
HANNAH WHITALL SMITH

We should learn to live in the presence of the living God. He should be a well for
us—delightful, comforting, unfailing, springing up to eternal life (John 4:14).
When we rely on other people, their water supplies ultimately dry up. But the
well of the Creator never fails to nourish us.

CHARLES HADDON SPURGEON

Because of who he is, I can trust him for everything I need.
When I rely on myself, God's perfect answer is lost. When I rely on God, my
shortsighted answer is lost.

GOD PROVIDES

But Moses said [to God], "The people I am with number six hundred thousand on foot; and you say, 'I will give them meat, that they may eat for a whole month!' Are there enough flocks and herds to slaughter for them? Are there enough fish in the sea to catch for them?" The LORD said to Moses, "Is the LORD's power limited? Now you shall see whether my word will come true for you or not." ❖ He took the seven loaves, and having given thanks he broke them and gave them to his disciples to set before the people. . . . And they ate, and were satisfied. ❖ Blessed is he whose help is the God of Jacob, whose hope is in the LORD his God, the Maker of heaven and earth, the sea, and everything in them— the LORD, who remains faithful forever. ❖ You sent a gift more than once for my needs. ❖ And Abraham called the name of the place, The-LORD-Will-Provide; as it is said to this day, "In the Mount of The LORD it shall be provided."

NUM. 11:21–23 NRSV; MARK 8:6, 8 RSV; PS. 146:5–6 NIV; PHIL. 4:16 NASB; GEN. 22:14 NKJV

How like Moses I am—assuming that since I can't figure out how a need can be met, then there must be no way. God always has ways that I can't imagine.

MMS

God was meeting the needs of the young church as surely as he had met the needs of the Israelites, but he was doing so indirectly, through fellow members of his body.

PHILIP YANCEY

When God, therefore, says to us, "I am He that seeth thy need," He in reality says also, "I am He that provideth," for He cannot see, and fail to provide.

HANNAH WHITALL SMITH

As I came to God in a helpless heap, he turned my life upside down and around and did amazing things I never could have imagined.

RONALD WILSON

Is the God of the universe able to meet my need?
Today I will focus on his greatness, his power, his love for me—and not on my need.

HE IS THE SOURCE

My God shall supply all your need according to his riches in glory by Christ Jesus. ❖ God is able to make all grace abound toward you, that you, always having all sufficiency in all things, may have an abundance for every good work. ❖ "Test Me now in this," says the LORD of hosts, "if I will not open for you the windows of heaven, and pour out for you a blessing until it overflows." ❖ The LORD has blessed his people. ❖ Your heavenly Father knows that you need all these things. ❖ With all my heart I praise the LORD. ❖ For he satisfieth the longing soul, and filleth the hungry soul with goodness. ❖ For the LORD has done marvelous things! ❖ The LORD has done great things for us, and we are filled with joy. ❖ Now unto him that is able to do exceeding abundantly above all that we ask or think, according to the power that worketh in us, unto him be glory in the church by Christ Jesus throughout all ages, world without end. Amen.

PHIL. 4:19; 2 COR. 9:8 NKJV; MAL. 3:10 NASB; 2 CHRON. 31:10 RSV; MATT. 6:32 NRSV; PS. 103:1 CEV; PS. 107:9; JOEL 2:21 NKJV; PS. 126:3 NIV; EPH. 3:20–21

The more I have, the less I depend on him. And as I grasp how truly poor and needy I am, then I can let God's power come to full strength in me.

RONALD WILSON

He doesn't give us what we need once for all. He wants us to keep coming back to him.

MMS

We do not need to beg Him to bless us, He simply cannot help it.

HANNAH WHITALL SMITH

What is the evidence in my life that I am relying on God to supply my need? How has God shown me that he wants what's best for me?

HE SHOWS THE WAY

I will instruct you and teach you the way you should go; I will counsel you with my eye upon you. ❖ The LORD shall preserve your going out and your coming in from this time forth, and even forevermore. ❖ And the LORD, He is the one who goes before you. He will be with you, He will not leave you nor forsake you; do not fear nor be dismayed. ❖ Your ears will hear a word behind you, "This is the way, walk in it." ❖ I am sending an angel ahead of you to guard you along the way and to bring you to the place I have prepared. ❖ During the day the LORD went ahead of his people in a thick cloud, and during the night he went ahead of them in a flaming fire. That way the LORD could lead them at all times, whether day or night. ❖ The hand of the LORD my God was upon me. ❖ It is good for me to draw near to God: I have put my trust in the Lord GOD.

PS. 32:8 RSV; PS. 121:8 NKJV; DEUT. 31:8 NKJV; ISA. 30:21 NASB; EXOD. 23:20 NIV; EXOD. 13:21–22 CEV; EZRA 7:28; PS. 73:28

His hand on me is a father's hand, gently guiding and encouraging. His hand lets me know he is with me, so I am not afraid. I know that if there is danger or a need to turn, his hand will make it clear.

MMS

Make my path sure, O Lord. Establish my goings. Send me when and where You will and manifest to all that Thou art my guide.

JIM ELLIOT

Let me abandon myself to his direction, his guidance, his knowledge of the way.
May your guidance, O Lord, be as real as a column of fire ahead of me, illuminating the path I should take.

GOD IS LOVE

But you, O Lord, are a God merciful and gracious, slow to anger and abounding in steadfast love and faithfulness. ❖ All my bones shall say, "Lord, who is like You, delivering the poor from him who is too strong for him." ❖ He raises the poor from the dust, and lifts the needy from the ash heap. ❖ Because of your great mercy, you sent leaders to rescue them. ❖ As a father has compassion for his children, so the Lord has compassion for those who fear him. For he knows how we were made; he remembers that we are dust. ❖ Not one [sparrow] falls to the ground apart from your Father's will. But the very hairs of your head are all numbered. Do not fear therefore; you are of more value than many sparrows. ❖ Jesus, moved with compassion, put out His hand and touched him, and said to him, "I am willing; be cleansed." ❖ Have mercy on me, O God, according to your unfailing love; according to your great compassion blot out my transgressions. ❖ And when Jesus saw their faith, he said to the paralytic, "My son, your sins are forgiven." ❖ God is love.

Ps. 86:15 nrsv; Ps. 35:10 nkjv; Ps. 113:7 rsv; Neh. 9:27 cev;
Ps. 103:13–14 nrsv; Matt. 10:29–31 nkjv; Mark 1:41 nkjv; Ps. 51:1 niv;
Mark 2:5 rsv; 1 John 4:16

When God scooped out the valleys and created the mountains, when He hung the stars and blew the wind, you were on His mind.

Steve Brown

Love, for instance, is not something God has which may grow or diminish or cease to be. His love is the way God is, and when He loves He is simply being Himself.

A. W. Tozer

If God is love, there is nothing about him that is unloving.
If God is love, he can't help but love me.

UNFAILING LOVE

LORD God of Israel, there is no God in heaven or on earth like You, who keep Your covenant and mercy with Your servants who walk before You with all their hearts. ❖ You should praise the LORD for his love and for the wonderful things he does for all of us. ❖ His mercies never come to an end. ❖ Though he cause grief, yet will he have compassion according to the multitude of his mercies. ❖ "Though the mountains be shaken and the hills be removed, yet my unfailing love for you will not be shaken nor my covenant of peace be removed," says the LORD, who has compassion on you. ❖ Your steadfast love, O LORD, extends to the heavens, your faithfulness to the clouds. ❖ For as the heaven is high above the earth, so great is his mercy toward them that fear him. ❖ How precious is Your lovingkindness, O God!

2 CHRON. 6:14 NKJV; PS. 107:8 CEV; LAM. 3:22 RSV; LAM. 3:32; ISA. 54:10 NIV; PS. 36:5 NRSV; PS. 103:11; PS. 36:7 NKJV

This is the very essence of who the Holy One is—extravagantly, sacrificially, passionately loving.

TREVOR HUDSON

To be loved by God is the highest relationship, the highest achievement, and the highest position of life.

BLACKABY AND KING

He is "for us" with all the infinity of His being; with all the omnipotence of His love; with all the infallibility of His wisdom; arrayed in all His divine attributes, He is "for us,"—eternally and immutably "for us," . . . throughout eternity.

CHARLES HADDON SPURGEON

Knowing he loves me like this, can I trust him?
What can I do but love him back?

WHAT GOD REQUIRES

Without faith it is impossible to please him. For whoever would draw near to God must believe that he exists and that he rewards those who seek him. ❖ And you will seek Me and find Me, when you search for Me with all your heart. ❖ For in Christ Jesus neither circumcision nor uncircumcision means anything, but faith working through love. ❖ By [Jesus Christ] also we have access by faith into this grace wherein we stand. ❖ For by grace are ye saved through faith; and that not of yourselves: it is the gift of God: Not of works, lest any man should boast. ❖ See, I lay in Zion a stone that causes men to stumble and a rock that makes them fall, and the one who trusts in him will never be put to shame. ❖ The scripture was fulfilled that says, "Abraham believed God, and it was reckoned to him as righteousness," and he was called the friend of God. ❖ Where is your faith? ❖ You, my people, don't know what I demand.

HEB. 11:6 RSV; JER. 29:13 NKJV; GAL. 5:6 NASB; ROM. 5:2; EPH. 2:8–9; ROM. 9:33 NIV; JAMES 2:23 NRSV; LUKE 8:25; JER. 8:7 CEV

The answer of the Bible is simply "through Jesus Christ our Lord." In Christ and by Christ, God effects complete self-disclosure, although He shows Himself not to reason but to faith and love. Faith is an organ of knowledge, and love an organ of experience. God came to us in the incarnation; in atonement He reconciled us to Himself, and by faith and love we enter and lay hold on Him.

A. W. TOZER

Following God will require faith and action. Without faith you will not be able to please God. When you act in faith, God is pleased.

BLACKABY AND KING

Faith is the only way to please God because in faith we show that circumstances cannot sway us. Our life and hope are built on the perfect knowledge that he's in control.

MMS

Am I trusting in your grace alone, Lord, and not in my ability to save myself? Am I seeking to follow you with all my heart?

ONLY GOD

I, even I, am the LORD, and besides Me there is no savior. ❖ Behold, this is our God; we have waited for Him, and He will save us. ❖ I will be your God through all your lifetime, yes, even when your hair is white with age. I made you and I will care for you. I will carry you along and be your Savior. ❖ The LORD our God is one LORD. ❖ I am the LORD: that is my name: and my glory will I not give to another. ❖ The LORD is God; there is no other besides him. ❖ The LORD he is God in heaven above, and upon the earth beneath: there is none else. ❖ You alone are the LORD. ❖ There is one God, the Father, from whom are all things and for whom we exist, and one Lord, Jesus Christ, through whom are all things and through whom we exist. ❖ I and my Father are one. ❖ We have only one Lord, one faith, and one baptism. There is one God who is the Father of all people. . . . and he lives in all of us. ❖ I am the First, I am also the Last. ❖ "I am the Alpha and the Omega, the Beginning and the End," says the Lord, "who is and who was and who is to come, the Almighty."

ISA. 43:11 NKJV; ISA. 25:9 NKJV; ISA. 46:4 TLB; DEUT. 6:4; ISA. 42:8; DEUT. 4:35 RSV; DEUT. 4:39; NEH. 9:6 NIV; 1 COR. 8:6 NRSV; JOHN 10:30; EPH. 4:5–6 CEV; ISA. 48:12 NKJV; REV. 1:8 NKJV

Souls must look upon everything as though it were a matter of complete indifference, and, seeing only him in all things, must take or leave them as he wishes so as to live, be nourished by, and hope in him alone and not by any power or virtue which does not come from him.

JEAN-PIERRE DE CAUSSADE

God desires that we find our fulfillment and satisfaction first in him—not in a husband or children or a job or even in our service to him. He is the true source of all that is good.

MMS

Is he my beginning and my end? Is he everything to me?
Help me, Lord, to find my all in you.

TO GLORIFY GOD

God wants you to be holy. ❖ For we are His workmanship, created in Christ Jesus for good works, which God prepared beforehand that we should walk in them. ❖ May the God of steadfastness and encouragement grant you to live in such harmony with one another, in accord with Christ Jesus, that together you may with one voice glorify the God and Father of our Lord Jesus Christ. ❖ You are . . . God's instruments to do his work and speak out for him, to tell others of the night-and-day difference he made for you—from nothing to something, from rejected to accepted. ❖ Whosoever shall do the will of God, the same is my brother, and my sister, and mother. ❖ He who does the will of God abides forever. ❖ Now the God of peace . . . equip you in every good thing to do His will, working in us that which is pleasing in His sight, through Jesus Christ, to whom be the glory forever and ever. Amen.

1 Thess 4:3 tlb; Eph. 2:10 nkjv; Rom. 15:5–6 rsv; 1 Peter 2:9–10 the message; Mark 3:35; 1 John 2:17 nkjv; Heb. 13:20–21 nasb

God is far more interested in your having an experience with Him than He is interested in getting the job done.

Blackaby and King

It is the will of God that gives everything, whatever it may be, the power to form Jesus Christ in the center of our being. This will knows no limits.

Jean-Pierre de Caussade

God's purpose accomplished in His way brings Him glory.

Blackaby and King

Am I doing his will, being obedient, bringing him glory?
My deepest desire should be to do only that which points to him and to how wonderful he is.

GOD'S GLORY

Out of Zion, the perfection of beauty, God hath shined. ❖ He wraps himself in light as with a garment. ❖ The glory of the LORD stood there . . . and I fell on my face. ❖ The earth shone with His glory. ❖ Let the light of your face shine on us, O LORD! ❖ The people which sat in darkness saw great light; and to them which sat in the region and shadow of death light is sprung up. ❖ The true light now shineth. ❖ Jesus said to the people, "I am the Light of the world. So if you follow me, you won't be stumbling through the darkness, for living light will flood your path." ❖ The LORD is my light and my salvation. ❖ The LORD will be your everlasting light, and your God will be your glory. ❖ Holy, holy, holy, is the LORD of hosts: the whole earth is full of his glory. ❖ Glorious are you, more majestic than the everlasting mountains. ❖ Let them praise the name of the LORD: for his name alone is excellent; his glory is above the earth and heaven.

Ps. 50:2; Ps. 104:2 NIV; EZEK. 3:23; EZEK. 43:2 NASB; Ps. 4:6 NRSV; MATT. 4:16; 1 JOHN 2:8; JOHN 8:12 TLB; Ps. 27:1; ISA. 60:19 RSV; ISA. 6:3; Ps. 76:4 NRSV; Ps. 148:13

A new longing begins to fill my soul, that every day, every hour, that in every prayer the glory of the Father may be everything to me.

ANDREW MURRAY

The splendor of God's beauty satisfies every appetite we have. He is more beautiful than a waterfall, than the softness of a baby's skin, than the aroma of baking bread, than the taste of chocolate, than the sound of a symphony. His beauty fills us up so that we long for nothing more.

MMS

Christ Jesus is the purest gold, light without darkness, bright glory unclouded. He is altogether lovely.

CHARLES HADDON SPURGEON

All our thoughts about Him will be less than He, and our loftiest utterances will be trivialities in comparison with Him.

NOVATIAN

What is keeping me from appreciating his glory?
Are the artificial beauties of the world getting in the way?

GOD HIGHLY EXALTED

The glory of the LORD filled the tabernacle. ❖ The temple was filled with smoke from the glory of God. ❖ I saw the Lord sitting upon a throne, high and lifted up. ❖ The glory of the LORD filled the house of the LORD. ❖ They shall see the glory of the LORD, and the excellency of our God. ❖ For great in your midst is the Holy One of Israel. ❖ Out of the north comes golden splendor; around God is awesome majesty. ❖ Power belongs to God! His majesty shines down on Israel; his strength is mighty in the heavens. What awe we feel, kneeling here before him in the sanctuary. The God of Israel gives strength and mighty power to his people. Blessed be God! ❖ Give unto the LORD, O you mighty ones, give unto the LORD glory and strength. Give unto the LORD the glory due to His name; worship the LORD in the beauty of holiness.

EXOD. 40:35; REV. 15:8; ISA. 6:1 RSV; 1 KINGS 8:11 NKJV; ISA. 35:2; ISA. 12:6 NASB; JOB 37:22 NRSV; PS. 68:34–35 TLB; PS. 29:1–2 NKJV

Before that burning bush we ask not to understand, but only that we may fitly adore Thee, One God in Persons Three. Amen.

A. W. TOZER

Such an One is to be revered, worshipped, adored. He is solitary in His majesty, unique in His excellency, peerless in His perfections. He sustains all, but is Himself independent of all. He gives to all, but is enriched by none.

ARTHUR W. PINK

How can I approach one so glorious? Praise God, he has made it possible through Christ Jesus, my Lord!

GOD MOST GLORIOUS

Great and marvelous are Your works, Lord God Almighty! . . . For You alone are holy. ❖ Your lovingkindness, O LORD, extends to the heavens, Your faithfulness reaches to the skies. Your righteousness is like the mountains of God; Your judgments are like a great deep. ❖ O LORD God of hosts, who is mighty like You, O LORD? ❖ I am the root and the offspring of David, and the bright and morning star. ❖ The Ancient of Days was seated . . . His throne was a fiery flame. ❖ Holy, holy, holy, Lord God Almighty, which was, and is, and is to come. ❖ It is he alone who has immortality and dwells in unapproachable light, whom no one has ever seen or can see; to him be honor and eternal dominion. ❖ Now unto the King eternal, immortal, invisible, the only wise God, be honour and glory for ever and ever. ❖ For of him, and through him, and to him, are all things: to whom be glory for ever. Amen.

REV. 15:3–4 NKJV; PS. 36:5–6 NASB; PS. 89:8 NKJV; REV. 22:16; DAN. 7:9 NKJV; REV. 4:8; 1 TIM. 6:16 NRSV; 1 TIM. 1:17; ROM. 11:36

Forever God stands apart, in light unapproachable.
A. W. TOZER

> Immortal, invisible, God only wise,
> In light inaccessible hid from our eyes,
> Most blessed, most glorious, the Ancient of Days,
> Almighty, victorious, Thy great Name we praise.
> WALTER CHALMERS SMITH

I bow before you, Almighty God, in awe and wonder.
You are the God of the universe. You are my Savior and Friend.

HE IS OVER ALL

Heaven is my throne, and the earth is my footstool. ❖ The Most High is ruler over the realm of mankind. ❖ The LORD is exalted, for he dwells on high. ❖ O LORD of hosts, God of Israel, the One who dwells between the cherubim, You are God, You alone, of all the kingdoms of the earth. You have made heaven and earth. ❖ And God has put all things under his feet and made him the supreme Head of the Church. ❖ Now is come salvation, and strength, and the kingdom of our God, and the power of his Christ. ❖ The kingdoms of this world are become the kingdoms of our Lord, and of his Christ; and he shall reign for ever and ever. ❖ The LORD reigns forever. ❖ Alleluia! For the Lord God Omnipotent reigns! Let us be glad and rejoice and give Him glory.

ISA. 66:1; DAN. 4:25 NASB; ISA. 33:5 RSV; ISA. 37:16 NKJV; EPH. 1:22 TLB; REV. 12:10; REV. 11:15; PS. 9:7 NIV; REV. 19:6–7 NKJV

As there is but one God and Father of us all, whose glory gives light and life to everything that lives, whose presence fills all places, whose power supports all beings, whose providence ruleth all events, so everything that lives whether in Heaven or earth, whether they be thrones or principalities, men or angels, they must all with one spirit live wholly to the praise and glory of this one God and Father of them all.

WILLIAM A. LAW

Let my world be centered not in myself but in Thee.
JOHN BAILLIE

I praise you, God of the universe;
God of all there is, God of all that isn't;
God of all.

I praise you, Alpha and Omega,
God at the beginning, God at the end;
Always God.

MMS

Am I trusting in his goodness, resting in his power, rejoicing in his love?

GOD'S POWER

For since the creation of the world His invisible attributes, His eternal power and divine nature, have been clearly seen, being understood through what has been made, so that they are without excuse. ❖ "To whom will you compare me? Or who is my equal?" says the Holy One. Lift your eyes and look to the heavens: Who created all these? He who brings out the starry host one by one, and calls them each by name. Because of his great power and mighty strength, not one of them is missing. ❖ The heavens keep telling the wonders of God, and the skies declare what he has done. ❖ Awesome is God in his sanctuary. ❖ How excellent is Your name in all the earth. ❖ Jehovah sits in majesty in Zion, supreme above all rulers of the earth. Let them reverence your great and holy name. ❖ The LORD your God, the great and awesome God, is among you. ❖ The LORD is the strength of his people. ❖ He worked [His mighty power] in Christ when He raised Him from the dead and seated Him at His right hand in the heavenly places, far above all principality and power and might and dominion, and every name that is named, not only in this age but also in that which is to come. And He put all things under His feet, and gave Him to be head over all things. ❖ Then they will see the Son of man coming in clouds with great power and glory. ❖ I am God Almighty [El Shaddai].

ROM. 1:20 NASB; ISA. 40:25–26 NIV; PS. 19:1 CEV; PS 68:35 NRSV; PS. 8:1 NKJV; PS. 99:2–3 TLB; DEUT. 7:21 NKJV; PS. 28:8 RSV; EPH. 1:20–22 NKJV; MARK 13:26 RSV; GEN. 35:11

God freely admits he is holding back his power, but he restrains himself for our benefit. For all scoffers who call for direct action from the heavens, the prophets have ominous advice: Just wait.

PHILIP YANCEY

So God's patience is His power over Himself. Great is that God who, having all power, yet keeps all power subject to Himself.

JIM ELLIOT

Is he El Shaddai to me?
Do I know him in his great power as well as in his never failing love?

HE REVEALS HIMSELF TO US

And the LORD appeared to Abram and said, "To your descendants I will give this land." ❖ When Abram was ninety-nine years old the LORD appeared to Abram, and said to him, "I am God Almighty; walk before me, and be blameless." ❖ I am . . . the God of Abraham, the God of Isaac, and the God of Jacob. ❖ Israel saw that great work which the LORD did upon the Egyptians. ❖ For this purpose I have raised you up, that I may show My power in you, and that My name may be declared in all the earth. ❖ I revealed myself to those who did not ask for me; I was found by those who did not seek me. ❖ No one has ever seen God. The only Son, who is truly God and is closest to the Father, has shown us what God is like. ❖ Jesus . . . revealed his glory; and his disciples believed in him. ❖ For my eyes have seen Your salvation . . . a light to bring revelation to the Gentiles. ❖ The earth shall be full of the knowledge of the LORD, as the waters cover the sea. ❖ And all flesh shall see the salvation of God. ❖ And the glory of the LORD shall be revealed, and all flesh shall see it together.

GEN. 12:7 NASB; GEN. 17:1 RSV; EXOD. 3:6; EXOD. 14:31; EXOD. 9:16 NKJV; ISA. 65:1 NIV; JOHN 1:18 CEV; JOHN 2:11 NRSV; LUKE 2:30, 32 NKJV; ISA. 11:9; LUKE 3:6; ISA. 40:5

Nowhere else in the Semitic world has a similar higher type of religion made its appearance, except in Israel. The only reasonable explanation for the uniqueness of Israel in this respect is that here another factor was at work, the factor of supernatural revelation.

GERHARDUS VOS

Christianity, in its purest form, is nothing more than seeing Jesus. Christian service, in its purest form, is nothing more than imitating him who we see. To see his Majesty and to imitate him . . . that is the sum of Christianity.

MAX LUCADO

God revealed himself to Moses and he saw his glory; God revealed himself to the Samaritan woman and she knew that Jesus was the Christ; God revealed himself to me and I became his child.

MMS

Help me, Lord, to see you in your beauty, holiness, and power.

HE COMES DOWN TO US

The LORD has bared his holy arm before the eyes of all the nations; and all the ends of the earth shall see the salvation of our God. ❖ I will cause them to know My hand and My might; and they shall know that My name is the LORD. ❖ He . . . declares to man what are His thoughts . . . the LORD God of hosts is His name. ❖ You explain deep mysteries, because even the dark is light to you. ❖ Prophecy never came by the will of man, but holy men of God spoke as they were moved by the Holy Spirit. ❖ Then opened he their understanding, that they might understand the scriptures. ❖ God has deliberately chosen to use ideas the world considers foolish and of little worth in order to shame those people considered by the world as wise and great. ❖ For God, who said, "Let there be light in the darkness," has made us understand that this light is the brightness of the glory of God that is seen in the face of Jesus Christ. ❖ No one knows the Son except the Father, and no one knows the Father except the Son and anyone to whom the Son chooses to reveal him. ❖ "No eye has seen, no ear has heard, no mind has conceived what God has prepared for those who love him"—but God has revealed it to us by his Spirit.

ISA. 52:10 RSV; JER. 16:21 NKJV; AMOS 4:13 NASB; DAN. 2:22 CEV; 2 PETER 1:21 NKJV; LUKE 24:45; 1 COR. 1:27 TLB; 2 COR. 4:6 NLT; MATT. 11:27 NRSV; 1 COR. 2:9–10 NIV

We do not ascend to the absolute in faith, but the absolute descends to our level. He enters our personal history and speaks to us in our time-conditioned language.
DONALD G. BLOESCH

You are searching for God, the idea of God in his essential being. You seek perfection and it lies in everything that happens to you—your suffering, your actions, your impulses are the mysteries under which God reveals himself to you.
JEAN-PIERRE DE CAUSSADE

The God of the universe has seen fit to reveal himself to me. Am I listening? Do I hear his voice? Do I see his power in my life?

THE TRINITY

And immediately, coming up from the water, He saw the heavens parting and the Spirit descending upon Him like a dove. Then a voice came from heaven, "You are My beloved Son, in whom I am well pleased." ❖ [God] has spoken to us in His Son. ❖ Praise God, the Father of our Lord Jesus Christ. ❖ Now the Lord is the Spirit. ❖ And I will pray the Father, and He will give you another Helper, that He may abide with you forever—the Spirit of truth. ❖ We ought always to thank God for you, brothers loved by the Lord, . . . saved through the sanctifying work of the Spirit. ❖ God the Father chose you long ago and knew you would become his children. And the Holy Spirit has been at work in your hearts, cleansing you with the blood of Jesus Christ. ❖ Now there are varieties of gifts, but the same Spirit; and there are varieties of service, but the same Lord; and there are varieties of working, but it is the same God who inspires them all in every one. ❖ The grace of the Lord Jesus Christ and the love of God and the fellowship of the Holy Spirit be with you all.

MARK 1:10–11 NKJV; HEB. 1:2 NASB; 1 PETER 1:3 CEV; 2 COR. 3:17 RSV; JOHN 14:16–17 NKJV; 2 THESS. 2:13 NIV; 1 PETER 1:2 TLB; 1 COR. 12:4–6 RSV; 2 COR. 13:14 RSV

In this Trinity, nothing is before or after, nothing is greater or less: but all three Persons coeternal, together and coequal.

FROM THE ATHANASIAN CREED

Father, Son, and Holy Spirit—One
One God of glory
One Savior, Redeemer, Friend.

MMS

This beautiful Mystery—our God, Three in One.
Thank you for gracious glimpses of insight into the mystery that is you. Grant
me increased understanding of who you are.

HE IS WORTHY

Not to us, O LORD, not to us, but to thy name give glory, for the sake of thy steadfast love and thy faithfulness! ❖ The LORD is exalted, for He dwells on high; He has filled Zion with justice and righteousness. ❖ The battle shields of all the armies of the world are his trophies. He is highly honored everywhere. ❖ All worshipers of images are put to shame. ❖ For his images are false, and there is no breath in them. They are worthless, a work of delusion. ❖ Those who choose another god multiply their sorrows. ❖ But the LORD is the true God, he is the living God, and an everlasting king. ❖ For You, LORD, are most high above all the earth; You are exalted far above all gods. ❖ The heavens declare his righteousness, and all the people see his glory. ❖ Give unto the LORD the glory due unto his name; worship the LORD in the beauty of holiness. ❖ Give to the LORD, O families of the peoples, give to the LORD glory and strength. ❖ But the LORD of hosts is exalted in justice, and the Holy God shows himself holy in righteousness.

PS. 115:1 RSV; ISA. 33:5 NKJV; PS. 47:9 TLB; PS. 97:7 RSV; JER. 10:14–15 RSV; PS. 16:4 NRSV; JER. 10:10; PS. 97:9 NKJV; PS. 97:6; PS. 29:2; PS. 96:7 NKJV; ISA. 5:16 RSV

The essence of idolatry is the entertainment of thoughts about God that are unworthy of Him.

A. W. TOZER

The glory of God has not been revealed to this generation of men. The God of contemporary Christianity is only slightly superior to the gods of Greece and Rome, if indeed He is not actually inferior to them in that He is weak and helpless while they at least had power.

A. W. TOZER

God's glory is the result of his nature and his actions. He is glorious in his character, for he holds within him everything that is holy, good, and lovely.

CHARLES HADDON SPURGEON

Do I recognize him as the almighty, omniscient God of the universe? Let me attribute to God the glory due his holy name. Let me honor him and worship him as God of all.

ZEALOUS FOR HOLINESS

I am the LORD: that is my name: and my glory will I not give to another. ❖ I will be jealous for my holy name. ❖ I, the LORD your God, am a jealous God. ❖ For the LORD your God is a devouring fire, a jealous God. ❖ He is a holy God. ❖ The light of Israel will become a fire, and his Holy One a flame. ❖ Who among us can live with the consuming fire? . . . He who walks righteously, and speaks with sincerity. ❖ Surely the LORD our God has shown us His glory and His greatness, and we have heard His voice from the midst of the fire. We have seen this day that God speaks with man; yet he still lives. ❖ LORD, our Sovereign, how majestic is your name in all the earth! You have set your glory above the heavens. ❖ I will not let my holy name be profaned any more; and the nations shall know that I am the LORD, the Holy One in Israel. ❖ Our Father in heaven, we honor your holy name. ❖ Worship the LORD in the beauty of holiness. Fear before him, all the earth. ❖ O magnify the LORD with me, and let us exalt his name together.

ISA. 42:8; EZEK. 39:25 RSV; EXOD. 20:5 NKJV; DEUT. 4:24 RSV; JOSH. 24:19 RSV; ISA. 10:17 RSV; ISA. 33:14–15 NASB; DEUT. 5:24 NKJV; PS. 8:1 NRSV; EZEK. 39:7 RSV; MATT. 6:9 TLB; 1 CHRON. 16:29–30; PS. 34:3

Holiness . . . is represented as the light of divine glory turned into a flame devouring the sinful.

GERHARDUS VOS

For if we are worldly or earthly minded in our employments, if they are carried on with vain desires and covetous tempers only to satisfy ourselves, we can no more be said to live to the glory of God than gluttons and drunkards can be said to eat and drink to the glory of God.

WILLIAM A. LAW

God needs no defenders. He is the eternal Undefended.

A. W. TOZER

Is my life different from the life of those who don't know Christ as Savior? Is his name honored through me?
Lord God, give me a zeal for holiness.

THE DEPTH OF GOD'S WISDOM

O the depth of the riches and wisdom and knowledge of God! How unsearchable are his judgments and how inscrutable his ways! For who has known the mind of the Lord, or who has been his counselor? ❖ Who has directed the Spirit of the LORD, or as His counselor has taught Him? With whom did He take counsel, and who instructed Him, and taught Him in the path of justice? Who taught Him knowledge, and showed Him the way of understanding? ❖ For as the heavens are higher than the earth, so are my ways higher than your ways, and my thoughts than your thoughts. ❖ His understanding is infinite. ❖ And the spirit of the LORD shall rest upon him, the spirit of wisdom and understanding, the spirit of counsel and might, the spirit of knowledge. ❖ A King shall reign and prosper, and shall execute judgment and justice in the earth.

ROM. 11:33–34 RSV; ISA. 40:13–14 NKJV; ISA. 55:9; PS. 147:5; ISA. 11:2; JER. 23:5

Because God knows all things perfectly, He knows no thing better than any other thing, but all things equally well. He never discovers anything, He is never amazed. He never wonders about anything nor (except when drawing men out for their own good) does He seek information or ask questions.

A. W. TOZER

Christ's death freed God to show His loving and forgiving grace to sinners who come to Him, confess their sins, and receive Jesus as Savior. This is the manifold wisdom of God.

TONY EVANS

All God's acts are done in perfect wisdom, first for His own glory, and then for the highest good of the greatest number for the longest time.

A. W. TOZER

Can I trust that in his great wisdom, God will do what is best for me?
If I depend on the counsel of his Holy Spirit, I will choose the right path and go the right way.

GOD KNOWS US

The LORD does not see as mortals see; they look on the outward appearance, but the LORD looks on the heart. ❖ I'm an open book to you; even from a distance, you know what I'm thinking. ❖ And there is no creature hidden from His sight, but all things are naked and open to the eyes of Him to whom we must give account. ❖ Can any hide himself in secret places that I shall not see him? saith the LORD. Do not I fill heaven and earth? ❖ I, the LORD, search the heart, I test the mind. ❖ For a man's ways are before the eyes of the LORD, and he watches all his paths. ❖ You spread out our sins before you—our secret sins—and see them all. ❖ I know also, my God, that You test the heart and have pleasure in uprightness. ❖ But, O LORD of hosts, You who test the righteous, and see the mind and heart, . . . I have pleaded my cause before You.

1 SAM. 16:7 NRSV; PS. 139:2 THE MESSAGE; HEB. 4:13 NKJV; JER. 23:24; JER. 17:10 NASB; PROV. 5:21 RSV; PS. 90:8 TLB; 1 CHRON. 29:17 NKJV; JER. 20:12 NKJV

God is so compassionate and ready to forgive! He sees our heart and knows when we have humbled ourselves in repentance. Then he immediately forgives. It doesn't matter how terrible the sin; he's looking for a repentant heart that he can forgive.

MMS

Hold fast to the Lord Jesus. As He teaches you to shun the world and its attractions, your love will go out to Him in loyal-hearted service. But remember— there must be daily fellowship with Jesus. His love alone can expel the love of the world. Take time to be alone with your Lord.

ANDREW MURRAY

We have depths we ourselves have never seen or felt.
RAYMOND C. ORTLUND

What am I trying to hide from God? It is comforting to remember that he knows all about me and loves me still.

GOD REVEALS HIS WILL

He leads the humble in justice, and He teaches the humble His way. ❖ The friendship of the LORD is for those who fear him, and he makes known to them his covenant. ❖ Understand what the will of the Lord is. ❖We have not ceased to pray for you and to ask that you may be filled with the knowledge of His will in all spiritual wisdom and understanding. ❖ Your ears shall hear a word behind you, saying, "This is the way, walk in it," whenever you turn to the right hand or whenever you turn to the left. ❖ God is working in you to make you willing and able to obey him. ❖ It is God's will that you should be sanctified. ❖ In every thing give thanks: for this is the will of God in Christ Jesus concerning you. ❖ Teach me, O LORD, the way of Your statutes, and I shall keep it to the end.

PS. 25:9 NASB; PS. 25:14 RSV; EPH. 5:17 NKJV; COL. 1:9 NASB; ISA. 30:21 NKJV; PHIL. 2:13 CEV; 1 THESS. 4:3 NIV; 1 THESS. 5:18; PS. 119:33 NKJV

We must remember that God is not attempting to conceal himself or his will. Biblical history is the record of his desire to reveal, not to conceal.

R. C. SPROUL

He says to me: Spend time with me in the morning. Spend time with me in the evening. Think about me throughout the day. And I will show you all you need to know.

MMS

It is in a prayer relationship that God gives further direction.
BLACKABY AND KING

Our ways may seem good to us. We may even enjoy some moderate successes. But when we do the work of God in our own ways, we will never see the power of God in what we do. God reveals His ways because that is the only way to accomplish His purposes.

BLACKABY AND KING

I don't need to worry about finding out what God's will is. He wants me to know and will reveal it to me.
My concern must be to prepare my heart for hearing what God is saying to me.

SEEK HIS WILL

Now devote your heart and soul to seeking the LORD your God. ❖ If you seek Him, He will be found by you. ❖ Show me Your ways, O LORD; teach me Your paths. ❖ Make thy way straight before my face. ❖ Teach me thy way, O LORD; and lead me on a level path. ❖ Teach me to do Your will, for You are my God. ❖ I delight to do your will, O my God; your law is within my heart. ❖ And this is the confidence which we have in him, that if we ask anything according to his will he hears us. ❖ Since we first heard about you we have kept on praying and asking God to help you understand what he wants you to do. ❖ I keep asking that the God of our Lord Jesus Christ, the glorious Father, may give you the Spirit of wisdom and revelation, so that you may know him better.

1 CHRON. 22:19 NIV; 1 CHRON. 28:9 NKJV; PS. 25:4 NKJV; PS. 5:8; PS. 27:11 RSV; PS. 143:10 NKJV; PS. 40:8 NRSV; 1 JOHN 5:14 RSV; COL. 1:9 TLB; EPH. 1:17 NIV

God is longing to bless you, but is unable to do so as long as you are not willing to give yourself unreservedly, and with all the strength of your will, to let Him work out His will in you. Speak it out in God's presence: "Father, I will seek Thee with all my heart and will."

ANDREW MURRAY

Whenever God gives a vision to a saint, He puts him, as it were, in the shadow of His hand, and the saint's duty is to be still and listen.

OSWALD CHAMBERS

Am I seeking his will with all my heart? Or is my will still most important? May my relationship with you deepen, O Lord, so that I will know your will and desire to do it.

A LIVING RELATIONSHIP

For whoever does the will of My Father in heaven is My brother and sister and mother. ❖ You are my friends if you do what I command you. ❖ Whoever obeys his word, truly in this person the love of God has reached perfection. By this we may be sure that we are in him. ❖ Because I live, you also will live. ❖ If anyone desires to come after Me, let him deny himself, and take up his cross daily, and follow Me. For whoever desires to save his life will lose it, but whoever loses his life for My sake will save it. ❖ My sheep hear my voice, and I know them, and they follow me. ❖ He who has My commandments and keeps them, he it is who loves Me; and he who loves Me shall be loved by My Father, and I will love him, and will disclose Myself to him. ❖ May they be brought to complete unity to let the world know that you sent me and have loved them even as you have loved me. ❖ For this finds favor, if for the sake of conscience toward God a man bears up under sorrows when suffering unjustly. ❖ If you find life difficult because you're doing what God said, take it in stride. Trust him. He knows what he's doing, and he'll keep on doing it. ❖ For to this you have been called, because Christ also suffered for you, leaving you an example, that you should follow in his steps.

MATT. 12:50 NKJV; JOHN 15:14 RSV; 1 JOHN 2:5 NRSV; JOHN 14:19 NRSV; LUKE 9:23–24 NKJV; JOHN 10:27; JOHN 14:21 NASB; JOHN 17:23 NIV; 1 PETER 2:19 NASB; 1 PETER 4:19 THE MESSAGE; 1 PETER 2:21 RSV

"What is God's will for my life?" is not the best question to ask. I think the right question is simply, "What is God's will?" Once I know God's will, then I can adjust my life to Him and His purposes. In other words, what is it that God is purposing where I am? Once I know what God is doing, then I know what I need to do. The focus needs to be on God and His purposes, not my life!

BLACKABY AND KING

The will of God is a living relationship between God and the believer.

WARREN W. WIERSBE

Am I content to do something "small" for the Lord if that is his will?
Do I obey him because I love him or because I'm afraid of the consequences if I don't?

DISCOVERING GOD'S WILL FOR ME

Lead me, O LORD, in thy righteousness . . . make thy way straight before my face. ❖ You lead humble people to do what is right and to stay on your path. ❖ So then do not be foolish, but understand what the will of the Lord is. ❖ Try to learn what is pleasing to the Lord. ❖ My child, keep your father's commandment, and do not forsake your mother's teaching. . . . When you walk, they will lead you; when you lie down, they will watch over you; and when you awake, they will talk with you. For the commandment is a lamp and the teaching a light, and the reproofs of discipline are the way of life. ❖ He will teach us of his ways, and we will walk in his paths. ❖ I will instruct you and teach you the way you should go; I will counsel you with my eye upon you. ❖ When he, the Spirit of truth, is come, he will guide you into all truth. ❖ Your will be done on earth as it is in heaven. ❖ You ought to say, "If the Lord wills, we shall live and do this or that." ❖ I want your will, not mine.

PS. 5:8; PS. 25:9 CEV; EPH. 5:17 NASB; EPH. 5:10 RSV; PROV. 6:20, 22–23 NRSV; MICAH 4:2; PS. 32:8 RSV; JOHN 16:13; MATT. 6:10 NKJV; JAMES 4:15 NKJV; MATT. 26:39 TLB

God wants his people to earnestly seek his will and pray for it and thus become agents of the blessing God brings.

JAMES MONTGOMERY BOICE

"If the Lord will" is not just a statement on a believer's lips: it is the constant attitude of his heart.

WARREN W. WIERSBE

We learn to determine the will of God by working at it. The more we obey, the easier it is to discover what God wants us to do.

WARREN W. WIERSBE

What are you doing, Lord? Help me focus on you.
Teach me your ways. Teach me obedience.

GIVE IT YOUR ALL

May the God of hope fill you with all joy and peace in believing, that you may abound in hope by the power of the Holy Spirit. ❖ Live in a right way in undivided devotion to the Lord. ❖ She did not depart from the temple, worshiping with fasting and prayer night and day. ❖ [She] is concerned about the things of the Lord, that she may be holy both in body and spirit. ❖ They have devoted themselves to the ministry of the saints. ❖ Let each of you look not only to his own interests, but also to the interests of others. ❖ Let no one seek his own good, but the good of his neighbor. ❖ Love one another with mutual affection. ❖ Love rejoices in the truth, but not in evil. Love is always supportive, loyal, hopeful, and trusting. ❖ Now may the God who gives perseverance and encouragement grant you to be of the same mind with one another according to Christ Jesus, so that with one accord you may with one voice glorify the God and Father of our Lord Jesus Christ.

ROM. 15:13 NKJV; 1 COR. 7:35 NIV; LUKE 2:37 RSV; 1 COR. 7:34 NASB; 1 COR. 16:15 NKJV; PHIL. 2:4 RSV; 1 COR. 10:24 RSV; ROM. 12:10 NRSV; 1 COR. 13:6–7 CEV; ROM. 15:5–6 NASB

First, strive to do another's will rather than your own. Second, choose always to have less than more. Third, seek the lower places in life, dying to the need to be recognized and important. Fourth, always and in everything desire that the will of God may be completely fulfilled in you.

THOMAS À KEMPIS

Wherever you are, be all there. Live to the hilt every situation you believe to be the will of God.

JIM ELLIOT

Am I content to be where God has placed me or do I long to be somewhere else?

Am I devoted to serving the Lord, devoted to my fellow believers, devoted to spreading the good news?

GOD IS GRACIOUS

The LORD longs to be gracious to you, and therefore He waits on high to have compassion on you. For the LORD is a God of justice; how blessed are all those who long for Him. ❖ The Lord is not slack concerning His promise, as some count slackness, but is longsuffering toward us, not willing that any should perish but that all should come to repentance. ❖ For You, Lord, are good, and ready to forgive, and abundant in mercy to all those who call upon You. ❖ You, O Lord, are a God merciful and gracious, slow to anger and abounding in steadfast love and faithfulness. ❖ We believe that through the grace of the Lord Jesus Christ we shall be saved. ❖ Grace and truth came by Jesus Christ. ❖ The word of his grace . . . is able to build you up, and to give you an inheritance among all them which are sanctified. ❖ All . . . [are] justified freely by his grace through the redemption that is in Christ Jesus.

ISA. 30:18 NASB; 2 PETER 3:9 NKJV; PS. 86:5 NKJV; PS. 86:15 NRSV;
ACTS 15:11; JOHN 1:17; ACTS 20:32; ROM. 3:23–24

Grace: a gift that costs everything for the giver and nothing for the recipient.
PHILIP YANCEY

God is so gracious that He will even take us when we use Him as our last resort.
C. S. LEWIS

The purpose of grace is the perfection of the heart, not the mind.
JEAN-PIERRE DE CAUSSADE

Where would I be without the grace of God? It is by his grace that I realized my need for him and by his grace that I am saved.
We are all in the same boat, all dependent on God's grace for our salvation.

ETERNAL BLESSINGS

This is the day which the LORD hath made; we will rejoice and be glad in it. ❖ For the LORD your God will bless you just as He promised you. ❖ You will be blessed when you come in and blessed when you go out. ❖ Blessed be the God and Father of our Lord Jesus Christ, the Father of mercies and God of all comfort, who comforts us in all our affliction. ❖ The LORD my God illumines my darkness. ❖ I satisfy the weary ones and refresh everyone who languishes. ❖ Everlasting joy shall be theirs. ❖ The Lord GOD will cause righteousness and praise to spring forth before all the nations. ❖ You shall rejoice in every good thing which the LORD your God has given to you. ❖ Blessed be the God and Father of our Lord Jesus Christ, who has blessed us in Christ with every spiritual blessing in the heavenly places. ❖ I am the living bread which came down from heaven; if any one eats of this bread, he will live for ever; and the bread which I shall give for the life of the world is my flesh. ❖ To those who have, more will be given, and they will have abundance. ❖ The LORD your God will bless you in all your produce and in all the work of your hands, so that you will be altogether joyful. ❖ O LORD my God, I will give thanks unto thee for ever.

Ps. 118:24; DEUT. 15:6 NKJV; DEUT. 28:6 NIV; 2 COR. 1:3–4 RSV; Ps. 18:28 NASB; JER. 31:25 NASB; ISA. 61:7 NKJV; ISA. 61:11; DEUT. 26:11 NKJV; EPH. 1:3 NRSV; JOHN 6:51 RSV; MATT. 13:12 NRSV; DEUT. 16:15 RSV; Ps. 30:12

The secret of a happy life is to delight in duty. When duty becomes delight, then burdens become blessings.

WARREN W. WIERSBE

We look for material blessings—worldly blessings—and the Lord is longing to give us spiritual blessings that are eternal and of infinitely more value.

MMS

His presence goes with me. His Spirit is within. I can feel his hands of blessing on my head. He will lead me and protect me, rejoicing over me in love. And though I am completely unworthy, he has rescued and redeemed me. Praise you, the God who is real and true and love.

HE KNOWS WHAT WE NEED

The LORD is my shepherd; I shall not want. ❖ My soul shall be satisfied. ❖ Your Father knows the things you have need of before you ask Him. ❖ And the LORD will continually guide you, and satisfy your desire in scorched places. ❖ I will refresh the weary and satisfy the faint. ❖ Come away by yourselves to a lonely place, and rest a while. ❖ And when He went ashore, He saw a great multitude, and He felt compassion for them because they were like sheep without a shepherd; and He began to teach them many things. ❖ He gave thanks and broke the loaves. . . . He also divided the two fish among them all. They all ate and were satisfied, and the disciples picked up twelve basketfuls of broken pieces of bread and fish. ❖ Let them thank the LORD for his steadfast love, for his wonderful works to humankind. For he satisfies the thirsty, and the hungry he fills with good things. ❖ We give thanks to thee, O God; we give thanks; we call on thy name and recount thy wondrous deeds.

PS. 23:1; PS. 63:5; MATT. 6:8 NKJV; ISA. 58:11 NASB; JER. 31:25 NIV; MARK 6:31 RSV; MARK 6:34 NASB; MARK 6:41–43 NIV; PS. 107:8–9 NRSV; PS. 75:1 RSV

At the time of the feeding of the five thousand (Mark 6:30–44), Jesus was aware of more than a need for food. Earlier he knew the disciples needed rest. He met their physical need. He knew the crowd needed teaching. He met their spiritual need. Now he knew they needed food and he met their physical need. He knew the disciples needed to grow in their belief that he was God. He gave them a lesson to increase their faith. As the twelve baskets of leftovers symbolize, he meets our needs abundantly.

MMS

When we are full, we tend to forget God. We grow satisfied with earth; we can do without heaven.

CHARLES HADDON SPURGEON

Am I afraid that God doesn't understand my needs; do I worry that he won't meet them?
Can I trust him to know what I need even better than I know myself?

THE BLESSING OF SUFFERING

Steep your life in God-reality, God-initiative, God-provisions. Don't worry about missing out. You'll find all your everyday human concerns will be met. Give your entire attention to what God is doing right now, and don't get worked up about what may or may not happen tomorrow. God will help you deal with whatever hard things come up when the time comes. ❖ Those who suffer he delivers. ❖ Since Christ suffered and underwent pain, you must have the same attitude he did; you must be ready to suffer, too. For remember, when your body suffers, sin loses its power. ❖ Discipline yourselves, keep alert. Like a roaring lion your adversary the devil prowls around, looking for someone to devour. Resist him, steadfast in your faith, for you know that your brothers and sisters in all the world are undergoing the same kinds of suffering. And after you have suffered for a little while, the God of all grace, who has called you to his eternal glory in Christ, will himself restore, support, strengthen, and establish you. ❖ The grace of our Lord was more than abundant, with the faith and love which are found in Christ Jesus.

MATT. 6:33–34 THE MESSAGE; JOB 36:15 NIV; 1 PETER 4:1 TLB; 1 PETER 5:8–10 NRSV; 1 TIM. 1:14 NASB

God withholds blessing only in wisdom, never in spite or aloofness.

JIM ELLIOT

I discovered that sorrow was not to be feared but rather endured with hope and expectancy that God would use it to visit and bless my life.

JILL BRISCOE

Am I willing to suffer if it means growing to be more like Jesus?
Can I be sure that the suffering I endure is perfecting his nature in me?

HE CAN GIVE ONLY THE BEST

He who did not spare His own Son, but delivered Him up for us all, how will He not also with Him freely give us all things? ❖ Those who seek the LORD shall not lack any good thing. ❖ I am unworthy of all the lovingkindness and of all the faithfulness which You have shown to Your servant. ❖ He has delivered us from the power of darkness and conveyed us into the kingdom of the Son of His love, in whom we have redemption through His blood, the forgiveness of sins. ❖ My God shall supply all your need according to his riches in glory by Christ Jesus. ❖ For the LORD God is a sun and shield: the LORD will give grace and glory: no good thing will he withhold from them that walk uprightly. ❖ They shall celebrate the fame of your abundant goodness, and shall sing aloud of your righteousness. . . . The LORD is good to all, and his compassion is over all that he has made. ❖ Now to Him who is able to do exceeding abundantly above all that we ask or think, according to the power that works in us, to Him be glory in the church by Christ Jesus to all generations forever and ever! Amen.

ROM. 8:32 NASB; PS 34:10 NKJV; GEN. 32:10 NASB; COL. 1:13–14 NKJV; PHIL. 4:19; PS. 84:11; PS. 145:7, 9 NRSV; EPH. 3:20–21 NASB

However things may look, we always know that God must give the best because He is God and could do no other.

HANNAH WHITALL SMITH

God is so good that he only awaits our desire to overwhelm us with this gift which is himself.

FRANÇOIS FÉNELON

Have I begun to understand how abundantly and generously God gives to me?
When I have Jesus Christ, I have everything.

GOD'S SON

You will conceive in your womb, and bear a son, and you shall name Him Jesus. He will be great, and will be called the Son of the Most High . . . and His kingdom will have no end. . . . The Holy Spirit will come upon you, and the power of the Most High will overshadow you; and for that reason the holy offspring shall be called the Son of God. ❖ This is how much God loved the world: He gave his Son, his one and only Son. ❖ When his firstborn Son came to earth, God said, "Let all the angels of God worship him." ❖ To the Son He says: "Your throne, O God, is forever and ever; a scepter of righteousness is the scepter of Your Kingdom." ❖ Behold my servant, whom I have chosen; my beloved, in whom my soul is well pleased. ❖ You are My beloved Son; in You I am well pleased. ❖ [He] was put to death for our trespasses. ❖ For our sake he made him to be sin who knew no sin, so that in him we might become the righteousness of God. ❖ This is my body which is given for you. . . . This cup which is poured out for you is the new covenant in my blood. ❖ Christ died for the ungodly. ❖ Christ Jesus, who died—more than that, who was raised to life—is at the right hand of God and is also interceding for us.

Luke 1:31–33, 35 nasb; John 3:16 the message; Heb. 1:6 tlb; Heb. 1:8 nkjv; Matt. 12:18; Luke 3:22 nkjv; Rom. 4:25 rsv; 2 Cor. 5:21 nrsv; Luke 22:19–20 rsv; Rom. 5:6; Rom. 8:34 niv

In astounding tandem a human body housed divinity. Holiness and earthiness intertwined.

Max Lucado

How could [Jesus] have known what he knew and yet done such menial things in the carpenter's shop? Yet the Father said, "You are my Son, whom I love; with you I am well pleased" (Luke 3:22) when he had not yet preached a sermon or worked a miracle. This was probably not the first time God the Father assured Jesus of his love and thus liberated him to do little things for his pleasure before he went on to much bigger things.

R. Paul Stevens

The very Son of God, Jesus Christ, the Lord, died for me!
How can I thank him; how can I praise him enough?

GOD SHOWS HIS LOVE IN JESUS' BIRTH

Because of God's tender mercy, the light from heaven is about to break upon us. ❖ For God so loved the world, that he gave his only begotten Son, that whosoever believeth in him should not perish, but have everlasting life. ❖ He first loved us. ❖ This is how God showed his love among us: He sent his one and only Son into the world that we might live through him. ❖ For there is born to you this day in the city of David a Savior, who is Christ the Lord. ❖ But God, being rich in mercy, because of His great love with which He loved us, even when we were dead in our transgressions, made us alive together with Christ.

LUKE 1:78 NLT; JOHN 3:16; 1 JOHN 4:19; 1 JOHN 4:9 NIV; LUKE 2:11 NKJV; EPH. 2:4–5 NASB

The stunning point of Christmas is that God considered my needs and the worth of my relationship to Him to be sufficient cause to go through the trauma of changing places.

JOE STOWELL

Those who believe in God can never in a way be sure of him again. Once they have seen him in a stable, they can never be sure where he will appear or to what lengths he will go or to what ludicrous depths of self-humiliation he will descend in his wild pursuit of man.

FREDERICK BUECHNER

Jesus, the proof of God's love . . .
PHILIP YANCEY

"How can I give you up, Ephraim? How can I hand you over, Israel?" Substitute your own name for Ephraim and Israel. At the heart of the gospel is a God who deliberately surrenders to the wild, irresistible power of love.

PHILIP YANCEY

Have I considered the implications of his changing places with me? How much has he loved me? How far has he pursued me?

JESUS IS THE WAY

God did not send the Son into the world to judge the world, but that the world might be saved through Him. ❖ So it is written, "The first man Adam became a living being." The last Adam became a life-giving spirit. ❖ Now all of us, whether Jews or Gentiles, may come to God the Father with the Holy Spirit's help because of what Christ has done for us. ❖ In him and through faith in him we may approach God with freedom and confidence. ❖ Jesus said to him, "I am the way, the truth, and the life. No one comes to the Father except through Me." ❖ Only Jesus has the power to save! His name is the only one in all the world that can save anyone. ❖ I am the door; if any one enters by me, he will be saved. ❖ In him was life; and the life was the light of men. ❖ The Son gives life. ❖ The life which I now live in the flesh I live by the faith of the Son of God, who loved me, and gave himself for me.

JOHN 3:17 NASB; 1 COR. 15:45 NKJV; EPH. 2:18 TLB; EPH. 3:12 NIV;
JOHN 14:6 NKJV; ACTS 4:12 CEV; JOHN 10:9 RSV; JOHN 1:4; JOHN 5:21 RSV;
GAL. 2:20

The incarnation speaks to us of God humbling himself in order to make himself known to us, to call us back to him, to reveal the full extent of his love towards us.

ALISTER E. MCGRATH

The Christian man possesses God's own life and shares His infinitude with Him.

A. W. TOZER

The same voice that brought Lazarus out of the tomb raised us to newness of life.

CHARLES HADDON SPURGEON

I'm amazed when I think that God lives within me in all of his power and wisdom.
How has his life changed mine?

JESUS DID IT ALL

Christ died only once to take away the sins of many people. ❖ He was numbered with the transgressors, and He bore the sin of many. ❖ So Jesus also suffered outside the gate in order to sanctify the people through his own blood. ❖ God presented him as a sacrifice of atonement, through faith in his blood. ❖ And the LORD hath laid on him the iniquity of us all. ❖ He that spared not his own Son, but delivered him up for us all, how shall he not with him also freely give us all things? ❖ In Him we have redemption through His blood, the forgiveness of our trespasses, according to the riches of His grace. ❖ To Him who loved us and washed us from our sins in His own blood . . . to Him be glory and dominion forever and ever. Amen.

HEB. 9:28 CEV; ISA. 53:12 NKJV; HEB. 13:12 RSV; ROM. 3:25 NIV; ISA. 53:6; ROM. 8:32 KJV; EPH. 1:7 NASB; REV. 1:5–6 NKJV

Jesus did not identify the person with his sin, but rather saw in this sin something alien, something that really did not belong to him, something that merely chained and mastered him and from which he could free him and bring him back to his real self.

PAUL THIELICKE

God said in effect, "It is done! I have fulfilled the requirements for you." But that has no effect on me personally unless I believe it is done. If I don't believe it is done and done effectively, I'll go on trying to do it myself. I must believe that it is done and that Jesus was able to do it.

MMS

Do I believe what God says, that he has done it all?
There's nothing left for me to do but believe.

GOD INITIATES SALVATION

While we were yet sinners, Christ died for us. ❖ For the grace of God that brings salvation has appeared to all men. ❖ Not that we loved God, but that he loved us and sent his Son as an atoning sacrifice for our sins. ❖ The Father has sent the Son to be the Savior of the world. ❖ In Christ God was reconciling the world to himself, not counting their trespasses against them. ❖ And you who once were estranged and hostile in mind, doing evil deeds, he has now reconciled in his fleshly body through death, so as to present you holy and blameless and irreproachable before him. ❖ For if, when we were enemies, we were reconciled to God by the death of his Son, much more, being reconciled, we shall be saved by his life. ❖ But when the kindness of God our Savior and His love for mankind appeared, He saved us, not on the basis of deeds which we have done in righteousness, but according to His mercy.

ROM. 5:8; TITUS 2:11 NKJV; 1 JOHN 4:10 NIV; 1 JOHN 4:14 NASB;
2 COR. 5:19 RSV; COL. 1:21–22 NRSV; ROM. 5:10; TITUS 3:4–5 NASB

The step into the situation where faith is possible is not an offer which we can make to Jesus, but always his gracious offer to us. His initiative—our obedience.

DIETRICH BONHOEFFER

[God] takes the initiative in approaching us, in disclosing to us that he wants us to know him.

ALISTER E. MCGRATH

All of us begin our Christian life instantly by a work God accomplishes without human means.

R. C. SPROUL

I can take no credit for my salvation. He did it all and gave it to me. What amazing love makes him care about me?

THE PERFECT PLAN

But when the fullness of time had come, God sent his Son, born of a woman, born under the law, in order to redeem those who were under the law, so that we might receive adoption as children. ❖ There is one God, and one mediator between God and men, the man Christ Jesus. ❖ Christ has redeemed us from the curse of the law, having become a curse for us. ❖ He is able also to save forever those who draw near to God through Him, since He always lives to make intercession for them. ❖ He sacrificed for their sins once for all when he offered himself. ❖ We are sanctified through the offering of the body of Jesus Christ once for all. ❖ This salvation, which was first announced by the Lord, was confirmed by those who heard him. God also testified to it by signs, wonders and various miracles, and gifts of the Holy Spirit distributed according to his will. ❖ And the LORD their God shall save them in that day as the flock of his people: for they shall be as the stones of a crown.

GAL. 4:4–5 NRSV; 1 TIM. 2:5; GAL. 3:13 NKJV; HEB. 7:25 NASB; HEB. 7:27 NIV; HEB. 10:10; HEB. 2:3–4 NIV; ZECH. 9:16

[The incarnation] tells us that the God with whom we are dealing is no distant ruler who remains aloof from the affairs of his creatures, but one who is passionately concerned with them to the extent that he takes the initiative in coming to them. God doesn't just reveal things about himself—he reveals himself in Jesus Christ.

ALISTER E. MCGRATH

God's plan of salvation was perfect. He didn't abolish the world system; he entered into it and showed man what was necessary: first, very personally, as he drew people like Abraham into a special understanding of who he is and what he requires; then very graphically, as he delivered his people from Egypt, gave them the Ten Commandments, and taught them the need of sacrifice and forgiveness; and finally very effectively, as he provided in Jesus the eternal and perfect sacrifice for our sin.

MMS

How complete and wonderful is your plan, heavenly Father.
Has God revealed himself to me? Am I seeking more of the revelation of
*   himself?*

PERFECT LOVE

But God demonstrates His own love toward us, in that while we were still sinners, Christ died for us. ❖ In this act we see what real love is: it is not our love for God but his love for us when he sent his Son to satisfy God's anger against our sins. ❖ God is love. ❖ Greater love hath no man than this, that a man lay down his life for his friends. ❖ This is how we know what love is: Jesus Christ laid down his life for us. ❖ For I am persuaded, that neither death, nor life, nor angels, nor principalities, nor powers, nor things present, nor things to come, nor height, nor depth, nor any other creature, shall be able to separate us from the love of God, which is in Christ Jesus our Lord.

ROM. 5:8 NKJV; 1 JOHN 4:10 TLB; 1 JOHN 4:8; JOHN 15:13; 1 JOHN 3:16 NIV; ROM. 8:38–39

In the wounds of the dying Savior, see the love of the great I AM.
CHARLES HADDON SPURGEON

The spectacle of the Cross, the most public event of Jesus' life, reveals the vast difference between a god who proves himself through power and One who proves himself through love.
PHILIP YANCEY

Love so amazing, so divine
Demands my love, my life, my all.
ISAAC WATTS

We are astonished and marvel that one so holy and dread should invite us into Thy banqueting house and cause love to be the banner over us. We cannot express the gratitude we feel, but look Thou on our hearts and read it there.
A. W. TOZER

Have I properly responded to God's great love by receiving the One who died for me?
How can I show my gratitude to God?

HIS MERCIFUL LOVE

The LORD, the LORD God, merciful and gracious, longsuffering, and abundant in goodness and truth. ❖ He took note of their distress when he heard their cry; for their sake he remembered his covenant and out of his great love he relented. ❖ Where is another God like you . . . ? You cannot stay angry with your people forever, because you delight in showing mercy. ❖ As a father has compassion on his children, so the LORD has compassion on those who fear Him. ❖ The beloved of the LORD rests in safety—the High God surrounds him all day long—the beloved rests between his shoulders. ❖ God, who is rich in mercy, because of His great love with which He loved us, even when we were dead in trespasses, made us alive together with Christ. ❖ Blessed be the God and Father of our Lord Jesus Christ! By his great mercy we have been born anew to a living hope through the resurrection of Jesus Christ from the dead.

EXOD. 34:6; PS. 106:44–45 NIV; MICAH 7:18 NLT; PS. 103:13 NASB; DEUT. 33:12 NRSV; EPH. 2:4–5 NKJV; 1 PETER 1:3 RSV

Though our feelings come and go, His love for us does not. It is not wearied by our sins, or our indifference; and, therefore, it is quite relentless in its determination that we shall be cured of those sins, at whatever cost to us, at whatever cost to Him.

C. S. LEWIS

His call is not judgment, but sheer mercy.
R. PAUL STEVENS

After ten thousand insults, he still loves you as infinitely as ever.
CHARLES HADDON SPURGEON

Does realizing how much God loves me affect the way I live?
Help me, Lord Jesus, to love you as I should.

HIS HEART OF LOVE

The LORD your God loves you. ❖ The kindness of God leads you to repentance. ❖ If we confess our sins, he is faithful and just to forgive us our sins, and to cleanse us from all unrighteousness. ❖ The Lord our God is merciful and pardons even those who have rebelled against him. ❖ God will be merciful if you confess your sins and give them up. ❖ Blessed is he whose transgression is forgiven, whose sin is covered. ❖ You forgave the iniquity of my sin. ❖ In You the fatherless finds mercy. ❖ Return to the LORD, your God, for he is gracious and merciful, slow to anger, and abounding in steadfast love. ❖ I will heal their faithlessness; I will love them freely. ❖ His steadfast love endures for ever! ❖ For great is your love, higher than the heavens; your faithfulness reaches to the skies.

DEUT. 23:5 NKJV; ROM. 2:4 NASB; 1 JOHN 1:9; DAN. 9:9 TLB; PROV. 28:13 CEV; PS. 32:1; PS. 32:5 NKJV; HOSEA 14:3 NKJV; JOEL 2:13; HOSEA 14:4 RSV; 1 CHRON. 16:34 RSV; PS. 108:4 NIV

The whole of my life stood open to His view from the beginning. He foresaw my every fall, my every sin, my every backsliding; yet, nevertheless, fixed His heart upon me. Oh, how the realization of this should bow me in wonder and worship before Him!

ARTHUR W. PINK

The King, full of mercy and goodness, very far from chastising me [for my sin], embraces me with love, makes me eat at His table, serves me with His own hands, gives me the key of His treasures; He converses and delights Himself with me incessantly . . . and treats me in all respects as His favorite.

BROTHER LAWRENCE

His heart is fixed on me! How amazing!
Help me to understand, O God, how great your love is for me.

GOD WANTS ME

The LORD is . . . abounding in steadfast love. ❖ The LORD your God, He is God, the faithful God who keeps covenant and mercy for a thousand generations with those who love Him and keep His commandments. ❖ How often I wanted to gather your children together, the way a hen gathers her chicks under her wings. ❖ He will love you and bless you. ❖ My presence shall go with thee. ❖ You are a chosen race, . . . God's own people. ❖ You are precious in my eyes, and honored, and I love you. ❖ See how great a love the Father has bestowed on us, that we would be called children of God; and such we are. ❖ For I am honored in the eyes of the LORD. ❖ "My heart yearns for him; I will surely have mercy on him," declares the LORD. ❖ Come unto me . . . and I will give you rest. ❖ The beloved of My soul.

NUM. 14:18 RSV; DEUT. 7:9 NKJV; MATT. 23:37 NASB; DEUT. 7:13 NKJV; EXOD. 33:14; 1 PETER 2:9 NRSV; ISA. 43:4 RSV; 1 JOHN 3:1 NASB; ISA. 49:5 RSV; JER. 31:20 NASB; MATT. 11:28; JER. 12:7 NASB

God's promises are . . . overflowings from his great heart.
CHARLES HADDON SPURGEON

God calls you into a relationship with Himself.
BLACKABY AND KING

It is a strange and beautiful eccentricity of the free God that He has allowed His heart to be emotionally identified with men. Self-sufficient as He is, He wants our love and will not be satisfied till He gets it. Free as He is, He has let His heart be bound to us forever.

A. W. TOZER

We may often forget to think of our Lord, but he never ceases to remember us.
CHARLES HADDON SPURGEON

Am I running from God or have I let him have me?
How can I ignore him when his love for me is so relentless?

HE SEEKS US

When you were dead in your sins and in the uncircumcision of your sinful nature, God made you alive with Christ. He forgave us all our sins. ❖ But when he was yet a great way off, his father saw him, and had compassion, and ran, and fell on his neck, and kissed him. ❖ What man among you, if he has a hundred sheep and has lost one of them, does not leave the ninety-nine in the open pasture and go after the one which is lost until he finds it? And when he has found it, he lays it on his shoulders, rejoicing. ❖ Or what woman, having ten silver coins, if she loses one coin, does not light a lamp and sweep the house and seek diligently until she finds it? ❖ For you know the grace of our Lord Jesus Christ, that though He was rich, yet for your sakes He became poor, that you through His poverty might become rich. ❖ He came to His own, and those who were His own did not receive Him. But as many as received Him, to them He gave the right to become children of God.

COL. 2:13 NIV; LUKE 15:20; LUKE 15:4–5 NASB; LUKE 15:8 RSV; 2 COR. 8:9 NKJV; JOHN 1:11–12 NASB

When it is a question of a sinner He does not merely stand still, open his arms and say, "Come hither"; no, He stands there and waits, as the father of the son waited, rather He does not stand and wait, He goes forth to seek, as the shepherd sought the lost sheep, as the woman sought the lost coin. He goes—yet no, He has gone, but infinitely farther than any shepherd or any woman, He went, in sooth, the infinitely long way from being God to becoming man, and that way He went in search of sinners.

SØREN KIERKEGAARD

The scope of God's redeeming work is always larger than we allow ourselves to believe.

R. C. SPROUL

Thank you, Lord Jesus, for coming in search of me.
There is no one like you, my Savior. No one could love me as you do.

LOOK ONLY TO HIM

You are my hiding place; You shall preserve me from trouble; You shall surround me with songs of deliverance. ❖ O that my people would listen to me, that Israel would walk in my ways! Then I would quickly subdue their enemies, and turn my hand against their foes. ❖ Oh, that they had such a heart in them that they would fear Me and always keep all My commandments, that it might be well with them and with their children forever! ❖ For God is at work within you, helping you want to obey him, and then helping you do what he wants. ❖ The Spirit helps us in our weakness. ❖ Call on His name. ❖ Deliver us from the evil one. ❖ Your God whom you constantly serve will Himself deliver you. ❖ On him we have set our hope that he will deliver us again. ❖ I am thy shield, and thy exceeding great reward. ❖ Shout aloud and sing for joy, O royal Zion, for great in your midst is the Holy One of Israel. ❖ The LORD is my rock, and my fortress, and my deliverer.

Ps. 32:7 NKJV; Ps. 81:13–14 NRSV; DEUT. 5:29 NKJV; PHIL. 2:13 TLB; ROM. 8:26 RSV; ISA. 12:4 NASB; MATT. 6:13 NKJV; DAN. 6:16 NASB; 2 COR. 1:10 RSV; GEN. 15:1; ISA. 12:6 NRSV; Ps. 18:2

When we think of being delivered from sin, of being filled with the Spirit, and of walking in the light, we picture the peak of a great mountain, very high and wonderful, and we say—"Oh, but I could never live up there!" But when we do get there by God's grace, we find it is not a mountain peak, but a plateau where there is ample room to live and to grow.

OSWALD CHAMBERS

Do not fight the thing [the temptation] in detail. Turn from it. Look ONLY at your Lord. Sing. Read. Work.

AMY CARMICHAEL

He will bring me safe to heaven at last, unhurt by the way.

CHARLES HADDON SPURGEON

He is my Savior, meeting my greatest need for deliverance—deliverance from the power of sin.
Is my trust in him alone?

THE AUTHOR OF MY FAITH

Let us fix our eyes on Jesus, the author and perfecter of our faith. ❖ That your faith would not rest on the wisdom of men, but on the power of God. ❖ A man can receive nothing, except it be given him from heaven. ❖ He which hath begun a good work in you will perform it until the day of Jesus Christ. ❖ For it is God who works in you both to will and to do for His good pleasure. ❖ Do not think of yourself more highly than you ought, but rather think of yourself with sober judgment, in accordance with the measure of faith God has given you. ❖ Faith comes from what is heard, and what is heard comes by the preaching of Christ. ❖ When we told you the good news, it was with the power and assurance that come from the Holy Spirit, and not simply with words. ❖ After beginning with the Spirit, are you now trying to attain your goal by human effort? ❖ Now may the God of hope fill you with all joy and peace in believing, that you may abound in hope by the power of the Holy Spirit.

HEB. 12:2 NIV; 1 COR. 2:5 NASB; JOHN 3:27; PHIL. 1:6; PHIL. 2:13 NKJV; ROM. 12:3 NIV; ROM. 10:17 RSV; 1 THESS. 1:5 CEV; GAL. 3:3 NIV; ROM. 15:13 NKJV

God in Christ is the author and finisher of my faith. He knows exactly what needs to happen in my life for my faith to grow. He designs the perfect program for me.

MMS

Faith views each promise in connection with the Promise Giver, and says with assurance, "Surely goodness and love will follow me all the days of my life" (Psalm 23:6).

CHARLES HADDON SPURGEON

Are my eyes on the Promise Giver?
Am I working with his program so that my faith will grow and I will be pleasing to him?

BELIEVING

God wants you to have faith in the one he sent. ❖ We have believed in Jesus Christ, that we might be justified by the faith of Christ. ❖ [Jesus] said to him, "Do you believe in the Son of God?" He answered and said, "Who is He, Lord, that I may believe in Him?" And Jesus said to him, "You have both seen Him and it is He who is talking with you." Then he said, "Lord, I believe!" ❖ It is this God who has made you and me into faithful Christians. ❖ The Son of man [must] be lifted up, that whoever believes in him may have eternal life. ❖ Build yourselves up on your most holy faith. ❖ Have faith in the LORD your God and you will be upheld. ❖ Our eyes are on you. ❖ Did not God choose the poor of this world to be rich in faith and heirs of the kingdom which He promised to those who love Him? ❖ If you have faith as a grain of mustard seed, you will say to this mountain, "Move from here to there," and it will move; and nothing will be impossible to you. ❖ Whatever things you ask in prayer, believing, you will receive. ❖ I know the one in whom I trust, and I am sure that he is able to guard what I have entrusted to him until the day of his return.

JOHN 6:29 CEV; GAL. 2:16; JOHN 9:35–38 NKJV; 2 COR. 1:21 TLB; JOHN 3:14–15 RSV; JUDE 20 RSV; 2 CHRON. 20:20 NIV; 2 CHRON. 20:12 NRSV; JAMES 2:5 NASB; MATT. 17:20 RSV; MATT. 21:22 NKJV; 2 TIM. 1:12 NLT

The measure of faith must always determine the measure of power and of blessing. . . . Faith can only live by feeding on what is Divine, on God Himself.

ANDREW MURRAY

The Holy Spirit has taken a set of historic, space/time events and so applied those events to my mind and heart that it is impossible for me not to believe.

STEVE BROWN

Do I rely on God for the faith I need?
Can I trust him every day for everything?

BOUND BY SIN

No one can come to Me unless the Father who sent Me draws him. ❖ I have drawn you with lovingkindness. ❖ No one can come to Me unless it has been granted to him by My Father. ❖ The mind that is set on the flesh is hostile to God; it does not submit to God's law—indeed it cannot, and those who are in the flesh cannot please God. ❖ For all have sinned, and come short of the glory of God. ❖ Jews and Gentiles alike are all under sin. ❖ There is no one who does not sin. ❖ Sin controls everyone. ❖ For the wages of sin is death; but the gift of God is eternal life through Jesus Christ our Lord. ❖ If any man sin, we have an advocate with the Father, Jesus Christ the righteous.

JOHN 6:44 NKJV; JER. 31:3 NASB; JOHN 6:65 NKJV; ROM. 8:7–8 NRSV; ROM. 3:23; ROM. 3:9 NIV; 1 KINGS 8:46 NRSV; GAL. 3:22 CEV; ROM. 6:23; 1 JOHN 2:1

Sin taints every thought, word, and act, including the seemingly best deeds.
R. C. SPROUL

We are so depraved that God must drag us to himself. The beauty of the gospel, however, is that at the same time, the Spirit's work is to make us willing to come.
R. C. SPROUL

The wrath of God is a perfection of the Divine character upon which we need to frequently meditate. First, that our hearts may be duly impressed by God's detestation of sin. . . . The more we study and ponder God's abhorrence of sin and His frightful vengeance upon it, the more likely we are to realize its heinousness. Secondly, to beget a true fear in our souls for God: ". . . for our 'God is a consuming fire'" (Heb. 12:29). We cannot serve Him "acceptably" unless there is due "reverence" for His awful Majesty and "godly fear" of His righteous anger; and these are best promoted by frequently calling to mind that "our God is a consuming fire." Thirdly, to draw our souls, in fervent praise for our having been delivered from "the wrath to come" (1 Thess. 1:10).
ARTHUR W. PINK

Lord, impress on me the awfulness of sin and how you hate it. Give me a desire to forsake all that is sin in me. May I allow your Spirit to cleanse me, making me pure in your sight.

LIFE FROM GOD

I created you. I will carry you and always keep you safe. ❖ Uphold me according unto thy word, that I may live. ❖ He reached from on high, he took me, he drew me out of many waters. ❖The LORD is my light and my salvation; whom shall I fear? the LORD is the strength of my life; of whom shall I be afraid? ❖ With long life will I satisfy him, and shew him my salvation. ❖ He is not a God of the dead, but of the living. ❖ I am the Vine, you are the branches. When you're joined with me and I with you, the relation intimate and organic, the harvest is sure to be abundant. Separated, you can't produce a thing. ❖ Meditate upon all the laws I have given you today, and pass them on to your children. These laws are not mere words—they are your life! ❖ I am the bread of life; he who comes to Me will not hunger, and he who believes in Me will never thirst. ❖ I am the light of the world. He who follows Me shall not walk in darkness, but have the light of life. ❖ The LORD is your life. ❖ I came so they can have real and eternal life, more and better life than they ever dreamed of.

ISA. 46:4 CEV; PS. 119:116; PS. 18:16 RSV; PS. 27:1; PS. 91:16; LUKE 20:38; JOHN 15:5 THE MESSAGE; DEUT. 32:46–47 TLB; JOHN 6:35 NASB; JOHN 8:12 NKJV; DEUT. 30:20 NIV; JOHN 10:10 THE MESSAGE

We accept Jesus Christ, the living Word of God, as our life.
RICHARD FOSTER

He has transforming power—He can change the quality of our lives.
CHARLES SWINDOLL

We are created so as to receive life from God, who is Spirit, and to express that life through our bodies and in the physical world in which we live.
RICHARD FOSTER

Since I have known Christ, has he changed the quality of my life?
Am I experiencing his promise of a life that is better than I ever dreamed?

OUR LIFE IS IN HIM

My tabernacle also shall be with them: . . . I will be their God, and they shall be my people. . . . My sanctuary shall be in the midst of them for evermore. ❖ O Lord, . . . You have redeemed my life. ❖ For with You is the fountain of life. ❖ The breath of the Almighty hath given me life. ❖ You show me the path of life. In your presence there is fullness of joy; in your right hand are pleasures forevermore. ❖ Jesus said to her, "I am the resurrection and the life; he who believes in Me will live even if he dies, and everyone who lives and believes in Me will never die." ❖ Whoever believes in the Son has eternal life. ❖ And this is what he has promised us, eternal life. ❖ The LORD their God will save them on that day as the flock of his people. They will sparkle in his land like jewels in a crown. ❖ You shall also be a crown of glory in the hand of the LORD, and a royal diadem in the hand of your God.

EZEK. 37:27–28; LAM. 3:58 NKJV; PS. 36:9 NKJV; JOB 33:4; PS. 16:11 NRSV; JOHN 11:25–26 NASB; JOHN 3:36 NRSV; 1 JOHN 2:25 RSV; ZECH. 9:16 NIV; ISA. 62:3 NKJV

Salvation is a radical change, being thrust from the womb of sin into the life of God.

JOEY JOHNSON

Yet that God has made us of the stuff of eternity is both a glory and a prophecy, a glory yet to be realized and a prophecy yet to be fulfilled.

A. W. TOZER

Do I look forward to life with God throughout eternity?
Make me a crown of splendor in your hand, O Lord.

GOD DOES MORE THAN WE CAN IMAGINE

I watch, and am as a sparrow alone upon the house top. ❖ In all their affliction He was afflicted, and the angel of His presence saved them; in His love and in His mercy He redeemed them; and He lifted them and carried them all the days of old. ❖ The LORD your God carried you, as a man carries his son. ❖ Even to your old age, I am He, and even to gray hairs I will carry you! ❖ Even [Gentiles] will I bring to my holy mountain, and make them joyful in my house of prayer: their burnt offerings and their sacrifices shall be accepted upon mine altar; for mine house shall be called an house of prayer for all people. ❖ For they shall hear of your great name, your mighty hand, and your outstretched arm. ❖ And they were astonished beyond measure, saying, "He has done all things well; he even makes the deaf hear and the dumb speak." ❖ And God is able to make all grace abound toward you. ❖ He who supplies seed to the sower and bread for food will supply and multiply your resources and increase the harvest of your righteousness. ❖ Now to him who by the power at work within us is able to accomplish abundantly far more than all we can ask or imagine, to him be glory.

Ps. 102:7; Isa. 63:9 NASB; DEUT. 1:31 NKJV; ISA. 46:4 NKJV; ISA. 56:7;
1 KINGS 8:42 NRSV; MARK 7:37 RSV; 2 COR. 9:8; 2 COR. 9:10 RSV;
EPH. 3:20–21 NRSV

How great is the generosity of Jesus! He has given us his all. Even if he only donated a tenth of his possessions to our cause, it would make us rich beyond belief. But he was not content until he had given everything.

CHARLES HADDON SPURGEON

My pride is a burden I carry, a trap encircling me, a disease invading my body, mud holding my feet immobile. But, praise God, his Holy Spirit is able to lift the burden, open the trap, heal the disease, and pull me out of the mud. Praise him! He is able to rescue me from myself!

MMS

You have been with me; you have saved me; you have carried me through many difficulties; you have taught me that your love is everlasting and your mercy has no boundaries.
What will you do next that is beyond my imagination?

TRUST IN HIS DELIVERANCE

He has a great army, but they are all mere men, while we have the Lord our God to fight our battles for us! ❖ Do not be afraid of them, for I am with you to deliver you, says the LORD. ❖ Our God, make us strong again! Smile on us and save us. ❖ He clung to the LORD; he did not depart from following Him, but kept His commandments. ❖ The angel of the LORD encamps around those who fear Him, and rescues them. ❖ The LORD saved Hezekiah and the people of Jerusalem from the hand of Sennacherib . . . and from the hand of all others. He took care of them on every side. ❖ The name of the LORD is a strong tower; the righteous run to it and are safe. ❖ Many are the afflictions of the righteous: but the LORD delivereth him out of them all. ❖ Be brave and strong! . . . The LORD your God will always be at your side, and he will never abandon you. ❖ The LORD . . . will not forsake his faithful ones. ❖ You shall go out in joy, and be led forth in peace.

2 CHRON. 32:8 TLB; JER. 1:8 NRSV; PS. 80:3 CEV; 2 KINGS 18:6 NASB; PS. 34:7 NASB; 2 CHRON. 32:22 NIV; PROV. 18:10 NKJV; PS. 34:19; DEUT. 31:6 CEV; PS. 37:28 NIV; ISA. 55:12 RSV

In the face of the incredibly powerful army of Assyria, Hezekiah trusted God to protect Israel. It wasn't something he was matter-of-fact about. He and Isaiah cried out to the Lord for his protection. Trying to shake their faith in God, Sennacherib reminded them that no other nation was able to stand against his army, but Hezekiah stood firmly in his trust in God. And God came through in a miraculous way—an angel destroyed the enemy. Certainly this was not something Hezekiah could have done or perhaps even imagined. He just knew that in some way God would protect them.

MMS

> How often, when trials like sea billows roll,
> Have I hidden in Thee, O Thou Rock of my soul.
> WILLIAM O. CUSHING

My thoughts can be like the taunts of Sennacherib. I must ignore them and trust in my Savior.
Help me hide in you.

GOD IS MY SOURCE AND STRENGTH

The LORD has become my stronghold, and my God the rock of my refuge. ❖ Lead me to the rock that is higher than I. ❖ The God of my strength, in whom I will trust; my shield and the horn of my salvation, my stronghold and my refuge; my Savior. ❖ [Elisha] answered, "Do not fear, for those who are with us are more than those who are with them." . . . And the LORD opened the servant's eyes, and he saw; and behold, the mountain was full of horses and chariots of fire. ❖ By awesome deeds you answer us with deliverance, O God of our salvation. ❖ Happy is the man who has the God of Jacob as his helper, whose hope is in the Lord his God. . . He is the God who keeps every promise. ❖ For He who is mighty has done great things for me, and holy is His name. ❖ Blessed be the LORD God of Israel from everlasting, and to everlasting. Amen, and Amen.

PS. 94:22 RSV; PS. 61:2; 2 SAM. 22:3 NKJV; 2 KINGS 6:16–17 NASB; PS. 65:5 NRSV; PS. 146:5–6 TLB; LUKE 1:49 NKJV; PS. 41:13

When we reach the end of our hoarded resources
Our Father's full giving is only begun.

.   .   .   .

His love has no limit; His grace has no measure
His power has no boundary known unto men
For out of His infinite riches in Jesus
He giveth and giveth and giveth again!
ANNIE JOHNSON FLINT

With the goodness of God to desire our highest welfare, the wisdom of God to plan it, and the power of God to achieve it, what do we lack?
A. W. TOZER

What need do I have that he is incapable or unwilling to meet?
How can I follow his example and give and give and give again?

HE'S ALWAYS WITH US

I myself will tend my sheep and have them lie down, declares the Sovereign LORD. I will search for the lost and bring back the strays. I will bind up the injured and strengthen the weak. ❖ Thus shall they know that I the LORD their God am with them. ❖ As I was with Moses, so I will be with you. I will not leave you nor forsake you. ❖ I have not seen the righteous forsaken. ❖ The LORD is near to the brokenhearted, and saves the crushed in spirit. ❖ Now My eyes will be open and My ears attentive to prayer made in this place. . . . My eyes and My heart will be there perpetually. ❖ The LORD has heard my supplication; the LORD accepts my prayer. ❖ Christ Jesus is He who died, yes, rather who was raised, who is at the right hand of God, who also intercedes for us. ❖ For I am sure that neither death, nor life, nor angels, nor principalities, nor things present, nor things to come, nor powers, nor height, nor depth, nor anything else in all creation, will be able to separate us from the love of God in Christ Jesus our Lord. ❖ The LORD will be your everlasting light.

EZEK. 34:15–16 NIV; EZEK. 34:30; JOSH. 1:5 NKJV; PS. 37:25 RSV; PS. 34:18 RSV; 2 CHRON. 7:15–16 NKJV; PS. 6:9 NRSV; ROM. 8:34 NASB; ROM. 8:38–39 RSV; ISA. 60:19 NRSV

God said his name would be in the temple forever. Now *we* are the temple. He gives us his name forever and his heart is with us perpetually. Always his eyes watch over us. How blessed we are! His presence with us is unconditional, never leaving us no matter how far from him we try to go.

MMS

The next time you hear a baby laugh or see an ocean wave, take note. Pause and listen as his Majesty whispers ever so gently, "I'm here."

MAX LUCADO

I bask in the light of your presence! I delight in the warmth of your love! When I feel far from the Lord, who has moved?

GOD'S COMPASSION

The LORD your God is with you, he is mighty to save. He will take great delight in you, he will quiet you with his love, he will rejoice over you with singing. ❖ I will redeem you with an outstretched arm. ❖ Because of your great mercy, you never abandoned them in the desert. ❖ Their heart was not steadfast toward him; they were not true to his covenant. Yet he, being compassionate, forgave their iniquity, and did not destroy them; often he restrained his anger, and did not stir up all his wrath. ❖ Yet God does not take away a life; but He devises means, so that His banished ones are not expelled from Him. ❖ Therefore the LORD longs to be gracious to you, and therefore He waits on high to have compassion on you. ❖ In distress he entreated the favor of the LORD his God and humbled himself greatly before the God of his fathers. He prayed to him, and God received his entreaty and heard his supplication. ❖ Know therefore that the LORD your God is God, the faithful God who keeps covenant and steadfast love with those who love him and keep his commandments, to a thousand generations.

ZEPH. 3:17 NIV; EXOD. 6:6 NKJV; NEH. 9:19 CEV; PS. 78:37–38 NRSV; 2 SAM. 14:14 NKJV; ISA. 30:18 NASB; 2 CHRON. 33:12–13 RSV; DEUT. 7:9 RSV

Mercy is an attribute of God, an infinite and inexhaustible energy within the divine nature which disposes God to be actively compassionate.

A. W. TOZER

After each failure, ask forgiveness, pick yourself up and try again. Very often what God first helps us towards is not the virtue itself but just this power of always trying again. For however important chastity (or courage, or truthfulness, or any other virtue) may be, this process trains us in habits of the soul which are more important still. It cures our illusions about ourselves and teaches us to depend on God. We learn, on the one hand, that we cannot trust ourselves even in our best moments, and, on the other, that we need not despair even in our worst, for our failures are forgiven. The only fatal thing is to sit down content with anything less than perfection.

C. S. LEWIS

I'm beginning to realize how much the Father loves me, even though I am so unworthy of his love.
His love and compassion are boundless; they know no end.

HIS NATURE IS FORGIVING

The Lord is slow to anger, abounding in love and forgiving sin and rebellion. ❖ The Lord is full of compassion and is merciful. ❖ If You, Lord, should mark iniquities, O Lord, who could stand? But there is forgiveness with You. ❖ You are a God of forgiveness. ❖ I, even I, am He who blots out your transgressions for My own sake; and I will not remember your sins. ❖ I will cleanse them from all the guilt of their sin against me, and I will forgive all the guilt of their sin and rebellion against me. ❖ The Lord thy God is a merciful God. ❖ For you, O Lord, are good and forgiving, abounding in steadfast love to all who call on you. ❖ He saved us, not on the basis of deeds which we have done in righteousness, but according to His mercy. ❖ Through Jesus the forgiveness of sins is proclaimed. ❖ God in Christ forgave you.

Num. 14:18 niv; James 5:11 nasb; Ps. 130:3–4 nkjv; Neh. 9:17 tlb; Isa. 43:25 nkjv; Jer. 33:8 rsv; Deut. 4:31; Ps. 86:5 nrsv; Titus 3:5 nasb; Acts 13:38 niv; Eph. 4:32 rsv

Forgiveness is the divine miracle of grace; it cost God the Cross of Jesus Christ before He could forgive sin and remain a holy God.

Oswald Chambers

Miracles broke the physical laws of the universe; forgiveness broke the moral rules.

Philip Yancey

Forgiveness does not necessarily mean that sin is eliminated—it means that the *threat sin poses to man's relationship to God* is eliminated. There is all the difference in the world between being sinless and being forgiven!

Alister E. McGrath

How amazing that I, though so unworthy, so sinful, am the beneficiary of God's abounding love and unlimited forgiveness!

MMS

How should I respond to such mercy and grace?
I know that I am undeserving but I humbly bow before him and accept all that he has done for me.

JESUS' OBEDIENCE

Even though Jesus was God's Son, he had to learn from experience what it was like to obey when obeying meant suffering. ❖ Through the obedience of the One the many will be made righteous. ❖ Jesus said to them, "My food is to do the will of Him who sent Me, and to finish His work." ❖ I do as the Father has commanded me, so that the world may know that I love the Father. ❖ He went out into a mountain to pray, and continued all night in prayer to God. ❖ I want your will, not mine. ❖ He was led as a sheep to the slaughter; and like a lamb dumb before his shearer, so opened he not his mouth. ❖ He obediently humbled himself . . . by dying a criminal's death on a cross. ❖ For this reason the Father loves me, because I lay down my life in order to take it up again. No one takes it from me, but I lay it down of my own accord. ❖ He bore the sin of many, and made intercession for the transgressors. ❖ But all this was done, that the scriptures of the prophets might be fulfilled. ❖ It was the will of the LORD.

HEB. 5:8 TLB; ROM. 5:19 NASB; JOHN 4:34 NKJV; JOHN 14:31 RSV; LUKE 6:12; MATT. 26:39 TLB; ACTS 8:32; PHIL. 2:8 NLT; JOHN 10:17–18 NRSV; ISA. 53:12 NKJV; MATT. 26:56; ISA. 53:10 RSV

It is here, as Scripture saith [Heb. 5:8], that He learned obedience, and became the author of everlasting salvation to all that obey Him.

ANDREW MURRAY

Suffering teaches us to align our wills with his. Jesus too had to subdue his own will until he was able to say about the cross—not my will but yours. He had *learned* that obedience.

MMS

Both Adam and Jesus were tempted on the same point. The critical issue for both was: Would they trust God? The question was not whether they would believe that there is a God, but whether they would trust him.

R. C. SPROUL

Jesus is my teacher, my model of obedience.
Help me to be like you, Lord, knowing the Father's will is always best.

HE LEFT HIS HEAVENLY HOME

Though he was rich, yet for your sakes he became poor. ❖ Who, though he was in the form of God, did not count equality with God a thing to be grasped, but emptied himself, taking the form of a servant, being born in the likeness of men. ❖ You will . . . bring forth a Son, and shall call His name Jesus. He will be great, and will be called the Son of the Highest. ❖ But when the fullness of time had come, God sent his Son, born of woman, born under the law, in order to redeem those who were under the law. ❖ There has been born for you a Savior, who is Christ the Lord. ❖ Since we, God's children, are human beings—made of flesh and blood—he became flesh and blood too by being born in human form; for only as a human being could he die and in dying break the power of the devil who had the power of death.

2 COR. 8:9; PHIL. 2:6–7 RSV; LUKE 1:31–32 NKJV; GAL. 4:4–5 NRSV; LUKE 2:11 NASB; HEB. 2:14 TLB

Why would he come to earth as a frail human baby? Why would he suffer the frustrations of life on earth? Why would he subject himself to thirst and hunger, headaches, dusty roads, and hardheaded friends? Why would he be willing to die the death of a criminal, the agonizing crucifixion? There is no human explanation. It's beyond us but well within the heart of a loving God, a lovesick God, who would do what was necessary to bring his beloved back to him. Praise to the resurrected Christ who did it all for me!

MMS

Dorothy Sayers has said that God underwent three great humiliations in his efforts to rescue the human race. The first was the Incarnation, when he took on the confines of a physical body. The second was the Cross, when he suffered the ignominy of public execution. The third humiliation, Sayers suggested, is the church. In an awesome act of self-denial, God entrusted his reputation to ordinary people.

PHILIP YANCEY

He left the bosom of the Father and entered the womb of Mary.
He ascended from the cold rejection of earth and entered the warm adoration of heaven.

THE SACRIFICE THAT COVERS OUR SIN

Christ died for our sins according to the scriptures. ❖ For He made Him who knew no sin to be sin for us, that we might become the righteousness of God in Him. ❖ So the soldiers took charge of Jesus. . . . They crucified him. ❖ He was wounded for our transgressions, crushed for our iniquities; upon him was the punishment that made us whole, and by his bruises we are healed. ❖ You know that you were ransomed . . . with the precious blood of Christ. ❖ Christ was offered once to bear the sins of many. ❖ He himself bore our sins in his body on the tree, that we might die to sin and live to righteousness. ❖ Because of his great love for us, God, who is rich in mercy, made us alive with Christ even when we were dead in transgressions—it is by grace you have been saved.

1 Cor. 15:3; 2 Cor. 5:21 nkjv; John 19:16, 18 niv; Isa. 53:5 nrsv; 1 Peter 1:18–19 rsv; Heb. 9:28 nkjv; 1 Peter 2:24 rsv; Eph. 2:4–5 niv

---

In the crucifixion we are shown the full horror of the consequences of sin, and the urgency of the call to repent, to turn away from it to the one who alone may break its hold upon us. The cross reveals both the seriousness of sin, and the purpose and power of God to overcome it.

Alister E. McGrath

This is an eternal truth. Sin cannot be pardoned without atonement. That means that there is no hope for me outside of Christ, for there is no other blood that can truly take away my sin.

Charles Haddon Spurgeon

Ask God to give you a proper fear of his intolerance of sin, that you might cling to Jesus and his atonement with greater desperation.

R. C. Sproul

How could I ignore so great a sacrifice, so great a love?
I bow before you, my Savior, aware of my unworthiness, thankful for your
blood that covers my sin.

HE DID IT ALL

For as in Adam all die, even so in Christ shall all be made alive. ❖ For Christ also died for sins once for all, the righteous for the unrighteous. ❖ The Son of Man did not come to be served, but to serve, and to give His life a ransom for many. ❖ The blood of Jesus Christ His Son cleanses us from all sin. ❖ Without shedding of blood there is no forgiveness. ❖ He is able to save forever those who draw near to God through Him, since He always lives to make intercession for them. ❖ But you were washed, you were sanctified, you were justified in the name of the Lord Jesus Christ and in the Spirit of our God. ❖ Since we have now been justified by his blood, how much more shall we be saved from God's wrath through him! ❖ Therefore if any man be in Christ, he is a new creature: old things are passed away; behold, all things are become new.

1 Cor. 15:22; 1 Peter 3:18 rsv; Matt. 20:28 nkjv; 1 John 1:7 nkjv; Heb. 9:22 nasb; Heb. 7:25 nasb; 1 Cor. 6:11 rsv; Rom. 5:9 niv; 2 Cor. 5:17

This is not some small peephole, through which we may peer at the mercy seat. No, this veil has been ripped apart, from top to bottom. We may come boldly to the throne of heavenly grace.

Charles Haddon Spurgeon

The idea of a bloodthirsty, vengeful God has no place at all in the New Testament, which affirms that God himself entered into history in order to suffer for offending sinners. If *anyone* suffers, it is God himself who suffers on man's behalf and in man's place in order that justice and mercy might both be satisfied. It is the judge himself who suffers in order that his own law may be upheld and man truly and justly forgiven.

Alister E. McGrath

But blessed be His name, that which His holiness demanded His grace has provided in Christ Jesus our Lord.

Arthur W. Pink

I praise you, Lord Jesus. Your provision for my salvation is complete!
Jesus paid the price and redeemed me. Now I belong to him and will live with
    him eternally.

HE PAID THE PRICE

For as by one man's disobedience many were made sinners, so by the obedience of one shall many be made righteous. ❖ Since all have sinned and fall short of the glory of God, they are justified by his grace as a gift, through the redemption which is in Christ Jesus. ❖ He humbled himself, and became obedient unto death, even the death of the cross. ❖ Jesus also suffered outside the gate in order to sanctify the people through his own blood. ❖ God presented him as a sacrifice of atonement, through faith in his blood. ❖ In [Christ] we have redemption through his blood, the forgiveness of sins, according to the riches of his grace. ❖ He entered the Most Holy Place once for all, having obtained eternal redemption. ❖ For with the Lord there is lovingkindness, and with Him is abundant redemption. ❖ You, O Lord, are our Father; Our Redeemer from Everlasting is Your name.

Rom. 5:19; Rom. 3:23–24 rsv; Phil. 2:8; Heb. 13:12 rsv; Rom. 3:25 niv; Eph. 1:7; Heb. 9:12 nkjv; Ps. 130:7 nasb; Isa. 63:16 nkjv

---

Man is brought to God through God being brought to man.
Alister E. McGrath

We need no human mediator, for God himself became one.
Philip Yancey

It is a very precious thing to stand at the altar of our Good Shepherd, to see him bleeding there as a slaughtered priest, and then to hear his blood speaking peace to his whole flock.

Charles Haddon Spurgeon

Do I believe that he is my sacrificial Lamb, paying the price for my sin and that through him I am forgiven? I rejoice, for I am redeemed!
He gave his all for me; what do I give back in return?

HE SUFFERED FOR ME

Surely our griefs He Himself bore, and our sorrows He carried; yet we ourselves esteemed Him stricken, smitten of God, and afflicted. But He was pierced through for our transgressions, He was crushed for our iniquities; the chastening for our well-being fell upon Him, and by His scourging we are healed. ❖ I say unto you, that one of you shall betray me. ❖ Jesus began to show to His disciples that He must go to Jerusalem, and suffer many things . . . and be killed. . . . Peter took Him aside and began to rebuke Him, saying, "Far be it from You, Lord; this shall not happen to You!" ❖ The Son of Man . . . will be handed over to the Gentiles. They will mock him, insult him, spit on him, flog him and kill him. ❖ And he said to them, "My soul is very sorrowful, even to death; remain here, and watch." ❖ Then they spit on him. They took the stick from him and beat him on the head with it. When the soldiers had finished making fun of Jesus, they took off the robe. They put his own clothes back on him and led him off to be nailed to a cross.

Isa. 53:4–5 nasb; John 13:21; Matt. 16:21–22 nkjv; Luke 18:31–32 niv;
Mark 14:34 rsv; Matt. 27: 30–31 cev

Every part of his body suffered, but he came through it all, into his power and glory, uninjured.

Charles Haddon Spurgeon

The spirit of Peter, seeking to turn Him away from the cross and its suffering, was nothing but Satan tempting Him to turn aside from what God had appointed as our way of salvation.

Andrew Murray

They spit on you, Lord. They punched you and slapped you in the face. Do we, who *know* you are God, treat you any better?

MMS

Thank you, Lord, for suffering and dying in my place.

HE IS MY SAVIOR

This Man, delivered up by the predetermined plan and foreknowledge of God, you nailed to a cross by the hands of godless men and put Him to death. And God raised Him up again, putting an end to the agony of death, since it was impossible for Him to be held in its power. ❖ For while we were still helpless, at the right time Christ died for the ungodly. . . . God demonstrates His own love toward us, in that while we were yet sinners, Christ died for us. ❖ Therefore we are buried with him by baptism into death: that like as Christ was raised up from the dead by the glory of the Father, even so we also should walk in newness of life. ❖ And God hath both raised up the Lord, and will also raise up us by his own power. ❖ You have been raised with Christ. ❖ When he had made purification for sins, he sat down at the right hand of the Majesty on high. ❖ Christ died and was raised to life, and now he is at God's right side, speaking to him for us.

ACTS 2:23–24 NASB; ROM. 5:6, 8 NASB; ROM. 6:4; 1 COR. 6:14; COL. 3:1 RSV; HEB. 1:3 RSV; ROM. 8:34 CEV

Paul makes a clear distinction between the *event* of the death of Christ, and the *significance* of this event. That Christ died is a simple matter of history; that Christ died *for our sins* is the gospel itself.

ALISTER E. MCGRATH

Paul links Jesus' death and resurrection together as the two elements of his gospel. Jesus "was put to death for our trespasses and raised for our justification" (Rom. 4:25).

ALISTER E. MCGRATH

The resurrection . . . publicly proclaims that God has been completely satisfied, and redemption has been fully accomplished.

R. C. SPROUL

In the New Testament Jesus Christ is . . . salvation itself, He is the Gospel of God.

OSWALD CHAMBERS

I will never comprehend how much I owe you, my Savior.
May the fact that I have been raised with you impact my life today.

ONE AND ONLY SAVIOR

And there is no other God besides Me, a righteous God and a Savior; there is none except Me. ❖ You shall call His name Jesus, for He will save His people from their sins. ❖ For there is no other name under heaven that has been given among men, by which we must be saved. ❖ Everyone who believes in him receives forgiveness of sins through his name. ❖ Whoever believes in the Son has eternal life; whoever disobeys the Son will not see life, but must endure God's wrath. ❖ For there is one God, and one mediator between God and men, the man Christ Jesus. ❖ And God placed all things under his feet and appointed him to be head over everything for the church, which is his body. ❖ His dominion is an everlasting dominion, which shall not pass away, and his kingdom that which shall not be destroyed. ❖ Christ is the head of his body, the church; he gave his life to be her Savior. ❖ And Jesus came and spoke to them, saying, "All authority has been given to Me in heaven and on earth." ❖ I am with you always, to the close of the age.

ISA. 45:21 NASB; MATT. 1:21 NKJV; ACTS 4:12 NASB; ACTS 10:43 RSV; JOHN 3:36 NRSV; 1 TIMOTHY 2:5; EPH. 1:22–23 NIV; DAN. 7:14; EPH. 5:23 NLT; MATT. 28:18 NKJV; MATT. 28:20 RSV

Christians did not come up with the idea that Jesus is the only way to God. That idea originated with Jesus. If he was wrong, then Christianity has no validity at all. If he was right, then there is no other way to be saved.

R. C. SPROUL

After I have tried every circuitous path, I find that you, Lord, are the way.

MMS

Thy work alone, O Christ, can ease this weight of sin;
Thy blood alone, O Lamb of God, can give me peace within.

HORATIUS BONAR

Is Christ the only way for me? Am I hedging my bets, putting my trust in other less efficacious saviors?
Only when I abandon myself, my life, all that I love to him can he shower on me the blessings of his salvation.

CHRIST OUR EXAMPLE

For you have been called for this purpose, since Christ also suffered for you, leaving you an example for you to follow in His steps. ❖ For as we share abundantly in Christ's sufferings, so through Christ we share abundantly in comfort too. ❖ For consider Him who endured such hostility from sinners against Himself, lest you become weary and discouraged in your souls. ❖ For to be sure, he was crucified in weakness, yet he lives by God's power. Likewise, we are weak in him, yet by God's power we will live with him. ❖ For we do not have a High Priest who cannot sympathize with our weaknesses, but was in all points tempted as we are, yet without sin. ❖ Although He was a Son, He learned obedience from the things which He suffered. ❖ I want to know Christ and the power of his resurrection and the fellowship of sharing in his sufferings, becoming like him in his death, and so, somehow, to attain to the resurrection from the dead. ❖ But rejoice in so far as you share Christ's sufferings, that you may also rejoice and be glad when his glory is revealed. ❖ And since we are his children, we will share his treasures—for all God gives to his Son Jesus is now ours too. But if we are to share his glory, we must also share his suffering.

1 Peter 2:21 nasb; 2 Cor. 1:5 rsv; Heb. 12:3 nkjv; 2 Cor. 13:4 niv;
Heb. 4:15 nkjv; Heb. 5:8 nasb; Phil. 3:10–11 niv; 1 Peter 4:13 rsv; Rom.
8:17 tlb

In the hour of the cruellest torture they bear for his sake, they are made partakers in the perfect joy and bliss of fellowship with him.

Dietrich Bonhoeffer

In leaning upon His Cross, let me not refuse my own; yet in bearing mine, let me bear it by the strength of His.

John Baillie

How can I rejoice in suffering, Lord? Only as I suffer in your strength. I rejoice when I see that suffering has made me more like you.

JESUS' AUTHORITY

Do not be afraid; only believe. ❖ Say the word, and my servant will be healed. ❖ "That you may know that the Son of man has authority on earth to forgive sins"—he then said to the paralytic—"Rise, take up your bed and go home." ❖ When the multitudes saw this, they were filled with awe. ❖ He rebuked the wind and said to the sea, "Hush, be still." And the wind died down and it became perfectly calm. . . . And they became very much afraid and said to one another, "Who then is this, that even the wind and the sea obey Him?" ❖ And Jesus came and said to them, "All authority in heaven and on earth has been given to me. . . . I am with you always, to the close of the age." ❖ For this reason the Father loves me, because I lay down my life in order to take it up again. No one takes it from me, but I lay it down of my own accord. I have power to lay it down, and I have power to take it up again. I have received this command from my Father. ❖ Suffering made Jesus perfect, and now he can save forever all who obey him. This is because God chose him to be a high priest like Melchizedek. ❖ The government shall be upon his shoulder. ❖ When I open a door, no one can close it. And when I close a door, no one can open it. ❖ To the only God our Savior be glory, majesty, power and authority, through Jesus Christ our Lord, before all ages, now and forevermore!

LUKE 8:50 NKJV; LUKE 7:7 NKJV; MATT. 9:6 RSV; MATT. 9:8 NASB; MARK 4:39, 41 NASB; MATT. 28:18, 20 RSV; JOHN 10:17–18 NRSV; HEB. 5:9–10 CEV; ISA. 9:6; REV. 3:7 CEV; JUDE 25 NIV

Jesus told the girl's father, "Don't be afraid; only believe" (Luke 8:50). When it comes to God's ability to intervene, nothing is over and settled. Everything is subject to his reversal, even death. Only believe!

MMS

We'll vanquish all the hosts of night,
In Jesus' conquering name.
JOHN H. YATES

Who but God has authority over illness, over death, over nature?
Will I trust in Jesus' power and authority?

JESUS IS GOD

He is the reflection of God's glory and the exact imprint of God's very being. ❖ He is the image of the invisible God. ❖ "Tell us if You are the Christ, the Son of God!" Jesus said to him, "It is as you said." ❖ To see me is to see the Father. ❖ I and my Father are one. ❖ He claimed to be the Son of God. ❖ [He] called God his Father, making himself equal with God. ❖ For a child has been born for us, a son given to us . . . and he is named Wonderful Counselor, Mighty God, Everlasting Father, Prince of Peace. ❖ And on His robe and on His thigh He has a name written, "KING OF KINGS, AND LORD OF LORDS."

HEB. 1:3 NRSV; COL. 1:15 RSV; MATT. 26:63–64 NKJV; JOHN 14:9 THE MESSAGE; JOHN 10:30; JOHN 19:7 NIV; JOHN 5:18 RSV; ISA. 9:6 NRSV; REV. 19:15 NASB

I believe in one Lord Jesus Christ,
The only-begotten Son of God,
Begotten of Him before all ages,
God of God, Light of Light,
Very God of Very God,
Begotten, not made,
Being of one substance with the Father,
By whom all things were made.

FROM THE NICENE CREED

In His incarnation the Son veiled His deity, but He did not void it. The unity of the Godhead made it impossible that He should surrender anything of His deity. When He took upon Him the nature of man, He did not degrade Himself or become even for a time less than He had been before. God can never become less than Himself. For God to become anything that He has not been is unthinkable.

A. W. TOZER

O Lord Jesus, the wonder of you!
You are my Savior; you are God of the universe; you are my friend; you are
eternal God.

SON OF MAN

Jesus Christ . . . is gone into heaven, and is on the right hand of God; angels and authorities and powers being made subject unto him. ❖ No one has ascended to heaven but He who came down from heaven, that is, the Son of Man. ❖ For the Son of man shall come in the glory of his Father with his angels. ❖ He received honor and glory from God the Father, such an utterance as this was made to Him by the Majestic Glory, "This is My beloved Son with whom I am well-pleased." ❖ The God of Abraham, Isaac, and Jacob, the God of our fathers, has glorified His servant Jesus. ❖ We see Jesus, who for a little while was made lower than the angels, crowned with glory and honor because of the suffering of death, so that by the grace of God he might taste death for every one. ❖ Jesus said to them, "Very truly, I tell you, before Abraham was, I am." ❖ Since the world began it has been unheard of that anyone opened the eyes of one who was born blind. If this Man were not from God, He could do nothing."

1 PETER 3:21–22; JOHN 3:13 NKJV; MATT. 16:27; 2 PETER 1:17 NASB; ACTS 3:13 NASB; HEB. 2:9 RSV; JOHN 8:58 NRSV; JOHN 9:32–33 NKJV

The truth is that the Man who walked among us was a demonstration, not of unveiled deity but of perfect humanity.

A. W. TOZER

Equal to His Father, as touching His Godhead; less than the Father, as touching His manhood.

FROM THE ATHANASIAN CREED

He came the first time in humiliation to die on Calvary. He will come the second time in visible glory and irresistible power as KING OF KINGS (Rev. 19:16), Lord of the whole universe (Phil. 2:10–11).

HAROLD LINDSELL

How thankful I am to know you, Son of Man, Lord of lords.
I look forward to your coming again, to seeing you in your glory.

WE SEE HIS GLORY

Moses was there with the LORD forty days and forty nights. . . . He was not aware that his face was radiant because he had spoken with the LORD. ❖ We are . . . not like Moses, who put a veil over his face so that the Israelites might not see the end of the fading splendor. But their minds were hardened; for to this day, when they read the old covenant, that same veil remains unlifted, because only through Christ is it taken away. ❖ Father, the hour is come; glorify thy Son, that thy Son also may glorify thee. ❖ He was transfigured before them. His face shone like the sun, and His clothes became as white as the light. ❖ And His head and His hair were white like white wool, like snow; and His eyes were like a flame of fire; and His feet were like burnished bronze, when it has been caused to glow in a furnace, and His voice was like the sound of many waters. . . . His face was like the sun shining in its strength. ❖ Blessed be his glorious name for ever: and let the whole earth be filled with his glory.

EXOD. 34:28–29 NIV; 2 COR. 3:12–14 RSV; JOHN 17:1; MATT. 17:2 NKJV; REV. 1:14–16 NASB; PS. 72:19

Jesus Himself predicts that He will build the O.T. temple . . . through the resurrection. This affirms the continuity between the O.T. sanctuary and His glorified Person. In Him will be forever perpetuated all that the tabernacle and temple stood for. The structure of stone may disappear; the essence proves itself eternal.

GERHARDUS VOS

Praise be to his glorious name forever; may the whole earth be filled with his glory. The eyes of the Israelites were veiled to the truth. But for all of us who believe in Christ, the veil has been lifted—we see in him the glory of God.

MMS

Do I see in Christ the glory of God? Do I let his glory impact me?
Help me to know you, Lord, in all your glory and splendor.

LIVING IN HIS PRESENCE

I tell you the truth: it is to your advantage that I go away, for if I do not go away, the Counselor will not come to you; but if I go, I will send him to you. ❖ Another Counselor, to be with you for ever, even the Spirit of truth. ❖ It is the Spirit that beareth witness, because the Spirit is truth. ❖ Now He who establishes us with you in Christ and has anointed us is God, who also has sealed us and given us the Spirit in our hearts as a guarantee. ❖ The Spirit Himself bears witness with our spirit that we are children of God. ❖ As you, Father, are in me, and I am in you, may they also be in us, so that the world may believe that you have sent me. ❖ The grace of the Lord Jesus Christ, and the love of God, and the fellowship of the Holy Spirit, be with you all.

JOHN 16:7 RSV; JOHN 14:16–17 RSV; 1 JOHN 5:6; 2 COR. 1:21–22 NKJV;
ROM. 8:16 NASB; JOHN 17:21 NRSV; 2 COR. 13:14 NASB

Christ is my King and my High Priest and the Holy Spirit dwells in me—all because Christ "went away."

MMS

It is the Spirit who makes Christ present to us, and us to him.

R. C. SPROUL

As the Spirit of the Father, and of the Son, the whole life and love of the Father and the Son are in Him; and, coming down into us, He lifts us up into their fellowship.

ANDREW MURRAY

There can be no more intimate fellowship than between me and my God dwelling within me.
Do I live daily with the realization that I live always in his presence?

GOD IN ME

Do you not know that you are the temple of God and that the Spirit of God dwells in you? ❖ God has given us his Spirit. That is how we know that we are one with him, just as he is one with us. ❖ Everyone who confesses that Jesus is God's Son participates continuously in an intimate relationship with God. ❖ "I am with you," declares the LORD. ❖ My Spirit remains among you. ❖ The gift of the Holy Spirit had been poured out even on the Gentiles. ❖ You also are built together spiritually into a dwelling place for God. ❖ I pray that the eyes of your heart may be enlightened, so that you may know what is the hope of His calling, what are the riches of the glory of His inheritance in the saints, and what is the surpassing greatness of His power toward us who believe. ❖ We will walk in the name of the LORD our God for ever and ever. ❖ The LORD, the King of Israel, is with you.

1 COR. 3:16 NKJV; 1 JOHN 4:13 CEV; 1 JOHN 4:15 THE MESSAGE; HAG. 1:13 NASB; HAG. 2:5 NKJV; ACTS 10:45 RSV; EPH. 2:22 NRSV; EPH. 1:18–19 NASB; MICAH 4:5; ZEPH. 3:15 NIV

For the blessed news is that the God who needs no one has in sovereign condescension stooped to work by and in and through His obedient children.

A. W. TOZER

God cannot be expressed but only experienced.

FREDERICK BUECHNER

I want to experience you, Lord God of the universe. Can it be that you can accomplish your work through me? Help me to be obedient and useful.

THE SOURCE OF LIFE AND POWER

Let them make me a sanctuary; that I may dwell among them. ❖ You are blessed, for the Spirit of glory and of God rests on you. ❖ The kingdom of God is within you. ❖ Jesus Christ is in you. ❖ You shall know that I am in My Father, and you in Me, and I in you. ❖ It is Christ who lives in me. ❖ They were all filled with the Holy Spirit, and they spoke the word of God with boldness. ❖ My mother and My brothers are these who hear the word of God and do it. ❖ The Son also gives life to whom He wishes. ❖ All of them were filled with the Holy Spirit and began to speak in other languages, as the Spirit gave them ability. ❖ He will baptize you with the Holy Spirit and with fire. ❖ Be filled with the Spirit.

EXOD. 25:8; 1 PETER 4:14 NIV; LUKE 17:21; 2 COR. 13:5 THE MESSAGE; JOHN 14:20 NASB; GAL. 2:20 NRSV; ACTS 4:31 NKJV; LUKE 8:21 NASB; JOHN 5:21 NASB; ACTS 2:4 NRSV; LUKE 3:16 RSV; EPH. 5:18

Jesus has brought to us a new relationship—one that is deeper than that of mother and son or brother with brother. In this relationship he knows us completely and loves us thoroughly and we desire only to hear his voice and obey. It's the only relationship where the Spirit of one indwells the other.

MMS

In him I have *depth* of life—I don't have to search for meaning. Incredible meaning dwells within me.

MMS

God shares himself generously and graciously.
EUGENE H. PETERSON

If he is the source of all I need, why do I so often feel empty and alone?
May your Spirit move within me today with such strength and fervor that
nothing can diminish your voice—not busyness or interactions with others
or my own attitudes.

THE POWER OF HIS SPIRIT

I pray that, according to the riches of his glory, he may grant that you may be strengthened in your inner being with power through his Spirit. ❖ For God has not given us a spirit of timidity, but of power and love and discipline. ❖ I can do all things through Christ who strengthens me. ❖ Greater is He who is in you than he who is in the world. ❖ "Not by might nor by power, but by my Spirit," says the LORD Almighty. ❖ May the God of green hope fill you up with joy, fill you up with peace, so that your believing lives, filled with the life-giving energy of the Holy Spirit, will brim over with hope!

EPH. 3:16 NRSV; 2 TIM. 1:7 NASB; PHIL. 4:13 NKJV; 1 JOHN 4:4 NASB; ZECH. 4:6 NIV; ROM. 15:13 THE MESSAGE

. . . those souls who abandon the self-life, and give themselves up to the Lord to be fully possessed by Him, do find that He takes possession of the inner springs of their being, and works there to will and to do of His good pleasure.

HANNAH WHITALL SMITH

God knew that, though he had redeemed us, as long as we remained in this world, we would be unable to keep the commandments. So he made a way for that too. He chose to live in us, to indwell us. There could be no greater power than that— Christ in me! What a mystery! I am still me but I am me with his power and all that he is.

MMS

Take hold, God of Eternal Counsel! Carry on Your great purpose in me. You have certainly set a task for Yourself!

JIM ELLIOT

Let him live in me richly—not in just a small part of my life but richly indwelling every part of me.

MMS

Am I allowing Christ to dwell in me richly, extravagantly, or do I allow him only a tiny part of me?
He wants to do in me and be in me all that is needed.

THE INDWELLING SPIRIT

And I will ask the Father, and He will give you another Helper, that He may be with you forever; that is the Spirit of truth . . . you know Him because He abides with you, and will be in you. ❖ It is best for you that I go away, for if I don't, the Comforter won't come. If I do, he will—for I will send him to you. ❖ Repent, and be baptized every one of you in the name of Jesus Christ for the forgiveness of your sins; and you shall receive the gift of the Holy Spirit. ❖ Now we have received, not the spirit of the world, but the spirit which is of God; that we might know the things that are freely given to us of God. ❖ We know that we live in him and he in us, because he has given us of his Spirit. ❖ If the Spirit of Him who raised Jesus from the dead dwells in you, He who raised Christ Jesus from the dead will also give life to your mortal bodies through His Spirit who indwells you. ❖ No one has seen God at any time. If we love one another, God abides in us, and His love has been perfected in us. ❖ Following after the Holy Spirit leads to life and peace.

JOHN 14:16–17 NASB; JOHN 16:7 TLB; ACTS 2:38 RSV; 1 COR. 2:12; 1 JOHN 4:13 NIV; ROM. 8:11 NASB; 1 JOHN 4:12 NKJV; ROM. 8:6 TLB

The great mystical work of the Holy Spirit is in the dim regions of our personality which we cannot get at. Read the 139th Psalm; the Psalmist implies, "Thou art the God of the early mornings, the God of the late at nights, the God of the mountain peaks, and the God of the sea; but, my God, my soul has further horizons than the early mornings, deeper darkness than the nights of earth, higher peaks than any mountain peaks, greater depths than any sea in nature—Thou who art the God of all these, be my God. I cannot reach to the heights or to the depths; there are motives I cannot trace, dreams I cannot get at—my God, search me out."

OSWALD CHAMBERS

There can be only so much faith as there is of the Living Word dwelling in the soul.

ANDREW MURRAY

Have full sway in my inner being, Holy Spirit!
Am I depending on Christ's Spirit for help? If so, I will know his peace.

DEPENDING ON THE SPIRIT

I am filled with power, with the Spirit of the LORD. ❖ Do not cast me away from Your presence, and do not take Your Holy Spirit from me. ❖ The Spirit helps us in our weakness; for we do not know how to pray as we ought, but the Spirit himself intercedes for us with sighs too deep for words. And he who searches the hearts of men knows what is the mind of the Spirit, because the Spirit intercedes for the saints according to the will of God. ❖ The Helper, the Holy Spirit, whom the Father will send in My name, He will teach you all things, and bring to your remembrance all that I said to you. ❖ You received the word with joy inspired by the Holy Spirit. ❖ The law of the Spirit of life in Christ Jesus has made me free from the law of sin and death. ❖ When he, the Spirit of truth, is come, he will guide you into all truth. ❖ You have an anointing from the Holy One, and all of you know the truth.

MICAH 3:8 RSV; PS. 51:11 NKJV; ROM. 8:26–27 RSV; JOHN 14:26 NASB;
1 THESS. 1:6 NRSV; ROM. 8:2 NKJV; JOHN 16:13; 1 JOHN 2:20 NIV

Father, for this new day renew within me the gift of the Holy Spirit.
ANDREW MURRAY

And in truth, if we only knew it, our chief fitness is our utter helplessness. His strength is made perfect, not in our strength, but in our weakness. Our strength is only a hindrance.
HANNAH WHITALL SMITH

The Holy Spirit would not be in them as a power which they could possess. But He would possess them and their work would be the work of the Almighty Christ. Their posture each day would be that of dependence and prayer, and of confident expectation.
ANDREW MURRAY

I look forward to what you're going to do in me today, Holy Spirit. Fill me with your joy, peace, and wisdom.

RIVERS OF LIVING WATER

As the scripture has said, "Out of the believer's heart shall flow rivers of living water." Now he said this about the Spirit. ❖ You show that you are a letter of Christ, prepared by us, written not with ink but with the Spirit of the living God, not on tablets of stone but on tablets of human hearts. ❖ The Spirit of glory and of God rests upon you. ❖ I will pour out My Spirit. ❖ The love of God has been poured out in our hearts by the Holy Spirit who was given to us. ❖ God is love, and the one who abides in love abides in God, and God abides in him. ❖ Love one another. As I have loved you, so you must love one another. ❖ Be imitators of God, as beloved children. And walk in love, as Christ loved us. ❖ Love one another earnestly from the heart.

JOHN 7:38–39 NRSV; 2 COR. 3:3 NRSV; 1 PETER 4:14 NKJV; JOEL 2:28 NASB; ROM. 5:5 NKJV; 1 JOHN 4:16 NASB; JOHN 13:34 NIV; EPH. 5:1–2 RSV; 1 PETER 1:22 RSV

May the meek, innocent, tender, righteous life that reigns within you and governs you, shine through you into the eyes of all with whom you speak.

ISAAC PENINGTON

We're riverbeds, carrying the life-giving water of the Holy Spirit to everyone around us.

JOEY JOHNSON

For God himself works in our souls, in their deepest depths, taking increasing control as we are progressively willing to be prepared for his wonder.

THOMAS KELLY

Is Christ living in me? Is he preparing me for his wonder?
Is his Spirit evident in me, producing goodness, peace, and joy?
Does his Spirit flow from me to touch the lives of others?

HIS SPIRIT IN ME

Turn from sin, return to God, and be baptized in the name of Jesus Christ for the forgiveness of your sins; then you also shall receive this gift, the Holy Spirit. ❖ He saved us, through the washing of regeneration and renewing of the Holy Spirit, whom He poured out on us abundantly through Jesus Christ our Savior. ❖ If anyone acknowledges that Jesus is the Son of God, God lives in him and he in God. ❖ We know how dearly God loves us, and we feel this warm love everywhere within us because God has given us the Holy Spirit to fill our hearts with his love. ❖ By this we know that we abide in Him and He in us, because He has given us of His Spirit. ❖ The Advocate, the Holy Spirit, whom the Father will send in my name, will teach you everything. ❖ The Spirit will take from what is mine and make it known to you. ❖ I will put My Spirit within you and cause you to walk in My statutes. ❖ Those who obey God's commandments live in fellowship with him, and he with them. And we know he lives in us because the Holy Spirit lives in us.

Acts 2:38 tlb; Titus 3:5–6 nkjv; 1 John 4:15 niv; Rom. 5:5 tlb; 1 John 4:13 nasb; John 14:26 nrsv; John 16:15 niv; Ezek. 36:27 nkjv; 1 John 3:24 nlt

I believe in the Holy Spirit
The Lord and giver of life,
Which proceed from the Father and the Son,
Who with the Father and Son together
Is worshipped and glorified.
From the Nicene Creed

Discovery of the fact that his heart is God's dwelling-place will revolutionize the life of any Christian.
Watchman Nee

What stands in the way of my assurance that the Spirit lives in me?
I praise you and worship you, Holy Spirit.

PURITY THROUGH THE SPIRIT

The LORD your God will circumcise your heart and the heart of your descendants, to love the LORD your God with all your heart and with all your soul, that you may live. ❖ In him also you were circumcised with a circumcision made without hands, by putting off the body of flesh in the circumcision of Christ. ❖ For we are the circumcision, which worship God in the spirit, and rejoice in Christ Jesus, and have no confidence in the flesh. ❖ But now we have been released from the Law, having died to that by which we were bound, so that we serve in newness of the Spirit and not in oldness of the letter. ❖ For the law of the Spirit of life in Christ Jesus has made me free from the law of sin and death. ❖ Those who belong to Christ Jesus have nailed the passions and desires of their sinful nature to his cross and crucified them there. If we are living now by the Holy Spirit, let us follow the Holy Spirit's leading in every part of our lives. ❖ Having been freed from sin, you became slaves of righteousness.

DEUT. 30:6 NKJV; COL. 2:11 RSV; PHIL. 3:3; ROM. 7:6 NASB; ROM. 8:2 NKJV; GAL. 5:24–25 NLT; ROM. 6:18 NASB

We will not truly repent and forsake our sins until our hearts are regenerated by the Holy Spirit as we hear the message of the Gospel.

DONALD G. BLOESCH

It is the Spirit who brings us into ever-deeper, ever-fuller purity of heart.

RICHARD FOSTER

In the beginning and in the end it is the Spirit. Am I listening for and responding to his voice?
Purify me, Lord. Spirit, wash me clean.

HE REVEALS HIMSELF IN HIS WORD

We have the prophetic message more fully confirmed. You will do well to be attentive to this as to a lamp shining in a dark place, until the day dawns and the morning star rises in your hearts. First of all you must understand this, that no prophecy of scripture is a matter of one's own interpretation, because no prophecy ever came by human will, but men and women moved by the Holy Spirit spoke from God. ❖ It started when God said, "Light up the darkness!" and our lives filled up with light as we saw and understood God in the face of Christ, all bright and beautiful. ❖ [Jesus] explained to them the things concerning Himself in all the Scriptures. ❖ We have found the Messiah!—the very person Moses and the prophets told about! His name is Jesus!

2 Peter 1:19–21 nrsv; 2 Cor. 4:6 the message; Luke 24:27 nasb;
John 1:45 tlb

If you want to see the glory of Jesus today, Peter exhorts you to find it in the pages of the Bible [2 Peter 1:19–21]. This is a remarkable promise from one who personally witnessed the transfiguration and post-resurrection accounts of Jesus.
R. C. Sproul

If you want to know God as he speaks to you through the Bible, you should study the Bible daily, systematically, comprehensively, devotionally, and prayerfully.
James Montgomery Boice

The Bible tells us that it is primarily a Story about God and the new community he is creating and about what he is doing in history. The Bible is about God, not us.
Hahn and Verhaagen

Am I reading the Bible to see myself or to see Jesus?
Jesus, show me yourself in the pages of your Word.

KNOWING GOD'S WORD

Open my eyes, that I may behold wonderful things from Your law. ❖ Your decrees are wonderful; therefore my soul keeps them. ❖ I have made up my mind to obey your laws forever, no matter what. ❖ Just tell me what to do and I will do it, Lord. ❖ I will put My law in their minds, and write it on their hearts; and I will be their God, and they shall be My people. ❖ Impress these words of mine on your heart. ❖ Your law is within my heart. ❖ I treasure your word in my heart, so that I may not sin against you. ❖ The word is very near you; it is in your mouth and in your heart, so that you can do it. ❖ The Holy Scriptures . . . are able to make you wise for salvation through faith which is in Christ Jesus. ❖ Let the word of Christ richly dwell within you, with all wisdom teaching and admonishing one another with psalms and hymns and spiritual songs, singing with thankfulness in your hearts to God.

Ps. 119:18 NASB; Ps. 119:129 NRSV: Ps. 119:112 CEV; Ps. 119:33 TLB; Jer. 31:33 NKJV; Deut. 11:18 NASB; Ps. 40:8 NKJV; Ps. 119:11 NRSV; Deut. 30:14 RSV; 2 Tim. 3:15 NKJV; Col. 3:16 NASB

At Sinai God wrote the law on tablets of stone, but since Pentecost he's been writing his Word on the hearts of his people.

WARREN W. WIERSBE

In reading the Bible we study to know God, hear his voice, and be changed by him as we grow in holiness.

JAMES MONTGOMERY BOICE

Is God's Word written on my heart? Does it have an impact on my life? If I find God's Word wonderful, then I must share it with others.

LIGHT AND TRUTH

O Lord GOD, You are God, and Your words are true. ❖ Your word is truth. ❖ The unfolding of your words gives light; it imparts understanding to the simple. ❖ The statutes of the LORD are right, rejoicing the heart: the commandment of the LORD is pure, enlightening the eyes. ❖ For the commandment is a lamp; and the law is light. ❖ Is not my word like fire, says the LORD, and like a hammer which breaks the rock in pieces? ❖ Teach [God's laws] to your children. Talk about them all the time—whether you're at home or walking along the road or going to bed at night, or getting up in the morning. ❖ Blessed are those who hear God's word and guard it with their lives! ❖ For whatever was written in earlier times was written for our instruction, so that through perseverance and the encouragement of the Scriptures we might have hope. ❖ The word of God lives in you.

2 SAM. 7:28 NKJV; JOHN 17:17 NKJV; PS. 119:130 NRSV; PS. 19:8; PROV. 6:23; JER. 23:29 RSV; DEUT. 11:19 CEV; LUKE 11:28 THE MESSAGE; ROM. 15:4 NASB; 1 JOHN 2:14 NIV

Our nighttime passage through the dark and dangerous journey of this life is illumined by God's Word, the Bible. . . . "Your word is a lamp to my feet and a light for my path" (Ps. 119:105).
   . . . It is a light for our darkness and for our brighter times as well.

JAMES MONTGOMERY BOICE

Try to state to yourself what you feel implicitly to be God's truth, and you give God a chance to pass it on to someone else through you.

OSWALD CHAMBERS

How can God's Word impact my life if I don't read it?
I desire your truth, Lord. I long for your light.

GOD'S WORD CHANGES US

All the people wept, when they heard the words of the law. ❖ For the word of God is quick, and powerful, and sharper than any twoedged sword, piercing even to the dividing asunder of soul and spirit, and of the joints and marrow, and is a discerner of the thoughts and intents of the heart. ❖ So will My word be which goes forth from My mouth; it will not return to Me empty, without accomplishing what I desire, and without succeeding in the matter for which I sent it. ❖ The word of God . . . is at work in you believers. ❖ As the Spirit of the Lord works within us, we become more and more like him. ❖ Blessed rather are those who hear the word of God and obey it! ❖ Your decrees are my heritage forever; they are the joy of my heart.

NEH. 8:9; HEB. 4:12; ISA. 55:11 NASB; 1 THESS 2:13 RSV; 2 COR. 3:18 TLB; LUKE 11:28 NRSV; PS. 119:111 NRSV

In Nehemiah 8, when Ezra read the Law to the people in Jerusalem, they wept. Then they celebrated because they understood the words. They were obedient to what they heard, they rejoiced, and they listened to the Word every day. The Word should have the same impact on me—it should be able to penetrate me, give me a desire for more insight, fill me with joy, and inspire me to obedience. Praise God, whose Holy Spirit causes the Word to do these things in me.

MMS

Perhaps one reason we glance into the Word instead of gaze into the Word is that we are afraid of what we might see.

WARREN W. WIERSBE

When the child of God looks into the Word of God (the glass, the mirror), he sees the Son of God, and he is transformed by the Spirit of God to share in the glory of God!

WARREN W. WIERSBE

Do I dare look into the Word of God and see myself as I am?
Praise God, he not only shows me who I am but how to be like him.

THE POWER OF GOD'S WORD

For truly I say to you, until heaven and earth pass away, not the smallest letter or stroke shall pass from the Law, until all is accomplished. ❖ The scripture cannot be broken. ❖ The word of the Lord endureth for ever. ❖ But the word of God continued to increase and spread. ❖ Take the helmet of salvation, and the sword of the Spirit, which is the word of God. ❖ Man shall not live by bread alone, but by every word that proceedeth out of the mouth of God. ❖ Order my steps in thy word: and let not any iniquity have dominion over me. ❖ May your laws sustain me. ❖ You have been born anew . . . through the living and enduring word of God. ❖ He gave us birth by the word of truth. ❖ Great peace have those who love Your law, and nothing causes them to stumble.

MATT. 5:18 NASB; JOHN 10:35; 1 PETER 1:25; ACTS 12:24 NIV; EPH. 6:17 NASB; MATT. 4:4; PS. 119:133; PS. 119:175 NIV; 1 PETER 1:23 NRSV; JAMES 1:18 NRSV; PS. 119:165 NKJV

Amazingly, all that it took [for Jesus] to defeat the devil was "every word that proceedeth out of the mouth of God." . . . We dare not be careless or lazy about storing God's Word in our minds.

R. ARTHUR MATHEWS

Basic to all victory over the devil is the unashamed use of the Word of God and the application of its absolute and objective truth and promises in a direct confrontation against the lies, deceits, and misquotes of the devil. Satan cannot face the Word of God thrust at him by the believing heart in the power of the Spirit.

R. ARTHUR MATHEWS

It is wonderful that God should have borne testimony at all to sinful men, and more wonderful still that his testimony should be of such a character, so clear, so full, so gracious, so mighty.

CHARLES HADDON SPURGEON

The Bible is alive, it speaks to me; it has feet, it runs after me; it has hands, it lays hold of me. The Bible is not antique or modern. It is eternal.

MARTIN LUTHER

Do I realize the power of the Word to fight Satan's attacks? To have access to its power, I must know the Word.

HIS WORD ALONE

God said, Let there be light: and there was light. ❖ By the word of the LORD were the heavens made. ❖ For He spoke, and it was done; He commanded, and it stood fast. ❖ In the beginning was the Word, and the Word was with God, and the Word was God. . . . All things were made by him; and without him was not any thing made that was made. ❖ [The Son] reflects the glory of God and bears the very stamp of his nature, upholding the universe by his word of power. ❖ I the LORD have spoken, and I will do it. ❖ [Jesus] touched him, and said to him, "I am willing; be cleansed." And immediately the leprosy left him and he was cleansed. ❖ Only speak a word, and my servant will be healed. ❖ He cried with a loud voice, "Lazarus, come out!" The dead man came out. ❖ The disciples went to him and wakened him, shouting, "Lord, save us! We're sinking!" . . . Then he stood up and rebuked the wind and waves, and the storm subsided and all was calm. The disciples just sat there, awed! "Who is this," they asked themselves, "that even the winds and the sea obey him?" ❖ The LORD also will roar from Zion, and utter His voice from Jerusalem; the heavens and earth will shake; but the LORD will be a shelter for His people.

GEN. 1:3; PS. 33:6; PS. 33:9 NKJV; JOHN 1:1, 3; HEB. 1:3 RSV; EZEK. 17:24 RSV; MARK 1:41–42 NASB; MATT. 8:8 NKJV; JOHN 11:43–44 NRSV; MATT. 8:25–27 TLB; JOEL 3:16 NKJV

We don't seem to believe God is strong enough to do what he says he will do. God, however, has not changed. He has not stopped exercising his power, nor has his strength diminished.

R. C. SPROUL

Religious belief exists not in its last analysis on what we can prove to be so, but on the fact of God having declared it to be so.

GERHARDUS VOS

What powerful word do I need to hear from the Lord?
Whatever he has promised, he will do.

THE CONSUMING FIRE

The LORD is exalted, for he dwells on high; he will fill Zion with justice and righteousness. He will be the sure foundation for your times, a rich store of salvation and wisdom and knowledge; the fear of the LORD is the key to this treasure. ❖ Nothing is hidden from God! He sees through everything, and we will have to tell him the truth. ❖ The Lord God gives just punishment. ❖ The LORD looks at the heart. ❖ The eyes of the LORD are in every place, watching the evil and the good. ❖ His eyes were as a flame of fire. ❖ For the LORD your God is a consuming fire, a jealous God. ❖ It is a fearful thing to fall into the hands of the living God. ❖ Who is like you, majestic in holiness, awesome in splendor, doing wonders? ❖ Our God is a consuming fire. ❖ The sinners in Zion are afraid; trembling has seized the godless: "Who among us can dwell with the devouring fire? Who among us can dwell with everlasting burnings?" He who walks righteously and speaks uprightly. ❖ We have an advocate with the Father, Jesus Christ the righteous.

ISA. 33:5–6 NIV; HEB. 4:13 CEV; JER. 51:56 TLB; 1 SAM. 16:7 NKJV; PROV. 15:3 NASB; REV. 1:14; DEUT. 4:24 NKJV; HEB. 10:31; EXOD. 15:11 NRSV; HEB. 12:29; ISA. 33:14–15 RSV; 1 JOHN 2:1

The holy love of God is inseparably related to his wrath.
DONALD G. BLOESCH

Jehovah, according to Amos, executed righteousness, not from any lower motive, such as safeguarding the structure of society, or converting the sinner, but from the supreme motive of giving free sway to the infinite force of his ethical indignation.

GERHARDUS VOS

To know God fully is to know him as a consuming fire.
MMS

When I think of your righteous judgment of sin, I am comforted in the knowledge that you see me in love through the blood of your Son.

HE IS EVERYWHERE

The highest heaven cannot contain you. ❖ "Can anyone hide himself in secret places, So I shall not see him?" says the LORD; "Do I not fill heaven and earth?" says the LORD. ❖ Heaven is my throne, and earth is my footstool. ❖ The LORD is in his holy temple; the LORD's throne is in heaven. His eyes behold, his gaze examines humankind. ❖ Where can I go from Your Spirit? Or where can I flee from Your presence? ❖ The LORD sees everything, whether good or bad. ❖ The LORD watches over you. . . . The LORD will keep you from all harm—he will watch over your life.

1 KINGS 8:27 NRSV; JER. 23:24 NKJV; ACTS 7:49; PS. 11:4 NRSV; PS. 139:7 NKJV; PROV. 15:3 CEV; PS. 121:5, 7 NIV

Because his presence permeates every corner of the world, there is no refuge from his eye. Flight from his presence and authority is futile, as is attempting to hide.

R. C. SPROUL

Live every day *coram Deo*—practicing the presence of God—growing in your awareness of his awesome glory, and bringing all aspects of your life into greater conformity to his will. Please God (Heb. 11:6a) in your faithful response to his Lordship.

R. C. SPROUL

What do I try to do in secret, away from God's sight?
His love envelopes me. His Spirit fills me.

HIS PRESENCE WITH ME

You, O LORD, are in our midst, and we are called by Your name. ❖ I am with you and will keep you wherever you go. ❖ My Presence will go with you. ❖ The LORD is for me; I will not fear; what can man do to me? ❖ God . . . has been with me wherever I have gone. ❖ The LORD will be your everlasting light. ❖ He does not take his eyes off the righteous. ❖ The LORD will guard your going out and your coming in from this time forth and forever. ❖ In the shelter of your presence you hide them. ❖ You are the Christ, the Son of God, even He who comes into the world. ❖ I am in my Father, and ye in me, and I in you. ❖ When I go and prepare a place for you, I will come again and will take you to myself, that where I am you may be also. ❖ Now to him who is able to keep you from falling, and to make you stand without blemish in the presence of his glory with rejoicing, to the only God our Savior, through Jesus Christ our Lord, be glory.

JER. 14:9 NKJV; GEN. 28:15 NKJV; EXOD. 33:14 NKJV; PS. 118:6 NASB; GEN. 35:3 RSV; ISA. 60:20 RSV; JOB 36:7 NIV; PS. 121:8 NASB; PS. 31:20 NRSV; JOHN 11:27 NASB; JOHN 14:20; JOHN 14:3 RSV; JUDE 24–25 NRSV

When we reflect on the Tabernacle in the wilderness and all that it represents, we realize that in the fullness of time Mary's womb became the dwelling place, the "tabernacle" of God. Even more, we see that in Jesus Christ, God has truly "tabernacled" among us. And as if that were not enough, we are to be the dwelling place of the Holy Spirit, making the reality of God visible and manifest everywhere we go and in everything we do.

RICHARD FOSTER

That all my life may be filled by the radiance of Thy presence. . . . Let the Spirit of Him whose life was the light of men rule within my heart till eventide.

JOHN BAILLIE

God is with me—there is no reason to be afraid.
Do others see your light in me?

NO FEAR

Do not fear, for I am with you; do not anxiously look about you, for I am your God. I will strengthen you, surely I will help you, surely I will uphold you with My righteous right hand. ❖ For I am the LORD your God, who upholds your right hand, Who says to you, "Do not fear, I will help you." ❖ Do not be afraid, nor be dismayed, for the LORD your God is with you wherever you go. ❖ Jesus spoke to them, saying, "Take courage, it is I; do not be afraid." ❖ There is no fear in love; but perfect love casts out fear. ❖ For the mountains may be removed and the hills may shake, but My lovingkindness will not be removed from you. ❖ Lift up your eyes to the heavens, and look at the earth beneath; for the heavens will vanish like smoke, the earth will wear out like a garment, and those who live on it will die like gnats; but my salvation will be forever, and my deliverance will never be ended. ❖ Therefore let us be grateful for receiving a kingdom that cannot be shaken, and thus let us offer to God acceptable worship, with reverence and awe.

ISA. 41:10 NASB; ISA. 41:13 NASB; JOSH. 1:9 NKJV; MATT. 14:27 NASB; 1 JOHN 4:18 NKJV; ISA. 54:10 NASB; ISA. 51:6 NRSV; HEB. 12:28 RSV

God constantly encourages us to trust Him in the dark. "I will go before thee, and make the crooked places straight . . ."

A. W. TOZER

To fear and not be afraid—that is the paradox of faith.
A. W. TOZER

He treats us as sons, and all He asks in return is that we shall treat Him as a Father, whom we can trust without anxiety. We must take the son's place of dependence and trust, and must let Him keep the father's place of care and responsibility.

HANNAH WHITALL SMITH

You cannot fear and have faith in God at the same time. What you fear is what you have faith in.

JOEY JOHNSON

Help me to have the confidence, Lord, that even if the mountains move into the sea, I have nothing to fear. My eyes are on you and you made the mountains and hold me in your hand. Praise you!

OUR VALUE IS IN HIM

Then Job arose and tore his robe and shaved his head, and he fell to the ground and worshiped. . . ."Blessed be the name of the LORD." In all this Job did not sin nor charge God with wrong. ❖ God is the Judge: He puts down one, and exalts another. ❖ Submit yourselves therefore to God. ❖ To keep me from exalting myself, there was given me a thorn in the flesh. . . . I implored the Lord three times that it might depart from me. And He has said to me, "My grace is sufficient for you, for power is perfected in weakness." Most gladly, therefore, I will rather boast about my weaknesses, so that the power of Christ may dwell in me. ❖ Humble yourselves therefore under the mighty hand of God, that he may exalt you in due time. ❖ My soul makes its boast in the LORD. ❖ In God we boast all the day long. ❖ His praise is not from men, but from God. ❖ You deliver the weak from those too strong for them. ❖ Who is like the LORD our God, who is seated on high, who looks far down on the heavens and the earth? He raises the poor from the dust, and lifts the needy from the ash heap.

JOB 1:20–22 NKJV; PS. 75:7 NKJV; JAMES 4:7; 2 COR. 12:7–9 NASB;
1 PETER 5:6; PS. 34:2 RSV; PS. 44:8; ROM. 2:29 NASB; PS. 35:10 NRSV;
PS. 113:5–7 NRSV

We are not our own ends. Our value is our worth to God, and our end is "to glorify God and enjoy him forever."

WILLIAM TEMPLE

We may lose all that we have on this earth—family, friends, material possessions—but in the midst of our grief we must fall to the ground and worship God, like Job. The fact that he is Almighty God overshadows all other reality.

MMS

Am I trying to exalt myself or am I willing to humble myself so that Christ can exalt me?
What am I willing to bear so that I can realize his power in the midst of my weakness?

KNOWING GOD

And the LORD said, "I will cause all my goodness to pass in front of you, and I will proclaim my name, the LORD, in your presence." ❖ When You said, "Seek My face," my heart said to You, "Your face, LORD, I will seek." ❖ "Let him who boasts boast of this, that he understands and knows Me, that I am the LORD who exercises lovingkindness, justice, and righteousness on earth; for I delight in these things," declares the LORD. ❖ This is eternal life, that they may know You, the only true God, and Jesus Christ whom You have sent. ❖ I want to know Christ and the power of his resurrection and the sharing of his sufferings by becoming like him in his death. ❖ O righteous Father, . . . these disciples know you sent me. And I have revealed you to them and will keep on revealing you so that the mighty love you have for me may be in them, and I in them.

EXOD. 33:19 NIV; PS. 27:8 NKJV; JER. 9:24 NASB; JOHN 17:3 NKJV; PHIL. 3:10 NRSV; JOHN 17:25–26 TLB

God is *everything.* My focus must be on him, seeking to know him more completely and allowing him full possession of my life.

MMS

We have tasted "that the Lord is good" (Psalm 34:8), but we don't yet know *how* good he is. We only know that his sweetness makes us long for more.

CHARLES HADDON SPURGEON

It is Thy will, O God, to be found that Thou mayest be sought, to be sought that Thou mayest more truly be found.

ST. BERNARD OF CLAIRVAUX

Do I long to know him better?
What in my life is drowning out that longing?

MY DIVIDED HEART

Teach me your way, O LORD, that I may walk in your truth; give me an undivided heart to revere your name. ❖ Draw near to God and He will draw near to you. Cleanse your hands, you sinners; and purify your hearts, you double-minded. ❖ I will give them an heart to know me, that I am the LORD. ❖ I will give them one heart, and put a new spirit within them. ❖ Serve the Lord without distraction. ❖ Do not love the world or the things in the world. The love of the Father is not in those who love the world; for all that is in the world—the desire of the flesh, the desire of the eyes, the pride in riches—comes not from the Father but from the world. ❖ Do not conform any longer to the pattern of this world, but be transformed by the renewing of your mind. Then you will be able to test and approve what God's will is—his good, pleasing and perfect will.

PS. 86:11 NRSV; JAMES 4:8 NKJV; JER. 24:7; EZEK. 11:19 NASB; 1 COR. 7:35 NKJV; 1 JOHN 2:15–16 NRSV; ROM. 12:2 NIV

I have had a divided heart, trying to love God and the world at the same time. God says, You can't love me as you should if you love this world too.

MMS

What God wants is not a good performance [free of sin], but my heart.

PHILIP YANCEY

So purify and sanctify my heart, make it so tenderly susceptible of Thyself and Thy love, that believing on Thee may be the very life it breathes.

ANDREW MURRAY

Can I give him my undivided heart as he desires?
What has a hold on my heart when I am trying to love God with all of it?

GOD CHANGES ME

But now he has reconciled you by Christ's physical body through death to present you holy in his sight, without blemish and free from accusation. ❖ Therefore you shall be perfect, just as your Father in heaven is perfect. ❖ You shall be holy; for I the LORD your God am holy. ❖ Consecrate yourselves therefore, and be holy. ❖ It is by God's will that we have been sanctified through the offering of the body of Jesus Christ once for all. ❖ Christ also loved the church, and gave himself for it; that he might sanctify and cleanse it . . . that he might present it to himself a glorious church, not having spot, or wrinkle, or any such thing; but that it should be holy and without blemish. ❖ He chose us . . . that we would be holy and blameless before Him. ❖ May the God of peace himself sanctify you entirely; and may your spirit and soul and body be kept sound and blameless at the coming of our Lord Jesus Christ. The one who calls you is faithful, and he will do this.

COL. 1:22 NIV; MATT. 5:48 NKJV; LEV. 19:2–3 RSV; LEV. 20:7 NKJV;
HEB. 10:10 NRSV; EPH. 5:25–27; EPH. 1:4 NASB; 1 THESS 5:23–24 NRSV

In God's sight, you are "complete in him." Right now, you stand accepted by God.

CHARLES HADDON SPURGEON

God has charged Himself with full responsibility for our eternal happiness and stands ready to take over the management of our lives the moment we turn in faith to Him.

A. W. TOZER

What is both Good and New about the Good News is the wild claim that Jesus did not simply tell us that God loves us even in our wickedness and folly and wants us to love each other the same way and to love him too, but that if we will let him, God will actually bring about this unprecedented transformation of our hearts himself.

FREDERICK BUECHNER

Am I letting him transform me?
Am I clinging to things of this world that prevent the complete transformation of my heart?

MY FOCUS IS THE LORD

Seek the LORD your God, and you will find Him if you seek Him with all your heart and with all your soul. ❖ They sought God eagerly, and he was found by them. ❖ With all my heart I have sought You. ❖ Make Your face shine upon Your servant. ❖ Whom have I in heaven but you? And there is nothing on earth that I desire other than you. My flesh and my heart may fail, but God is the strength of my heart and my portion forever. ❖ I count all things to be loss in view of the surpassing value of knowing Christ Jesus my Lord. ❖ But it is good for me to draw near to God: I have put my trust in the Lord GOD, that I may declare all thy works.

DEUT. 4:29 NKJV; 2 CHRON. 15:15 NIV; PS. 119:10 NASB; PS. 119:135 NKJV; PS. 73:25–26 NRSV; PHIL. 3:8 NASB; PS. 73:28

Let this be your chief object in prayer, to realize the presence of your heavenly Father. Let your watchword be: Alone with God.

ANDREW MURRAY

As we find that it is not easy to persevere in this being "alone with God," we begin to realize that it is because we are not "wholly for God." God has a right to demand that *He should have us completely for Himself.*

ANDREW MURRAY

Our relationship with God must be a constant thing if it is to impact our life and the lives of others. Our faith may be a way of life, but until Jesus has access to every aspect of our life, we are not truly his. There must be constant awareness of his presence, constant dependence on him for guidance, and constant praise.

MMS

Do I keep God relegated to one small area of my life?
How can I be more aware of his presence with me and more dependent on his guidance?

PUTTING GOD FIRST

"I am the Alpha and the Omega, the Beginning and the End," says the Lord, "who is and who was and who is to come, the Almighty." ❖ Love the Lord your God with all your heart, and with all your soul, and with all your mind, and with all your strength. ❖ What does the LORD your God require of you, but to fear the LORD your God, to walk in all his ways, to love him, to serve the LORD your God with all your heart and with all your soul. ❖ Hold fast to Him. ❖ Seek first His kingdom and His righteousness. ❖ For those who want to save their life will lose it, and those who lose their life for my sake, and for the sake of the gospel, will save it. ❖ Lead a life worthy of the Lord, fully pleasing to him.

REV. 1:8 NKJV; MARK 12:30 NASB; DEUT. 10:12 RSV; JOSH. 22:5 NKJV;
MATT. 6:33 NASB; MARK 8:35 NRSV; COL. 1:10 RSV

We can't live with God closeted away in the center of our life. He must be all of our life. Everything else is peripheral, dependent on him. We are to love him with all that we are.

MMS

We can't have the promises without the presence of the Promiser.
JOEY JOHNSON

I renounced, for the love of Him, everything that was not He, and I began to live as if there was none but He and I in the world.

BROTHER LAWRENCE

God is everything. He deserves my attention.
What part of my life am I holding back from God?

DRAWING NEAR

Since . . . we have confidence to enter the holy place by the blood of Jesus . . . let us draw near with a sincere heart. ❖ Through Him we . . . have access by one Spirit to the Father. ❖ Now we can come fearlessly right into God's presence, assured of his glad welcome when we come with Christ and trust in him. ❖ He has delivered us from the power of darkness and conveyed us into the kingdom of the Son of His love. ❖ Be all the more eager to make your calling and election sure. . . . and you will receive a rich welcome into the eternal kingdom of our Lord and Savior Jesus Christ. ❖ I bore you on eagles' wings and brought you to myself. ❖ Remain in my love.

HEB. 10:19, 22 NASB; EPH. 2:18 NKJV; EPH. 3:12 TLB; COL. 1:13 NKJV;
2 PETER 1:10–11 NIV; EXOD. 19:4 RSV; JOHN 15:9 NIV

There is a mystical oneness between Christ's followers, Christ, and the Father, so that what is done to Christ's followers is done to him.

MMS

I know that for the right practice of [the presence of God] the heart must be empty of all other things, because God will possess the heart *alone;* and as he cannot possess it *alone* without emptying it of all besides, so neither can He act *there,* and do in it what He pleases, unless it be left vacant to Him.

BROTHER LAWRENCE

Without solitude it is virtually impossible to live a spiritual life. Solitude begins with a time and a place for God, and him alone.

HENRI J. M. NOUWEN

The real test of being in the presence of God is that you either forget about yourself altogether or see yourself as a small, dirty object. It is better to forget about yourself altogether.

C. S. LEWIS

If I want to experience the presence of God, I must spend some time quiet and alone.
Am I willing to make my heart empty and available to him?

GREAT CONFIDENCE

Truly, truly, I say to you, he who hears My word, and believes Him who sent Me, has eternal life, and does not come into judgment, but has passed out of death into life. ❖ Let us therefore come boldly unto the throne of grace, that we may obtain mercy, and find grace to help in time of need. ❖ The effect of righteousness will be quietness and confidence forever. ❖ Out of my distress I called on the LORD; the LORD answered me and set me free. ❖ The LORD is my strength and my song; he has become my salvation. ❖ My soul waits in silence for God only; from Him is my salvation. He only is my rock and my salvation, my stronghold; I shall not be greatly shaken. ❖ Be strong in the Lord, and in the power of his might. ❖ You can be sure that the LORD will protect you from harm.

JOHN 5:24 NASB; HEB. 4:16; ISA. 32:17 NIV; PS. 118:5 RSV; PS. 118:14 RSV; PS. 62:1–2 NASB; EPH. 6:10; PROV. 3:26 CEV

The repeated emphasis on "stand" and "withstand" [in Eph. 6] . . . suggests that the Christian's danger and the devil's advantage lie in the believer's relinquishing his position and attempting to tackle some problem from the human, flesh-and-blood level. . . . The devil is a panic artist and plays heavily on our self-consciousness in emergency situations.

R. ARTHUR MATHEWS

God will not change his mind regarding our salvation; once in Christ we will never be forsaken. As we cannot earn our way into his favor, so we cannot sin our way out of it.

R. C. SPROUL

I pray that God will convince you of your security in Christ. I pray that he will remind you that your name is engraved on his hands. I pray that you will hear him whisper, "So do not fear, for I am with you" (Isaiah 41:10).

CHARLES HADDON SPURGEON

I have nothing to fear now and throughout eternity. Praise God! He is the great and faithful Promiser. All he has said, he will do.

FAITH IN CHRIST

Believe on the Lord Jesus Christ, and you will be saved. ❖ We have believed in Christ Jesus, in order to be justified by faith in Christ, and not by works of the law, because by works of the law shall no one be justified. ❖ The disciples went and woke him, saying, "Master, Master, we're going to drown!" He got up and rebuked the wind and the raging waters; the storm subsided, and all was calm. "Where is your faith?" he asked his disciples. ❖ Whosoever shall call upon the name of the Lord shall be saved. ❖ Lord, I believe; help my unbelief! ❖ He said, "Lord, I believe"; and he worshiped him. ❖ Truly, I say to you, not even in Israel have I found such faith. ❖ I believe that you are the Christ, the Son of God. ❖ We believe that Jesus died and rose again. ❖ For the love of Christ controls us, having concluded this, that one died for all. ❖ I know the one in whom I trust, and I am sure that he is able to safely guard all that I have given him until the day of his return. ❖ These are written so that you may come to believe that Jesus is the Messiah, the Son of God, and that through believing you may have life in his name.

ACTS 16:31 NKJV; GAL. 2:16 RSV; LUKE 8:24–25 NIV; ROM. 10:13; MARK 9:24 NKJV; JOHN 9:38 RSV; MATT. 8:10 RSV; JOHN 11:27 CEV; 1 THESS. 4:14; 2 COR. 5:14 NASB; 2 TIM. 1:12 TLB; JOHN 20:31 NRSV

When Jesus stilled the storm in Luke 8:22–25, it was a lesson for his disciples. He was showing them what faith can do; he was teaching them to trust God; he was revealing to them that he *is* God.

MMS

My faith does not rest on what I am or will be or will feel or will know, but in what Christ is, in what he has done, and in what he is now doing for me.

CHARLES HADDON SPURGEON

Do I trust Christ and his work alone? Lord, help my unbelief!
He does it all. There is nothing left for me to do but trust in what he's already done.

WHAT HE'S DONE FOR ME

God sent Jesus to take the punishment for our sins and to satisfy God's anger against us. We are made right with God when we believe that Jesus shed his blood, sacrificing his life for us. ❖ He . . . was delivered up because of our transgressions, and was raised because of our justification. ❖ Therefore we are buried with him by baptism into death: that like as Christ was raised up from the dead by the glory of the Father, even so we also should walk in newness of life. ❖ Christ lives in you, and he is your hope of sharing in God's glory. ❖ He finished all sacrifices, once and for all, when he sacrificed himself on the cross. ❖ He is the atoning sacrifice for our sins. ❖ For by one offering He has perfected for all time those who are sanctified. ❖ Our Passover lamb is Christ, who has already been sacrificed. ❖ Behold! The Lamb of God who takes away the sin of the world! ❖ Worthy is the Lamb that was slain to receive power, and riches, and wisdom, and strength, and honour, and glory, and blessing.

ROM. 3:25 NLT; ROM. 4:25 NASB; ROM. 6:4; COL. 1:27 CEV; HEB. 7:27 TLB;
1 JOHN 2:2 NIV; HEB. 10:14 NASB; 1 COR. 5:7 CEV; JOHN 1:29 NKJV;
REV. 5:12

'Tis Jesus, the first and the last,
　　Whose Spirit shall guide us safe home;
We'll praise Him for all that is past,
　　And trust Him for all that's to come.
JOSEPH HART

Christianity is not the sacrifice we make, but the sacrifice we trust, not the victory we win, but the victory we inherit. That is the evangelical principle.
P. T. FORSYTH

Lord, I look forward to the prize you have won for me.
I want nothing but to celebrate with you the victory.

HE REDEEMS US

You must redeem every firstborn son. ❖ Christ has redeemed us from the curse of the law, having become a curse for us. ❖ For He made Him who knew no sin to be sin for us, that we might become the righteousness of God in Him. ❖ When the fullness of time had come, God sent his Son, born of woman, born under the law, in order to redeem those who were under the law, so that we might receive adoption as children. ❖ For there is one God, and one mediator between God and men, the man Christ Jesus; who gave himself a ransom for all. ❖ In Him we have redemption through His blood, the forgiveness of our trespasses, according to the riches of His grace, which He lavished on us. ❖ By his own blood he entered in once into the holy place, having obtained eternal redemption for us. ❖ He saved them from the hand of him that hated them, and redeemed them from the hand of the enemy. ❖ They shall be called the holy people, the redeemed of the LORD. ❖ My salvation lasts forever; my righteous rule will never die nor end.

NUM. 18:15 NIV; GAL. 3:13 NKJV; 2 COR. 5:21 NKJV; GAL. 4:4–5 NRSV; 1 TIM. 2:5–6; EPH. 1:7–8 NASB; HEB. 9:12; PS. 106:10; ISA. 62:12 RSV; ISA. 51:6 TLB

Our greatest problems seem to be political, but the Bible teaches the real problem is sin, and the solution is redemption and sanctification.

R. C. SPROUL

The redemption accomplished for us by our Lord Jesus Christ on the cross at Calvary, is a redemption from the power of sin as well as from its guilt, and that He *is* able to save to the uttermost all who come unto God by Him.

HANNAH WHITALL SMITH

The term "redemption" describes the loving reacquisition of something formerly possessed.

GERHARDUS VOS

You had no need, Lord Jesus, to pay for sin, except the need engendered by your great love for me.
I praise you that through your precious blood, my sin debt was canceled.

THE SON OF GOD

She will bear a son, and you shall call his name Jesus, for he will save his people from their sins. ❖ By His knowledge the Righteous One, My Servant, will justify the many, as He will bear their iniquities. ❖ And all peoples on earth will be blessed through you. ❖ Christ Jesus came into the world to save sinners. ❖ For God sent not his Son into the world to condemn the world; but that the world through him might be saved. ❖ Therefore he had to become like his brothers and sisters in every respect, so that he might be a merciful and faithful high priest in the service of God, to make a sacrifice of atonement for the sins of the people. ❖ The Son of man [must] be lifted up, that whoever believes in him may have eternal life. ❖ I, if I am lifted up from the earth, will draw all peoples to Myself. ❖ They put him to death by hanging him on a tree; but God raised him on the third day. ❖ He died for our sins and rose again to make us right with God.

MATT. 1:21 RSV; ISA. 53:11 NASB; GEN. 12:3 NIV; 1 TIM. 1:15; JOHN 3:17; HEB. 2:17 NRSV; JOHN 3:14–15 RSV; JOHN 12:32 NKJV; ACTS 10:39–40 RSV; ROM. 4:25 TLB

Come to Bethlehem and see him whose birth the angels sing;
Come adore on bended knee Christ the Lord, the newborn King.
OLD FRENCH CAROL

We need God incarnate for redemptive reasons. The whole incarnation, with all that pertains to it, is one great sacrament of redemption.
GERHARDUS VOS

He, who will come again in splendor and majesty to shake the earth (Isa. 2:19), first came gently, as a little baby, to save us (Luke 2:11).
MMS

Do I see in the beautiful baby Jesus the Savior who died for me?
Jesus grew up to die on the cross. The purpose of his life was to be my Savior.

THE LAMB OF GOD

Redeem every firstborn among your sons. ❖ God will provide himself a lamb for a burnt offering. ❖ Christ, God's Lamb, has been slain for us. ❖ He was led as a lamb to the slaughter, and as a sheep before its shearers is silent, so He opened not His mouth. ❖ So He became their Savior. ❖ For the LORD GOD is my strength and my song, and he has become my salvation. ❖Here is the Lamb of God who takes away the sin of the world! ❖ He died for all, that those who live should live no longer for themselves, but for Him who died for them and rose again. ❖ My heart shall rejoice in Your salvation. ❖ You were ransomed . . . with the precious blood of Christ, like that of a lamb without blemish or spot. He was destined before the foundation of the world but was made manifest at the end of the times for your sake. ❖ And for this reason He is the mediator of a new covenant, so that, since a death has taken place for the redemption of the transgressions that were committed under the first covenant, those who have been called may receive the promise of the eternal inheritance. ❖ Worthy is the Lamb, who was slain, to receive power and wealth and wisdom and strength and honor and glory and praise!

EXOD. 13:13 NIV; GEN. 22:8; 1 COR. 5:7 TLB; ISA. 53:7 NKJV; ISA. 63:8 NASB; ISA. 12:2 RSV; JOHN 1:29 NRSV; 2 COR. 5:15 NKJV; PS. 13:5 NKJV; 1 PETER 1:18–20 RSV; HEB. 9:15 NASB; REV. 5:12 NIV

Jesus, my lamb-like Jesus,
Shivering as the nails go through his hands;

. . . .

What a day! Lord, what a day!
When my blessed Jesus died.
JAMES WELDON JOHNSON

Forbid it, Lord, that I should boast,
Save in the death of Christ, my God.
ISAAC WATTS

What a wondrous thought: You, Lord Jesus, are the required sacrificial Lamb by whom I am redeemed. No further sacrifice is required.

HE REDEEMED ME

You in Your mercy have led forth the people whom You have redeemed. ❖ It was necessary for the Christ to suffer and to rise from the dead the third day, and that repentance and remission of sins should be preached in His name. ❖ This is how God showed his love for us: God sent his only son into the world so we might live through him. This is the kind of love we are talking about—not that we once upon a time loved God, but that he loved us and sent his Son as a sacrifice to clear away our sins and the damage they've done to our relationship with God. ❖ The Lord is not slow about His promise, as some count slowness, but is patient toward you, not wishing for any to perish but for all to come to repentance. ❖ God does not take away life, but plans ways so that the banished one may not be cast out from him. ❖ My lips shall greatly rejoice when I sing unto thee; and my soul, which thou hast redeemed. ❖ Therefore the redeemed of the Lord shall return, and come with singing unto Zion; and everlasting joy shall be upon their head: they shall obtain gladness and joy; and sorrow and mourning shall flee away.

Exod. 15:13 nkjv; Luke 24:46–47 nkjv; 1 John 4:9–10 the message;
2 Peter 3:9 nasb; 2 Sam. 14:14 nasb; Ps. 71:23; Isa. 51:11

The whole cause of that suffering was that Jesus loved us and could not help us in any way except through his sacrifice. As a result, he rather gave himself up to the deep and heaviest suffering rather than to allow us to lose our salvation. . . .
Philipp Jacob Spener

It was not the soldiers who killed him, nor the screams of the mob: It was his devotion to us.

Max Lucado

When you hung on the cross, your mind was on me. You could have called ten thousand angels to come to your rescue, but your love for me did not allow you to utter a cry for help.

OUR REDEEMER

By one offering He has perfected for all time those who are sanctified. ❖ He Himself bore our sins in His body on the cross, so that we might die to sin and live to righteousness. ❖ The LORD has laid on Him the iniquity of us all. ❖ One man's act of righteousness leads to justification and life for all. . . . by the one man's obedience the many will be made righteous. ❖ But you were washed, you were sanctified, you were justified in the name of the Lord Jesus Christ and in the Spirit of our God. ❖ God will credit righteousness—for us who believe in him who raised Jesus our Lord from the dead. ❖ Now, therefore, you are no longer strangers and foreigners, but fellow citizens with the saints and members of the household of God, having been built on the foundation of the apostles and prophets, Jesus Christ Himself being the chief cornerstone.

HEB. 10:14 NASB; 1 PETER 2:24 NASB; ISA. 53:6 NKJV; ROM. 5:18–19 NRSV; 1 COR. 6:11 RSV; ROM. 4:24 NIV; EPH. 2:19–20 NKJV

The miracle of Redemption is that God turns me, the unholy one, into the standard of Himself, the Holy One, by putting into me a new disposition, the disposition of Jesus Christ.

OSWALD CHAMBERS

Because He took their place, they now share His. His righteousness is theirs, His standing before God is theirs, His life is theirs. There is not a single condition for them to meet, not a single responsibility for them to discharge in order to attain their eternal bliss.

ARTHUR W .PINK

When God's Son took on flesh, he truly and bodily took on, out of pure grace, our being, our nature, ourselves. This was the eternal counsel of the triune God. Now we are in him. Where he is, we are too, in the incarnation, on the Cross, and in his resurrection. We belong to him because we are in him. That is why the Scriptures call us the Body of Christ.

DIETRICH BONHOEFFER

Praise God for his incredible gift! He has made me his own. He has made me like him.

ALL FOR ME

You were slain, and have redeemed us to God by Your blood out of every tribe and tongue and people and nation. ❖ He . . . was delivered over because of our transgressions, and was raised because of our justification. ❖ For God did not appoint us to wrath, but to obtain salvation through our Lord Jesus Christ, who died for us, that whether we wake or sleep, we should live together with Him. ❖ Then he said to Thomas, "Put your finger here, and see my hands." ❖ I have inscribed you on the palms of My hands. ❖ You were bought with a price. ❖ At just the right time, when we were still powerless, Christ died for the ungodly. ❖ He is able for all time to save those who approach God through him, since he always lives to make intercession for them. ❖ That I may gain Christ and be found in him, not having a righteousness of my own that comes from the law, but one that comes through faith in Christ, the righteousness from God based on faith. ❖ How shall we escape, if we neglect so great salvation?

REV. 5:9 NKJV; ROM. 4:25 NASB; 1 THESS 5:9–10 NKJV; JOHN 20:27 RSV; ISA. 49:16 NASB; 1 COR. 6:20 RSV; ROM. 5:6 NIV; HEB. 7:25 NRSV; PHIL. 3:8–9 NRSV; HEB. 2:3

The man who knows God but does not know his own misery, becomes proud. The man who knows his own misery but does not know God, ends in despair. The incarnation shows man the greatness of his own misery by the greatness of the remedy which he acquired.

BLAISE PASCAL

> Arise, my soul, arise;
>   Shake off thy guilty fears;
> Thy bleeding Sacrifice
>   In my behalf appears:
> Before the throne my Surety stands,
> My name is written on His hands.
> CHARLES WESLEY

You died for me, dear Lord Jesus, without taking into account how long it would take me to forsake the world and cling to you alone.

HE MADE THE WAY

Thomas said to Him, "Lord, we do not know where You are going, how do we know the way?" Jesus said to him, "I am the way, and the truth, and the life; no one comes to the Father but through Me." ❖ I am the door: by me if any man enter in, he shall be saved. ❖ This hope we have as an anchor of the soul, a hope both sure and steadfast and one which enters within the veil, where Jesus has entered as a forerunner for us, having become a high priest forever according to the order of Melchizedek. ❖ He entered once for all into the Holy Place, taking not the blood of goats and calves but his own blood, thus securing an eternal redemption. ❖ Therefore, my friends, since we have confidence to enter the sanctuary by the blood of Jesus, by the new and living way that he opened for us through the curtain (that is, through his flesh), and since we have a great priest over the house of God, let us approach with a true heart in full assurance of faith. ❖ But now in Christ Jesus you who once were far off have been brought near in the blood of Christ. ❖ You make me glad by your deeds, O Lord; I sing for joy at the works of your hands.

JOHN 14:5–6 NASB; JOHN 10:9; HEB. 6:19–20 NASB; HEB. 9:12 RSV;
HEB. 10:19–22 NRSV; EPH. 2:13 RSV; PS. 92:4 NIV

The God-man then is the gateway between God and man. Through Him God has found His way back to man, from whom He had been excluded by his rebellion. In Him man finds his way back to God from Whom he had been alienated by the darkening of his intelligence, the death of his love, and the disobedience of his will. God finds Himself in this Person and is with men. Man finds himself in this Person, and is with God.

G. CAMPBELL MORGAN

The same Divine Artist again forms a body. This time his own. Fleshly divinity. Skin layered on spirit.

MAX LUCADO

You are the way for me, dear Lord. Without you there would be no way.
Impress on me the wonder of what you have done, the glory of your great love.

JOY OF THE REDEEMED

Has God not chosen the poor of this world to be rich in faith and heirs of the kingdom which He promised to those who love Him? ❖ What God has planned for people who love him is more than eyes have seen or ears have heard. It has never even entered our minds! ❖ Although you have not seen him, you love him; and even though you do not see him now, you believe in him and rejoice with an indescribable and glorious joy. ❖ Blessed is anyone who endures temptation. Such a one has stood the test and will receive the crown of life that the Lord has promised to those who love him. ❖ A highway will be there, a roadway, and it will be called the Highway of Holiness. The unclean will not travel on it. . . . But the redeemed will walk there, and the ransomed of the LORD will return and come with joyful shouting to Zion, with everlasting joy upon their heads. They will find gladness and joy, and sorrow and sighing will flee away.

JAMES 2:5 NKJV; 1 COR. 2:9 CEV; 1 PETER 1:8 NRSV; JAMES 1:12 NRSV;
ISA. 35:8–10 NASB

As Catherine of Siena said, "All the way to heaven is heaven." A joyful end requires a joyful means. Bless the Lord.

EUGENE H. PETERSON

The glory that belongs to the honored saints belongs to us as well, for we are already the children of God, princes and princesses of imperial blood. . . . We share the honors of citizenship, for we have joined the assembly of those whose names are written in heaven.

CHARLES HADDON SPURGEON

Am I filled with joy by the realization that I am redeemed, to say nothing of my heavenly inheritance?
How thankful I am that my name is written in heaven. I will be there some day.

UNDESERVED LOVE

Blessed be God, even the Father of our Lord Jesus Christ, the Father of mercies, and the God of all comfort. ❖ It is his boundless mercy that has given us the privilege of being born again so that we are now members of God's own family. Now we live in the hope of eternal life because Christ rose again from the dead. ❖ The Lord our God is merciful and forgiving, even though we have rebelled against him. ❖ For the LORD delights in you. ❖ Out of all the peoples on the face of the earth, the LORD has chosen you to be his treasured possession. ❖ The LORD your God loves you. ❖ I will not forget you.

2 COR. 1:3; 1 PETER 1:3 TLB; DAN. 9:9 NIV; ISA. 62:4 NASB; DEUT. 14:2 NIV; DEUT. 23:5 NKJV; ISA. 49:15 NKJV

You have been faithful though I have often been faithless. You have never left me or forsaken me though I have often neglected you. You have patiently urged me to get to know you better though I have resisted you. You have forgiven me over and over though over and over I have sinned against you.

MMS

God's love . . . is always for nothing. Nothing in any of us can arouse it, and nothing in us can destroy it. His love is for nothing.

AUGUSTINE

If nothing in us can win Thy love, nothing in the universe can prevent Thee from loving us. Thy love is uncaused and undeserved. Thou art Thyself the reason for the love wherewith we are loved.

A. W. TOZER

You fill me with your Spirit, Lord. You honor me with your love.
In light of your great love for me, I must give you all I am.

HIS SACRIFICIAL LOVE

I will heal their backsliding, I will love them freely. ❖ In this was manifested the love of God toward us, because that God sent his only begotten Son into the world, that we might live through him. Herein is love, not that we loved God, but that he loved us, and sent his Son to be the propitiation for our sins. ❖ Consider the steadfast love of the LORD. ❖ If, when we were enemies, we were reconciled to God by the death of his Son, much more, being reconciled, we shall be saved by his life. ❖ Greater love has no one than this, than to lay down one's life for his friends. You are My friends if you do whatever I command you. ❖ We know what real love is from Christ's example in dying for us. ❖ I am the good shepherd. The good shepherd gives His life for the sheep. ❖ The LORD your God carried you, just as one carries a child. ❖ Christ's love compels us, because we are convinced that one died for all. ❖ Shout praises to the LORD! He is good to us, and his love never fails.

HOSEA 14:4; 1 JOHN 4:9–10; PS. 107:43 RSV; ROM. 5:10; JOHN 15:13–14 NKJV; 1 JOHN 3:16 TLB; JOHN 10:11 NKJV; DEUT. 1:31 NRSV; 2 COR. 5:14 NIV; PS. 107:1 CEV

God's free forgiving love is the sole source of salvation.
GERHARDUS VOS

You have shown us love
in your blood,
and in your blood
you have shown us your mercy
and generosity.
CATHERINE OF SIENA

If it were not for your great love, dear Lord Jesus, I would be lost.
How I praise you! Your love, your death, your resurrection, my life!

ALL–ENCOMPASSING LOVE

With everlasting love I will have compassion on you, says the LORD, your Redeemer. ❖ I have loved you with an everlasting love; therefore with lovingkindness I have drawn you. ❖ I pray that you, being rooted and established in love, may have power, together with all the saints, to grasp how wide and long and high and deep is the love of Christ, and to know this love that surpasses knowledge—that you may be filled to the measure of all the fullness of God. ❖ For your steadfast love is as high as the heavens; your faithfulness extends to the clouds. ❖ Great is Your mercy toward me. ❖ Because Your lovingkindness is better than life, my lips shall praise You. ❖ The mercy of the LORD is from everlasting to everlasting upon them that fear him. ❖ Think how much the Father loves us. He loves us so much that he lets us be called his children, as we truly are. ❖ Praise the LORD of hosts: for the LORD is good; for his mercy endureth for ever. ❖ You led me to your banquet room and showered me with love.

ISA. 54:8 RSV; JER. 31:3 NKJV; EPH. 3:17–19 NIV; PS. 57:10 NRSV;
PS. 86:13 NKJV; PS. 86:13 NKJV; PS. 103:17; 1 JOHN 3:1 CEV; JER. 33:11;
SONG OF SOL. 2:4 CEV

May the love of Jesus fill me
As the waters fill the sea;
Him exalting, self abasing—
This is victory.
KATE B. WILKINSON

You had shot my heart through with the arrows of your love, and I carried your words thrust deep into my inner being.

AUGUSTINE

Do I allow his love to encompass me so that I have no earthly craving?
Your arms of love carry me; your voice of love comforts me.

GRACE FOR ALL

The hand of our God is gracious to all who seek him. ❖ The LORD has chosen you to be a people for Himself, a special treasure. ❖ I will also make you a light of the nations so that My salvation may reach to the end of the earth. ❖ And now God can always point to us as examples of how very, very rich his kindness is, as shown in all he has done for us through Jesus Christ. ❖ The LORD your God is a merciful God. ❖ The LORD is gracious, and full of compassion; slow to anger, and of great mercy. The LORD is good to all: and his tender mercies are over all his works. ❖ But to each one of us grace was given according to the measure of Christ's gift. ❖ God's abundant provision of grace and of the gift of righteousness reign in life through the one man, Jesus Christ. ❖ For the grace of God has appeared, bringing salvation to all.

EZRA 8:22 NRSV; DEUT. 14:2 NKJV; ISA. 49:6 NASB; EPH. 2:7 TLB; DEUT. 4:31 RSV; PS. 145:8–9; EPH. 4:7 NKJV; ROM. 5:17 NIV; TITUS 2:11 NRSV

God is round about us in Christ on every hand, with His many-sided and all-sufficient grace. All we need to do is to open our hearts.

O. HALLESBY

No one is beyond his grace. No situation, anywhere on earth, is too hard for God.

JIM CYMBALA

You are gracious, Lord. You have been gracious to me. You have loved me, protected me, lifted me up, encouraged me, comforted me, forgiven me, and used me. How wonderful you are! I love you and praise you.

ALL-SUFFICIENT GRACE

We do not present our supplication before you on the ground of our righteousness, but on the ground of your great mercies. ❖ Show us thy steadfast love, O LORD. ❖ For all have sinned, and come short of the glory of God; being justified freely by his grace through the redemption that is in Christ Jesus. ❖ The LORD is gracious and full of compassion. . . . he will ever be mindful of his covenant. ❖ Everything depends on having faith in God, so that God's promise is assured by his great kindness. ❖ God from the beginning chose you for salvation through sanctification by the Spirit and belief in the truth. ❖ And the grace of our Lord was exceedingly abundant, with faith and love which are in Christ Jesus. ❖ And of his fulness have all we received, and grace for grace. . . . grace and truth came by Jesus Christ. ❖ Now may our Lord Jesus Christ Himself, and our God and Father, who has loved us and given us everlasting consolation and good hope by grace, comfort your hearts and establish you in every good word and work.

DAN. 9:18 NRSV; PS. 85:7 RSV; ROM. 3:23–24; PS. 111:4–5; ROM. 4:16 CEV; 2 THESS. 2:13 NKJV; 1 TIM. 1:14 NKJV; JOHN 1:16–17; 2 THESS. 2:16–17 NKJV

The good news is that man's free will enthralled by sin can be turned around by grace.

DONALD G. BLOESCH

Our transformation of heart is utterly and completely a work of grace.

RICHARD FOSTER

He is merciful to the very depths of his being.

RAYMOND C. ORTLUND

O merciful Lord, thank you for dying to save me.
Thank you for freely giving me what I don't deserve.

WHOLLY GOD

The goodness of God leads you to repentance. ❖ In Your great mercy You did not utterly consume them nor forsake them; for You are God, gracious and merciful. ❖ [God] has saved us, and called us with a holy calling, not according to our works, but according to His own purpose and grace which was granted us in Christ Jesus from all eternity, but now has been revealed by the appearing of our Savior Christ Jesus, who abolished death, and brought life and immortality to light through the gospel. ❖ At the present time there is a remnant, chosen by grace. But if it is by grace, it is no longer on the basis of works, otherwise grace would no longer be grace. ❖ Where sin abounded, grace abounded much more, so that as sin reigned in death, even so grace might reign through righteousness to eternal life through Jesus Christ our Lord. ❖ But even though we were dead in our sins God, who is rich in mercy, because of the great love he had for us, gave us life together with Christ—it is, remember, by grace and not by achievement that you are saved—and has lifted us right out of the old life to take our place with him in Christ in the Heavens.

ROM. 2:4 NKJV; NEH. 9:31 NKJV; 2 TIM. 1:9–10 NASB; ROM. 11:5–6 NRSV; ROM. 5:20–21 NKJV; EPH. 2:4–6 PHILLIPS

[Abraham] felt he could still do something to produce a child, as indeed he could, and did. At eighty-six he yet had that capacity.

There followed a further long wait, until at an age of a hundred Abraham could no longer do even this; his body was "as good as dead" (Romans 4:19). It was to such a man, powerless now in himself to please God, that the marvellous gift of grace came in the person of Isaac. This was wholly God's doing and well worth waiting for. To have God do His own work through us, even once, is better than a lifetime of human striving.

WATCHMAN NEE

Thank you, Lord Jesus, for doing what I could not do. You saved me through your great sacrifice on the cross. It was you alone.

THE FREE GIFT

"I will have mercy on whom I have mercy, and I will have compassion on whom I have compassion." So it depends not on human will or exertion, but on God who shows mercy. ❖ So the last shall be first, and the first last. ❖ Let him return unto the LORD, and he will have mercy upon him; and to our God, for he will abundantly pardon. ❖ In You the fatherless finds mercy. ❖ The Lord is full of compassion and mercy. ❖ Since I was worse than anyone else, God had mercy on me and let me be an example of the endless patience of Christ Jesus. He did this so that others would put their faith in Christ and have eternal life. ❖ I became a minister according to the gift of the grace of God given to me by the effective working of His power. ❖ They also, by prayer on your behalf, yearn for you because of the surpassing grace of God in you. Thanks be to God for His indescribable gift! ❖ For by grace you have been saved through faith, and that not of yourselves; it is the gift of God, not of works, lest anyone should boast.

ROM. 9:15–16 NRSV; MATT. 20:16; ISA. 55:7; HOSEA 14:3 NKJV; JAMES 5:11 NIV; 1 TIM. 1:16 CEV; EPH. 3:7 NKJV; 2 COR. 9:14–15 NASB; EPH. 2:8–9 NKJV

God does not begin with working upon the inward physical states of the patriarchs, as though they were subjects for reform. . . . He begins with giving them promises. The keynote is not what Abraham has to do for God, but what God will do for Abraham. Then, in response to this, the subjective frame of mind that changes the inner and outer life is cultivated.

GERHARDUS VOS

Grace is not about finishing last or first; it is about not counting. We receive grace as a gift from God, not as something we toil to earn.

PHILIP YANCEY

Grace is God's free, spontaneous, unsolicited, even unreturned love, which finds its origin in itself, not in its object.

JOHN STOTT

I am thankful, Lord, that your grace doesn't depend on what I do. I am undeserving but your grace is abundant nevertheless.

ALWAYS THE BEST

Gracious is the LORD, and righteous; yes, our God is merciful. ❖ Rejoice in the LORD, your God; for he has given the early rain for your vindication, he has poured down for you abundant rain, the early and the latter rain. ❖ [Peter] and all who were with him were astonished at the catch of fish which they had taken. ❖ How blessed is God! And what a blessing he is! He's the Father of our Master, Jesus Christ, and takes us to the high places of blessing in him. Long before he laid down earth's foundations, he had us in mind, had settled on us as the focus of his love, to be made whole and holy by his love. Long, long ago he decided to adopt us into his family through Jesus Christ. (What pleasure he took in planning this!) He wanted us to enter into the celebration of his lavish gift-giving by the hand of his beloved Son. ❖ For the LORD is good; his mercy is everlasting. ❖ Be still, and know that I am God.

Ps. 116:5 NKJV; JOEL 2:23 RSV; LUKE 5:9 NKJV; EPH. 1:3–6 THE MESSAGE; Ps. 100:5; Ps. 46:10

Even when our hearts are connected to God and to His Christ, we think we can bless Him more with our doing than with our receiving. Needing His grace runs counter to our determination to earn His favor by our own best efforts.

NANCY GROOM

The catch of fish in Luke 5:1–11 illustrates the difference between our work on our own and his work through us. When he directs our work, it is very fruitful. What we do in our own strength is often unproductive. When we see what God does—using our hands, head, feet—we too should be awestruck.

MMS

God Almighty, maker of heaven and earth, what a wonder you are! Help me, Father, to realize how much I need your grace and where I would be without it.

RELAXING IN HIS GRACE

Return to the LORD, your God, for he is gracious and merciful, slow to anger, and abounding in steadfast love. ❖ For sin shall not be master over you, for you are not under law, but under grace. ❖ Be strong in the grace that is in Christ Jesus. ❖ The LORD your God, who goes before you, He will fight for you, according to all He did for you in Egypt before your eyes, and in the wilderness where you saw how the LORD your God carried you, as a man carries his son. ❖ I led them with cords of compassion, with the bands of love. ❖ In his love and mercy he redeemed them; he lifted them up and carried them all the days of old. ❖ Save Your people, and bless Your inheritance; shepherd them also, and bear them up forever. ❖ The eternal God is thy refuge, and underneath are the everlasting arms. ❖ I will comfort you . . . like a mother comforting her child. ❖ I will betroth you to Me forever; yes, I will betroth you to Me in righteousness and justice, in lovingkindness and mercy; I will betroth you to Me in faithfulness, and you shall know the LORD. ❖ The LORD your God in your midst, The Mighty One, will save; He will rejoice over you with gladness, He will quiet you with His love, He will rejoice over you with singing.

JOEL 2:13 NRSV; ROM. 6:14 NASB; 2 TIM. 2:1; DEUT. 1:30–31 NKJV; HOSEA 11:4 RSV; ISA. 63:9 NIV; PS. 28:9 NKJV; DEUT. 33:27; ISA. 66:13 CEV; HOSEA 2:19–20 NKJV; ZEPH. 3:17 NKJV

[Jesus] stooped into an actual identification with human nature, and by that stoop lifted human nature into the spaciousness of fellowship with God.

G. CAMPBELL MORGAN

God has two outstretched arms. One is strong enough to surround us with justice, and one is gentle enough to embrace us with grace.

MARTIN LUTHER KING JR.

Stretch out in God's grace.

JOEY JOHNSON

Do I feel safe and secure in God's embrace?
Do I trust his unfailing love and his never-ending grace?

MY GRACIOUS GOD

Have mercy upon me, O God, according to Your lovingkindness; according to the multitude of Your tender mercies, blot out my transgressions. ❖ He will again have compassion on us, and will subdue our iniquities. You will cast all our sins into the depths of the sea. ❖ Let us fall now into the hand of the LORD; for his mercies are great. ❖ But you are merciful and gentle, Lord, slow in getting angry, full of constant loving-kindness and of truth. ❖ Have mercy upon me, and hear my prayer. ❖ LORD God, you are merciful and forgiving, even though we have rebelled against you. ❖ If he cries to me, I will hear, for I am compassionate. ❖ With great compassion I will gather you. ❖ God our Savior . . . desires all men to be saved and to come to the knowledge of the truth. ❖ Let the wicked forsake their way, and the unrighteous their thoughts; let them return to the LORD, that he may have mercy on them, and to our God, for he will abundantly pardon.

Ps. 51:1 NKJV; MICAH 7:19 NKJV; 2 SAM. 24:14; Ps. 86:15 TLB; Ps. 4:1; DAN. 9:9 CEV; EXOD. 22:27 RSV; ISA. 54:7 RSV; 1 TIM. 2:3–4 NKJV; ISA. 55:7 NRSV

If you have a true faith that Christ is your Saviour, then at once you have a gracious God, for faith leads you in and opens up God's heart and will, that you should see pure grace and overflowing love. This it is to behold God in faith that you should look upon his fatherly, friendly heart, in which there is no anger nor ungraciousness.

MARTIN LUTHER

But God is also good, kind, and gracious. He loves sinners and wants to show mercy. He sent Jesus to uphold his integrity and justice and to show his mercy. The cross of Christ is the crossroad where God's justice and mercy meet. It demonstrates how serious God is in dealing with sin, yet it also proves how earnest he is in giving mercy.

GERALD L. SITTSER

*Almighty God has shown me his merciful, compassionate heart.
How I long to please him with my righteousness; how thankful I am that he deals with me in grace.*

MY LORD AND MASTER

He said to them, "But who do you say that I am?" Peter answered and said, "The Christ of God." ❖ You are the Christ. ❖ Jesus [spoke to] them, saying, All power is given unto me in heaven and in earth. ❖ My Lord and my God. ❖ Why do you keep on saying that I am your Lord, when you refuse to do what I say? ❖ We believe and know that you are the Holy One of God. ❖ If you confess with your lips that Jesus is Lord and believe in your heart that God raised him from the dead, you will be saved. ❖ No one can say that Jesus is Lord except by the Holy Spirit. ❖ You have accepted Christ Jesus as your Lord. Now keep on following him. Plant your roots in Christ and let him be the foundation for your life. ❖ There is but one God, the Father, of whom are all things, and we in him; and one Lord Jesus Christ, by whom are all things. ❖ For the LORD is great, and greatly to be praised. ❖ That at the name of Jesus every knee should bow, of things in heaven, and things in earth, and things under the earth. And that every tongue should confess that Jesus Christ is Lord, to the glory of God the Father.

LUKE 9:20 NKJV; MARK 8:27 NKJV; MATT. 28:18; JOHN 20:28; LUKE 6:46 CEV; JOHN 6:69 NIV; ROM. 10:9 NRSV; 1 COR. 12:3 NKJV; COL. 2:6–7 CEV; 1 COR. 8:6; PS. 96:4; PHIL. 2:10–11

Christ must be Lord, and the practical evidence that he is your Savior necessarily gives evidence in a life growing into conformity to the life of Christ.

R. C. SPROUL

Our wrestling with the enemy can never hope for victory unless this Man has first wrestled with us, has dealt with all that hinders His control, and has reduced us to complete surrender.

R. ARTHUR MATHEWS

Because of their experience with him, Peter, Martha, and Thomas knew that Jesus was the Christ. Allow me, Lord, to have such experience with you. I kneel before you, Lord Jesus, and ask you to master me.

REPENTANCE AND DELIVERANCE

So My people are bent on turning from Me. ❖ They cling to deceit; they refuse to return. . . . But my people do not know the requirements of the LORD. ❖ They are wise to do evil, but to do good they have no knowledge. ❖ Rend your heart . . . and turn unto the LORD your God: for he is gracious and merciful, slow to anger, and of great kindness. ❖ For thus says the High and Lofty One Who inhabits eternity, whose name is Holy: "I dwell in the high and holy place, with him who has a contrite and humble spirit, to revive the spirit of the humble, and to revive the heart of the contrite ones." ❖ The LORD our God be with us . . . that he may incline our hearts unto him, to walk in all his ways. ❖ Help us, O God of our salvation, for the glory of Your name; and deliver us, and provide atonement for our sins, for Your name's sake! ❖ Because Your mercy is good, deliver me. ❖ Wash me thoroughly from my iniquity, and cleanse me from my sin! ❖ If we confess our sins, he is faithful and just to forgive us our sins, and to cleanse us from all unrighteousness. ❖ So I confessed my sins and told them all to you. . . . Then you forgave me and took away my guilt.

HOSEA 11:7 NASB; JER. 8:5, 7 NIV; JER. 4:22; JOEL 2:13; ISA. 57:15 NKJV; 1 KINGS 8:57–58; PS. 79:9 NKJV; PS. 109:21 NKJV; PS. 51:2 RSV; 1 JOHN 1:9; PS. 32:5 CEV

I grieve and lament before Thee that I am still so prone to sin and so little inclined to obedience. . . . So helpless apart from Thee, and yet so little willing to be bound to Thee.

JOHN BAILLIE

You can claim the promises for deliverance when you know God's Word, want to be delivered for his glory, and are not overwhelmed by fear.

JOEY JOHNSON

Have I faced up to my sin and asked for forgiveness and deliverance?
Am I willing to be bound to him, to do his will, and be pleasing to him
regardless of what that involves?

HE FORGIVES MY SIN

Your sins have deprived you of good. ❖ If you repent, I will restore you that you may serve me. ❖ David said to Nathan, "I have sinned against the LORD." And Nathan said to David, "The LORD also has put away your sin." ❖ I confess my iniquity, I am sorry for my sin. ❖ There is forgiveness with You. ❖ Hear in heaven Your dwelling place; and when You hear, forgive. ❖ You are merciful, and you treat people better than they deserve. So please forgive these people. . . . Then the LORD said to Moses: In answer to your prayer, I do forgive them. ❖ I came not to call the righteous, but sinners to repentance. ❖ Father, forgive them; for they know not what they do. ❖ Let us lift our hearts and hands to God in heaven.

JER. 5:25 NRSV; JER. 15:19 NIV; 2 SAM. 12:13 NKJV; PS. 38:18 RSV; PS. 130:4 NKJV; 1 KINGS 8:30 NKJV; NUM. 14:19–20 CEV; LUKE 5:32; LUKE 23:34; LAM. 3:41 NKJV

It is said that forgiveness is the fragrance the violet sheds on the heel that has crushed it. If so, could there be a fragrance as sweet in all the Bible as that of Jesus washing the feet of the very one whose heel was raised against Him?

CHARLES R. SWINDOLL

My God, shall sin its power maintain
And in my soul defiant live!
'Tis not enough that Thou forgive,
The cross must rise and self be slain.

GREEK HYMN

I am so like Israel, sinful and disobedient. God is always the same, forgiving a repentant heart.

BEING FORGIVEN

I will forgive their iniquity, and I will remember their sin no more. ❖ I will cleanse them from all the guilt of their sin against me, and I will forgive all the guilt of their sin and rebellion against me. ❖ He does not treat us as our sins deserve. ❖ For the wages of sin is death; but the gift of God is eternal life through Jesus Christ our Lord. ❖ You shall call His name JESUS, for He will save His people from their sins. ❖ The Messiah is to suffer and to rise from the dead on the third day, and . . . repentance and forgiveness of sins is to be proclaimed in his name. ❖ The Lord isn't slow about keeping his promises. . . . In fact, God is patient, because he wants everyone to turn from sin and no one to be lost. ❖ They must turn to God in repentance and have faith in our Lord Jesus. ❖ "Blessed and to be envied," he said, "are those whose sins are forgiven and put out of sight. Yes, what joy there is for anyone whose sins are no longer counted against him by the Lord." ❖ As far as the east is from the west, so far has He removed our transgressions from us.

JER. 31:34; JER. 33:8 RSV; PS. 103:10 NIV; ROM. 6:23; MATT. 1:21 NKJV; LUKE 24:46–47 NRSV; 2 PETER 3:9 CEV; ACTS 20:21 NIV; ROM. 4:7–8 TLB; PS. 103:12 NKJV

You are so quick to forgive, Lord—no matter what evil has been committed—when there is true repentance. A humble heart turns away your wrath.

MMS

Repentance becomes a way of life—a lifelong process of turning towards the Holy One that happens one day at a time.

TREVOR HUDSON

In terms of the parable of the Prodigal Son, repentance is the flight home that leads to joyful celebration. It opens the way to a future, to a relationship restored.

PHILIP YANCEY

If we repent and believe that Christ's blood covers our sin, God never withholds his forgiveness from us.

THE CROSS OF CHRIST

The Son of man shall be betrayed . . . and they shall condemn him to death, and shall deliver him to the Gentiles to mock, and to scourge, and to crucify him. ❖ They were insistent, demanding with loud voices that He be crucified. And the voices of these men and of the chief priests prevailed. ❖ This Man, delivered up by the predetermined plan and foreknowledge of God, you nailed to a cross by the hands of godless men and put Him to death. ❖ For in him all the fulness of God was pleased to dwell, and through him to reconcile to himself all things, whether on earth or in heaven, making peace by the blood of his cross. ❖ He forgave us all our trespasses, erasing the record that stood against us with its legal demands. He set this aside, nailing it to the cross. ❖ The third day he shall rise again. ❖ He is risen; he is not here. ❖ God raised him from the dead, freeing him from the agony of death, because it was impossible for death to keep its hold on him. ❖ God has made this Jesus, whom you crucified, both Lord and Christ. ❖ For You were slain, and have redeemed us to God by Your blood out of every tribe and tongue and people and nation.

MATT. 20:18–19; LUKE 23:23 NKJV; ACTS 2:23 NASB; COL. 1:19–20 RSV; COL. 2:13–14 NRSV; MATT. 20:19; MARK 16:6; ACTS 2:24 NIV; ACTS 2:36 NKJV; REV. 5:9 NKJV

God acts justly in dealing with sin and redeeming mankind. The cross demonstrates that the guilt of sin is really forgiven, and makes clear the full cost of this forgiveness.

ALISTER E. McGRATH

To be a Christian means to forgive the inexcusable, because God has forgiven the inexcusable in you.

C. S. LEWIS

Help me to understand the extent of your suffering, Lord Jesus, that I may understand the extent of your love.
Can I remain unmoved when I think about the agony, the pain, the death that he suffered for me?

MY EYES ARE ON YOU

O LORD, there is no difference for you between helping the mighty and the weak. Help us, O LORD our God, for we rely on you. ❖ My eyes are ever looking to the Lord for help. ❖ I will look unto the LORD; I will wait for the God of my salvation: my God will hear me. ❖ Let integrity and uprightness preserve me, for I wait for You. ❖ And Abraham said, My son, God will provide himself a lamb for a burnt offering. ❖ We must keep our eyes on Jesus, who leads us and makes our faith complete. ❖ Let the light of your face shine on us, O LORD! ❖ For consider Him who endured such hostility from sinners against Himself, lest you become weary and discouraged in your souls. ❖ I can lie down and sleep soundly because you, LORD, will keep me safe. ❖ The LORD make His face shine upon you, and be gracious to you; the LORD lift up His countenance upon you, and give you peace.

2 CHRON. 14:11 NRSV; PS. 25:15 TLB; MICAH 7:7; PS. 25:21 NKJV; GEN. 22:8; HEB. 12:2 CEV; PS. 4:6 NRSV; HEB. 12:3 NKJV; PS. 4:8 CEV; NUM. 6:25–26 NKJV

It is what *Jesus* is, not what we are, that gives rest to the soul. If we really want to overcome Satan and have peace with God, we must "fix our eyes on Jesus." Let his death, his suffering, his glories, and his intercession be fresh on your mind.
CHARLES HADDON SPURGEON

It ought to be remembered that Isaac was surrendered to God not merely as an object of paternal affection, but as an exponent and instrument and pledge of the fulfillment of all the promises, which thus appeared to perish with his death.
GERHARDUS VOS

It is our willingness to let God be God in our lives that sustains our walk with Him, and this submission alone allows us to find our rest in Him.
NANCY GROOM

May my vision be unfocused except when I gaze upon you.
Am I willing to let God be God of my life?

CHRIST IS MY FOCUS

Your face, LORD, I will seek. ❖ I shall behold your face in righteousness; when I awake I shall be satisfied, beholding your likeness. ❖ Our eyes look to the LORD our God. ❖ Keep your eyes on Jesus, who both began and finished this race we're in. Study how he did it. ❖ No one has ever seen God; the only Son, who is in the bosom of the Father, he has made him known. ❖ The Word became flesh and blood, and moved into the neighborhood. We saw the glory with our own eyes, the one-of-a-kind glory, like Father, like Son, generous inside and out, true from start to finish. ❖ I am in the Father, and the Father in me. ❖ The Son is the radiance of God's glory and the exact representation of his being. ❖ He who believes in Me, believes not in Me but in Him who sent Me. And he who sees Me sees Him who sent Me. ❖ Eternal life is to know you, the only true God, and to know Jesus Christ, the one you sent.

PS. 27:8 NKJV; PS. 17:15 NRSV; PS. 123:2 NKJV; HEB. 12:2 THE MESSAGE; JOHN 1:18 RSV; JOHN 1:14 THE MESSAGE; JOHN 14:10; HEB. 1:3 NIV; JOHN 12:44–45 NKJV; JOHN 17:3 CEV

God calls us to holiness—to bring every aspect of our lives in submission to him, so that we think his thoughts and do his deeds. We are not selfish or self-centered but are concerned only with submission to God's will and service to others. We don't seek the place of leadership or recognition but happily perform in obscurity whatever tasks he has given us to do. Our delight and reward come when he is glorified.

How do we come to this place—the place of holiness? By seeking his face, staying focused on him, and praising him. Making him the center, the focus, is essential to holiness. We must seek to let him control our thoughts, our emotions, and our use of resources. Under grace, he doesn't forsake us when we don't focus on him, but with our attention straying, we cannot grow in him.

MMS

When my attention wanders from his face, I must quickly draw it back before self and the world capture my full devotion.
This focusing on him is a constant, conscious effort, a continual sense of being in his presence.

ALONE WITH HIM

Jesus often withdrew to lonely places and prayed. ❖ Peter went up upon the housetop to pray. ❖ When you pray, go into a room alone and close the door. Pray to your Father in private. He knows what is done in private, and he will reward you. ❖ "I am with you," declares the LORD. ❖ My soul yearns for you in the night, my spirit within me earnestly seeks you. ❖ My soul thirsts for God, for the living God. When shall I come and behold the face of God? ❖ When I remember You on my bed, I meditate on You in the night watches. Because You have been my help, therefore in the shadow of Your wings I will rejoice. My soul follows close behind You; Your right hand upholds me. ❖ I reach out for you. ❖ Listen! I am standing at the door, knocking; if you hear my voice and open the door, I will come in to you and eat with you, and you with me. ❖ Blessed are those who dwell in your house; they are ever praising you.

LUKE 5:16 NIV; ACTS 10:9; MATT. 6:6 CEV; HAG. 1:13 NASB; ISA. 26:9 NRSV; PS. 42:2 RSV; PS. 63:6–8 NKJV; PS. 143:6 TLB; REV. 3:20 NRSV; PS. 84:4 NIV

If we center down and live in that holy Silence that is dearer than life, and take our life program into the silent places of the heart, with complete openness, ready to do, ready to renounce according to His leading, then many of the things we are doing lose their vitality for us.

THOMAS KELLY

. . . what is it that keeps me—and you—close to God in the good times? . . . It is in solitude. Quietness. Waiting and listening. . . . Seeking before anything and everything the face and the voice of God in long encounters with him.

RONALD E. WILSON

Do I long for him? Does my soul thirst for him?
Do I invite him in to have supper with me?

HIS DAILY PRESENCE

By day the LORD directs his love, at night his song is with me—a prayer to the God of my life. ❖ You have granted me life and favor, and Your care has preserved my spirit. ❖ I am with you, says the LORD. ❖ I am with you always, even to the end of the age. ❖ Surely goodness and mercy shall follow me all the days of my life: and I will dwell in the house of the LORD for ever. ❖ You, O LORD, are in the midst of this people; for you, O LORD, are seen face to face, and your cloud stands over them and you go in front of them, in a pillar of cloud by day and in a pillar of fire by night. ❖ My presence will go with you, and I will give you rest. ❖ The LORD your God will always be at your side, and he will never abandon you. ❖ I will not fail thee, nor forsake thee. ❖ God is with us. ❖ He will be called Immanuel, which means "God is with us."

Ps. 42:8 NIV; JOB 10:12 NKJV; HAG. 1:13 NKJV; MATT. 28:20 NKJV; Ps. 23:6; NUM. 14:14 NRSV; EXOD. 33:14 RSV; DEUT. 31:6 CEV; JOSH. 1:5; ISA. 8:10; MATT. 1:23 CEV

Jesus is the tabernacle of God on earth, and we are his tabernacle, the dwelling place of God.

JOEY JOHNSON

Our body [is] a portable sanctuary through which we are daily experiencing the pre1sence of God.

RICHARD FOSTER

Christianity is neither a set of beliefs nor a moral code for living but the condition of having God present within us.

TIM RITER

Lead me by day and by night, O Lord.
He is with us now; he is with us forever.

HE IS MY SHEPHERD

The LORD is my shepherd; I shall not want. ❖ In times of trouble, you will protect me. You will hide me in your tent and keep me safe on top of a mighty rock. ❖ For you were like sheep going astray, but have now returned to the Shepherd and Overseer of your souls. ❖ His voice you shall obey, him you shall serve, and to him you shall hold fast. ❖ We are His people and the sheep of His pasture. . . . For the LORD is good; His mercy is everlasting, and His truth endures to all generations. ❖ I myself will be the shepherd of my sheep, and I will make them lie down, says the Lord GOD. ❖ I will also hold you by the hand and watch over you. ❖ I am the good shepherd. The good shepherd gives His life for the sheep. ❖ May he who became the great Shepherd of the sheep by an everlasting agreement between God and you, signed with his blood, produce in you through the power of Christ all that is pleasing to him.

PS. 23:1; PS. 27:5 CEV; 1 PETER 2:25 NKJV; DEUT. 13:4 NRSV; PS. 100:3, 5 NKJV; EZEK. 34:15 NRSV; ISA. 42:6 NASB; JOHN 10:11 NKJV; HEB. 13:20–21 TLB

He asks all, but he gives all.
THOMAS KELLY

People get tired of our leaning on them. They don't want us to "cling." We become "parasites." Parents encourage their children to become independent—that's healthy. But it's the opposite with God. He wants us to *cling* to him and depend on him for everything. We *can't* become *too* dependent on him. As we get to know him, we depend on him more and more and find that we can do less and less in ourselves—that's spiritually healthy.

MMS

Leaning on the everlasting arms.
ELISHA A. HOFFMAN

Have I found him to be an attentive and faithful Shepherd?
Help me, Lord, to reject my self-reliance and cling to you.

HE IS MY ROCK

The name of the LORD is a strong tower; the righteous run to it and are safe. ❖ The joy of the LORD is your strength. ❖ The LORD is my rock, and my fortress, and my deliverer. ❖ His truth shall be your shield. ❖ He only is my rock and my salvation, my fortress; I shall not be shaken. ❖ I long to dwell in your tent forever and take refuge in the shelter of your wings. ❖ You are my mighty rock and my fortress. ❖ There is no Rock like our God. ❖ For who is God, save the LORD? and who is a rock, save our God? God is my strength and power. ❖ Behold, I lay in Zion a chief cornerstone, elect, precious, and he who believes on Him will by no means be put to shame. ❖ All drank the same spiritual drink, for they were drinking from a spiritual rock which followed them; and the rock was Christ. ❖ The stone that the builders rejected has become the very head of the corner.

PROV. 18:10 NKJV; NEH. 8:10; 2 SAM. 22:2; PS. 91:4 NKJV; PS. 62:6 RSV; PS. 61:4 NIV; PS. 71:3 CEV; 1 SAM. 2:2 NRSV; 2 SAM. 22:32–33; 1 PETER 2:6 NKJV; 1 COR. 10:4 NASB; 1 PETER 2:7 NRSV

You are mighty, Lord, you are mighty. Nothing compares to you in power. No one can equal the strength of your hand.

MMS

Jesus wanted the disciples to huddle together for self-protection until they had received the power of the Holy Spirit. Then they would be able to take on Satan. But in themselves they could do nothing but huddle together and wait.

That's how we are. In ourselves we are afraid and weak. All we can do is find a corner to hide in and wait. But in Christ and his power we are fearless and fit to do what he's called us to—go into all the world.

MMS

I'll strengthen thee, help thee, and cause thee to stand,
Upheld by my gracious, omnipotent hand.

HOW FIRM A FOUNDATION

Do I realize that I can't be my own rock?
Am I hiding in a corner or am I finding strength in him to step out boldly?

IN HIS PRESENCE IS JOY

The LORD your God in your midst, the Mighty One, will save; He will rejoice over you with gladness, He will quiet you with His love, He will rejoice over you with singing. ❖ They feast on the abundance of your house, and you give them drink from the river of your delights. ❖ In Your presence is fullness of joy; at Your right hand are pleasures forevermore. ❖ Surely goodness and mercy shall follow me all the days of my life: and I will dwell in the house of the LORD for ever. ❖ Now unto him that is able to keep you from falling, and to present you faultless before the presence of his glory with exceeding joy, to the only wise God our Saviour, be glory and majesty, dominion and power, both now and ever. ❖ You have made him exceedingly glad with Your presence. ❖ I will go to the altar of God, to God my exceeding joy; and on the harp I will praise You, O God, my God.

ZEPH. 3:17 NKJV; PS. 36:8 NRSV; PS. 16:11 NKJV; PS. 23:6; JUDE 24–25;
PS. 21:6 NKJV; PS. 43:4 NKJV

Help us make at once such amendment of life as is necessary before we can experience the true meaning of the words "in thy presence is fulness of joy."

A. W. TOZER

God intervenes in every day, but often I'm not aware of it. I'm insensitive to his working, to his Spirit, to his voice. Yet he is there and I'm so busy, I don't know it. Or I'm so self-absorbed, I don't want to be bothered.

MMS

Just because your heart is cold and prayerless, get you into the presence of the loving Father. . . . Just place yourself before, and look up into, His face; think of His love, His wonderful, tender, pitying love.

ANDREW MURRAY

Let my response to life be regulated by your presence.
Help me seek your presence, Lord, and discover your true joy, not the
counterfeit joy of this world.

A VITAL CONNECTION TO HIM

Delight yourself also in the LORD. . . . Commit your way to the LORD, trust also in Him. ❖ A new heart also will I give you, and a new spirit will I put within you. ❖ If anyone is in Christ, he is a new creation; old things have passed away; behold, all things have become new. ❖ You are living a brand new kind of life that is continually learning more and more of what is right, and trying constantly to be more and more like Christ who created this new life within you. ❖ You . . . keep Your covenant and mercy with Your servants who walk before You with all their hearts. ❖ You have made him exceedingly glad with Your presence. ❖ You are a holy people to the LORD your God. ❖ The friend who attends the bridegroom waits and listens for him, and is full of joy when he hears the bridegroom's voice. ❖ I have walked before you in faithfulness with a whole heart, and have done what is good in your sight. ❖ Keep me as the apple of the eye, hide me under the shadow of thy wings. ❖ Greater love has no man than this, that a man lay down his life for his friends. . . . I have called you friends, for all that I have heard from my Father I have made known to you.

PS. 37:4–5 NKJV; EZEK. 36:26; 2 COR. 5:17 NKJV; COL. 3:10 TLB; 2 CHRON. 6:14 NKJV; PS. 21:6 NKJV; DEUT. 7:6 NASB; JOHN 3:29 NIV; 2 KINGS 20:3 NRSV; PS. 17:8; JOHN 15:13, 15 RSV

In order to maintain this friendship to the Bridegroom, we have to be more careful of our moral and vital relationship to Him than of any other thing, even of obedience. Sometimes there is nothing to obey, the only thing to do is to maintain a vital connection with Jesus Christ, to see that nothing interferes with that.

OSWALD CHAMBERS

To be transformed means to go above and beyond the forms of the world. Christians should neither conform nor react. They should transform.

R. C. SPROUL

What do I consider important and valuable? Is it my intimate connection with the Savior?
Am I really his friend?

I NEED HIM

Let Your tender mercies come speedily to meet us, for we have been brought very low. ❖ When I was in great need, he saved me. ❖ I proclaimed a fast there . . . that we might deny ourselves before our God, to seek from him a safe journey. ❖ [They] sought him with their whole desire; and he was found of them. ❖ God, who comforts the downcast, comforted us. ❖ It is time to seek the LORD, till he come and rain righteousness upon you. ❖ Now I take limitations in stride, and with good cheer, these limitations that cut me down to size— abuse, accidents, opposition, bad breaks. I just let Christ take over! And so the weaker I get, the stronger I become. ❖ Now may our Lord Jesus Christ Himself, and our God and Father . . . comfort your hearts and establish you in every good word and work.

PS. 79:8 NKJV; PS. 116:6 NIV; EZRA 8:21 NRSV; 2 CHRON. 15:15; 2 COR. 7:6 NKJV; HOSEA 10:12; 1 COR. 12:9–10 THE MESSAGE; 2 THESS. 2:16–17 NKJV

God is attracted to weakness. He can't resist those who humbly and honestly admit how desperately they need him.

JIM CYMBALA

It is not the self-sufficient who are found by God, but those who embrace their own weakness, who would rather limp their way into the Promised Land, like Jacob, with a song of praise on their lips than to stride faultlessly in their own confidence.

R. PAUL STEVENS

I am wearied and burdened trying to attain recognition and riches in this world. When I rest in him, I don't have to seek worldly prestige. He wants me to be humble like he is—that's an easy "burden"—being yoked to him in humility, losing my life—not trying to be honored by the world. As far as what is really important is concerned, I've already made it—I'm his child. Nothing else matters but to live as his child in obedience.

MMS

How can I be glad about my weaknesses? Help me, Lord!
God wants me to need him so that he can be involved in my life. He wants me
*   to be unsure of the way so that he can lead.*

MY HIGH PRIEST

The priest shall offer the sin offering . . . the priest shall make an atonement for him, and he shall be clean. ❖ When Christ appeared as a high priest . . . he entered once for all into the Holy Place, taking not the blood of goats and calves but his own blood, thus securing an eternal redemption. ❖ He sacrificed for their sins once for all when he offered himself. ❖ He had to be one of us, so that he could serve God as our merciful and faithful high priest and sacrifice himself for the forgiveness of our sins. ❖ Seeing then that we have a great High Priest who has passed through the heavens, Jesus the Son of God, let us hold fast our confession. For we do not have a High Priest who cannot sympathize with our weaknesses, but was in all points tempted as we are, yet without sin. Let us therefore come boldly to the throne of grace, that we may obtain mercy and find grace to help in time of need. ❖ He is, therefore, exactly the kind of High Priest we need. ❖ We have such a high priest, one who is seated at the right hand of the throne of the Majesty in the heavens. ❖ Through him we . . . have equal access to the Father.

LEV. 14:19–20; HEB. 9:11–12 RSV; HEB. 7:27 NIV; HEB. 2:17 CEV; HEB. 4:14–16 NKJV; HEB. 7:26 TLB; HEB. 8:1 NRSV; EPH. 2:18 THE MESSAGE

Realize that he was once brought far lower, in mental distress and inward anguish, than any of us. See how well he qualifies to be our High Priest—for he has felt our infirmities.

CHARLES HADDON SPURGEON

It is from the entire surrender of His will in Gethsemane that the High Priest on the throne has the power to ask what He will, has the right to make His people share in that power too, and ask what they will.

ANDREW MURRAY

He has made it possible for me to approach, without fear, the very throne of God.
My High Priest forever. Thank you, Lord Jesus.

MY LIFE HAS MEANING

I am come that they might have life, and that they might have it more abundantly. ❖ Whoever drinks of the water that I shall give him will never thirst. But the water that I shall give him will become in him a fountain of water springing up into everlasting life. ❖ Go your way, sell whatever you have and give to the poor, and you will have treasure in heaven; and come, take up the cross, and follow Me. ❖ Follow me, and I will make you fishers of men. ❖ We have left everything and followed You. ❖ Let us not grow weary in doing what is right, for we will reap at harvest time, if we do not give up. So then, whenever we have an opportunity, let us work for the good of all. ❖ Therefore we do not lose heart. Though outwardly we are wasting away, yet inwardly we are being renewed day by day. For our light and momentary troubles are achieving for us an eternal glory that far outweighs them all. ❖ For to me to live is Christ, and to die is gain. ❖ The God of love and peace shall be with you.

JOHN 10:10; JOHN 4:14 NKJV; MARK 10:21 NKJV; MATT. 4:19; MATT. 19:27 NASB; GAL. 6:9–10 NRSV; 2 COR. 4:16–17 NIV; PHIL. 1:21; 2 COR. 13:11

If the Word became flesh cosmically, physically, personally, aesthetically, spiritually, and eternally, then ordinary life has meaning.

R. PAUL STEVENS

There would be only this difference [if we begin to scorn earthly things], that instead of being devoured by our pride, by our overbearing passions, and by the malicious criticism of the world, we shall act instead with liberty, courage, and hope in God.

FRANÇOIS FÉNELON

As Jesus walked this earth, living and working among all kinds and classes of people, he gave us the divine paradigm for conjugating all the verbs of our living.

RICHARD FOSTER

How could I live without you, Lord? How could I be satisfied with a life that is not vitalized by your Spirit and infused with your love?

MY HELPER

I have taught you in the way of wisdom; I have led you in right paths. When you walk, your steps will not be hindered, and when you run, you will not stumble. ❖ Obey My voice, and I will be your God, and you shall be My people. And walk in all the ways that I have commanded you, that it may be well with you. ❖ You enlarged my path under me; so my feet did not slip. ❖ The LORD watches over the way of the righteous. ❖ Stand by the roads, and look, and ask for the ancient paths, where the good way is; and walk in it, and find rest for your souls. ❖ Take the yoke I give you. Put it on your shoulders and learn from me. I am gentle and humble, and you will find rest.

PROV. 4:11–12 NKJV; JER. 7:23 NKJV; 2 SAM. 22:37 NKJV; PS. 1:6 NRSV;
JER. 6:16 RSV; MATT. 11:29 CEV

He is the "ancient path." He will teach the way in which there is rest.
MMS

Jehoshaphat: *Do not be afraid . . . for the battle is not yours, but God's* (2 Chron. 20:15).

Moses: *Do not fear! . . . The LORD will fight for you while you keep silent* (Exod. 14:13–14 NASB).

Hezekiah: *Be strong and courageous. . . . for there is a greater power with us than with him. . . . with us is the LORD our God to help us and to fight our battles* (2 Chron. 32:7–8).

David: *The battle is the LORD's* (1 Sam. 17:47).

Asa: *LORD, there is no one besides Thee to help in the battle between the powerful and those who have no strength. . . . we trust in Thee* (2 Chron. 14:11 NASB).

He takes us by the hand and leads us from where we were. He gives us of himself. We are filled with his Spirit and are able to see.

NO FEAR

Our steps are made firm by the LORD, when he delights in our way; though we stumble, we shall not fall headlong, for the LORD holds us by the hand. ❖ He is a shield unto them that put their trust in him. ❖ Call upon Me in the day of trouble; I will deliver you, and you shall glorify Me. ❖ The LORD is my light and my salvation; Whom shall I fear? ❖ Surrender your heart to God, turn to him in prayer. . . . Then you won't be ashamed; you will be confident and fearless. . . . You will rest safe and secure, filled with hope and emptied of worry. ❖ Fear not, for I am with you; be not dismayed, for I am your God. I will strengthen you, yes, I will help you, I will uphold you with My righteous right hand.

Ps. 37:23–24 NRSV; PROV. 30:5; Ps. 50:15 NKJV; Ps. 27:1 NKJV; JOB 11:13, 15, 18 CEV; ISA. 41:10 NKJV

I am convinced that none of us have appreciated how deeply it wounds the loving heart of our Lord, when He finds that His people do not feel safe in His care.

HANNAH WHITALL SMITH

For many of us the great obstacle to charity lies not in our luxurious living or desire for more money, but in our fear—fear of insecurity.

C. S. LEWIS

We cannot have faith that certain things won't happen to us, because we don't know what the future holds. Our faith must be in the goodness and mercy of God. We must not doubt that he loves us and knows what is best for us. Our faith is in his steadfastness in watching over us and in his power. So we don't need to fear the future; in fact we can't fear it if our trust is in God. The future will be just right for us.

MMS

Why am I worried when my Guardian, Defender, Shield, and Shepherd is watching over me and has my best interests at heart?
Help me, O Lord, to honor your great power and your love for me with my trust that you will work on my behalf.

OUR CITIZENSHIP IS IN HEAVEN

He was in the world, and though the world was made through him, the world did not recognize him. ❖ He shall judge the world with righteousness. ❖ Your kingdom come. Your will be done on earth as it is in heaven. ❖ For what profit is it to a man if he gains the whole world, and loses his own soul? ❖ If you belonged to the world, its people would love you. But you don't belong to the world. I have chosen you to leave the world behind, and that is why its people hate you. ❖ [You] are not of the world, just as I am not of the world. ❖ You are no longer strangers and aliens, but you are citizens with the saints and also members of the household of God. ❖ Our citizenship is in heaven, and it is from there that we are expecting a Savior, the Lord Jesus Christ. ❖ In my Father's house are many rooms; if it were not so, would I have told you that I go to prepare a place for you? And when I go and prepare a place for you, I will come again and will take you to myself, that where I am you may be also.

JOHN 1:10 NIV; PS. 96:13; MATT. 6:10 NKJV; MATT. 16:26 NKJV; JOHN 15:19 CEV; JOHN 17:16 NKJV; EPH. 2:19 NRSV; PHIL. 3:20 NRSV; JOHN 14:2–3 RSV

The world is that sphere, or group of people that has no affection for the things of God. The world, in this sense, exists in tension with the kingdom of God.

R. C. SPROUL

I wonder about the enormous energy being devoted these days to restoring morality to the United States. Are we concentrating more on the kingdom of this world than on the kingdom that is not of this world?

PHILIP YANCEY

I want to live in another dimension—one that has as its chief motivation pleasing God and adoring him!

MMS

Let me be productive in the tension of living in this world but belonging to heaven.
Am I in love with the world or am I in love with Jesus? I can't love both.

IN HIS PRESENCE

Now we see in a mirror, dimly, but then face to face. ❖ Then shall the righteous shine forth as the sun in the kingdom of their Father. ❖ There shall be no night there: They need no lamp nor light of the sun, for the Lord God gives them light. ❖ For I will be a wall of fire all around it, says the LORD, and I will be the glory within it. ❖ They shall come from the east, and from the west, and from the north, and from the south, and shall sit down in the kingdom of God. ❖ Blessed are those who are invited to the wedding supper of the Lamb! ❖ But our homeland is in heaven, where our Savior, the Lord Jesus Christ, is; and we are looking forward to his return from there. When he comes back, he will take these dying bodies of ours and change them into glorious bodies like his own. ❖ When Christ who is our life appears, then you also will appear with Him in glory. ❖ God shall wipe away all tears from their eyes; and there shall be no more death, neither sorrow, nor crying, neither shall there be any more pain: for the former things are passed away. And he that sat upon the throne said, Behold, I make all things new.

1 COR. 13:12 NKJV; MATT. 13:43; REV. 22:5 NKJV; ZECH. 2:5 NRSV; LUKE 13:29; REV. 19:9 NIV; PHIL. 3:20–21 TLB; COL. 3:4 NKJV; REV. 21:4–5

In heaven we will be face-to-face with the light of God.
R. C. SPROUL

While all mankind is created in God's image, only those re-created by the Son will behold the unveiled glory of the Father.

R. C. SPROUL

It is impossible for us to imagine how glorious it will be in the presence of our Lord, to see him face-to-face.
Am I prepared to stand before him?

HE PREPARES US FOR WORK

[David prayed:] "O LORD our God, as for all this abundance that we have provided for building you a temple for your Holy Name, it comes from your hand, and all of it belongs to you." ❖ All Scripture is given by inspiration of God, and is profitable for . . . instruction in righteousness, that the man of God may be complete, thoroughly equipped for every good work. ❖ I have received everything in full, and have an abundance; I am amply supplied. ❖ It is God who arms me with strength, and makes my way perfect. He makes my feet like the feet of deer, and sets me on my high places. ❖ And after you have suffered for a little while, the God of all grace, who has called you to his eternal glory in Christ, will himself restore, support, strengthen, and establish you. ❖ Now may our Lord Jesus Christ Himself, and our God and Father, who has loved us and given us everlasting consolation and good hope by grace, comfort your hearts and establish you in every good word and work. ❖ May the God of peace . . . make you complete in everything good so that you may do his will, working among us that which is pleasing in his sight, through Jesus Christ, to whom be the glory forever and ever.

1 CHRON. 29:16 NIV; 2 TIM. 3:16–17 NKJV; PHIL. 4:18 NASB; PS. 18:32–33 NKJV; 1 PETER 5:10 NRSV; 2 THESS. 2:16–17 NKJV; HEB. 13:20–21 NRSV

Every time God asks us to do something, he supplies all we need. Solomon had the supplies (assembled by David), the plans (given by God), and the people (skilled workmen) to build the temple.

MMS

His name is Shaddai, the all-sufficient God.
CHARLES HADDON SPURGEON

What do I need?
Can El Shaddai supply it?

HUMBLE SERVICE

He has shown you, O man, what is good; and what does the LORD require of you but to do justly, to love mercy, and to walk humbly with your God? ❖ The sacrifices of God are a broken spirit, a broken and a contrite heart—these, O God, You will not despise. ❖ This is the one to whom I will look, to the humble and contrite in spirit, who trembles at my word. ❖ From the first day that you set your heart to understand, and to humble yourself before your God, your words were heard. ❖ Because you humbled yourself before me . . . I have heard you, declares the LORD. ❖ Show perfect courtesy toward all men. ❖ For he that is least among you all, the same shall be great. ❖ Humble yourselves in the sight of the Lord, and he shall lift you up. ❖ To the humble he shows favor. ❖ Finally, all of you should agree and have concern and love for each other. Your should also be kind and humble.

MICAH 6:8 NKJV; Ps. 51:17 NKJV; ISA. 66:2 NRSV; DAN. 10:12 NKJV; 2 CHRON. 34:27 NIV; TITUS 3:2 RSV; LUKE 9:48; JAMES 4:10; PROV. 3:34 NRSV; 1 PETER 3:8 CEV

God the Creator is transcendent, mysterious, and inscrutable, beyond the range of any imagining or philosophical guesswork of which we are capable; and hence [the second commandment is] a summons to us to humble ourselves, to listen and learn of Him, and to let Him teach us what He is like and how we should think of Him.

J. I. PACKER

After his resurrection, Jesus honored the women by appearing to them first. He didn't overlook them even though they would never be great preachers like Peter or write books of the Bible like Matthew or John. They were simple, humble women who loved Jesus and served him with all that they had, and he took note of that.

MMS

Am I serving God with humility, without concern for recognition or position? Am I sitting at the Master's feet, realizing how little I understand and how much I need to learn?

DEPENDENT ON THE LORD

In God is my salvation and my glory: the rock of my strength, and my refuge, is in God. ❖ You shall receive power when the Holy Spirit has come upon you; and you shall be My witnesses . . . to the remotest part of the earth. ❖ I decided to know nothing among you except Jesus Christ, and him crucified. And I came to you in weakness and in fear and in much trembling. ❖ To the weak I became weak, so that I might win the weak. I have become all things to all people, that I might by all means save some. ❖ Most gladly I will rather boast in my infirmities, that the power of Christ may rest upon me. Therefore I take pleasure in infirmities, in reproaches, in needs, in persecutions, in distresses, for Christ's sake. For when I am weak, then I am strong. ❖ We are fools for Christ's sake. ❖ I pray that God, who gives hope, will bless you with complete happiness and peace because of your faith. And may the power of the Holy Spirit fill you with hope.

Ps. 62:7; Acts 1:8 NASB; 1 Cor. 2:2–3 NRSV; 1 Cor. 9:22 NRSV; 2 Cor. 12:9–10 NKJV; 1 Cor. 4:10; Rom. 15:13 CEV

If you are weak, limited, ordinary, you are the best material through which God can work!

BLACKABY AND KING

There are two things we are called to do: we are to depend on His strength and be obedient to His Word. If we can't handle being dependent and obedient . . . we will never become the kind of people who have a heart for God.

STUART BRISCOE

When we follow Jesus, we give up our dependence on and security in the past. He wants total abandonment to him.
Have I learned that my weakness can be used to God's glory?

BEING LIKE HIM

Stay joined to me, and I will stay joined to you. Just as a branch cannot produce fruit unless it stays joined to the vine, you cannot produce fruit unless you stay joined to me. ❖ You shall receive power when the Holy Spirit has come upon you. ❖ I have loved you, just as my Father has loved me. So remain faithful to my love for you. ❖ I am the light of the world. He who follows Me shall not walk in darkness, but have the light of life. ❖ You are the light of the world. ❖ The path of the righteous is like the first gleam of dawn, shining ever brighter till the full light of day. ❖ The LORD has set apart the faithful for himself. ❖ Dear friends, while you are waiting for . . . [Jesus] to come, try hard to live without sinning; and be at peace with everyone so that he will be pleased with you when he returns. ❖ Serve and honor God by the way you live. ❖ Godliness is of value in every way, as it holds promise for the present life and also for the life to come. ❖ Grow in grace, and in the knowledge of our Lord and Saviour Jesus Christ.

JOHN 15:4 CEV; ACTS 1:8 NKJV; JOHN 15:9 CEV; JOHN 8:12 NKJV; MATT. 5:14 NKJV; PROV. 4:18 NIV; PS. 4:3 NRSV; 2 PETER 3:14 TLB; 2 PETER 3:11 CEV; 1 TIM. 4:8 RSV; 2 PETER 3:18

Power with God is the highest attainment of the life of full abiding.
ANDREW MURRAY

We simply cannot consider the earth apart from Christ's footsteps imprinted upon it. "Christ's manger stands on the earth, his cross is rammed into the earth, his grave is dug into the earth." This being so, the community of faith must recognize Christ's personal presence in the world today and set out to follow him in all things.
RICHARD FOSTER

Is God's power evident in my daily life?
Help me follow in your steps, Lord, willing to stay close to you in sacrificial obedience.

REACHING OUT TO GOD

For I will not trust in my bow, nor shall my sword save me. But You have saved us from our enemies. . . . In God we boast all day long. ❖ Thus says the LORD, "Let not a wise man boast of his wisdom, and let not the mighty man boast of his might, let not a rich man boast of his riches." ❖ My soul shall make its boast in the LORD. ❖ Let the one who boasts, boast in the Lord. ❖ Rescue me and deliver me. ❖ The LORD your God will fight alongside you and help you win the battle. ❖ The LORD will fight for you, and you have only to keep still. ❖ O Lord GOD, remember me. ❖ Arise, O LORD; save me, O my God. ❖ Say to them that are of a fearful heart, Be strong, fear not: behold, your God will come. ❖ The LORD will surely deliver us. ❖ And lead us not into temptation, but deliver us from evil. ❖ My hope is in you. ❖ This is the LORD; we have waited for him, we will be glad and rejoice in his salvation.

Ps. 44:6–8 NKJV; Jer. 9:23 NASB; Ps. 34:2 NKJV; 1 Cor. 1:31 NRSV;
Ps. 144:11 NKJV; Deut. 20:4 CEV; Exod. 14:14 NRSV; Judg. 16:28; Ps. 3:7;
Isa. 35:4; Isa. 36:15; Matt. 6:13; Ps. 25:21 NIV; Isa. 25:9

Faith is like an empty, open hand stretched out towards God, with nothing to offer and everything to receive.

JOHN CALVIN

True faith must always be measured by self-despair; or in other words, the measure of your trust in Christ must be the measure of your distrust in self.

STEPHEN F. OLFORD

I grew up learning to be self-reliant, but now to grow up in Christ, I must unlearn self-reliance and learn self-distrust in light of his all-sufficiency.

MMS

The answers are not always logical; the direction often cannot be determined through a formula. So I must dwell in your love, feel your peace, and trust in your sure guidance.
Where is my trust? In what do I boast?

GOD'S STRENGTH ALONE

God is our refuge and strength, an ever-present help in trouble. Therefore we will not fear, though the earth give way and the mountains fall into the heart of the sea. ❖ Our God whom we serve is able to deliver us. ❖ We do not know what to do, but our eyes are on you. ❖ David encouraged himself in the LORD his God. ❖ Commit your way to the LORD; trust in him, and he will act. ❖ My health fails; my spirits droop, yet God remains! He is the strength of my heart; he is mine forever! ❖ God . . . has been my shepherd all my life to this day. ❖ Trust in Him at all times, you people; pour out your heart before Him; God is a refuge for us. ❖ He knows those who trust in Him. ❖ Why am I discouraged? Why am I restless? I trust you! And I will praise you again because you help me, and you are my God. ❖ I will love You, O LORD, my strength.

Ps. 46:1–2 NIV; Dan. 3:17; 2 Chron. 20:12 NRSV; 1 Sam. 30:6; Ps. 37:5 RSV; Ps. 73:26 TLB; Gen. 48:15 NRSV; Ps. 62:8 NKJV; Nahum 1:7 NKJV; Ps. 42:5–6 CEV; Ps. 18:1 NKJV

We must understand that the first and chief thing for every one who would do the work of Jesus, is to believe, and so to get linked to Him, the Almighty One, and then to pray the prayer of faith in His Name.

Andrew Murray

We do not need an overwhelming amount of faith for God to hear us, since the believer's strength is not in his or her faith but in God, who is faith's object.

James Montgomery Boice

"But David encouraged himself in the Lord his God"; and the result was a magnificent victory, in which all that they had lost was more than restored to them. This always will be, and always must be the result of a courageous faith, because faith lays hold of the omnipotence of God.

Hannah Whitall Smith

Through small faith and weak trust, I see you working.
Whatever faith I have is enough to claim God's mercy and help.

GOD IS ENOUGH

Whom have I in heaven but You? And there is none upon earth that I desire besides You. My flesh and my heart fail; but God is the strength of my heart and my portion forever. ❖ And My people shall be satisfied with My goodness, says the LORD. ❖ Every good thing I have is a gift from you. ❖ I count all things to be loss in view of the surpassing value of knowing Christ Jesus my Lord. ❖ In him we live, and move, and have our being. ❖ Christ is all, and in all. ❖ There is one body and one Spirit, . . . one Lord, one faith, one baptism, one God and Father of all, who is above all and through all and in all. ❖ Love the LORD your God, listen to his voice, and hold fast to him. For the LORD is your life.

Ps. 73:25–26 NKJV; JER. 31:14 NKJV; Ps. 16:2 CEV; PHIL. 3:8 NASB; ACTS 17:28; COL. 3:11; EPH. 4:4–6 NRSV; DEUT. 30:20 NIV

We know God too little. In our prayer, we are concerned less with His presence than the thing on which our heart is set. We think mostly of ourselves, our need, and weakness, our desire and prayer. But we forget that in every prayer God must be First, must be All.

ANDREW MURRAY

God will call you to obey Him and do whatever He asks of you. However, you do not need to be doing something to feel fulfilled. You are fulfilled completely in a relationship with God. When you are filled with Him, what else do you need?

BLACKABY AND KING

The last and greatest lesson that the soul has to learn is the fact that God, and God alone, is enough for all its needs. This is the lesson that all His dealings with us are meant to teach; and this is the crowning discovery of our whole Christian life. God is enough!

HANNAH WHITALL SMITH

Have I found that God is enough for me?
God must be first for me; he must be enough.

CONTENT WITH HIS SUPPLY

The rabble with them began to crave other food, and again the Israelites started wailing and said, "If only we had meat to eat! . . . We never see anything but this manna!" ❖ They spoke against God: They said, "Can God prepare a table in the wilderness?" ❖ I am the LORD your God, Who brought you out of the land of Egypt; open your mouth wide, and I will fill it. ❖ For he satisfies him who is thirsty, and the hungry he fills with good things. ❖ Be satisfied with what you have. ❖ I have learned in whatever state I am, to be content. ❖ I love the LORD, because he has heard my voice and my supplications. Because he inclined his ear to me, therefore I will call on him as long as I live. ❖ Godliness with contentment is great gain. ❖ I have learned the secret of contentment in every situation, . . . I can do everything God asks me to with the help of Christ who gives me the strength and power.

Num. 11:4, 6 NIV; Ps. 78:19 NKJV; Ps. 81:10 NKJV; Ps. 107:9 RSV; Heb. 13:5 CEV; Phil. 4:11 NKJV; Ps. 116:1–2 NRSV; 1 Tim. 6:6; Phil. 4:12–13 TLB

In the midst of our complaining he supplies what we need. Sometimes we're so into our complaints we don't recognize that what he has supplied *is* what we need.

MMS

Not, what they have to bring the Father, but what the Father waits to give them.
ANDREW MURRAY

How delightful a teacher, but gentle a provider, how bountiful a giver is my Father! Praise, praise to Thee, O manifested Most High.

JIM ELLIOT

What do I need that he doesn't supply?
What do I want that he doesn't supply?

HE MEETS MY DAILY NEEDS

Feed me with the food that is my portion. ❖ Stay joined to me and let my teachings become part of you. Then you can pray for whatever you want, and your prayer will be answered. ❖ The LORD will . . . satisfy your needs. ❖ For your Father knows the things you have need of before you ask Him. ❖ Strive first for the kingdom of God and his righteousness, and all these things will be given to you as well. ❖ Then my Father will give you whatever you ask in my name. ❖ He that spared not his own Son, but delivered him up for us all, how shall he not with him also freely give us all things? ❖ For through Him we . . . have access by one Spirit to the Father. ❖ Let us then approach the throne of grace with confidence, so that we may receive mercy and find grace to help us in our time of need. ❖ His compassions fail not. They are new every morning; great is Your faithfulness.

PROV. 30:8 NASB; JOHN 15:7 CEV; ISA. 58:11 NRSV; MATT. 6:8 NKJV; MATT. 6:33 NRSV; JOHN 15:16 CEV; ROM. 8:32; EPH. 2:18 NKJV; HEB. 4:16 NIV; LAM. 3:22–23 NKJV

Christ is the answer to all our questions.
WATCHMAN NEE

We have a sense of "coming to him daily" as the right way to live, when in fact we shouldn't have to *come* to him. We should never leave him. Our life in him should be ongoing, never stopping—not with him and then away from him. His all-sufficiency is always a part of us. We don't have to stop and ask for it in the midst of trouble.

MMS

Having loved us and made us one with Himself, what could He do but give those who bear His name the right to present it before the Father, or to come with it to Himself for all they need.

ANDREW MURRAY

Every day God's love and compassion are just as strong as ever and available and sufficient to meet the needs, whatever they are, of the day.

MMS

Every day God's supply is fresh and abundant—all I need.
Where is my confidence? On whom am I relying?

HE MEETS MY NEEDS PERFECTLY

My people have committed two evils: They have forsaken Me, the fountain of living waters, and hewn themselves cisterns—broken cisterns that can hold no water. ❖ For with You is the fountain of life. ❖ All who forsake You shall be ashamed. . . . Because they have forsaken the LORD, the fountain of living waters. ❖ The water I give is like a flowing fountain that gives eternal life. ❖ To the thirsty I will give water as a gift from the spring of the water of life. ❖ Every one who thirsts, come to the waters. ❖ With joy you will draw water from the wells of salvation. ❖ No one who has faith in me will ever be thirsty. ❖ Streams of living water will flow from within him. ❖ For the Lamb which is in the midst of the throne shall feed them, and shall lead them unto living fountains of waters. ❖ There shall be showers of blessing. ❖ Whoever wishes, let him take the free gift of the water of life.

JER. 2:13 NKJV; PS. 36:9 NKJV; JER. 17:13 NKJV; JOHN 4:14 CEV; REV. 21:6 NRSV; ISA. 55:1 RSV; ISA. 12:3 NRSV; JOHN 6:35 CEV; JOHN 7:38 NIV; REV. 7:17; EZEK. 34:26; REV. 22:17 NIV

God has the water we need, but we try to dig for our own water. Even if we could get water on our own, his is *living* water. We prefer our own substitute for God's best.

MMS

"Come," Jesus says to us in our paralysis, "your efforts to be perfectly in control, to have mastered your own righteousness, these torment you. All your efforts to be God are forgiven. Nurture yourselves in the celebration of my gospel. Remember, remind each other, that you are my friends. I call you to be beautifully human, to walk with me in the ambiguity of finitude, to accept your helplessness. I will show you the way."

MARGARET GRAMATKY

If I rely on myself, I rely on weakness. I must daily face my helplessness and rely on him. I must daily confess that without him, I am nothing.
Am I trying to quench my thirst with Kool-Aid when living water is available?

JUNE 8

IN MY WEAKNESS GOD MEETS MY NEED

God is my helper; the Lord is the sustainer of my soul. ❖ We have no power against this great multitude that is coming against us; nor do we know what to do, but our eyes are upon You. ❖ I am the LORD, the God of all flesh. Is there anything too hard for Me? ❖ Without Me you can do nothing. ❖ My grace is sufficient for you, for power is made perfect in weakness. ❖ I pray that, according to the riches of his glory, he may grant that you may be strengthened in your inner being. ❖ Christ gives me the strength to face anything. ❖ When I am weak, then am I strong. ❖ The Lord stood with me, and strengthened me. ❖ I thank Christ Jesus our Lord, who has given me strength.

Ps. 54:4 NASB; 2 Chron. 20:12 NKJV; Jer. 32:27 NKJV; John 15:5 NKJV; 2 Cor. 12:9 NRSV; Eph. 3:16 NRSV; Phil. 4:13 CEV; 2 Cor. 12:10; 2 Tim. 4:17; 1 Tim. 1:12 NIV

Jacob had to see himself before he could turn to God—like the Prodigal. When he wrestled with God he was ready to admit his need.

R. Paul Stevens

My burden carries me daily to Jesus, who transforms my burden daily into a sacrament of Christ's power and grace made perfect through weakness.

R. Paul Stevens

As we are reminded through our burden of our utter weakness without Christ, we are given strength to go on.

MMS

He provides for those who will be helpless enough to come to him for refuge, helpless enough to pour out their heart.

Pastor Anthes

Do I feel helpless enough to let God help?
I must stop trying to do it myself; then God will do it for me.

HAVING THE WISDOM OF CHRIST

The fear of the LORD is the beginning of wisdom; all those who practice it have a good understanding. ❖ Wisdom is worth much more than precious jewels. ❖ Teach me wisdom in my secret heart. ❖ The spiritual man has insight into everything, and that bothers and baffles the man of the world, who can't understand him at all. . . . Strange as it seems, we Christians actually do have within us a portion of the very thoughts and mind of Christ. ❖ All things that I have heard of my Father I have made known unto you. ❖ For the LORD gives wisdom. ❖ I do not cease to give thanks for you, remembering you in my prayers, that the God of our Lord Jesus Christ, the Father of glory, may give you a spirit of wisdom and of revelation in the knowledge of him. ❖ And this I pray, that your love may abound still more and more in knowledge and all discernment, that you may approve the things that are excellent, that you may be sincere and without offense till the day of Christ.

Ps. 111:10 NRSV; Prov. 8:11 CEV; Ps. 51:6 NRSV; 1 Cor. 2:15–16 TLB; John 15:15; Prov. 2:6 NKJV; Eph. 1:16–17 RSV; Phil. 1:9–10 NKJV

What a nation needs more than anything else is not a Christian ruler in the palace but a Christian prophet within earshot.

KENNETH KAUNDA

God never gives us discernment in order that we may criticize, but that we may intercede.

OSWALD CHAMBERS

The fruit of wisdom is Christlikeness—peace, and humility, and love—and the root of it is faith in Christ as the manifested wisdom of God.

J. I. PACKER

Lord, I long for your wisdom, your discernment. May I rely more and more on your thoughts within me.
With your thoughts, Lord, humility; with your wisdom, grace.

FOCUS ON HIM

The Lord answered and said to her, "Martha, Martha, you are worried and bothered about so many things; but only a few things are necessary, really only one, for Mary has chosen the good part, which shall not be taken away from her." ❖ "Come, follow me," Jesus said. ❖ I will follow You wherever You go. ❖ If we live in the Spirit, let us also walk in the Spirit. ❖ Everyone who looks to the Son and believes in him shall have eternal life, and I will raise him up at the last day. ❖ He who believes in Me, believes not in Me but in Him who sent Me. And he who sees Me sees Him who sent Me. I have come as a light into the world, that whoever believes in Me should not abide in darkness. ❖ If you have seen me, you have seen the Father. ❖ We have seen his glory, the glory as of a father's only son, full of grace and truth. ❖ For it is the God who said, "Let light shine out of darkness," who has shone in our hearts to give the light of the knowledge of the glory of God in the face of Jesus Christ.

LUKE 10:41–42 NASB; MATT. 4:19 NIV; MATT. 8:19 NKJV; GAL. 5:25;
JOHN 6:40 NIV; JOHN 12:44–46 NKJV; JOHN 14:9 CEV; JOHN 1:14 NRSV;
2 COR. 4:6 NRSV

We are told in Scripture to focus on the Lord—not on self or our circumstances. Focusing on self is sin; dwelling on our own attributes is pride; bemoaning our situation is lack of trust. None of that matters. All that matters is Christ. When we focus on him and are obedient to him, our thoughts and our actions will be what they should be.

MMS

Aim at Heaven and you will get earth "thrown in": aim at earth and you will get neither.

C. S. LEWIS

Jesus says: Sit at my feet and let me teach you; don't try to teach yourself (as is your tendency). Be like Mary—eager, committed, undistracted, recognizing what is top priority.
May my only goal be to praise, worship, and serve you.

HIS PURPOSE FOR ME

Work hard and cheerfully at whatever you do, as though you were working for the Lord rather than for people. ❖ Be dressed for action. ❖ For everyone to whom much is given, from him much will be required. ❖ When you eat or drink or do anything else, always do it to honor God. ❖ I desire that you insist on these things, so that those who have come to believe in God may be careful to devote themselves to good works; these things are excellent and profitable to everyone. ❖ I have no greater joy than to hear that my children walk in truth. ❖ He taught us to give up our wicked ways and our worldly desires and to live decent and honest lives in this world. ❖ He sought his God and worked wholeheartedly. And so he prospered. ❖ As long as he sought the LORD, God made him prosper. ❖ By works was faith made perfect. ❖ Let the words of my mouth, and the meditation of my heart, be acceptable in thy sight, O LORD, my strength, and my redeemer.

COL. 3:23 NLT; LUKE 12:35 NRSV; LUKE 12:48 NKJV; 1 COR. 10:31 CEV;
TITUS 3:8 NRSV; 3 JOHN 3 NKJV; TITUS 2:12 CEV; 2 CHRON. 31:21 NIV;
2 CHRON. 26:5 NKJV; JAMES 2:22; PS. 19:14

Have I today done anything to fulfil the purpose for which Thou didst cause me to be born?

JOHN BAILLIE

Of all today's miracles, the greatest is this: To know that I find Thee best when I work listening, not when I am still or meditative or even on my knees in prayer, but when I *work* listening and co-operating.

FRANK LAUBACK

What is God's purpose for me?
May my work be for your glory; may my words be to your praise.

SEEK HIM

But seek first the kingdom of God and His righteousness, and all these things shall be added to you. ❖ Seek the LORD and his strength, seek his face continually. ❖ You will seek Me and find Me, when you search for Me with all your heart. ❖ If my people, which are called by my name, shall humble themselves, and pray, and seek my face, and turn from their wicked ways; then will I hear from heaven, and will forgive their sin. ❖ When in their trouble they turned to the LORD God of Israel, and sought Him, He was found by them. ❖ You did not let them down when they depended on you. ❖ I sought the LORD, and he heard me, and delivered me from all my fears. ❖ And when he was in distress he entreated the favor of the LORD his God and humbled himself greatly before the God of his fathers. He prayed to him, and God received his entreaty and heard his supplication. ❖ May your eyes be open to your servant's plea. ❖ With all my heart I want your blessings. Be merciful just as you promised. ❖ I give thanks to you, O Lord my God, with my whole heart. ❖ Let the heart of them rejoice that seek the LORD.

MATT. 6:33 NKJV; 1 CHRON. 16:11; JER. 29:13 NKJV; 2 CHRON. 7:14; 2 CHRON. 15:4 NKJV; PS. 22:5 CEV; PS. 34:4; 2 CHRON. 33:12–13 RSV; 1 KINGS 8:52 NIV; PS. 119:58 TLB; PS. 86:12 NRSV; 1 CHRON. 16:10

How can I make my life today, amid all my duties, a platform for being with God? How can I take the raw materials of this day and dignify them with the underlying purpose of seeking the face of God?

RAYMOND C. ORTLUND

I sought the Lord, and afterward I knew
He moved my heart to seek him, seeking me.

ANONYMOUS

Today, Lord, my desire is to seek your face and hear your voice. So that your presence with me will not be impeded, I will keep ungodly attitudes out of my mind, I will not let anxiety take over, I will not be concerned for my own "rights," and I will take time to remember you.

CHOOSE HIS WAY

I pondered the direction of my life, and I turned to follow your statutes. ❖ If you give yourself to the hungry, and satisfy the desire of the afflicted, then your light will rise in darkness, and your gloom will become like midday. And the LORD will continually guide you. ❖ If you keep your feet from breaking the Sabbath and from doing as you please on my holy day, if you call the Sabbath a delight and the LORD's holy day honorable, and if you honor it by not going your own way and not doing as you please or speaking idle words, then you will find your joy in the LORD. ❖ Do not be hard-hearted or tightfisted toward your needy neighbor. You should rather open your hand, willingly lending enough to meet the need, whatever it may be. ❖ Love should be your guide. ❖ Let nothing be done through selfish ambition or conceit, but in lowliness of mind let each esteem others better than himself. . . . Let this mind be in you which was also in Christ Jesus. ❖ I am the way, the truth, and the life.

Ps. 119:59 NLT; Isa. 58:10–11 NASB; Isa. 58:13–14 NIV; Deut. 15:7–8 NRSV; 1 Cor. 14:1 CEV; Phil. 2:3 NKJV; John 14:6

I have to choose thoughts that are your thoughts, words that are your words, and actions that are your actions. There are no times or places without choices. And I know how deeply I resist choosing you.

HENRI J. M. NOUWEN

Live in such a way that any day would make a suitable topstone for life. Live so that you need not change your mode of living, even if your sudden departure were immediately predicted to you.

CHARLES HADDON SPURGEON

I hear him say, "Spend more time listening to me."
I have so many choices, but there is only one way pleasing to the Lord. May I not resist it. May I walk in it.

LETTING HIM HAVE CONTROL

How can young people keep their way pure? By guarding it according to your word. ❖ Let me know what your plans are, then I can obey and continue to please you. ❖ Show me Your ways, O LORD; teach me Your paths. ❖ Direct my steps by Your word. ❖ He leads me in the paths of righteousness for His name's sake. ❖ My foot has held fast to his steps; I have kept his way and have not turned aside. ❖ My steps have held fast to your paths; my feet have not slipped. ❖ Let us walk in the light of the LORD. ❖ He is our God forever and ever, and he will be our guide until we die. ❖ I trust you, LORD. . . . My life is in your hands. ❖ Commit your way to the LORD; trust in him and he will do this: He will make your righteousness shine like the dawn, the justice of your cause like the noonday sun.

Ps. 119:9 NRSV; EXOD. 33:13 CEV; Ps. 25:4 NKJV; Ps. 119:133 NKJV; Ps. 23:3 NKJV; JOB 23:11 RSV; Ps. 17:5 NRSV; ISA. 2:5; Ps. 48:14 NLT; Ps. 31:14–15 CEV; Ps. 37:5–6 NIV

To wait on the Lord, to live the life of prayer, to abide in Christ, to walk in the Spirit, the modus operandi of the open Bible with the open heart, is a way of doing the business of life that does not come naturally to us.

RAYMOND C. ORTLUND

Having, therefore, taken the step of faith by which you have put yourself wholly and absolutely into His hands, you must now expect Him to begin to work. His way of accomplishing that which you have entrusted to Him may be different from your way; but He knows, and you must be satisfied.

HANNAH WHITALL SMITH

I open my heart to you, Lord, that your Spirit may have control.
Am I satisfied with what God is doing in my life?

SINGLE-MINDED

Let the Lord Jesus Christ be as near to you as the clothes you wear. Then you won't try to satisfy your selfish desires. ❖ Those who are Christ's have crucified the flesh with its passions and desires. ❖ Each of you is now a new person. You are becoming more and more like your Creator. ❖ For as many of you as have been baptized into Christ have put on Christ. ❖ Seek those things which are above, where Christ is, sitting at the right hand of God. Set your mind on things above, not on things on the earth. ❖ Test me, O LORD, and try me, examine my heart and my mind. ❖ For we are what he has made us, created in Christ Jesus for good works, which God prepared beforehand to be our way of life. ❖ Walk in the Spirit. ❖ Let the peace of God rule in your hearts. . . . Let the word of Christ dwell in you richly. . . . And whatever you do in word or deed, do all in the name of the Lord Jesus, giving thanks to God the Father through Him. ❖ Those of steadfast mind you keep in peace—in peace because they trust in you.

ROM. 13:14 CEV; GAL. 5:24 NKJV; COL. 3:10 CEV; GAL. 3:27; COL. 3:1–2 NKJV; PS. 26:2 NIV; EPH. 2:10 NRSV; GAL. 5:16; COL. 3:15–17 NKJV; ISA. 26:3 NRSV

We "wear him." We are hidden in him; we are covered by him.
MAX LUCADO

Dressed in his righteousness alone,
faultless to stand before the throne.
EDWARD MOTE

"What, Father, do you desire said? What, Father, do you desire done this minute?
FRANK LAUBACH

If I am single-minded in my devotion to God, everything else takes second place.
Why do I change my clothes? Why am I not content with wearing him alone?

WE REPRESENT HIM

Behold what manner of love the Father has bestowed on us, that we should be called children of God! Therefore the world does not know us, because it did not know Him. ❖ His Holy Spirit speaks to us deep in our hearts and tells us that we are God's children. ❖ For those God foreknew he also predestined to be conformed to the likeness of his Son, that he might be the firstborn among many brothers. ❖ But we all, with open face beholding as in a glass the glory of the Lord, are changed into the same image from glory to glory, even as by the Spirit of the Lord. ❖ Whoever does not practice righteousness is not of God, nor is he who does not love his brother. ❖ You shall be My witnesses. ❖ Everyone therefore who acknowledges me before others, I also will acknowledge before my Father in heaven.

1 JOHN 3:1–2 NKJV; ROM. 8:16 NLT; ROM. 8:29 NIV; 2 COR. 3:18;
1 JOHN 3:10 NKJV; ACTS 1:8 NASB; MATT. 10:32 NRSV

There is a glorified Man on the right hand of the Majesty in heaven faithfully representing us there. We are left for a season among men; let us faithfully represent Him here.

A. W. TOZER

Presenting myself before God, I ask Him to form His perfect image in my soul and make me entirely like Himself.

BROTHER LAWRENCE

God has revealed to us a new reality that the world does not understand: In his eternal kingdom, what matters is being like our Father. That is the way to success and peace. We don't have to struggle to make it. We're already there.

MMS

How well do I represent my Lord Jesus here on earth?
Is there a family resemblance? Would people know by looking at me that I am his child?

LIVING FOR HIM IN THE WORLD

Blessed are the peacemakers. . . . Blessed are they which are persecuted for righteousness' sake. ❖ Love your enemies and pray for those who persecute you. ❖ And the fruit of righteousness is sown in peace of them that make peace. ❖ Therefore, whether you eat or drink, or whatever you do, do all to the glory of God. ❖ Say the right thing at the right time and help others by what you say. . . . Be kind and merciful, and forgive others, just as God forgave you because of Christ. ❖ If anybody asks why you believe as you do, be ready to tell him, and do it in a gentle and respectful way. ❖ Let your speech always be with grace, seasoned with salt, that you may know how you ought to answer each one. ❖ Our great God and Savior, Jesus Christ . . . gave himself for us to redeem us from all wickedness and to purify for himself a people that are his very own, eager to do what is good.

MATT. 5:9–10; MATT. 5:44 RSV; JAMES 3:18; 1 COR. 10:31 NKJV; EPH. 4:29, 32; 1 PETER 3:15 TLB; COL. 4:6 NKJV; TITUS 2:13–14 NIV

Jesus' images portray the Kingdom as a kind of secret force. Sheep among wolves, treasure hidden in a field, the tiniest seed in a garden, wheat growing among weeds, a pinch of yeast worked into bread dough, a sprinkling of salt on meat— all these hint at a movement that works within society, changing it from inside out.

PHILIP YANCEY

All too often the church holds up a mirror reflecting back the society around it, rather than a window revealing a different way.

PHILIP YANCEY

Does my life simply mirror what is in the world or am I a window, revealing the love and grace of God?
Am I working where I am—a tiny seed beginning to grow, later to bloom?

WE ARE LIGHT

I am the light that has come into the world. No one who has faith in me will stay in the dark. ❖ While you have the light, believe in the light, so that you may become children of light. ❖ For you were once darkness, but now you are light in the Lord. Walk as children of light. ❖ Sow for yourselves righteousness; reap steadfast love; break up your fallow ground; for it is time to seek the LORD, that he may come and rain righteousness upon you. ❖ You are the salt of the earth. ❖ You are the light of the world. ❖ Let your light shine before others, so that they may see your good works and give glory to your Father in heaven. ❖ Whatsoever ye do, do all to the glory of God. ❖ You are a chosen race, a royal priesthood, a holy nation, a people for God's own possession, that you may proclaim the excellencies of Him who has called you out of darkness into His marvelous light.

JOHN 12:46 CEV; JOHN 12:36 NRSV; EPH. 5:8 NKJV; HOS. 10:12 NRSV;
MATT. 5:13 NKJV; MATT. 5:14 NKJV; MATT. 5:16 NRSV; 1 COR. 10:31;
1 PETER 2:9 NASB

So, let your lives preach, let your light shine, that your works may be seen, that your Father may be glorified. This has the praise of God, and they who do so come to answer that which God requires, to love mercy, do justly, and to walk humbly with God.

GEORGE FOX

Is my light dim and useless or does Jesus shine brightly through all I say and do?
What crop is my life producing?

WALKING AS HE WOULD

For the ways of the LORD are right; the righteous walk in them, but transgressors stumble in them. ❖ LORD, walking in the way of your laws, we wait for you. ❖ My foot stands on level ground. ❖ Blessed is the man who walks not in the counsel of the ungodly, nor stands in the path of sinners, nor sits in the seat of the scornful. ❖ If we walk in the light, as he is in the light, we have fellowship one with another, and the blood of Jesus Christ his Son cleanseth us from all sin. ❖ Let us walk in the light of the LORD. ❖ If you refuse to take up your cross and follow me, you are not worthy of being mine. ❖ Whoever desires to save his life will lose it, but whoever loses his life for My sake will find it. ❖ Our LORD, you always do right, and you make the path smooth for those who obey you. ❖ You meet him who rejoices and does righteousness, who remembers You in Your ways. ❖ The joy of the LORD is your strength.

HOSEA 14:9 NKJV; ISA. 26:8 NIV; PS. 26:12 RSV; PS. 1:1 NKJV; 1 JOHN 1:7; ISA. 2:5; MATT. 10:38 TLB; MATT. 16:25 NKJV; ISA. 26:7 CEV; ISA. 64:5 NKJV; NEH. 8:10

True Christlikeness, true companionship with Christ, comes at the point where it is hard not to respond as he would.

DALLAS WILLARD

The spiritual life is a life beyond moods. It is a life in which we choose joy and do not allow ourselves to become victims of passing feelings of happiness or depression.

. . . To choose joy [means] the determination to let whatever takes place bring us one step closer to the God of life.

HENRI J. M. NOUWEN

What do I need to give up so that my heart can be more committed to Christ? Why do I go kicking and screaming when his will is best and he knows all that I go through? I should bear my burden and go my way rejoicing!

GIVE HIM GLORY

You are my God. I worship you. In my heart, I long for you, as I would long for a stream in a scorching desert. . . . Your love means more than life to me, and I praise you. ❖ How my heart yearns within me! ❖ Our heart's desire is to glorify your name. ❖ I will strengthen them in the LORD; and they shall walk up and down in his name. ❖ Do you not know that your body is the temple of the Holy Spirit who is in you, whom you have from God, and you are not your own? For you were bought at a price; therefore glorify God in your body and in your spirit, which are God's. ❖ Put on the new self, which in the likeness of God has been created in righteousness and holiness of the truth. ❖ To grant us that we . . . might serve Him without fear, in holiness and righteousness before Him all the days of our life. ❖ I eagerly expect and hope that I will in no way be ashamed, but will have sufficient courage so that now as always Christ will be exalted in my body, whether by life or by death. ❖ I wait for the LORD. ❖ In your generous love I am really living at last! My lips brim praises like fountains. I bless you every time I take a breath; my arms wave like banners of praise to you. ❖ We will walk in the name of the LORD our God for ever and ever.

PS. 63:1, 3 CEV; JOB 19:27 NKJV; ISA. 26:8 NLT; ZECH. 10:12;
1 COR. 6:19–20 NKJV; EPH. 4:24 NASB; LUKE 1:74–75 NKJV; PHIL. 1:20 NIV;
PS. 130:5; PS. 63:3–4 THE MESSAGE; MICAH 4:5

God doth not need
Either man's work or his own gifts; who best
Bear his mild yoke, they serve him best.
JOHN MILTON

Shape my thoughts; form my words; guide my acts that all of my life may glorify you.

MMS

That my life would give you pleasure, that my words would rise to you like sweet-smelling perfume, that my thoughts would align with your will for me—this is my prayer.

DEVOTED TO HIM

Hannah answered, . . ." I . . . have poured out my soul before the LORD."
. . . Her face was no longer sad. ❖ [Anna] departed not from the temple,
but served God with fastings and prayers night and day. ❖ [Caleb] wholly
followed the LORD. ❖ As for me and my house, we will serve the LORD.
❖ Paul answered, . . ."For I am ready not only to be bound, but also
to die at Jerusalem for the name of the Lord Jesus." ❖ [Job] fell down
upon the ground, and worshipped. ❖ Then I lift my hands in prayer,
because my soul is a desert, thirsty for water from you. ❖ Whom have
I in heaven but you? And earth has nothing I desire besides you. ❖ As
the deer pants for water, so I long for you, O God. I thirst for God, the
living God.

1 SAM. 1:15, 18 NKJV; LUKE 2:37; DEUT. 1:36 NKJV; JOSH. 24:15; ACTS 21:13
NKJV; JOB 1:20; PS. 143:6 CEV; PS. 73:25 NIV; PS. 42:1–2 TLB

After her prayer, Hannah knew once again that she was loved by God. . . . Her
happiness was no longer dependent upon having a child, but only upon the total
and unlimited love of God. . . . God's goodness, not her own, was the main source
of her joy.

HENRI J. M. NOUWEN

> In Thy will, O Lord, is my peace.
> In Thy love is my rest.
> In Thy service is my joy.
> Thou art all my heart's desire.
> *Whom have I in heaven but Thee?*
> *And there is none upon earth that I desire besides Thee.*
> JOHN BAILLIE

*What of my devotion, Lord? When have I devoted myself to prayer, when have
I committed myself to service, when have I fallen before you in worship,
when have I been willing to die for you?*

PRAYER AND FASTING

"Now, therefore," says the LORD, "turn to Me with all your heart, with fasting, with weeping, and with mourning." ❖ You must deny yourselves. ❖ I humbled my soul with fasting. ❖ Therefore, prepare your minds for action; be self-controlled; set your hope fully on the grace to be given you when Jesus Christ is revealed. ❖ Be serious and watchful in your prayers. ❖ Is this not the fast that I have chosen: To loose the bonds of wickedness, to undo the heavy burdens, to let the oppressed go free. . . . Is it not to share your bread with the hungry? ❖ They were worshiping the Lord and fasting. ❖ When they had ordained them elders in every church, and had prayed with fasting, they commended them to the Lord.

JOEL 2:12 NKJV; LEV. 16:29 NIV; PS. 35:13; 1 PETER 1:13 NIV; 1 PETER 4:7 NKJV; ISA. 58:6–7 NKJV; ACTS 13:2 RSV; ACTS 14:23

Fasting helps to express, to deepen, and to confirm the resolution that we are ready to sacrifice anything, to sacrifice ourselves, to attain what we seek for the kingdom of God.

ANDREW MURRAY

Food is ultimately not about food, but about God. The meaning of hunger— indeed, of all desire—is to point us to God, our only true Provider. We shouldn't be too quick to make hunger go away, for it can teach us much about our frailty, need, and emptiness apart from God.

BEN PATTERSON

However little we can understand it, in the spiritual husbandry . . . the seed we sow in the soil of heaven, the efforts we put forth, and the influence we seek to exert in the world above, need our whole being; we must give ourselves to prayer. But let us hold fast the great confidence, that in due season we shall reap, if we faint not.

ANDREW MURRAY

Lord, you are calling me into a deeper relationship with you. Let me do what it takes to get there.

WHAT SACRIFICE AM I WILLING TO MAKE?

If any of you want to be my followers, you must forget about yourself. You must take up your cross and follow me. If you want to save your life, you will destroy it. But if you give up your life for me, you will find it. ❖ If your hand or foot causes you to sin, cut it off and cast it from you. ❖ Anyone who does not take his cross and follow me is not worthy of me. ❖ If anyone serves Me, let him follow Me. ❖ Take my yoke upon you, and learn of me; for I am meek and lowly in heart. . . . For my yoke is easy, and my burden is light. ❖ Has the LORD as great delight in burnt offerings and sacrifices, as in obeying the voice of the LORD? Behold, to obey is better than sacrifice. ❖ I urge you therefore, brethren, by the mercies of God, to present your bodies a living and holy sacrifice, acceptable to God, which is your spiritual service of worship.

MATT. 16:24–25 CEV; MATT. 18:8 NKJV; MATT. 10:38 NIV; JOHN 12:26 NKJV; MATT. 11:29–30; 1 SAM. 15:22 NKJV; ROM. 12:1 NASB

The sacrifice is gone through in will before it is performed actually.
OSWALD CHAMBERS

We must make a decision of whether or not we want a life of devotion. If we do, it means being sold out to Christ. Our life then revolves around him, not ourselves or our family or work or any other thing.

We will need the nearness of his presence so much that we will not consider it a sacrifice to spend hours in Bible study and prayer and we will want every thought and act to come under the scrutiny of the Spirit.

How many of us are willing? How many of us even know that that's what God desires?

MMS

What holds me back from committing myself completely to the Master? Do the things of the world still have a hold on my heart?

CONSECRATED THROUGH OBEDIENCE

Noah did everything the LORD told him to do. ❖ By faith Noah, being warned of God of things not seen as yet, moved with fear, prepared an ark to the saving of his house. ❖ As the LORD commanded his servant Moses, so Moses commanded Joshua, and Joshua did it. ❖ You need only to be strong and courageous and to obey to the letter every law Moses gave you, for if you are careful to obey every one of them, you will be successful in everything you do. ❖ He wholly followed the LORD God of Israel. ❖ Keeping the commandments of God is what matters. ❖ You are My friends if you do whatever I command you. ❖ Anyone who obeys my Father in heaven is my brother or sister or mother. ❖ If anyone loves Me, he will keep My word. ❖ For not the hearers of the law are just before God, but the doers of the law shall be justified.

GEN. 6:22 CEV; HEB. 11:7; JOSH. 11:15 NIV; JOSH. 1:7 TLB; JOSH. 14:14;
1 COR. 7:19–20 NKJV; JOHN 15:14 NKJV; MATT. 12:50 CEV; JOHN 14:23 NKJV;
ROM. 2:13

God asked both Noah and Joshua to do something unusual and difficult. They did it, and their obedience brought them deliverance.

MMS

We offend God if we feel that he is cheating us out of life, as if obeying him were a fast rather than a feast. Obedience is a privilege not granted to everyone. After all, God "comes to the help" of obedient people.

RAYMOND C. ORTLUND

Make this day a day of obedience, a day of spiritual joy and peace. Make this day's work a little part of the work of the Kingdom of my Lord Christ.

JOHN BAILLIE

How far does my obedience go? Until I forget about myself? Until it hurts? I know that my consecration to Christ, allowing his Spirit full possession of me, will be my deliverance.

THE BLESSINGS OF OBEDIENCE

If you keep looking steadily into God's perfect law—the law that sets you free—and if you do what it says and don't forget what you heard, then God will bless you for doing it. ❖ They glorify God for the obedience of your confession to the gospel of Christ. ❖ We are taking every thought captive to the obedience of Christ. ❖ Therefore prepare your minds for action; discipline yourselves; set all your hope on the grace that Jesus Christ will bring you when he is revealed. ❖ Whoever hears these sayings of Mine, and does them, I will liken him to a wise man who built his house on the rock. ❖ If anyone serves Me, let him follow Me; and where I am, there My servant will be also. ❖ This is love, that we walk after his commandments. ❖ If you know these things, blessed are you if you do them.

JAMES 1:25 NLT; 2 COR. 9:13 NKJV; 2 COR. 10:5 NASB; 1 PETER 1:13 NRSV; MATT. 7:24 NKJV; JOHN 12:26 NKJV; 2 JOHN 6; JOHN 13:17 NKJV

Only he who believes is obedient, and only he who is obedient believes.
DIETRICH BONHOEFFER

May this day be for me a day of obedience and of charity, a day of happiness and of peace. May all my walk and conversation be such as becometh the gospel of Christ.

JOHN BAILLIE

What does my obedience say about my faith?
May my disobedience be to me salt in a wound, nails scratching on a blackboard, the taste of cod liver oil on my tongue.

FULLY CONSECRATED

Sanctify yourselves: for to morrow the LORD will do wonders among you. ❖ Consecrate yourselves therefore, and be holy, for I am the LORD your God. ❖ As He who called you is holy, you also be holy in all your conduct. ❖ I was perfect in obedience and kept myself from sin. ❖ Noah walked with God. ❖ LORD, who may abide in Your tabernacle? Who may dwell in Your holy hill? He who walks uprightly, and works righteousness, and speaks the truth in his heart; he who does not backbite with his tongue, nor does evil to his neighbor. ❖ I am the LORD, who makes you holy. ❖ A new heart also will I give you, and a new spirit will I put within you. . . . And I will put my spirit within you, and cause you to walk in my statutes . . . and ye shall be my people, and I will be your God. ❖ And the very God of peace sanctify you wholly; and I pray God your whole spirit and soul and body be preserved blameless unto the coming of our Lord Jesus Christ.

JOSH. 3:5; LEV. 20:7 NKJV; 1 PETER 1:15 NKJV; 2 SAM. 22:24 TLB; GEN. 6:9; PS. 15:1–3 NKJV; EXOD. 31:13 NIV; EZEK. 36:26–28; 1 THESS. 5:23

[God] is able to do anything He pleases with one ordinary person fully consecrated to Him.

BLACKABY AND KING

God is not satisfied in the religious converse between Himself and man with anything short of the consecration of life itself.

GERHARDUS VOS

Take my life, and let it be
Consecrated, Lord, to Thee;

Take myself and I will be
Ever, only, all for Thee.

FRANCES R. HAVERGAL

What would God be able to do through me if I were totally committed and obedient to him? Surely more than he is able to do now!
What joy to know that all I am is his. I hold nothing back.

YIELDED

Yield your hearts to the LORD. ❖ May the LORD help us obey him. ❖ Submit yourselves therefore to God. ❖ There must be a spiritual renewal of your thoughts and attitudes. You must display a new nature because you are a new person, created in God's likeness—righteous, holy, and true. ❖ Put on the Lord Jesus Christ, and make no provision for the flesh, to gratify its desires. ❖ Draw near to God and He will draw near to you. ❖ Yield yourselves unto God, as those that are alive from the dead, and your members as instruments of righteousness unto God. ❖ Be subject to one another out of reverence for Christ. ❖ For the love of Christ compels us. . . . He died for all, that those who live should live no longer for themselves, but for Him who died for them and rose again. ❖ Grant us that we . . . might serve Him without fear, in holiness and righteousness before Him all the days of our life.

JOSH. 24:23 NIV; 1 KINGS 8:58 CEV; JAMES 4:7; EPH. 4:23–24 NLT; ROM. 13:14 RSV; JAMES 4:8 NKJV; ROM. 6:13; EPH. 5:21 NRSV; 2 COR. 5:14–15 NKJV; LUKE 1:74–75 NKJV

Readiness for God means that we are ready to do the tiniest little thing or the great big thing, it makes no difference.

OSWALD CHAMBERS

God is only asking for your heart. Everyone can aspire to the same love, the same surrender, the same God and his work.

JEAN-PIERRE DE CAUSSADE

When Jesus calls a man, He bids him come and die.
DIETRICH BONHOEFFER

> I wish Thy way
>> But when in me myself would rise
>> And long for something otherwise,
> Then, Holy One, take sword and spear
> And slay.

AMY CARMICHAEL

Have I committed myself to him alone; have I lost myself in his righteousness?

WHEN OTHER THINGS BECOME MORE IMPORTANT

My people have forgotten Me. ❖ This people honors Me with their lips, but their heart is far away from Me. ❖ We have not sought the favor of the LORD our God by turning from our sins and giving attention to your truth. ❖ You are not mindful of the things of God, but the things of men. ❖ Beware! Don't always be wishing for what you don't have. For real life and real living are not related to how rich we are. ❖ Do not be conformed to this world. ❖ Don't you know that if you love the world, you are God's enemies? ❖ They say they know God, but their actions speak louder than their words. ❖ Do not love the world or the things in the world. If anyone loves the world, the love of the Father is not in him. For all that is in the world—the lust of the flesh, the lust of the eyes, and the pride of life—is not of the Father but is of the world. And the world is passing away, and the lust of it; but he who does the will of God abides forever.

JER. 18:15 NKJV; MATT. 15:8 NASB; DAN. 9:13 NIV; MATT. 16:23 NKJV; LUKE 12:15 TLB; ROM. 12:2 NKJV; JAMES 4:4 CEV; TITUS 1:16 THE MESSAGE; 1 JOHN 2:15–17 NKJV

We are made spiritually lethargic by a steady diet of materialism.

MMS

Rituals can become rote; spontaneity can become superficial, and grace may not seem amazing any longer.

R. C. SPROUL

How easily I am pulled away from you. My thoughts don't turn to you and my affection is not centered on you. I so effortlessly stray back to my natural human state. It's like when the tires of my car need alignment. As soon as I take my hands off the steering wheel, the car starts straying to the right or left. I have to put my hands back on the wheel to make it go straight. Help me stay constantly aligned with you, Lord.

MMS

Protect me from spiritual lethargy that quickly leads to love for the world.

DON'T BE HINDERED BY WEALTH

We are merely moving shadows, and all our busy rushing ends in nothing. We heap up wealth for someone else to spend. ❖ Whoever loves money never has money enough; whoever loves wealth is never satisfied with his income. ❖ Better is a little with the fear of the LORD, than great treasure with trouble. ❖ Those who desire to be rich fall into temptation, into a snare, into many senseless and hurtful desires that plunge men into ruin and destruction. For the love of money is the root of all evils. ❖ It is hard for a rich man to enter the kingdom of heaven. ❖ Command those who are rich in this present age not to be haughty, nor to trust in uncertain riches but in the living God, who gives us richly all things to enjoy. Let them do good, that they be rich in good works, ready to give, willing to share, storing up for themselves a good foundation for the time to come, that they may lay hold on eternal life. ❖ Generosity will be rewarded. ❖ All to whom God gives wealth and possessions and whom he enables to enjoy them, and to accept their lot and find enjoyment in their toil—this is the gift of God.

Ps. 39:6 NLT; ECCLES. 5:10 NIV; PROV. 15:16 NKJV; 1 TIM. 6:9–10 RSV; MATT. 19:23 NKJV; 1 TIM. 6:17–19 NKJV; PROV. 11:25 CEV; ECCL. 5:19 NRSV

I saw that a humble man with the blessing of the Lord might live on a little, and that where the heart was set on greatness, success in business did not satisfy the craving, but that in common with an increase of wealth the desire of wealth increased. There was a care on my mind to so pass my time as to things outward that nothing might hinder me from the most steady attention to the voice of the True Shepherd.

JOHN WOOLMAN

Does my desire for wealth and possessions nullify my desire for God?
Am I willing to live in poverty or in wealth as Christ desires? Where is my treasure?

LOVING THE WORLD

Don't you realize that making friends with God's enemies—the evil pleasures of this world—makes you an enemy of God? ❖ The sinful mind is hostile to God. It does not submit to God's law, nor can it do so. Those controlled by the sinful nature cannot please God. ❖ Our foolish pride comes from this world, and so do our selfish desires and our desire to have everything we see. None of this comes from the Father. ❖ Let the Lord Jesus Christ take control of you, and don't think of ways to indulge your evil desires. ❖ Live according to your new life in the Holy Spirit. Then you won't be doing what your sinful nature craves. The old sinful nature loves to do evil, which is just opposite from what the Holy Spirit wants. ❖ When we are judged, we are chastened of the Lord, that we should not be condemned with the world. ❖ Now those who belong to Christ Jesus have crucified the flesh with its passions and desires. If we live by the Spirit, let us also walk by the Spirit.

JAMES 4:4 TLB; ROM. 8:7–8 NIV; 1 JOHN 2:16 CEV; ROM. 13:14 NLT; GAL. 5:16–17 NLT; 1 COR. 11:32; GAL. 5:24–25 NASB

First, there is "friendship with the world" (James 4:4), which can lead to a love for the world (1 John 2:15–17). If we are not careful, we will become conformed to this world (Rom. 12:1–2), and the result is being condemned with the world (1 Cor. 11:32).

WARREN W. WIERSBE

Generally speaking, if you want to know who you really are as distinct from who you like to think you are, keep an eye on where your feet take you.

FREDERICK BUECHNER

Where do my passions lie? Am I devoted to the things of the world or to the things of God?

Have I crucified my passions and desires so that I may be led by God's Holy Spirit, or do my passions and desires lead me?

SEPARATE FROM THE WORLD

I say, walk by the Spirit, and you will not carry out the desire of the flesh. ❖ Sin lies at the door. And its desire is for you, but you should rule over it. ❖ Do what is right and good in the sight of the LORD, that it may be well with you. ❖ Show me Your ways, O LORD; teach me Your paths. ❖ He guides me in the paths of righteousness for His name's sake. ❖ Repay no one evil for evil, if possible, so far as it depends upon you, live peaceably with all. ❖ You cannot be the slave of two masters! You will like one more than the other or be more loyal to one than the other. You cannot serve both God and money. ❖ You have been set free from sin and have become slaves to righteousness. ❖ So don't get tired of doing what is good. Don't get discouraged and give up, for we will reap a harvest of blessing at the appropriate time. ❖ Finally, beloved, whatever is true, whatever is honorable, whatever is just, whatever is pure, whatever is pleasing, whatever is commendable, if there is any excellence and if there is anything worthy of praise, think about these things.

GAL. 5:16 NASB; GEN. 4:7 NKJV; DEUT. 6:18 NKJV; PS. 25:4 NKJV; PS. 23:3 NASB; ROM. 12:17–18 RSV; MATT. 6:24 CEV; ROM. 6:18 NIV; GAL. 6:9 NLT; PHIL. 4:8 NRSV

You have loved us first, help us never to forget that You are love so that this sure conviction might triumph in our hearts over the seduction of the world, over the inquietude of the soul, over the anxiety for the future, over the fright of the past, over the distress of the moment.

SØREN KIERKEGAARD

Christians *do* hold absolutes and *must* hold to them. . . . We cannot hold to God's standards without separating from the contrary standards of the world. We cannot love the right path without hating the wrong ones.

JAMES MONTGOMERY BOICE

Have I yet realized that sin is anything that fails to glorify God?
Am I willing to resist the world's seduction and cling only to Christ?

ALL OF ME

Let your heart therefore be loyal to the LORD our God, to walk in His statutes and keep His commandments. ❖ [The king's] heart was fully committed to the LORD all his life. ❖ He walked in all the way of his father . . . ; he did not turn aside from it, doing what was right in the sight of the LORD. ❖ I have walked before You in truth and with a loyal heart, and have done what was good in Your sight. ❖ His heart took delight in the ways of the LORD. ❖ Whosoever shall seek to save his life shall lose it; and whosoever shall lose his life shall preserve it. ❖ For whoever desires to save his life will lose it, but whoever loses his life for My sake will save it. ❖ Jesus said to his disciples, "If anyone would come after me, he must deny himself and take up his cross and follow me. For whoever wants to save his life will lose it, but whoever loses his life for me will find it." ❖ If you refuse to take up your cross and follow me, you are not worthy of being mine. ❖ And whoever does not bear his cross and come after Me cannot be My disciple. ❖ The eyes of the LORD run to and fro throughout the whole earth, to show Himself strong on behalf of those whose heart is loyal to Him. ❖ Examine me, O LORD, and prove me; try my mind and my heart. For Your lovingkindness is before my eyes, and I have walked in Your truth.

1 KINGS 8:61 NKJV; 1 KINGS 15:14 NIV; 1 KINGS 22:43 NRSV; 2 KINGS 20:3 NKJV; 2 CHRON. 17:6 NKJV; LUKE 17:33; LUKE 9:24 NKJV; MATT. 16:24–25 NIV; MATT. 10:38 NLT; LUKE 14:27 NKJV; 2 CHRON. 16:9 NKJV; PS. 26:2–3 NKJV

> Fountain of good, all blessing flows
> From Thee; no want Thy fulness knows;
>   What but Thyself canst Thou desire?
> Yet, self-sufficient as Thou art,
> Thou dost desire my worthless heart;
>   This, only this, dost Thou require.
>   JOHANN SCHEFFLER

Show me, Lord, the level of my commitment to you.
Total commitment—what the Lord requires—nothing comes before him, not
*   self, not money, not ambition, not family.*

BEARING FRUIT

By this My Father is glorified, that you bear much fruit; so you will be My disciples. ❖ I am that glorious tree, the source of your fruit. ❖ You will know them by their fruits. ❖ There are different ways God works in our lives, but it is the same God who does the work through all of us. A spiritual gift is given to each of us as a means of helping the entire church. ❖ The ways of the LORD are right, and the just shall walk in them. ❖ And the work of righteousness shall be peace; and the effect of righteousness quietness and assurance for ever. ❖ Therefore, as the elect of God, holy and beloved, put on tender mercies, kindness, humility, meekness, longsuffering; bearing with one another, and forgiving one another . . . even as Christ forgave you, so you also must do. But above all these things put on love, which is the bond of perfection. And let the peace of God rule in your hearts. ❖ Let every detail in your lives—words, actions, whatever—be done in the name of the Master, Jesus, thanking God the Father every step of the way.

JOHN 15:8 NKJV; HOSEA 14:8 CEV; MATT. 7:16 NKJV; 1 COR. 12:6–7 NLT; HOSEA 14:9; ISA. 32:17; COL. 3:12–15 NKJV; COL. 3:17 THE MESSAGE

When the branch is truly integrated into the vine—united with the vine and receiving its life from the vine—then good spiritual fruit is a natural consequence. . . . Action follows essence.

RICHARD FOSTER

Being a Christian means accepting the terms of creation, accepting God as our maker and redeemer, and growing day by day into an increasingly glorious creature in Christ, developing joy, experiencing love, maturing in peace.

EUGENE H. PETERSON

Help me bear the fruit that you want me to bear—nothing more, nothing less. May I grow "day by day into an increasingly glorious creature in Christ."

THE FRUIT OF THE SPIRIT

When the Holy Spirit controls our lives, he will produce this kind of fruit in us: love, joy, peace, patience, kindness, goodness, faithfulness, gentleness, and self-control. ❖ You have died to the law through the body of Christ, so that you may belong to another, to him who has been raised from the dead in order that we may bear fruit for God. ❖ And the disciples were continually filled with joy and with the Holy Spirit. ❖ Since you are so anxious to have special gifts from the Holy Spirit, ask him for the very best, for those that will be of real help to the whole church. ❖ Lead a life worthy of the calling to which you have been called, with all humility and gentleness, with patience, bearing with one another in love, making every effort to maintain the unity of the Spirit in the bond of peace.

GAL. 5:22–23 NLT; ROM. 7:4 RSV; ACTS 13:52 NASB; 1 COR. 14:12 TLB;
EPH. 4:1–3 NRSV

Holy joy is one of the most common marks of those who walk in the power of the Spirit.

RICHARD FOSTER

If God fills us with his Spirit, then we should be living lives of powerful testimony and great effectiveness. But our self-centeredness and pride inhibit the Spirit's power in us. The culture that we live in urges us to focus on ourselves, to pamper ourselves because we deserve it and to demand everything from others because it is our right. This inhibits the power of the Spirit, because for him to work in us effectively, we must be submissive and humble. We have to admit that it's not us, not our ability, not our wisdom or strength—but it is all him. If we can freely submit to him long-term, he can do great things in us.

MMS

Fill me with your Spirit, Lord; bear in me your fruit.

OBEDIENCE

You shall follow the LORD your God and fear Him; and you shall keep His commandments, listen to His voice, serve Him, and cling to Him. ❖ All that the LORD our God says to you . . . we will hear and do it. ❖ We ought to obey God rather than men. ❖ I will obey your word. ❖ I shall keep Your law; indeed, I shall observe it with my whole heart. ❖ You are my portion, O LORD; I have said that I would keep Your words. ❖ Blessed are they that hear the word of God, and keep it. ❖ Jesus answered and said to him, "If anyone loves Me, he will keep My word." ❖ If you keep on obeying what I have said, you truly are my disciples. ❖ We know him, if we keep his commandments. ❖ Whoever keeps His word, truly the love of God is perfected in him. By this we know that we are in Him. He who says he abides in Him ought himself also to walk just as He walked.

DEUT. 13:4 NASB; DEUT. 5:27 NKJV; ACTS 5:29; PS. 119:17 NIV; PS. 119:34 NKJV; PS. 119:57 NKJV; LUKE 11:28; JOHN 14:23 NKJV; JOHN 8:31 CEV; 1 JOHN 2:3; 1 JOHN 2:5–6 NKJV

Mary, Jesus' mother, had to learn to stop being a mother and begin being a disciple. She had to learn to stop expecting obedience from him and start being obedient *to* him—the natural response of a disciple.

MMS

He expects me to say each morning, "Speak, Lord, Thy servant heareth, I yield myself to obey the prompting of Thy voice within me."

ANDREW MURRAY

Let your fellowship with the Father and with the Lord Jesus Christ have as its one aim and object—a life of quiet, determined, unquestioning obedience.

ANDREW MURRAY

For almighty God willeth that we be perfectly subject and obedient to him and that we rise high above our own will and above our own reason by a great burning love and a whole desire to him.

THOMAS À KEMPIS

Today, Lord, am I showing you my love by my obedience to you? Help me remember my promise to you—to let you live in me, to be your servant.

LEARNING TO OBEY

If a man observes [God's ordinances], he will live. ❖ Do not merely listen to the word, and so deceive yourselves. Do what it says. . . . The man who looks intently into the perfect law that gives freedom, and continues to do this, not forgetting what he has heard, but doing it—he will be blessed in what he does. ❖ [Abraham] was trusting God so much that he was willing to do whatever God told him to; his faith was made complete by what he did. ❖ Asa did that which was good and right in the eyes of the LORD his God. . . . And commanded Judah to seek the LORD God of their fathers, and to do the law and the commandment. ❖ David followed the LORD's instructions. ❖ We keep the command of the LORD our God. ❖ For it is not the hearers of the law who are righteous before God, but the doers of the law who will be justified. ❖ If you love me, show it by doing what I've told you.

EZEK. 20:21 NASB; JAMES 1:22, 25 NIV; JAMES 2:22 TLB; 2 CHRON. 14:2, 4;
1 CHRON. 21:19 CEV; 2 CHRON. 13:11 NKJV; ROM. 2:13 RSV; JOHN 14:15
THE MESSAGE

If there is one standard in the New Testament revealed by the light of God and you do not come up to it, and do not feel inclined to come up to it, that is the beginning of backsliding, because it means your conscience does not answer to the truth. You can never be the same after the unveiling of a truth. That moment marks you for going on as a more true disciple of Jesus Christ or for going back as a deserter.

OSWALD CHAMBERS

Father help me, I pray, be more thoughtful and considerate in speech, and in action be consistent. May my labors be attended with success and guide my pen in ways of wisdom and peace: and may my prayers be answered and may I be submissive to thy will.

IDA B. WELLS

Am I doing what God has told me to do?
My Lord and Savior, I long to please you by remembering your Word and obeying it.

BE MASTER OF MY BEING

Woe to him who strives with his Maker! . . . Shall the clay say to him who forms it, "What are you making?" ❖ Who are you, a man, to answer back to God? ❖ People are slaves of whatever controls them. ❖ As the clay is in the potter's hand, so are you in My hand. ❖ O LORD, you are our Father; we are the clay, and you are our potter; we are all the work of your hand. ❖ For one is your Master, even Christ. ❖ Scripture . . . straightens us out and teaches us to do what is right. It is God's way of preparing us in every way, fully equipped for every good thing God wants us to do. ❖ Whatever you do in word or deed, do all in the name of the Lord Jesus, giving thanks through Him to God the Father. ❖ For we are God's masterpiece. He has created us anew in Christ Jesus, so that we can do the good things he planned for us long ago.

ISA. 45:9 NKJV; ROM. 9:20 RSV; 2 PETER 2:19 CEV; JER. 18:6 NKJV; ISA. 64:8 NRSV; MATT. 23:8; 2 TIM. 3:17 NLT; COL. 3:17 NASB; EPH. 2:10 NLT

You will learn . . . that those who have persevered often and long before God, in pleading His promises, are those who have had the greatest power with God in prayer. . . .

How little we realize what we are losing in not living in fervent intercession! What we can gain for ourselves and for the world if we allow God's Spirit to master our whole being!

ANDREW MURRAY

Just as the potter, however skillful, cannot make a beautiful vessel out of a lump of clay that is never put into his hands, so neither can God make out of me a vessel unto His honor, unless I put myself into His hands.

HANNAH WHITALL SMITH

Am I a pliable lump of clay in the Father's hands?
If I let him master me, he will mold me into something beautiful and useful to him.

WHY PERSEVERE?

You have persevered and have patience, and have labored for My name's sake and have not become weary. ❖ To the degree that you share the sufferings of Christ, keep on rejoicing; so that also at the revelation of His glory, you may rejoice with exultation. ❖ You became slaves of righteousness. ❖ My righteous one shall live by faith. ❖ Let us throw off everything that hinders and the sin that so easily entangles, and let us run with perseverance the race marked out for us. ❖ Follow after righteousness, godliness, faith, love, patience, meekness. ❖ Do all to the glory of God. ❖ May the God of all grace, who called us to His eternal glory by Christ Jesus, after you have suffered a while, perfect, establish, strengthen, and settle you. To Him be the glory and the dominion forever and ever. Amen.

REV. 2:3 NKJV; 1 PETER 4:13 NASB; ROM. 6:18 NKJV; HEB. 10:38 RSV; HEB. 12:1 NIV; 1 TIM. 6:11; 1 COR. 10:31; 1 PETER 5:10–11 NKJV

There are four essentials for victory in trials: a joyful attitude, an understanding mind, a surrendered will, and a heart that wants to believe.

WARREN W. WIERSBE

It is when the answer to prayer does not come, . . . that the trial of faith, more precious than of gold, takes place. It is in this trial that the faith that has embraced the promise is purified and strengthened and prepared in personal, holy fellowship with the living God, to see the glory of God. It takes and holds the promise until it has received the fulfillment of what it had claimed in a living truth in the unseen but living God.

ANDREW MURRAY

Can I trust him in suffering and believe that it will work for good? How has his Spirit caused change, growth, maturity, and increased faith as I have patiently endured?

BE HUMBLE AND OBEDIENT

Whoever desires to become great among you, let him be your servant. And whoever desires to be first among you, let him be your slave—just as the Son of Man did not come to be served, but to serve, and to give His life a ransom for many. ❖ I then, your Lord and Teacher, have washed your feet, you also ought to wash one another's feet. For I have given you an example, that you also should do as I have done to you. ❖ If you don't change and become like a child, you will never get into the kingdom of heaven. But if you are as humble as this child, you are the greatest in the kingdom of heaven. ❖ Jesus said, "Let the children alone, and do not hinder them from coming to Me; for the kingdom of heaven belongs to such as these." ❖ Be gentle, and . . . show every courtesy to everyone. ❖ We should live soberly, righteously, and godly in the present age, looking for the blessed hope and glorious appearing of our great God and Savior Jesus Christ, who gave Himself for us, that He might redeem us from every lawless deed and purify for Himself His own special people, zealous for good works.

MATT. 20:26–28 NKJV; JOHN 13:14–15 RSV; MATT. 18:3–4 CEV; MATT. 19:14 NASB; TITUS 3:2 NRSV; TITUS 2:12–14 NKJV

Leadership in the church is predicated upon obedience, godly maturity, and a servant's heart. . . . Make yourself available to God by humble obedience.

R. C. SPROUL

The more meek that a man is in himself and the more obedient that he is to God, the more wise and the more peaceful shall he be in everything that he shall have to do.

THOMAS À KEMPIS

Is my service to God willing and self-sacrificing or am I careful to protect myself and my own interests?
How do I feel about servanthood?

THANKFUL FOR DIFFICULTIES

You should know in your heart that as a man chastens his son, so the LORD your God chastens you. ❖ As many as I love, I rebuke and chasten. ❖ Happy is the man whom God corrects; therefore do not despise the chastening of the Almighty. ❖ We gladly suffer, because we know that suffering helps us to endure. And endurance builds character, which gives us a hope that will never disappoint us. All of this happens because God has given us the Holy Spirit, who fills our hearts with his love. ❖ Count it all joy when you fall into various trials, knowing that the testing of your faith produces patience. But let patience have its perfect work, that you may be perfect and complete, lacking nothing. ❖ They that sow in tears shall reap in joy. ❖ Blessed is anyone who endures temptation. Such a one has stood the test and will receive the crown of life that the Lord has promised to those who love him. ❖ Through Jesus, therefore, let us continually offer to God a sacrifice of praise— the fruit of lips that confess his name.

DEUT. 8:5 NKJV; REV. 3:19; JOB 5:17 NKJV; ROM. 5:3–5 CEV; JAMES 1:2–4 NKJV; PS. 126:5; JAMES 1:12 NRSV; HEB. 13:15 NIV

God is my trainer. He knows what trials, experiences, and blessings I need to get in shape spiritually. Some of it is tough, but my Trainer knows what he's doing!
MMS

And surely we should . . . give thanks to our divine Physician, when He is obliged to give us bitter medicine to cure our spiritual diseases, or to perform a painful operation to rid us of something that harms.
HANNAH WHITALL SMITH

Suffering is not punishment—it is a work of grace meant to produce eternal fruit. God is preparing us for eternity.
JOEY JOHNSON

Am I complaining? Is the work too difficult for me? Are my eyes on my Trainer or on my aching muscles and tired feet?
I know, Lord, that all of my life is in your hands.

TRIALS HELP FAITH GROW

Let us not grow weary while doing good, for in due season we shall reap if we do not lose heart. ❖ "Shall we receive only pleasant things from the hand of God and never anything unpleasant?" So in all this Job said nothing wrong. ❖ Though he slay me, yet will I trust in him. ❖ Now when He got into a boat, His disciples followed Him. And suddenly a great tempest arose on the sea, so that the boat was covered with the waves. But He was asleep. ❖ Stand firm and don't be shaken. ❖ As an example of suffering and patience, beloved, take the prophets who spoke in the name of the Lord. Indeed we call blessed those who showed endurance. You have heard of the endurance of Job, and you have seen the purpose of the Lord, how the Lord is compassionate and merciful. ❖ For you have need of endurance, so that when you have done the will of God, you may receive what was promised. ❖ In this you greatly rejoice, though now for a little while, if need be, you have been grieved by various trials, that the genuineness of your faith, being much more precious than gold that perishes, though it is tested by fire, may be found to praise, honor, and glory at the revelation of Jesus Christ.

GAL. 6:9 NKJV; JOB 2:10 TLB; JOB 13:15; MATT. 8:23–24 NKJV; 1 COR. 15:58 CEV; JAMES 5:10–11 NRSV; HEB. 10:36 NASB; 1 PETER 1:6–7 NKJV

Jesus dwells within me, as he was in the boat with the disciples. He experienced the same thing they did. If they had perished, he would have also. He knew there was a storm but was able to sleep because he knew who was in control. He was surprised that the disciples didn't know this too. So often I forget that he's in the boat with me. He's in me, in my bones. What I go through, he experiences too, and he wants me to be at peace, knowing that the waves won't engulf me and at the right time he will still the storm.

MMS

In the Bible, *patience* is not a passive acceptance of circumstances. It is a courageous perseverance in the face of suffering and difficulty.

WARREN W. WIERSBE

How can I endure, dear God, unless you hold me up? How can I go on, unless you carry me?

BEING SET FREE

The person in charge of the Jewish meeting place was also there. His name was Jairus. . . . He knelt at Jesus' feet and started begging him for help. He said, "My daughter is about to die!" ❖ When she heard about Jesus, she came behind Him in the crowd and touched His garment; for she said, "If only I may touch His clothes, I shall be made well." ❖ Your faith has healed you. ❖ Martha said, "Master, if you'd been here, my brother wouldn't have died." . . . Jesus said, . . ."The one who believes in me, even though he or she dies, will live. And everyone who lives believing in me does not ultimately die at all. Do you believe this?" ❖ For [our parents] disciplined us for a short time as seemed best to them, but [God] disciplines us for our good, in order that we may share his holiness. Now, discipline always seems painful rather than pleasant at the time, but later it yields the peaceful fruit of righteousness to those who have been trained by it. ❖ For the sorrow that is according to the will of God produces a repentance without regret, leading to salvation.

MARK 5:22–23 CEV; MARK 5:27–28 NKJV; MATT. 9:22 NIV; JOHN 11:21, 25–26 THE MESSAGE; HEB. 12:10–11 NRSV; 2 COR. 7:10 NASB

Our trials are uniquely suited to us. They will not break us; they are what our particular makeup can bear as we trust in God, but they are severe enough to get our attention. They are in an area where we are vulnerable, so the suffering is meaningful to us.

MMS

> These inward trials I employ
> From self and pride to set thee free;
> And break thy schemes of earthly joy,
> That thou may'st seek thy all in me.
> JOHN NEWTON

Am I willing to go through difficulties and suffer pain if it will help my faith grow?
I will trust him through it all and enjoy my deepening relationship with the Father.

BEING POLISHED

He humbled you by letting you hunger, then by feeding you with manna, . . . to make you understand that one does not live by bread alone, but by every word that comes from the mouth of the LORD. ❖ I have gone astray like a lost sheep; seek Your servant, for I do not forget Your commandments. ❖ The LORD has chastened me severely. ❖ He has granted to us his precious and very great promises, that through these you may escape from the corruption that is in the world because of passion, and become partakers of the divine nature. ❖ We are chastened of the Lord, that we should not be condemned with the world. ❖ Let me not be ashamed, let not mine enemies triumph over me. ❖ Forgive me when I sin without knowing it. Don't let me do wrong on purpose, Lord, or let sin have control over my life. ❖ For whom the LORD loves He corrects, just as a father the son in whom he delights. ❖ Blessed is the man whom You instruct, O LORD, and teach out of Your law. ❖ The suffering you sent was good for me, for it taught me to pay attention to your principles. ❖ Let the words of my mouth, and the meditation of my heart, be acceptable in thy sight, O LORD, my strength, and my redeemer.

DEUT. 8:3 NRSV; PS. 119:176 NKJV; PS. 118:18 NKJV; 2 PETER 1:4 RSV;
1 COR. 11:32; PS. 25:2; PS. 19:12–13 CEV; PROV. 3:12 NKJV; PS. 94:12 NKJV;
PS. 119:71 NLT; PS. 19:14

Each individual believer is being prepared and polished, made ready for his place in the temple. Afflictions themselves cannot sanctify us—only when they are used by Christ to do so. Our prayers and efforts cannot make us ready for heaven, apart from the hand of Jesus, who is fashioning our hearts the way he wants them.
CHARLES HADDON SPURGEON

This is the goal of God's activity in your life—that you come to know Him.
BLACKABY AND KING

When I feel all alone, I will remember that you are holding me in your hand. When I feel lost, I will remember that you know the way.

THE SECRET OF ENDURANCE

Pray without ceasing. ❖ [Jesus] continued all night in prayer to God. ❖ These all with one mind were continually devoting themselves to prayer. ❖ With my whole heart I have sought You; oh, let me not wander from Your commandments! . . . I will meditate on Your precepts. ❖ These words which I command you today shall be in your heart. ❖ They delight in doing everything the LORD wants; day and night they think about his law. ❖ Your word I have hidden in my heart, that I might not sin against You! ❖ Open my mind and let me discover the wonders of your Law. ❖ I will praise thee, O LORD, with my whole heart. ❖ I will praise you as long as I live. ❖ Remember Jesus Christ, risen from the dead. ❖ Remember his marvellous works. ❖ Keep yourselves in the love of God. ❖ We ponder your steadfast love, O God. ❖ I will glorify Your name forevermore.

1 THESS. 5:17; LUKE 6:12; ACTS 1:14 NASB; PS. 119:10, 15 NKJV; DEUT. 6:6 NKJV; PS. 1:2 NLT; PS. 119:11 NKJV; PS. 119:18 CEV; PS. 9:1; PS. 63:4 NIV; 2 TIM. 2:8 RSV; 1 CHRON. 16:12; JUDE 21; PS. 48:9 NRSV; PS. 86:12 NKJV

It seems that affliction and trouble come to move us into the Lord's way—to discipline us and help us see our need to endure as we depend on him. Of course, living in this world means we're subject to the calamities of life, but God is in control and his purpose for us is to make us like him. So it seems reasonable that most of what we go through is designed to draw us close to him.

MMS

Here, then, is the secret of endurance when the going is tough: God is producing a harvest in our lives. He wants the "fruit of the Spirit" to grow (Gal. 5:22–23), and the only way He can do it is through trials and troubles.

WARREN W. WIERSBE

The Christian life is not simply a by-product or fruit of faith but the field or arena in which faith is worked out amid much tribulation and opposition.

DONALD G. BLOESCH

As I meditate on your great love, as I praise you for your mighty deeds, I find that I can endure.
Help me remember that, for God's child, there is a purpose in all of life.

GOD IS IN CONTROL

Are not two sparrows sold for a penny? And not one of them will fall to the ground without your Father's will. ❖ We know that God is always at work for the good of everyone who loves him. They are the ones God has chosen for his purpose. ❖ So if you are suffering according to God's will, keep on doing what is right and trust yourself to the God who made you, for he will never fail you. ❖ The LORD also will be a refuge for the oppressed, a refuge in times of trouble. ❖ My son, do not despise the chastening of the LORD, nor be discouraged when you are rebuked by Him; for whom the LORD loves He chastens, and scourges every son whom He receives. ❖ I know, O LORD, that your decisions are fair; you disciplined me because I needed it. Now let your unfailing love comfort me. ❖ [I] will refine them as silver is refined, and will try them as gold is tried: they shall call on my name, and I will hear them: I will say, It is my people: and they shall say, The LORD is my God. ❖ The Lord will deliver me from every evil work and preserve me for His heavenly kingdom. To Him be glory forever and ever. Amen!

MATT. 10:29 RSV; ROM. 8:28 CEV; 1 PETER 4:19 TLB; PS. 9:9; HEB. 12:5–6 NKJV; PS. 119:75–76 NLT; ZECH. 13:9; 2 TIM. 4:18 NKJV

If you are a true believer, and He still puts thorns in your bed, it is only to keep you from falling into the somnolence of complacency, and to ensure that you "continue in His goodness" by letting your sense of need bring you back constantly in self-abasement and faith to seek His face.

J. I. PACKER

When we are caught in rough country in the dark, with a storm getting up and our strength spent, and someone takes our arm to help us, we shall thankfully lean on Him. And God wants us to feel that our way through life is rough and perplexing, so that we may learn thankfully to lean on Him. Therefore He takes steps to drive us out of self-confidence to trust in Himself.

J. I. PACKER

Am I seeing in the burdens and troubles your perfect design for my life?
Lord, I trust you to make all that happens to me instrumental in shaping me
into the person you want me to be.

DISCIPLINED

We are instructed to turn from godless living and sinful pleasures. We should live in this evil world with self-control, right conduct, and devotion to God, while we look forward to that wonderful event when the glory of our great God and Savior, Jesus Christ, will be revealed. ❖ Be diligent to present yourself approved to God as a workman who does not need to be ashamed, handling accurately the word of truth. ❖ Let patience have her perfect work, that ye may be perfect and entire, wanting nothing. ❖ Take every thought captive to obey Christ. ❖ Train yourself in godliness; for while bodily training is of some value, godliness is of value in every way, as it holds promise for the present life and also for the life to come.

TITUS 2:12–13 NLT; 2 TIM. 2:15 NASB; JAMES 1:4; 2 COR. 10:5 RSV;
1 TIM. 4:7–8 NRSV

Spiritual disciplines are born of desperation.
R. PAUL STEVENS

A spiritual life without discipline is impossible. Discipline is the other side of discipleship. The practice of a spiritual discipline makes us more sensitive to the small, gentle voice of God.

HENRI J. M. NOUWEN

Jesus was the most disciplined Man who ever lived and yet the most joyful and passionately alive.

DONALD S. WHITNEY

Learning and following involve discipline, for those who only learn accidentally and follow incidentally are not true disciples.

DONALD S. WHITNEY

Are my prayer and Bible study sandwiched in around all the other parts of my life? Or are other parts of my life sandwiched in around my prayer, Bible study, meditation, and praise of God?

SIN INHIBITS MY GROWTH

Behold, the LORD's hand is not shortened, that it cannot save; neither his ear heavy, that it cannot hear: But your iniquities have separated between you and your God, and your sins have hid his face from you, that he will not hear. ❖ Your sins have withheld good from you. ❖ If your hand causes you to sin, cut it off. ❖ Why do you call Me, "Lord, Lord," and do not do what I say? ❖ The people of Israel went into exile for their sin, because they were unfaithful to me. ❖ Love the LORD and hate evil! ❖ You trusted in your own way. ❖ Let us strip off anything that slows us down or holds us back, and especially those sins that wrap themselves so tightly around our feet and trip us up; and let us run with patience the particular race that God has set before us. ❖ Let every man be swift to hear, slow to speak, slow to wrath; for the wrath of man does not produce the righteousness of God. ❖ The LORD will give grace and glory: no good thing will he withhold from them that walk uprightly.

ISA. 59:1–2; JER. 5:25 NKJV; MARK 9:43 NKJV; LUKE 6:46–47 NASB; EZEK. 39:23 NIV; PS. 97:10 CEV; HOSEA 10:13 NKJV; HEB. 12:1 TLB; JAMES 1:19–20 NKJV; PS. 84:11

Before we can experience even a little of God's love, we must be really turned to him, and, in mind at least, be wholly turned from every earthly thing.

RICHARD ROLLE

God blesses us *in spite* of our lives and not *because of* our lives.

MAX LUCADO

Do I ignore the parts of God's Word that show me my sin?
Help me see my sin, heavenly Father, and give me the strength to overcome it.

SIN INHIBITS MY WITNESS

When there are many words, transgression is unavoidable. ❖ On the day of judgment, everyone will have to account for every careless word they have spoken. ❖ He who loves purity of heart, and whose speech is gracious, will have the king as his friend. ❖ If anyone among you thinks he is religious, and does not bridle his tongue but deceives his own heart, this one's religion is useless. Pure and undefiled religion before God and the Father is this: to visit orphans and widows in their trouble, and to keep oneself unspotted from the world. ❖ Do not let any unwholesome talk come out of your mouths, but only what is helpful for building others up according to their needs, that it may benefit those who listen. ❖ Let there be tears for the wrong things you have done. Let there be sorrow and deep grief. ❖ Pursue peace with all people, and holiness. ❖ Walk as children of light: (For the fruit of the Spirit is in all goodness and righteousness and truth). ❖ So be careful how you live. . . . Make the most of every opportunity for doing good in these evil days. Don't act thoughtlessly, but try to understand what the Lord wants you to do.

PROV. 10:19 NASB; MATT. 12:36 CEV; PROV. 22:11 RSV; JAMES 1:26–27 NKJV;
EPH. 4:29 NIV; JAMES 4:9 NLT; HEB. 12:14 NKJV; EPH. 5:8–9; EPH. 5:15–17
NLT

The Lord spoke to me about my relationship with Mom. He said, "She interacts with you the same way you interact with me. She doesn't understand you, insults you, doesn't trust you, frustrates you by her forgetfulness." He said, "You don't understand me; you insult me, don't trust me, and frustrate me by your lack of understanding and faith. And yet I am never impatient, quick-tempered, or thoughtless with you!"

MMS

Grace dies when it becomes us versus them.
PHILIP YANCEY

Is my attitude humble, do I consider the needs of others, is my life a testimony of faithfulness?
Holy Spirit, be a light in me, shining into the lives of others.

TRUSTING SELF

Men will be lovers of themselves, lovers of money, boasters, proud, blasphemers, disobedient to parents, unthankful, unholy, unloving, unforgiving, slanderers, without self-control, brutal, despisers of good, traitors, headstrong, haughty, lovers of pleasure rather than lovers of God, having a form of godliness but denying its power. ❖ Those who are dominated by the sinful nature think about sinful things, but those who are controlled by the Holy Spirit think about things that please the Spirit. . . . if the Holy Spirit controls your mind, there is life and peace. For the sinful nature is always hostile to God. . . . That's why those who are still under the control of the sinful nature can never please God. ❖ You cannot fool God, so don't make a fool of yourself! You will harvest what you plant. If you follow your selfish desires, you will harvest destruction, but if you follow the Spirit, you will harvest eternal life. ❖ Knowing this, that our old man is crucified with him, that the body of sin might be destroyed, that henceforth we should not serve sin. For he that is dead is freed from sin. Now if we be dead with Christ, we believe that we shall also live with him. ❖ I delight in the law of God according to the inward man. But I see another law in my members, warring against the law of my mind, and bringing me into captivity to the law of sin which is in my members. O wretched man that I am! Who will deliver me from this body of death? I thank God—through Jesus Christ our Lord!

2 Tim. 3:2–5 nkjv; Rom. 8:5–8 nlt; Gal. 6:7–8 cev; Rom. 6:6–8; Rom. 7:22–25 nkjv

Sin is believing the lie that you are self-created, self-dependent, and self-sustained.

Augustine

Keep me, Lord, from focusing on myself, which always leads to sin. Thank you for the power to live for you.

PRIDE

The lofty looks of man shall be humbled, and the haughtiness of men shall be bowed down, and the LORD alone shall be exalted in that day. ❖ Yet they acted proudly, and did not heed Your commandments. ❖ "I am against you, O arrogant one," declares the Lord GOD of hosts, "for your day has come, the time when I shall punish you. And the arrogant one will stumble and fall." ❖ Rebelling against God or disobeying him because you are proud is just as bad as worshiping idols. ❖ The arrogant cannot stand in your presence. ❖ He is able to bring low those who walk in pride. ❖ For whoever exalts himself will be humbled, and he who humbles himself will be exalted. ❖ But many that are first shall be last; and the last shall be first. ❖ You rescue the humble, but you put down all who are proud. ❖ I bid every one among you not to think of himself more highly than he ought to think. ❖ Let nothing be done through selfish ambition or conceit, but in lowliness of mind let each esteem others better than himself. ❖ Let us not become conceited, provoking one another, envying one another. ❖ Love each other with brotherly affection and take delight in honoring each other.

ISA. 2:11; NEH. 9:29 NKJV; JER. 50:31–32 NASB; 1 SAM. 15:23 CEV; PS. 5:5 NIV; DAN. 4:37 NRSV; LUKE 14:11 NKJV; MATT. 19:30; PS. 18:27 CEV; ROM. 12:3 RSV; PHIL. 2:3 NKJV; GAL. 5:26 NKJV; ROM. 12:10 TLB

Great peace is with the meek man, but in the heart of a proud man is always envy and indignation.

THOMAS À KEMPIS

The moment we glorify ourselves, we set ourselves up as rivals to the Most High God.

CHARLES HADDON SPURGEON

A humility that afflicts itself with fasting, but indulges itself with the gains of injustice, means nothing to God.

RAYMOND C. ORTLUND

Am I guilty of idolatry?
Search me, O God. Show me what keeps us apart.

HE PRUNES ME

I am the true vine, and My Father is the vinedresser. . . . every branch that bears fruit He prunes, that it may bear more fruit. ❖ I will discipline you but only with justice. ❖ As a parent disciplines a child so the LORD your God disciplines you. ❖ Happy is the man whom God corrects; therefore do not despise the chastening of the Almighty. ❖ Do not regard lightly the discipline of the Lord. ❖ As many as I love, I rebuke and chasten. ❖ Count it all joy when you fall into various trials, knowing that the testing of your faith produces patience. ❖ Be patient when you are being corrected! This is how God treats his children. ❖ When your endurance is fully developed, you will be strong in character and ready for anything. ❖ Stand perfect and complete in all the will of God. ❖ We will be mature and full grown in the Lord, measuring up to the full stature of Christ. ❖ When He has tested me, I shall come forth as gold.

JOHN 15:1–2 NKJV; JER. 46:28 NIV; DEUT. 8:5 NRSV; JOB 5:17 NKJV; HEB. 12:5 RSV; REV. 3:19; JAMES 1:2–3 NKJV; HEB. 12:7 CEV; JAMES 1:4 NLT; COL. 4:12; EPH. 4:13 NLT; JOB 23:10 NKJV

God "longs to be gracious" to us (Isa. 30:18) and He carries out His judgment against our sin with holy sorrow, intending His discipline as a vehicle of mercy toward us.

NANCY GROOM

The pruning process cuts away what we do through self, allowing what we do through Christ to grow. If our self-shoots aren't pruned, they take over and no fruit is produced.

MMS

God cannot build our character without our cooperation. If we resist Him, then He chastens us into submission. But if we submit to Him, then He can accomplish His work. He is not satisfied with a halfway job. God wants a perfect work; He wants a finished product that is mature and complete.

WARREN W. WIERSBE

Help me to be willing to go round and round on the Potter's wheel until you're ready to take me off.
Take away all of self, Lord. Fill me with your joy.

LOOKING TO GOD

The foolishness of God is wiser than men; and the weakness of God is stronger than men. ❖ Come to Me, all you who labor and are heavy laden, and I will give you rest. Take My yoke upon you and learn from Me, for I am gentle and lowly in heart, and you will find rest for your souls. For My yoke is easy and My burden is light. ❖ Have this attitude in yourselves which was also in Christ Jesus, who, although He existed in the form of God, did not regard equality with God a thing to be grasped. ❖ Do you not realize that Jesus Christ is in you? ❖ We truly love God only when we obey him as we should, and then we know that we belong to him. If we say we are his, we must follow the example of Christ. ❖ Everyone born of God overcomes the world. This is the victory that has overcome the world, even our faith.

1 COR. 1:25; MATT. 11:28–30 NKJV; PHIL. 2:5–6 NASB; 2 COR. 13:5 RSV;
1 JOHN 2:5–6 CEV; 1 JOHN 5:4 NIV

Notice what Jesus had to say concerning those who have wearied themselves by trying to do things in their own strength: "Come to Me, all you who labor and are heavy laden, and I will give you rest."

BLACKABY AND KING

We can only see the things we look at, and while we are looking at ourselves, we simply cannot "behold God."

HANNAH WHITALL SMITH

If our burdens seem heavy, they must be ones we've taken on ourselves,
    because Jesus said his burden is light.
Am I walking as Jesus walked—trusting God to be all I need?

REMEMBERING GOD'S PRESENCE

My Presence will go with you, and I will give you rest. ❖ Hope in God. ❖ For God is greater than our worried hearts and knows more about us than we do ourselves. ❖ On God rests my deliverance and my honor. ❖ Whenever I am afraid, I will trust in You. ❖ When I remember You on my bed, I meditate on You in the night watches. Because You have been my help, therefore in the shadow of Your wings I will rejoice. My soul follows close behind You; Your right hand upholds me. ❖ God cares for you, so turn all your worries over to him. ❖ The LORD, the King of Israel, is with you; never again will you fear any harm. ❖ I will meditate on all your work, and muse on your mighty deeds. ❖ You will show me the way of life, granting me the joy of your presence and the pleasures of living with you forever. ❖ May [He] establish your hearts blameless in holiness before our God and Father at the coming of our Lord Jesus Christ.

EXOD. 33:14 NKJV; PS. 42:5 NKJV; 1 JOHN 3:20 THE MESSAGE; PS. 62:7 RSV; PS. 56:3 NKJV; PS. 63:6–8 NKJV; 1 PETER 5:7 CEV; ZEPH. 3:15 NIV; PS. 77:12 NRSV; PS. 16:11 NLT; 1 THESS. 3:13 NKJV

One thing that I long to develop in my walk with the Lord is a spiritual disposition that causes me to seek Him immediately in every single situation of life. I am so reactive by nature! So often I simply react to a situation rather than remembering how my God would have me respond because of who He is and because of what He has said.

KAY ARTHUR

How I hate being weak! I constantly fight God for control. If only I could learn to relax in his strength. He has shown me that he will be strong in me, but I keep depending on my own puny strength!

MMS

Do I treasure his presence?
Do I look to him for guidance, help, wisdom, protection, love, and all that I need? He must be my first resource.

CALLED TO BE HOLY

I the LORD your God am holy. ❖ Now you must be holy in everything you do, just as God—who chose you to be his children—is holy. ❖ God did not call us to impurity but in holiness. ❖ Present your bodies a living and holy sacrifice, acceptable to God, which is your spiritual service of worship. ❖ Pursue peace with all people, and holiness, without which no one will see the Lord. ❖ Blessed are they which do hunger and thirst after righteousness: for they shall be filled. ❖ Everyone who has this hope in Him purifies himself. ❖ For by a single offering he has perfected for all time those who are sanctified. ❖ Now you are free from the power of sin and are slaves of God, and his benefits to you include holiness and everlasting life. ❖ But grow in grace, and in the knowledge of our Lord and Saviour Jesus Christ. To him be glory both now and for ever. Amen.

LEV. 19:2; 1 PETER 1:15 NLT; 1 THESS. 4:7 NRSV; ROM. 12:1 NASB; HEB. 12:14 NKJV; MATT. 5:6; 1 JOHN 3:3 NKJV; HEB. 10:14 RSV; ROM. 6:22 TLB; 2 PETER 3:18

When there is sin in the camp of my heart, I must deal with it ruthlessly lest it contaminate and ultimately destroy me. The transgression may appear slight, but any forbidden thing, no matter how small, will grow to overwhelm me if left unrepented.

NANCY GROOM

Continually restate to yourself what the purpose of your life is. . . .

[God's] one aim is the production of saints. . . . He did not come to save men out of pity. He came to save men because He created them to be holy. . . .

Holiness is not only what God gives me, but what I manifest that God has given me.

OSWALD CHAMBERS

We trusted Him for forgiveness, and it became ours; now we trust Him for righteousness, and it shall become ours also.

HANNAH WHITALL SMITH

Help me to hunger and thirst after you, Lord.
Where is my pride and self-centeredness obscuring the holiness you have given me?

LIVING IN HOLINESS

Be holy, for I am holy. ❖ Fear the LORD, and turn away from evil. ❖ A virtuous and capable wife . . . is clothed with strength and dignity, and she laughs with no fear of the future. When she speaks, her words are wise. ❖ Keep away from worthless and useless talk. It only leads people farther away from God. ❖ His mouth is full of cursing and deceit and fraud: under his tongue is mischief and vanity. ❖ No man can tame the tongue. It is an unruly evil, full of deadly poison. ❖ Hold fast what is good. Abstain from every form of evil. ❖ The love of money is the root of all evil. ❖ Do not be overcome by evil, but overcome evil with good. ❖ Rejoice in the LORD, you who are righteous, and praise his holy name. ❖ Righteous are You, O LORD, and upright are Your judgments. Your testimonies, which You have commanded, are righteous and very faithful. ❖ Then all your people will be righteous; they will possess the land forever, the branch of My planting, the work of My hands, that I may be glorified.

1 PETER 1:16 NKJV; PROV. 3:7 RSV; PROV. 31:10, 25–26 NLT; 2 TIM. 2:16 CEV; PS. 10:7; JAMES 3:8 NKJV; 1 THESS. 5:21–22 NKJV; 1 TIM. 6:10; ROM. 12:21 NRSV; PS. 97:12 NIV; PS. 119:137–38 NKJV; ISA. 60:21 NASB

A holy life simply is a life that works.
RICHARD FOSTER

The things God delights in—kindness, justice, and righteousness—are the essence of Christianity. If he delights in "these things," then his followers must also.

MMS

Holiness *is* loving unity with God. It is an ever-expanding openness to the divine Center. It is a growing, maturing, freely given conformity to the will and ways of God. Holiness gives us our truest, fullest humanity. In holiness we become the persons we were created to be.

RICHARD FOSTER

Help me to be holy, focused on you, set apart for your service.
Am I letting you show me that my words, actions, thoughts, or attitudes are not holy?

MY HEART IN TRAINING

If you receive my words, and treasure my commands within you, so that you incline your ear to wisdom, and apply your heart to understanding; . . . then you will understand the fear of the LORD. ❖ Wisdom enters your heart, and knowledge is pleasant to your soul. ❖ Incline your ear and hear the words of the wise, and apply your heart to my knowledge. ❖ Apply your heart to discipline, and your ears to words of knowledge. ❖ Purify your hearts. ❖ Those who have clean hands and pure hearts . . . will receive blessing from the LORD. ❖ Keep your heart with all vigilance; for from it flow the springs of life. ❖ Now you can have sincere love for each other as brothers and sisters because you were cleansed from your sins when you accepted the truth of the Good News. So see to it that you really do love each other intensely with all your hearts. ❖ Create in me a clean heart, O God. ❖ He purified their hearts by faith. ❖ For it is by believing in his heart that a man becomes right with God; and with his mouth he tells others of his faith, confirming his salvation.

PROV. 2:1–2, 5 NKJV; PROV. 2:10 NKJV; PROV. 22:17 NKJV; PROV. 23:12 NASB; JAMES 4:8; PS. 24:4–5 NRSV; PROV. 4:23 RSV; 1 PETER 1:22 NLT; PS. 51:10; ACTS 15:9 NIV; ROM. 10:10 TLB

God wants us to adjust our lives to Him so He can do through us what He wants to do.

BLACKABY AND KING

We are to spend our time here on earth preparing for heaven, training our hearts and minds to be centered in him, learning to praise him and to desire the things that bring him glory.

MMS

Am I allowing the Holy Spirit to train me and change me?
My heart, O God, is yours. Make it pure and faithful.

WANTING TO PLEASE HIM

And those from all the tribes of Israel who set their hearts on seeking the LORD God of Israel, followed them to Jerusalem to sacrifice to the LORD God of their fathers. ❖ Sow for yourselves righteousness, reap the fruit of steadfast love; break up your fallow ground, for it is the time to seek the LORD. ❖ When a man's ways please the LORD, He makes even his enemies to be at peace with him. ❖ Walk as children of light, . . . finding out what is acceptable to the Lord. ❖ Take your everyday, ordinary life—your sleeping, eating, going-to-work, and walking-around life—and place it before God as an offering. Embracing what God does for you is the best thing you can do for him. Don't become so well-adjusted to your culture that you fit into it without even thinking. Instead, fix your attention on God. You'll be changed from the inside out.

2 CHRON. 11:16 NASB; HOSEA 10:12 RSV; PROV. 16:7 NKJV; EPH. 5:8, 10 NKJV; ROM. 12:1–2 THE MESSAGE

Discipleship is a decision to live by what I know about God, not by what I *feel* about him or myself or my neighbors.

EUGENE H. PETERSON

We have not piety enough to intend to be as good as we can or to please God in all the actions of our life. . . .

This doctrine does not suppose that we have no need of divine grace, or that it is in our own power to make ourselves perfect. It only supposes that through the want of a sincere intention of pleasing God in all our actions we fall into such irregularities of life as by the ordinary means of grace we should have power to avoid.

WILLIAM A. LAW

Discipleship simply means the life which springs from grace.

CLIFFORD WILLIAMS

What have I decided to do? Will I live to please God or myself?
As I think about all that God has done for me through Christ Jesus my Lord,
my only desire is to be pleasing to him.

DENY SELF

Who is wise and understanding among you? Let him show it by his good life, by deeds done in the humility that comes from wisdom. ❖ The wisdom that is from above is first pure, then peaceable, gentle, willing to yield, full of mercy and good fruits, without partiality and without hypocrisy. ❖ If any want to become my followers, let them deny themselves and take up their cross daily and follow me. ❖ And whoever does not bear his cross and come after Me cannot be My disciple. ❖ Simply put, if you're not willing to take what is dearest to you, whether plans or people, and kiss it goodbye, you can't be my disciple. ❖ No one of you can be My disciple who does not give up all his own possessions. ❖ He who finds his life will lose it, and he who loses his life for My sake will find it. ❖ If any man desire to be first, the same shall be last of all, and servant of all. ❖ The most important one of you should be like the least important, and your leader should be like a servant. ❖ Your attitude should be the kind that was shown us by Jesus Christ. . . . He humbled himself . . . going so far as actually to die a criminal's death on a cross.

JAMES 3:13 NIV; JAMES 3:17 NKJV; LUKE 9:23 NRSV; LUKE 14:27 NKJV; LUKE 14:27 THE MESSAGE; LUKE 14:33 NASB; MATT. 10:39 NKJV; MARK 9:35; LUKE 22:26 CEV; PHIL. 2:5, 8 TLB

Jesus talked with his disciples about denying self and taking up the cross even before they understood the significance of the cross. What did the cross mean to them? Execution. Jesus is saying denying self is like being executed. We must carry the cross around with us daily so that, when necessary, we can execute self. Unfortunately it's not a onetime thing.

MMS

It is the secret of true discipleship, to bear the cross, to acknowledge the death sentence that has been passed on self, and to deny any right that self has to rule over us.

ANDREW MURRAY

Help me, Lord, to lose my life as far as this world is concerned. Help me to find it in your kingdom, the only place that matters.

A WORTHY FOCUS

Now devote your heart and soul to seeking the LORD your God. ❖ Only fear the LORD, and serve him faithfully with all your heart; for consider what great things he has done for you. ❖ Turn my heart to your decrees, and not to selfish gain. ❖ Show me now Your way, that I may know You and that I may find grace in Your sight. ❖ Teach me to do Your will, for You are my God. ❖ Seek righteousness, seek humility. ❖ I proclaimed a fast . . . that we might humble ourselves before our God. ❖ You, LORD, are my choice, and I will obey you. ❖ I have learned both to be full and to be hungry, both to abound and to suffer need. I can do all things through Christ who strengthens me.

1 CHRON. 22:19 NIV; 1 SAM. 12:24 RSV; PS. 119:36 NRSV; EXOD. 33:13 NKJV; PS. 143:10 NKJV; ZEPH. 2:3 NASB; EZRA 8:21 NKJV; PS. 119:57 CEV; PHIL. 4:12–13 NKJV

[The humble person] will not be thinking about humility: He will not be thinking about himself at all.

C. S. LEWIS

[God] wants you to know Him: wants to give you Himself. . . . If you really get into any kind of touch with Him you will, in fact, be humble—delightedly humble, feeling the infinite relief of having for once got rid of all the silly nonsense about your own dignity which has made you restless and unhappy all your life.

C. S. LEWIS

Humility begins as a *gift* from God, but it is increased as a *habit* we develop. That is, humility is increased by exercising it.

JEREMY TAYLOR

Am I feeling delightedly humble as I find all my fulfillment in the Lord? May I lose myself in you.

THE TEST OF FAITH

Truly I say to you, if you have faith, and do not doubt . . . even if you say to this mountain, "Be taken up and cast into the sea," it shall happen. And all things you ask in prayer, believing, you shall receive. ❖ If you have faith as a mustard seed, . . . nothing will be impossible for you. ❖ Anything is possible for someone who has faith! ❖ The apostles said to the Lord, "Increase our faith." ❖ Beloved, build yourselves up on your most holy faith; pray in the Holy Spirit; keep yourselves in the love of God; wait for the mercy of our Lord Jesus Christ unto eternal life. ❖ Contend earnestly for the faith which was once for all delivered to the saints. ❖ We look not at the things which are seen, but at the things which are not seen: for the things which are seen are temporal; but the things which are not seen are eternal. ❖ We walk by faith, not by sight. ❖ This calls for patient endurance and faithfulness on the part of the saints. ❖ Your faith in Christ is strong. ❖[You] are kept by the power of God through faith.

MATT. 21:21–22 NASB; MATT. 17:21 NKJV; MARK 9:23 CEV; LUKE 17:5 NKJV; JUDE 20–21 RSV; JUDE 3 NKJV; 2 COR. 4:18; 2 COR. 5:7; REV. 13:10 NIV; COL. 2:5 CEV; 1 PETER 1:5

Faith is obedience at home and looking to the Master: obedience is faith going out to do His will.

ANDREW MURRAY

We have a God who wants us to take risks, and we are accountable for the risks we do not take!

R. PAUL STEVENS

Only a person who dares to risk is free.

JOEY JOHNSON

A person who truly believes will set no limits on what God can do.

NIV STUDY BIBLE NOTE ON MARK 9:23

Does my lack of faith limit God? Am I willing to take risks, knowing that in him there is no risk?
Do I see the law of faith working in my life?

TRUST WITHOUT DOUBTING

Have faith in God. ❖ If any of you lacks wisdom, let him ask of God, who gives to all liberally and without reproach, and it will be given to him. But let him ask in faith, with no doubting, for he who doubts is like a wave of the sea driven and tossed by the wind. ❖ Commit your works to the LORD, and your thoughts will be established. ❖ Why do you have such little faith? ❖ Don't be faithless any longer. Believe! ❖ Beware lest thou forget the LORD. ❖ Remember the wonderful works he has done. ❖ When He had come into the house, the blind men came to Him. And Jesus said to them, "Do you believe that I am able to do this?" They said to Him, "Yes, Lord." Then He touched their eyes, saying, "According to your faith let it be to you." And their eyes were opened. ❖ Jesus said to the woman, "Your faith has saved you; go in peace." ❖ "Daughter," he said, "all is well! Your faith has healed you." And the woman was well from that moment. ❖ I will remember the works of the LORD: surely I will remember thy wonders of old.

MARK 11:22; JAMES 1:5–6 NKJV; PROV. 16:3 NKJV; MATT. 6:30 CEV; JOHN 20:27 NLT; DEUT. 6:12; 1 CHRON. 16:12 NRSV; MATT. 9:28–30 NKJV; LUKE 7:50 NIV; MATT. 9:22 TLB; PS. 77:11

All doubts are from an evil source, and they must always be treated as the suggestions of an enemy. We cannot, it is true, prevent the suggestions of doubt making themselves heard in our hearts, anymore than we can prevent our ears from hearing the oaths of wicked men in the streets. . . . So can we refuse to pay any attention to these suggestions of doubt.

HANNAH WHITALL SMITH

I will trust him if I remember what he has taught me, what he has done for me, and who he is.
Give me faith, Lord, you who are the author of faith.

HE IS MY CONFIDENCE

Happy are those who make the LORD their trust. ❖ Christ was faithful over God's house as a son. And we are his house if we hold fast our confidence and pride in our hope. ❖ And I am sure that he who began a good work in you will bring it to completion at the day of Jesus Christ. ❖ "For I know the plans I have for you," declares the LORD, "plans to prosper you and not to harm you, plans to give you hope and a future." ❖ The LORD will perfect that which concerns me. ❖ He is faithful that promised. ❖ Therefore being justified by faith, we have peace with God through our Lord Jesus Christ: By whom also we have access by faith into this grace wherein we stand. ❖ Faith makes us sure of what we hope for and gives us proof of what we cannot see. ❖ This hope we have as an anchor of the soul, both sure and steadfast. ❖ We put no confidence in human effort. Instead, we boast about what Christ Jesus has done for us. ❖ Many, O LORD my God, are Your wonderful works which You have done; and Your thoughts toward us cannot be recounted.

Ps. 40:4 NRSV; HEB. 3:6 RSV; PHIL. 1:6 RSV; JER. 29:11 NIV; PS. 138:8 NKJV;
HEB. 10:23; ROM. 5:1–2; HEB. 11:1 CEV; HEB. 6:19 NKJV; PHIL. 3:3 NLT;
PS. 40:5 NKJV

If we indulge in any confidence that is not grounded on the Rock of Ages, our confidence is worse than a dream—it will fall on us and cover us with its ruins, causing sorrow and confusion.

CHARLES HADDON SPURGEON

Did we in our own strength confide, our striving would be losing.

MARTIN LUTHER

*In what is my confidence? In my own efforts, in the help of others, or in my
God?*
Help me, dear Lord, to give up my own striving, realizing how feeble it is.

THE BLESSINGS OF FAITH

Blessed are those who trust in the LORD and have made the LORD their hope and confidence. ❖ Many blessings are given to those who trust the Lord. ❖ David strengthened himself in the LORD his God. ❖ The LORD God of Jacob blesses everyone who trusts him and depends on him. . . . God always keeps his word. ❖ Whoever believes on Him will not be put to shame. ❖ The LORD gives perfect peace to those whose faith is firm. So always trust the LORD because he is forever our mighty rock. ❖ So then those who are of faith are blessed with Abraham, the believer. ❖ He staggered not at the promise of God through unbelief; but was strong in faith, giving glory to God. And being fully persuaded that, what he had promised, he was able also to perform. ❖ Abraham believed God, and it was accounted to him for righteousness.❖ And if you belong to Christ, then you are Abraham's offspring, heirs according to the promise. ❖ Be faithful until death, and I will give you the crown of life. ❖ Blessings are on the head of the righteous.

JER. 17:7 NLT; PS. 40:4 TLB; 1 SAM. 30:6 NKJV; PS. 146:5–6 CEV; ROM. 10:11 NKJV; ISA. 26:3–4 CEV; GAL. 3:9 NASB; ROM. 4:20–21; GAL. 3:6; GAL. 3:29 NRSV; REV. 2:10 NKJV; PROV. 10:6 NKJV

Do we not continually pass by blessings innumerable without notice, and instead fix our eyes on what we feel to be our trials and our losses, and think and talk about these, until our whole horizon is filled with them, and we almost begin to think we have no blessings at all?

HANNAH WHITALL SMITH

God only knows when everything in and around is fully ripe for the manifestation of the blessing that has been given to faith [Mark 11:24]. . . . It is through *faith and patience* we inherit the promises.

ANDREW MURRAY

How do I know if I am fully trusting in the Lord? Am I experiencing peace in all circumstances?
When I am feeling anxious, help me, Lord, to fix my thoughts on you.

WHAT IS FAITH?

What is faith? It is the confident assurance that something we want is going to happen. It is the certainty that what we hope for is waiting for us, even though we cannot see it up ahead. ❖ Hope that is seen is not hope; for why does one still hope for what he sees? But if we hope for what we do not see, we eagerly wait for it with perseverance. ❖ Unless you turn and become like children, you will never enter the kingdom of heaven. ❖ Whoever does not receive the kingdom of God as a little child will by no means enter it. ❖ Though I have all faith, so that I could remove mountains, but have not love, I am nothing. ❖ The Spirit has given each of us a special way of serving others. . . . To [some] the Spirit has given great faith. ❖ Having the same spirit of faith, according as it is written, I believed, and therefore have I spoken; we also believe, and therefore speak; knowing that he which raised up the Lord Jesus shall raise up us also by Jesus, and shall present us with you. ❖ There is one body, and one Spirit, even as ye are called in one hope of your calling; one Lord, one faith, one baptism, one God and Father of all, who is above all, and through all, and in you all.

HEB. 11:1 TLB; ROM. 8:24–25 NKJV; MATT. 18:3 RSV; MARK 10:15 NKJV;
1 COR. 13:2 NKJV; 1 COR. 12:7, 9 CEV; 2 COR. 4:13–14; EPH. 4:4–6

The whole person plays a part in true saving faith. The mind understands the truth; the heart desires the truth; and the will acts upon the truth. . . . Faith is not believing in spite of evidence; faith is obeying in spite of consequence.

WARREN W. WIERSBE

Faith is not just believing; faith is being open to what God is doing, being willing to learn and grow.

MMS

Faith means believing in advance what will only make sense in reverse.

PHILIP YANCEY

Am I open to what you are doing, Lord Jesus?
Am I willing to be stretched by hoping for what I cannot see?

FAITH AND RIGHTEOUSNESS

Pursue righteousness, godliness, faith, love, perseverance and gentleness. ❖ Stir up the gift of God which is in you. ❖ You will fight like a good soldier. You will be faithful and have a clear conscience. ❖ I keep working toward that day when I will finally be all that Christ Jesus saved me for and wants me to be. ❖ I bow my knees to the Father of our Lord Jesus Christ, . . . that He would grant you, according to the riches of His glory, to be strengthened with might through His Spirit in the inner man, that Christ may dwell in your hearts through faith. ❖ If Christ is in you, . . . your spirits are alive because of righteousness. ❖ I count all things but loss for the excellency of the knowledge of Christ Jesus my Lord: that I may win Christ, and be found in him, not having mine own righteousness, which is of the law, but that which is through the faith of Christ, the righteousness which is of God by faith. ❖ The one who is righteous will live by faith. ❖ Faith is counted for righteousness. ❖ He will keep you strong to the end, so that you will be blameless on the day of our Lord Jesus Christ.

1 TIM. 6:11 NASB; 2 TIM. 1:6 NKJV; 1 TIM. 1:18–19 CEV; PHIL. 3:12 NLT; EPH. 3:14, 16–17 NKJV; ROM. 8:10 RSV; PHIL. 3:8–9; ROM. 1:17 NRSV; ROM. 4:5; 1 COR. 1:8 NIV

True faith does not so much attempt to manipulate God to do our will as it does to position us to do his will.

PHILIP YANCEY

Trusting God is the bottom line of Christian righteousness.

R. C. SPROUL

Am I thinking that wealth, prestige, hard work, or a good name will put me in a favorable position before God?

Forgive me, Father, for trying to come to you in any way other than by faith in Christ.

GROWING FAITH

The fear of the Lord, that is wisdom. ❖ For I am the LORD your God, the Holy One of Israel, your Savior. ❖ Many of the people believed on him. ❖ A lot of those people . . . put their faith in Jesus. ❖ My speech and my preaching were not with persuasive words of human wisdom, but in demonstration of the Spirit and of power, that your faith should not be in the wisdom of men but in the power of God. ❖ You also, after listening to the message of truth, the gospel of your salvation— having also believed, you were sealed in Him with the Holy Spirit of promise. ❖ Your faith in God and your love for each other keep growing all the time. ❖ I have come as a light into the world, that whoever believes in Me should not abide in darkness. ❖ For with God nothing shall be impossible. ❖ With God all things are possible. ❖ Is any thing too hard for the LORD? ❖ O great and powerful God, whose name is the LORD Almighty, great are your purposes and mighty are your deeds.

JOB 28:28; ISA. 43:3 NKJV; JOHN 7:31; JOHN 10:42 CEV; 1 COR. 2:4–5 NKJV; EPH. 1:13 NASB; 2 THESS. 1:3 CEV; JOHN 12:46 NKJV; LUKE 1:37; MATT. 19:26; GEN. 18:14; JER. 32:18–19 NIV

O Lord, give us faith within, which comes out in holy lives, glorifying you.
CHARLES HADDON SPURGEON

Christian faith needs continuous maintenance.
EUGENE H. PETERSON

The power of the promise, "Ask, and it shall be given you," lies in the loving relationship between us as children and the Father in heaven; when we live and walk in that relationship, the prayer of faith and its answer will be the natural result.
ANDREW MURRAY

You will never find a truly holy life that is not rooted in a living faith in Jesus.
CHARLES HADDON SPURGEON

Is my faith living and growing or is it lifeless and powerless?
Simple faith: believing that Jesus is the Son of God.

UNWAVERING FAITH

Take care, brothers and sisters, that none of you may have an evil, unbelieving heart that turns away from the living God. ❖ He was surprised that the people did not have any faith. ❖ I am the LORD, the God of all flesh; is anything too difficult for Me? ❖ No one can oppose you, because you have the power to do what you want. ❖ The things which are impossible with men are possible with God. ❖ Jesus stretched out His hand and caught him, and said to him, "O you of little faith, why did you doubt?" ❖ Do not be unbelieving, but believing. ❖ He who doubts is like a wave of the sea driven and tossed by the wind. For let not that man suppose that he will receive anything from the Lord; he is a double-minded man, unstable in all his ways. ❖ If you will not believe, surely you shall not be established. ❖ But they that wait upon the LORD shall renew their strength; they shall mount up with wings as eagles; they shall run, and not be weary; and they shall walk, and not faint.

HEB. 3:12 NRSV; MARK 6:6 CEV; JER. 32:27 NASB; JOB 42:2 CEV; LUKE 18:27; MATT. 14:31 NKJV; JOHN 20:27 NKJV; JAMES 1:6–8 NKJV; ISA. 7:9 RSV; ISA. 40:31

Where there is no longer any opportunity for doubt, there is no longer any opportunity for faith either.

PAUL TOURNIER

The man who wavers in his faith is upset by the smallest trifles; the man who is steadfast in his faith can look on calmly at the ruin of all the universe.

HANNAH WHITALL SMITH

[Jesus] has been consistently affectionate and true to us. He has shared his great wealth with us. How can we doubt the all-powerful, all-sufficient Lord?

CHARLES HADDON SPURGEON

Satan's schemes try to distract me and frighten me. He wants me to doubt that God will help me. He's always attempting to weaken my trust and dependence on God.

Forgive me, Lord, for doubting that you are there for me.

LIVING BY FAITH

The righteous live by their faith. ❖ This Good News tells us that God makes us ready for heaven—makes us right in God's sight—when we put our faith and trust in Christ to save us. This is accomplished from start to finish by faith. ❖ This righteousness from God comes through faith in Jesus Christ to all who believe. ❖ His faith is counted for righteousness. ❖ Whoever believes in Him will not be disappointed. ❖ Your faith has made it happen. ❖ Therefore being justified by faith, we have peace with God through our Lord Jesus Christ. ❖ The life which I now live in the flesh I live by the faith of the Son of God, who loved me, and gave himself for me. ❖ We have faith that assures our salvation. ❖ For it is by his grace you are saved, through trusting him; it is not your own doing. It is God's gift. ❖ We Christians receive the promised Holy Spirit through faith. ❖ As the outcome of your faith you obtain the salvation of your souls.

HAB. 2:4 NRSV; ROM. 1:17 TLB; ROM. 3:22 NIV; ROM. 4:5; ROM. 10:11 NASB; MATT. 8:13 CEV; ROM. 5:1; GAL. 2:20; HEB. 10:39 NLT; EPH. 2:8 NEB; GAL. 3:14 NLT; 1 PETER 1:9 RSV

And, at bottom, all complainings mean just this, that we do not believe in God, and do not trust in His salvation.

HANNAH WHITALL SMITH

There is a law of faith. Certain things happen as a result of it—we are empowered to live for Christ and bear fruit and our prayers are answered. These are just the natural consequences of faith. The first step of faith is believing that Christ lives in me. Christ living in my heart is not just a nice metaphor—it's a reality. When I grasp this, I will realize that with Christ actually in me, I can't help but live by faith and produce faith's fruit.

MMS

Job teaches that at the moment when faith is hardest and *least* likely, then faith is most needed.

PHILIP YANCEY

Have I realized yet that faith is a gift, a gift from God? It's not something that I have to try to manufacture.
He gives me faith but it's up to me to step out in it.

FAITH THROUGH DISCIPLINE

Examine yourselves to see whether you are living in the faith. Test yourselves. Do you not realize that Jesus Christ is in you?—unless, indeed, you fail to meet the test! ❖ Now for a little while, if need be, you have been grieved by various trials, that the genuineness of your faith, being much more precious than gold that perishes, though it is tested by fire, may be found to praise, honor, and glory at the revelation of Jesus Christ. ❖ The testing of your faith produces endurance. ❖ Be watchful, stand firm in your faith, be courageous, be strong. ❖ Stand fast in one spirit, with one mind striving together for the faith of the gospel, and not in any way terrified by your adversaries. ❖ Now you see how Abraham's faith and deeds worked together. He proved that his faith was real by what he did. ❖ By faith Abraham, when he was tested, offered up Isaac, . . . concluding that God was able to raise him up, even from the dead, from which he also received him in a figurative sense. ❖ Faith without works is dead.

2 COR. 13:5 NRSV; 1 PETER 1:6–7 NKJV; JAMES 1:3 NASB; 1 COR. 16:13 RSV; PHIL. 1:27–28 NKJV; JAMES 2:22 CEV; HEB. 11:17, 19 NKJV; JAMES 2:26

Gifts of faith are often given to those who discipline themselves to hear the Word of God.

DONALD S. WHITNEY

We cannot call up faith at our bidding; it needs close intercourse with God. It needs not only prayer, but fasting too in the larger and deeper meaning of that word. It requires doing away with pleasing the flesh and the pride of life which is the essence of a worldly spirit. To gain the prizes of the heavenly life here on earth means to sacrifice what earth offers.

ANDREW MURRAY

[Satan] will first of all oppose our breaking through to the place of a real living faith, by all means in his power. He detests the prayer of faith, for it is an authoritative "notice to quit." We often have to strive and wrestle in prayer before we attain this quiet, restful faith.

J. O. FRASER

May my faith grow as I remember what you have done.

SUSTAINING FAITH

If you had faith no bigger than a tiny mustard seed, you could tell this mulberry tree to pull itself up, roots and all, and to plant itself in the ocean. And it would! ❖ Anything is possible if you have faith. ❖ Be strong, and let your heart take courage, all you who hope in the LORD. ❖ Cast your burden on the LORD, and he will sustain you; he will never permit the righteous to be moved. ❖ He heeded their prayer, because they put their trust in Him. ❖ My God sent His angel and shut the lions' mouths. . . . No injury whatever was found on [Daniel], because he believed in his God. ❖ These trials are only to test your faith, to show that it is strong and pure. It is being tested as fire tests and purifies gold—and your faith is far more precious to God than mere gold. So if your faith remains strong after being tried by fiery trials, it will bring you much praise and glory and honor on the day when Jesus Christ is revealed to the whole world. ❖ Whenever I am afraid, I will trust in You. . . . In God I have put my trust; I will not fear. ❖ I have trusted you without doubting. ❖ Surely God is my salvation; I will trust, and will not be afraid, for the LORD GOD is my strength and my might; he has become my salvation.

LUKE 17:6 CEV; MARK 9:23 TLB; PS. 31:24 NASB; PS. 55:22 RSV; 1 CHRON. 5:20 NKJV; DAN. 6:22–23 NKJV; 1 PETER 1:7 NLT; PS. 56:3–4 NKJV; PS. 26:1 CEV; ISA. 12:2 NRSV

Having faith in God doesn't mean that everything is going to go your way. It simply means that you will have his peace and joy even on those days when you wonder why you ever got out of bed!

PAT WILLIAMS

Faith is believing that God will do it. We must not worry about our lack of faith but act on the faith we have.

MMS

When my faith feels small, you can enlarge it. When my trust in you is weak, you can make it strong.
Am I trusting God to increase my faith as I step out in what he wants me to do?

MY TRUST IS IN THE LORD

From ages past no one has heard, no ear has perceived, no eye has seen any God besides you, who works for those who wait for him. ❖ Wait on your God continually. ❖ The children of Judah prevailed, because they relied upon the LORD God of their fathers. ❖ You did not let them down when they depended on you. ❖ We ourselves boast of you among the churches of God for your patience and faith in all your persecutions and tribulations that you endure. ❖ Those who are men of faith are blessed. ❖ Abraham never doubted or questioned God's promise. His faith made him strong, and he gave all the credit to God. ❖ We walk by faith, not by sight. ❖ By faith we eagerly await through the Spirit the righteousness for which we hope. ❖ Eye has not seen, nor ear heard, nor have entered into the heart of man the things which God has prepared for those who love Him.

ISA. 64:4 NRSV; HOSEA 12:6 NKJV; 2 CHRON. 13:18; PS. 22:5 CEV; 2 THESS. 1:4 NKJV; GAL. 3:9 RSV; ROM. 4:20–21 CEV; 2 COR. 5:7; GAL. 5:5 NIV; 1 COR. 2:9 NKJV

When you realize that your circumstances, no matter how overwhelming or pressing, are ruled by a King who seeks your highest good, you can truly "consider it all joy . . . when you encounter various trials, knowing that the testing of your faith produces endurance . . . that you may be perfect and complete, lacking in nothing" (James 1:2–4).

CHARLES R. SWINDOLL

Christian discipleship is a process of paying more and more attention to God's righteousness and less and less attention to our own; finding the meaning of our lives not by probing our moods and motives and morals but by believing in God's will and purposes; making a map of the faithfulness of God, not charting the rise and fall of our enthusiasms.

EUGENE H. PETERSON

I come to you in my need, Lord Jesus, remembering that I am yours and you are mine.
I focus on your Spirit within, guiding me, blessing me.

COURAGE TO DO GOD'S WILL

For it is better to suffer for doing right, if that should be God's will, than for doing wrong. ❖ So if you are suffering according to God's will, keep on doing what is right and trust yourself to the God who made you, for he will never fail you. ❖ With us is the LORD our God to help us, and to fight our battles. ❖ O My Father, if this cup cannot pass away from Me unless I drink it, Your will be done. ❖ Be strong and of good courage, do not fear nor be afraid of them; for the LORD your God, He is the One who goes with you. He will not leave you nor forsake you. ❖ So be strong and brave! Be careful to do everything my servant Moses taught you. ❖ Be strong and brave and don't get discouraged. ❖ Be strong and of good courage, and do it; do not fear nor be dismayed, for the LORD God—my God—will be with you. He will not leave you nor forsake you, until you have finished all the work for the service of the house of the LORD. ❖ Faithful is He who calls you, and He also will bring it to pass.

1 PETER 3:17 RSV; 1 PETER 4:19 TLB; 2 CHRON. 32:8; MATT. 26:42 NKJV; DEUT. 31:6 NKJV; JOSH. 1:7 CEV; 1 CHRON. 22:13 CEV; 1 CHRON. 28:20 NKJV; 1 THESS. 5:24 NASB

The same admonition is given for building the temple as for conquering the land—be strong and courageous, for God is with you (Joshua 1:6–7, 9; 1 Chronicles 28:20). It takes courage to do God's will and accomplish his purpose.

MMS

The kind of assignments God gives in the Bible are always God-sized. They are always beyond what people can do because He wants to demonstrate His nature, His strength, His provision, and His kindness to His people and to a watching world. That is the only way the world will come to know Him.

BLACKABY AND KING

The will of God will never lead you where the grace of God cannot keep you.

WARREN W. WIERSBE

Where his finger points, his hand provides.

ROBERT SUGGS

May I have the attitude of Christ: wanting nothing but to do God's will.

PREPARED FOR DOING GOD'S WILL

All discipline for the moment seems not to be joyful, but sorrowful; yet to those who have been trained by it, afterwards it yields the peaceful fruit of righteousness. ❖ Do not lie to one another, seeing that you have put off the old nature with its practices and have put on the new nature, which is being renewed in knowledge after the image of its creator. ❖ Be transformed by the renewing of your mind, that you may prove what is that good and acceptable and perfect will of God. ❖ The ones who stop doing evil and make themselves pure will become special. Their lives will be holy and pleasing to their Master, and they will be able to do all kinds of good deeds. ❖ Be prepared in season and out of season. ❖ The end of all things is near; therefore be serious and discipline yourselves for the sake of your prayers. ❖ Always be ready to give a defense to everyone who asks you a reason for the hope that is in you.

HEB. 12:11 NASB; COL. 3:9–10 RSV; ROM. 12:2 NKJV; 2 TIM. 2:21 CEV; 2 TIM. 4:2 NIV; 1 PETER 4:7 NRSV; 1 PETER 3:15 NKJV

Let God use times of waiting to mold and shape your character. Let God use those times to purify your life and make you into a clean vessel for His service.

BLACKABY AND KING

We can delight in doing God's will when we have allowed him to prepare us for it. That's why it's important to daily seek his direction. He knows how to get us to the right place.

MMS

May I have an excitement and an expectancy about what you are doing in my life, Lord.
Do I think of this present time as a time of preparation for what he wants me to do in the future?

GOD'S PURPOSE

"For I know the plans that I have for you," declares the LORD, "plans for welfare and not for calamity to give you a future and a hope." ❖ We know that to those who love God, who are called according to his plan, everything that happens fits into a pattern for good. ❖ We may make a lot of plans, but the LORD will do what he has decided. ❖ It is the LORD who directs our steps. ❖ So teach us to number our days, that we may gain a heart of wisdom. ❖ In your book were written all the days that were formed for me, when none of them as yet existed. ❖ All things happen just as he decided long ago. ❖ What the LORD has planned will stand forever. His thoughts never change. ❖ All I say will come to pass, for I do whatever I wish.

JER. 29:11 NASB; ROM. 8:28 PHILLIPS; PROV. 19:21 CEV; PROV. 20:24 NLT; PS. 90:12 NKJV; PS. 139:16 NRSV; EPH. 1:11 NLT; PS. 33:11 CEV; ISA. 46:10 TLB

When God speaks to you through the Bible, prayer, circumstances, the church, or in some other way, He has a purpose in mind for your life.

BLACKABY AND KING

He [man] acts as though the will of God is something he can accept or reject. In reality, the will of God is not an option; it is an obligation.

WARREN WIERSBE

God is working for His highest ends until His purpose and man's purpose become one.

OSWALD CHAMBERS

What an awesome thought, that you, the God of the universe, have a purpose and a plan for me!
Will I be content with your purpose, Lord, or will I seek my own?

NOT MY WILL

For all who are led by the Spirit of God are children of God. ❖ Give me an undivided heart, that I may fear your name. ❖ It is written, "Be holy, for I am holy." ❖ You have turned from your own desires and want to obey God for the rest of your life. ❖ So Abram departed as the LORD had spoken to him. . . . Abram was seventy-five years old when he departed from Haran. ❖ Not as I will, but as You will. ❖ I heard the voice of the Lord, saying, Whom shall I send, and who will go for us? Then said I, Here am I; send me. ❖ The Lord said to him, "Arise and go to the street called Straight, and inquire at the house of Judas for one called Saul of Tarsus." . . . Then Ananias answered, "Lord, I have heard from many about this man, how much harm he has done to Your saints in Jerusalem." . . . But the Lord said to him, "Go, for he is a chosen vessel." . . . And Ananias went his way and entered the house. ❖ For to me to live is Christ, and to die is gain.

ROM. 8:14 NRSV; PS. 86:11 NIV; 1 PETER 1:16–17 NKJV; 1 PETER 4:2 CEV; GEN. 12:4 NKJV; MATT. 26:39 NKJV; ISA. 6:8; ACTS 9:11–17 NKJV; PHIL. 1:21

"Give me an undivided heart, that I may fear your name" (Ps. 86:11). An undivided heart has one goal, one love. With an undivided heart I'm not split between what I want and what God wants for me. I want what God wants.

RONALD E. WILSON

"True patience," Andrew Murray wrote, "is the losing of our self-will in His perfect will." It takes a great depth of humility to get to the point where we're truly afraid to exercise our own will because we're sure we'll mess things up.

RONALD E. WILSON

If in the integrity of my heart I speak the words, *Thy will be done,* I must be willing, if the answer requires it, that *my* will be undone. It is a prayer of commitment and relinquishment.

ELISABETH ELLIOT

Am I willing to do your will, O God? If you go with me, I am willing.

COMMITMENT TO HIS WILL

Time would fail me to tell of Gideon and Barak and Samson and Jephthah, also of David and Samuel. and the prophets: who through faith subdued kingdoms, worked righteousness, obtained promises. ❖ David . . . kept my commandments, and . . . followed me with all his heart, to do that only which was right in mine eyes. ❖Asa was wholly devoted to the LORD all his days. ❖ [The apostles] departed from the presence of the council, rejoicing that they were counted worthy to suffer shame for his name. ❖ God worked unusual miracles by the hands of Paul. ❖ Moses kept right on going; it seemed as though he could see God right there with him. ❖ Seek the LORD your God with all your heart. ❖ With my whole heart I have sought You; oh, let me not wander from Your commandments! ❖ Those who do the will of God live forever. ❖ O LORD, truly I am thy servant. ❖ I have done what is just and right. ❖ As for me and my house, we will serve the LORD. ❖ The LORD is constantly watching everyone, and he gives strength to those who faithfully obey him.

HEB. 11:32–33 NKJV; 1 KINGS 14:8; 1 KINGS 15:14 NASB; ACTS 5:41; ACTS 19:11 NKJV; HEB. 11:27 TLB; 1 CHRON. 22:19 NLT; PS. 119:10 NKJV; 1 JOHN 2:17 NRSV; PS. 116:16; PS. 119:121 RSV; JOSH. 24:15; 2 CHRON. 16:9 CEV

We sow our "seed"—whatever we have to give to the work of God—by seeking the Lord in prayer, serving his will with faithful effort, steadily believing God's promises without becoming cynical, declaring his reviving power to his worldly church, consecrating our money to his glory, waiting patiently for the divine visitation.

RAYMOND C. ORTLUND

I have the responsibility of keeping my spirit in agreement with His Spirit and by degrees Jesus lifts me up to where He lived—in perfect consecration to His Father's will, paying no attention to any other thing.

OSWALD CHAMBERS

Why am I so unwilling to take my eyes off my circumstances and gaze at Jesus?
He will strengthen me; he will use me; he will help me persevere.

I WILL FOLLOW

And God is able to make all grace abound toward you, that you, always having all sufficiency in all things, may have an abundance for every good work. ❖ I press on toward the goal for the prize of the upward call of God in Christ Jesus. Let those of us who are mature be thus minded. ❖ Who then is willing to consecrate himself this day to the LORD? ❖ Make me want to obey! ❖ I do Your commandments. ❖ Obeying your instructions brings as much happiness as being rich. ❖ I will follow You wherever You go. ❖ Tend the flock of God that is your charge, not by constraint but willingly. ❖ We cannot but speak the things which we have seen and heard. ❖ We ought to obey God rather than men. ❖ All that the LORD hath said will we do, and be obedient. ❖ You have obeyed with all your heart the new teaching God has given you. ❖ [You] have been chosen and destined by God the Father and sanctified by the Spirit to be obedient to Jesus Christ and to be sprinkled with his blood.

2 COR. 9:8 NKJV; PHIL. 3:14–15 RSV; 1 CHRON. 29:5 NKJV; PS. 51:12 CEV; PS. 119:166 NKJV; PS. 119:14 CEV; MATT. 8:19 NASB; 1 PETER 5:2 RSV; ACTS 4:20; ACTS 5:29; EXOD. 24:7; ROM. 6:17 NLT; 1 PETER 1:2 NRSV

We piously ask for his will and then have the audacity to pout if everything doesn't go our way.

MAX LUCADO

Either we are struggling to control our own lives—or we are learning to rest in God and take our cues from Him.

JAN JOHNSON

Am I still resisting God, trying to have my own way?
He is relentless about my doing his will. He will not let me rest in my
stubbornness but has countless ways to bend my will to his. O Lord, may I
realize that in relinquishing my will there is eternal blessing.

HIS WILL IS GOOD

This is what the LORD says—your Redeemer, the Holy One of Israel: "I am the LORD your God, who teaches you what is best for you, who directs you in the way you should go." ❖ My purpose shall stand, and I will fulfill my intention. . . . I have spoken, and I will bring it to pass; I have planned, and I will do it. ❖ Surely as I have thought, so shall it come to pass; and as I have purposed, so shall it stand. ❖ In Him also we have obtained an inheritance, being predestined according to the purpose of Him who works all things according to the counsel of His will . . . to the praise of His glory. ❖ The Lord himself is my inheritance, my prize. He is my food and drink, my highest joy! He guards all that is mine. ❖ As the clay is in the potter's hand, so are you in My hand. ❖ Lead me in the right path, O LORD. . . . Tell me clearly what to do, and show me which way to turn. ❖ God makes it possible for you and us to stand firmly together with Christ. God is also the one who chose us and put his Spirit in our hearts to show that we belong only to him. ❖ And we know that all things work together for good to them that love God, to them who are the called according to his purpose.

ISA. 48:17 NIV; ISA. 46:10–11 NRSV; ISA. 14:24; EPH. 1:11–12 NKJV; PS. 16:5 TLB; JER. 18:6 NKJV; PS. 5:8 NLT; 2 COR. 1:21–22 CEV; ROM. 8:28

God makes no ungraceful moves, and as we are individually embraced by His will, we find that our lives are richer, our former emptiness now full of grace.
MATTSON AND MILLER

The will of love is always blessing for its loved one.
HANNAH WHITALL SMITH

Each one of us is like Abraham. God chooses us, reveals himself to us, and then leads us to the place he wants us to be.

MMS

Am I like Abraham? Am I following in faith though I don't know where God is leading?
Do I trust that all God does is blessing and good?

WAIT FOR HIM

Let us hold fast the profession of our faith without wavering; (for he is faithful that promised). ❖ For I know the thoughts that I think toward you, says the LORD, thoughts of peace and not of evil, to give you a future and a hope. ❖ The One who called you is completely dependable. If he said it, he'll do it! ❖ I wait for the LORD, my soul waits, and in His word I do hope. ❖ Each morning you listen to my prayer, as I bring my requests to you and wait for your reply. ❖ Therefore the LORD longs to be gracious to you, and therefore He waits on high to have compassion on you. For the LORD is a God of justice; how blessed are all those who long for Him. ❖ He will fulfil the desire of them that fear him: he also will hear their cry, and will save them. ❖ Then you will know that I am the LORD. You won't be disappointed if you trust me. ❖ His divine power has given to us all things that pertain to life and godliness, through the knowledge of Him who called us by glory and virtue.

HEB. 10:23; JER. 29:11 NKJV; 1 THESS. 5:24 THE MESSAGE; PS. 130:5 NKJV; PS. 5:3 CEV; ISA. 30:18 NASB; PS. 145:19; ISA. 49:23 CEV; 2 PETER 1:3 NKJV

God says: Living your life in my presence is not something you do, but something I do in you. Let me! Surrender control to me. Be willing! Even the willingness, I will give.

MMS

What he ordains for us each moment is what is most holy, best, and most divine for us.

JEAN-PIERRE DE CAUSSADE

As a Christian, I am a prisoner of hope.
CORNEL WEST

If God is God anywhere, he has to be God in the face of death.
MAX LUCADO

Thank you, Lord Jesus, for being my Paracletos, *one called alongside to help me.*
Am I willing to surrender control to Christ?

WILLING TO KNOW HIM

I ask the glorious Father and God of our Lord Jesus Christ to give you his Spirit. The Spirit will make you wise and let you understand what it means to know God. My prayer is that light will flood your hearts and that you will understand the hope that was given to you when God chose you. Then you will discover the glorious blessings that will be yours together with all of God's people. I want you to know about the great and mighty power that God has for us followers. ❖ And this I pray, that your love may abound still more and more in knowledge and all discernment, that you may approve the things that are excellent, that you may be sincere and without offense till the day of Christ. ❖ The fear of the LORD is the beginning of wisdom: and the knowledge of the holy is understanding. ❖ Blessed are your eyes, for they see: and your ears, for they hear.

EPH. 17–19 CEV; PHIL. 1:9–11 NKJV; PROV. 9:10; MATT. 13:16

Knowledge of such a being cannot be gained by study alone. . . . To know God is at once the easiest and the most difficult thing in the world. It is easy because the knowledge is not won by hard mental toil, but it is freely given. . . . But this knowledge is difficult because there are conditions to be met and the obstinate nature of fallen man does not take kindly to them.

A. W. TOZER

There is enough light for those who desire only to see, and enough darkness for those of a contrary disposition.

BLAISE PASCAL

Every time we hear the Word of God and refuse to respond, something happens to our hearing. A kind of deafness sets in, and we become progressively unable to hear it at all. . . . As Christians, we have to cultivate a keen sense of hearing, so that we don't just tune out the things we don't want to hear.

R. C. SPROUL

Lord, I desire to see. Help me know you. Show me your face. Let me hear your voice.

SEEING GOD

He said, "I will make all My goodness pass before you, and I will proclaim the name of the LORD before you." ❖ And the glory of the LORD shall be revealed, and all flesh shall see it together. ❖ For the earth shall be filled with the knowledge of the glory of the LORD, as the waters cover the sea. ❖ That men may know from the rising to the setting of the sun that there is no one besides Me. I am the LORD, and there is no other. ❖ For in the gospel a righteousness from God is revealed. ❖ I will give them a heart to know Me, that I am the LORD. ❖ Then all mankind shall see the Savior sent from God. ❖ The LORD bless thee, and keep thee: the LORD make his face shine upon thee, and be gracious unto thee: the LORD lift up his countenance upon thee, and give thee peace.

EXOD. 33:19 NKJV; ISA. 40:5; HAB. 2:14; ISA. 45:6 NASB; ROM. 1:17 NIV; JER. 24:7 NKJV; LUKE 3:6 TLB; NUM. 6:24–26

God does the finding, and our seeking is—even from the first movement within our souls—an active response to his finding us.

R. PAUL STEVENS

Each moment is a moment God has given us, and it is there, in that place, and no place else, that we will at that moment find him.

RONALD WILSON

Everything we know about God he has allowed us to know through grace. We can know nothing through our own efforts.

SAM WINSTON

God doesn't reveal his grand design. He reveals himself. He doesn't show why things are the way they are. He shows his face.

FREDERICK BUECHNER

O Lord, may you find me. And when you have found me, may I seek you more and more.
I must not allow my eyes to be blinded to the truth you are revealing to me.

FOCUS ON HIM

Do not worship any other gods besides me. ❖ You shall fear only the LORD your God; and you shall worship Him. ❖ You will seek the LORD your God, and you will find Him if you seek Him with all your heart and with all your soul. ❖ Those who seek me diligently find me. ❖ Look to the LORD and his strength; seek his face always. ❖ "Come," my heart says, "seek his face!" Your face, LORD, do I seek. ❖ Seek the LORD and his strength, seek his face continually. ❖ In the day of my trouble I sought the Lord. ❖ I sought the LORD, and he heard me, and delivered me from all my fears. ❖ Our God takes care of everyone who truly worships him. ❖ Blessed are they that keep his testimonies, and that seek him with the whole heart. ❖ Trust in the LORD with all your heart, and lean not on your own understanding; in all your ways acknowledge Him, and He shall direct your paths.

EXOD. 20:3 NLT; DEUT. 6:13 NASB; DEUT. 4:29 NKJV; PROV. 8:17 RSV;
PS. 105:4 NIV; PS. 27:8 NRSV; 1 CHRON. 16:11; PS. 77:2; PS. 34:4; EZRA 8:22
CEV; PS. 119:2; PROV. 3:5–6 NKJV

Help me, Lord, to focus on you, to be silent before you—waiting for your direction, your blessing—to trust you—allowing my faith to be based in my heart and not in my mind, loving you more and more. Teach me how important it is to love, to feel, to trust you.

MMS

Have faith in God, the living God; let faith look to God more than the thing promised: it is His love, His power, His living presence will waken and work the faith. . . . Learn to believe in God, to take hold of God, to let God take possession of thy life, and it will be easy to take hold of the promise.

ANDREW MURRAY

How often my attention is diverted, Lord, and I lose my focus. I begin to trust in myself and my own abilities instead of waiting on you and your great power and wisdom. Help me to love you with my whole heart and never stop gazing at your beautiful face, so that I may know your promises fulfilled.

OUR GREAT BURNING DESIRE

My soul longs, yes, even faints for the courts of the LORD; my heart and my flesh cry out for the living God. ❖ Show love to the LORD your God by walking in his ways and clinging to him. ❖ Hold fast to Him, and . . . serve Him with all your heart and with all your soul. ❖ Do not worship any god except me. ❖ This one will say, "I am the Lord's"; . . . and another will write on his hand, "Belonging to the LORD." ❖ Incline your heart to the LORD, the God of Israel. ❖ Those who follow after the Holy Spirit find themselves doing those things that please God. ❖ What shall I render to the LORD for all His benefits toward me? ❖ I delight to do Your will, O my God, and Your law is within my heart. ❖ I delight in the law of God. ❖ With all my heart I praise the LORD, and with all that I am I praise his holy name! With all my heart I praise the LORD! I will never forget how kind he has been. ❖ He has put a new song in my mouth—praise to our God; many will see it and fear, and will trust in the LORD.

Ps. 84:2 NKJV; Deut 11:22 NLT; Josh. 22:5 NKJV; Exod. 20:3 CEV; Isa. 44:5 NASB; Josh. 24:23 RSV; Rom. 8:5 TLB; Ps. 116:12 NKJV; Ps. 40:8 NKJV; Rom. 7:22; Ps. 103:1–2 CEV; Ps. 40:3 NKJV

He demands that he himself be our great, burning desire, for he loves us with a flamingly intense love.

RAYMOND C. ORTLUND

If I allow him to be more and more a part of me, he will direct my thinking and impact my will so that I will know what he wants and I will do it. As Jeremiah said: "If I say, 'I will not mention him or speak any more in his name,' his word is in my heart like a fire, a fire shut up in my bones. I am weary of holding it in; indeed, I cannot" (Jer. 20:9). Oh, to be at the place where I can't help but do his will, speak for him, and sacrifice everything in his Name!

MMS

I want to know you better, Lord—there is so much of you to know!
May your "flamingly intense love" sear my heart, purifying it for yourself.

WITH ALL OF MY HEART

Love the LORD your God with all your heart, with all your soul, with all your mind, and with all your strength. ❖ The LORD is your God, so you must always love him and obey his laws and teachings. ❖ What does the LORD your God require of you, but to fear the LORD your God, to walk in all His ways and to love Him, to serve the LORD your God with all your heart and with all your soul, and to keep the commandments of the LORD. ❖ For the love of God is this, that we obey his commandments. ❖ And the LORD your God will circumcise your heart . . . so that you will love the LORD your God with all your heart and with all your soul, that you may live. ❖ I will love You, O LORD, my strength. ❖ Though you have not seen Him, you love Him. ❖ My soul yearns for you in the night; in the morning my spirit longs for you. ❖ I am faint with love. ❖ I love the LORD, because he hath heard my voice and my supplications. ❖ And the grace of our Lord was exceeding abundant with faith and love which is in Christ Jesus. ❖ Grace be with all them that love our Lord Jesus Christ in sincerity.

MARK 12:30 NKJV; DEUT. 11:1 CEV; DEUT. 10:12–13 NKJV; 1 JOHN 5:3 NRSV; DEUT. 30:6 RSV; PS. 18:1 NKJV; 1 PETER 1:8 NASB; ISA. 26:9 NIV; SONG 2:5 NIV; PS. 116:1; 1 TIM. 1:14; EPH. 6:24

Let me not seek to deaden or destroy the desire for Thee that disturbs my heart. Let me rather yield myself to its constraint and go where it leads me.

JOHN BAILLIE

I'm just flat out adoring God with all that I am, with the little I have.

JANET HOLM McHENRY

Am I ignoring a longing in my heart to know you more?
Am I as consumed with love for Jesus as he is with love for me?

GET INTO GOD

As the deer pants for the water brooks, so pants my soul for You, O God. My soul thirsts for God, for the living God. ❖ In heaven I have only you, and on this earth you are all I want. My body and mind may fail, but you are my strength and my choice forever. ❖ Compared to the high privilege of knowing Christ Jesus as my Master, firsthand, everything I once thought I had going for me is insignificant—dog dung. I've dumped it all in the trash so that I could embrace Christ and be embraced by him. ❖ I press on, that I may lay hold of that for which Christ Jesus has also laid hold of me. ❖ We take our lead from Christ, who is the source of everything we do. He keeps us in step with each other. His very breath and blood flow through us, nourishing us so that we will grow up healthy in God, robust in love. ❖ May grace and peace be multiplied to you in the knowledge of God and of Jesus our Lord.

Ps. 42:1–2 NKJV; Ps. 73:25–26 CEV; Phil. 3:8 THE MESSAGE; Phil. 3:12 NKJV;
Eph. 4:15–16 THE MESSAGE; 2 Peter 1:2 RSV

So I say to you, seek God and discover Him and make Him a power in your life. . . . With Him we are able to rise from the midnight of desperation to the daybreak of joy.

MARTIN LUTHER KING JR.

This is the whole of religion—to get out of self and self-love in order to get into God.

FRANÇOIS FÉNELON

An habitual, silent, and secret conversation of the soul with God.

BROTHER LAWRENCE

My commitment to you wavers, Lord. Sometimes I long for you but at other times I neglect you. Become so much a part of me that, unless we are in communion, life for me is meaningless.

OUR DWELLING PLACE

Gather the people together, men, and women, and children . . . that they may hear, and that they may learn, and fear the LORD your God. ❖ Everyone who has heard and learned from the Father, comes to Me. ❖ If you have ears, pay attention! ❖ I pray, if I have found grace in Your sight, show me now Your way, that I may know You and that I may find grace in Your sight. ❖ I will make them know my power and my might, and they shall know that my name is the LORD. ❖ For behold, He who forms mountains, and creates the wind, Who declares to man what his thought is . . . the LORD God of hosts is His name. ❖ Lord, you have been our dwelling place in all generations. ❖ We believe and are sure that thou art that Christ, the Son of the living God. ❖ This is how God showed his love among us: He sent his one and only Son into the world that we might live through him. ❖ We can understand these things, for we have the mind of Christ. ❖ I know whom I have believed, and am persuaded that he is able to keep that which I have committed unto him against that day. ❖ Grow in grace, and in the knowledge of our Lord and Saviour Jesus Christ. To him be glory both now and for ever. Amen.

DEUT. 31:12; JOHN 6:45 NASB; MATT. 11:15 CEV; EXOD. 33:13 NKJV;
JER. 16:21 RSV; AMOS 4:13 NKJV; PS. 90:1 NRSV; JOHN 6:69; 1 JOHN 4:9 NIV;
1 COR. 2:16 NLT; 2 TIM. 1:12; 2 PETER 3:18

There is no Christian virtue that is not advanced by the knowledge of God.
CHARLES HADDON SPURGEON

I think God is crying out and shouting to us, "Don't just do something. Stand there! Enter into a love relationship with Me. Get to know Me. Adjust your life to Me. Let Me love you and reveal Myself to you as I work through you." A time will come when the doing will be called for, but we cannot skip the relationship. The relationship with God must come first.
BLACKABY AND KING

Now I know that the purpose of all my experiences is to draw me to God, so that I will find his presence in my life a necessity.

THE BALANCED LIFE

L ORD God of Israel, your throne is above the winged creatures. You created the heavens and the earth, and you alone rule the kingdoms of this world. ❖ I know, my God, that you search the heart, and take pleasure in uprightness. . . . I have seen your people, who are present here, offering freely and joyously to you. ❖ Although they were going through hard times and were very poor, they were glad to give generously. . . . They gave themselves first to the Lord and then to us, just as God wanted them to do. ❖ Happy are those whom you discipline, L ORD , and those whom you teach from your law. ❖ He disciplines us for our good, that we may share His holiness. ❖ Make every effort to supplement your faith with virtue, and virtue with knowledge, and knowledge with self-control, and self-control with steadfastness, and steadfastness with godliness, and godliness with brotherly affection, and brotherly affection with love. For if these things are yours and abound, they keep you from being ineffective or unfruitful in the knowledge of our Lord Jesus Christ.

2 K INGS 19:15 CEV ; 1 C HRON . 29:17–18 NRSV ; 2 C OR . 8:2, 5 CEV ; P S . 94:12 NLT ; H EB . 12:10 NASB ; 2 P ETER 1:5–8 RSV

We were meant to experience a balanced life of living wholly and completely for God.

R. P AUL S TEVENS

Through it all, God gradually and slowly "captures" the inner faculties: first the heart and the will, then the mind, the imagination, and the passions. The result is the transformation of the entire personality into the likeness of Christ. More and more and more we take on his habits, feelings, hopes, faith, and love.

R ICHARD F OSTER

Do I welcome the Lord's discipline because I desire a balanced life?
How precious to know that I can be effective and productive as I yield more
and more of myself to God.

REMEMBER THE LORD

The LORD spoke to Moses, saying, "Speak to the children of Israel: Tell them to make tassels on the corners of their garments. . . . And you shall have the tassel, that you may look upon it and remember all the commandments of the LORD and do them." ❖ Only give heed to yourself and keep your soul diligently, lest you forget the things which your eyes have seen, and lest they depart from your heart all the days of your life. ❖ So commit yourselves completely to these words of mine. ❖ Be careful that you do not forget the LORD. ❖ Remember his marvellous works that he hath done, his wonders, and the judgments of his mouth. ❖ If you hear the message and don't obey it, you are like people who stare at themselves in a mirror and forget what they look like as soon as they leave. ❖ "You have forgotten Me," declares the Lord GOD. ❖ I will remember the works of the LORD; surely I will remember Your wonders of old. I will also meditate on all Your work, and talk of Your deeds. ❖ You, LORD God, have done many wonderful things, and you have planned marvelous things for us. No one is like you! I would never be able to tell all you have done.

NUM. 15:37–39 NKJV; DEUT. 4:9 NASB; DEUT. 11:18 NLT; DEUT. 6:12 NIV; 1 CHRON. 16:12; JAMES 1:23–24 CEV; EZEK. 22:12 NASB; PS. 77:11–12 NKJV; PS. 40:5 CEV

In the Old Testament, the people had things to remind them of God and his commands. We now have the Holy Spirit living within, but we're subject to the flesh—and forgetting. We need to remember what God has done for each of us. We need to write our own history of redemption—what he brought us through, how he helped us grow, the things that seemed hard that were actually for our benefit. Now we see that all the time he was working.

MMS

I need to be reminded of him throughout the day. I need to connect the events of my life to his intervention—to his goodness, mercy, forgiveness, love. The situations of my life must remind me of him.
Do I remember the image of myself that I see in God's Word?

HE BLESSES WHAT WE OFFER

You should be happy to give the poor what they need, because then the LORD will make you successful in everything you do. ❖ Give to him as the LORD your God has blessed you. ❖ Therefore be imitators of God as dear children. And walk in love, as Christ also has loved us and given Himself for us, an offering and a sacrifice to God. ❖ Even if I am to be poured as a libation upon the sacrificial offering of your faith, I am glad and rejoice with you all. ❖ Here am I; send me. ❖ [Your gifts] are a sweet-smelling sacrifice that pleases God well. ❖ Like living stones, let yourselves be built into a spiritual house, to be a holy priesthood, to offer spiritual sacrifices acceptable to God through Jesus Christ. ❖ For all things come from You, and of Your own we have given You.

DEUT. 15:10 CEV; DEUT. 15:14 NASB; EPH. 5:1–2 NKJV; PHIL. 2:17 RSV;
ISA. 6:8; PHIL. 4:18 TLB; 1 PETER 2:5 NRSV; 1 CHRON. 29:14 NKJV

Like the disciples (in Mark 6:38–42), who said there were five loaves, we too can count what we have and tell the Lord. We must then give it to him, so that he can bless it and use it. In the hands of the people, the loaves were nothing. In Christ's hands they were more than what was needed. He asks, "What do you have?" When we give it to him, he blesses it, breaks it, and uses it. Then we are satisfied.

MMS

It is when we give ourselves to be a blessing that we can specially count on the blessing of God. It is when we draw near to God as the friend of the poor and the perishing that we may count on His friendliness.

ANDREW MURRAY

What offering do I bring to my Savior? Do I bring my love, my energy, my prayers, myself? What have I offered that he can bless?

CHOOSING THE WAY OF HUMILITY

Then Jesus came from Galilee to John at the Jordan to be baptized by him. And John tried to prevent Him, saying, "I need to be baptized by You, and are You coming to me?" But Jesus answered and said to him, "Permit it to be so now, for thus it is fitting for us to fulfill all righteousness." ❖ He leads the humble in what is right, and teaches the humble his way. ❖ I ask you to listen, because Christ himself was humble and gentle. ❖ But I will leave among you a humble and lowly people, and they will take refuge in the name of the LORD. ❖ The meek shall inherit the earth; and shall delight themselves in the abundance of peace. ❖ You also must obey the LORD—you must worship him with all your heart and remember the great things he has done for you. ❖ It is not the one who commends himself who is approved, but the one whom the Lord commends. ❖ With the humble is wisdom. ❖ Serve each other in humility.

MATT. 3:13–15 NKJV; PS. 25:9 NRSV; 2 COR. 10:1 CEV; ZEPH. 3:12 NASB; PS. 37:11; 1 SAM. 12:24 CEV; 2 COR. 10:18 NIV; PROV. 11:2 NKJV; 1 PETER 5:5 NLT

We see how Jesus clearly chooses the way of humility. He does not appear with great fanfare as a powerful savior, announcing a new order. On the contrary, he comes quietly, with the many sinners who are receiving a baptism of repentance.

HENRI J. M. NOUWEN

It is because Christians so little bear the mark of this self-emptying and humiliation unto death, that the world refuses to believe in the possibility of a Christ-filled life.

ANDREW MURRAY

We must not sentimentalize Christian humility as a mood, a posture, a tone of voice, or a personality type. It is more rigorous. It is a divine instrument of peace in consoling, understanding, loving, giving, pardoning, and dying. It is cheerful hard work. It is thinking first of the other person. It is lifting my head from my own depressing self-concern to look around and care for others.

RAYMOND C. ORTLUND

Am I willing to be humble like Jesus or am I afraid that someone will take advantage of me?

REST IN THE LORD

Rest in the LORD, and wait patiently for him. ❖ Wait on the LORD: be of good courage, and he shall strengthen thine heart: wait, I say, on the LORD. ❖ The LORD will fight for you, and you have only to be still. ❖ Be still, and know that I am God. ❖ And those who know Your name will put their trust in You; for You, LORD, have not forsaken those who seek You. ❖ Here is rest, give rest to the weary. ❖ Return, O my soul, to your rest, for the LORD has dealt bountifully with you. ❖ Our soul waits for the LORD; He is our help and our shield. For our heart shall rejoice in Him, because we have trusted in His holy name. Let Your mercy, O LORD, be upon us, just as we hope in You. ❖ I will make you strong if you quietly trust me. ❖ I waited patiently for the LORD; and he inclined unto me, and heard my cry. And he . . . put a new song in my mouth, even praise unto our God.

Ps. 37:7; Ps. 27:14; Exod. 14:14 RSV; Ps. 46:10; Ps. 9:10 NKJV; Isa. 28:12 NASB; Ps. 116:7 NRSV; Ps. 33:20–22 NKJV; Isa. 30:15 CEV; Ps. 40:1, 3

Just because of His unfathomable love, the God of love, when He sees His children resting their souls on things that can be shaken, must necessarily remove those things from their lives in order that they may be driven to rest only on the things that cannot be shaken; and this process of removing is sometimes very hard.

HANNAH WHITALL SMITH

> God of our weary years,
> God of our silent tears,
> Thou who has brought us thus far on the way,
> Thou who hast by thy might
> Led us into the light,
> Keep us forever in the path, we pray.
> JAMES WELDON JOHNSON

Am I resting in the Lord, am I waiting patiently for him, or am I trying to fix it myself?

IN HIM ALONE

Be silent, all people, before the LORD. ❖ You shall have no other gods before Me. ❖ Truly my soul silently waits for God; from Him comes my salvation. He only is my rock and my salvation; He is my defense; I shall not be greatly moved. ❖ The Lord is a strong fortress. The godly run to him and are safe. ❖ Let me dwell in Thy tent forever; let me take refuge in the shelter of Thy wings. ❖ The Lord is my helper, and I will not fear. ❖ In him was life; and the life was the light of men. ❖ The Spirit helps us in our weakness. ❖ With all my heart, I am waiting, LORD, for you!

ZECH. 2:13 NRSV; EXOD. 20:3 NKJV; PS. 62:1–2 NKJV; PROV. 18:10 TLB; PS. 61:4 NASB; HEB. 13:6; JOHN 1:4; ROM. 8:26 RSV; PS. 130:5 CEV

Not until then [when things we depend on are taken away] will our souls learn to rejoice in the Lord only, and to joy in the God of our salvation.

HANNAH WHITALL SMITH

Thou hast formed us for Thyself, and our hearts are restless till they find rest in Thee.

AUGUSTINE

Help me to not get so busy with my life that I forget that you are my life. I have no life apart from you.

MMS

In you alone, O Lord, in you alone I find rest.
What keeps me from trusting God when he says he will be my helper, my strong tower?

WORRY—THE OPPOSITE OF REST

Be strong and courageous, and act; do not fear nor be dismayed, for the LORD God, my God, is with you. ❖ God is for me. ❖ Stand true to what you believe. Be courageous. Be strong. ❖ Therefore I say to you, do not worry about your life, what you will eat or what you will drink. . . . Which of you by worrying can add one cubit to his stature? . . . Do not worry. . . . But seek first the kingdom of God and His righteousness, and all these things shall be added to you. Therefore do not worry about tomorrow. ❖ When someone arrests you, don't worry about what you will say or how you will say it. At that time you will be given the words to say. But you will not really be the one speaking. The Spirit from your Father will tell you what to say. ❖ My Spirit remains among you. Do not fear. ❖ He will . . . strengthen you to the end. ❖ [May he] establish your hearts unblamable in holiness before our God and Father, at the coming of our Lord Jesus with all his saints.

1 CHRON. 28:20 NASB; PS. 56:9; 1 COR. 16:13 NLT; MATT. 6:25, 27, 31, 33–34 NKJV; MATT. 10:19–20 CEV; HAG. 2:5 NIV; 1 COR. 1:8 NRSV; 1 THESS. 3:13 RSV

The very essence of anxious care is imagining that we are wiser than God. When we worry, we put ourselves in his place and try to do for him what he intends to do for us.

CHARLES HADDON SPURGEON

It is extraordinary what an enormous power there is in simple things to distract our attention from God. Refuse to be swamped with the cares of this life.

OSWALD CHAMBERS

Dreaming the dream of God is not for cowards.

JOEY JOHNSON

Do I feel peace regardless of the circumstances or do my circumstances rob me of peace?
Does God love me? Does he promise to help me? Can I believe him? The answer to all these questions is yes.

YIELDING CONTROL

We are flowers that fade and shadows that vanish. ❖ The grass withers, the flower fades, but the word of our God stands forever. ❖ [God] brings princes to nought, and makes the rulers of the earth as nothing. ❖ Let those who boast boast in this, that they understand and know me, that I am the LORD; I act with steadfast love, justice, and righteousness in the earth. ❖ Solomon, my son, get to know the God of your fathers. Worship and serve him with a clean heart and a willing mind, for the Lord sees every heart and understands and knows every thought. ❖ I am trusting you, O LORD. . . . My future is in your hands. ❖ Commit your work to the LORD, and your plans will be established. ❖ Trust in the LORD with all thine heart; and lean not unto thine own understanding. In all thy ways acknowledge him, and he shall direct thy paths.

JOB 14:2 CEV; ISA. 40:8 NASB; ISA. 40:23 RSV; JER. 9:24 NRSV; 1 CHRON. 28:9 TLB; PS. 31:14–15 NLT; PROV. 16:3 NRSV; PROV. 3:5–6

The Lord had said to His disciples: "Without Me ye can do nothing." Why is it then that He chose these impotent, helpless men to send them out to conquer the world for Him? It was that in their feebleness they might yield themselves and give Him as Lord the opportunity to show His power working through them. . . . Their place would be to pray, to believe, and to yield themselves to the mighty power of Christ.

ANDREW MURRAY

A saint is never consciously a saint; a saint is consciously dependent on God.

OSWALD CHAMBERS

What could I accomplish if I yielded myself to the mighty power of Christ? May I progress to total dependence on you, Lord!

THE LORD OUR RIGHTEOUSNESS

I will greatly rejoice in the LORD, my soul shall be joyful in my God; for he hath clothed me with the garments of salvation, he hath covered me with the robe of righteousness. ❖ The father said to his servants, Bring forth the best robe, and put it on him; and put a ring on his hand, and shoes on his feet. ❖ We have believed in Christ Jesus, that we might be justified by faith in Christ and not by the works of the law; for by the works of the law no flesh shall be justified. . . . If righteousness comes through the law, then Christ died in vain. ❖ All our righteousnesses are as filthy rags. ❖ He is the source of your life in Christ Jesus, whom God made our wisdom, our righteousness and sanctification and redemption. ❖ By His knowledge the Righteous One, My Servant, will justify the many, as He will bear their iniquities. ❖ Who will not fear you, O Lord, and bring glory to your name? For you alone are holy. All nations will come and worship before you, for your righteous acts have been revealed.

ISA. 61:10; LUKE 15:22; GAL. 2:16, 21 NKJV; ISA. 64:6; 1 COR. 1:30 RSV; ISA. 53:11 NASB; REV. 15:4 NIV

He is the absolute quintessence of moral excellence, infinitely perfect in righteousness, purity, rectitude, and incomprehensible holiness. And in all this he is uncreated, self-sufficient and beyond the power of human thought to conceive or human speech to utter.

A. W. TOZER

God is not only the Greatest of all beings, but the Best. All the goodness there is in any creature has been imparted from the Creator, but God's goodness is underived, for it is the essence of His eternal nature.

ARTHUR W. PINK

I've been clutching filthy rags, thinking they would please God, and have been unable to grasp the pure, eternal, perfect righteousness of God that is mine.

MMS

What part of me do I cling to, thinking it is good?
Am I ready to let his righteousness be mine?

THE LORD OUR PEACE

When I was burdened with worries, you comforted me and made me feel secure. ❖ Peace I leave with you, My peace I give to you; not as the world gives do I give to you. Let not your heart be troubled, neither let it be afraid. ❖ Your life is hid with Christ in God. ❖ If only you had paid attention to My commandments! Then your well-being would have been like a river, and your righteousness like the waves of the sea. ❖ For I, the LORD your God, hold your right hand; it is I who say to you, "Fear not, I will help you." ❖ But let all who take refuge in you rejoice, let them ever sing for joy. ❖ Now the Lord of peace himself give you peace always by all means. ❖ We have peace with God through our Lord Jesus Christ. ❖ You will experience God's peace, which is far more wonderful than the human mind can understand. ❖ The God of peace shall be with you. ❖ This One shall be peace. ❖ And he will be the source of our peace.

Ps. 94:19 CEV; JOHN 14:27 NKJV; COL. 3:3; ISA. 48:18 NASB; ISA. 41:13 RSV; Ps. 5:11 NRSV; 2 THESS. 3:16; ROM. 5:1; PHIL. 4:7 TLB; PHIL. 4:9; MICAH 5:5 NKJV; MICAH 5:5 NLT

"My peace I give unto you"; it is a peace all over from the crown of the head to the sole of the feet, an irrepressible confidence. "Your life is hid with Christ in God," and the inperturbable peace of Jesus Christ is imparted to you.

OSWALD CHAMBERS

Anxiety or care is a form of sin in the believer.
HAROLD LINDSELL

For Jesus peace seems to have meant not the absence of struggle but the presence of love.

FREDERICK BUECHNER

If God is with me and he's promised me peace, why do I feel so anxious? I can live in the knowledge that he goes before me in everything. I can have perfect trust in him.

HIS NEARNESS IS COMFORT

Let the smile of your face shine on us, LORD. ❖ Make Your face shine upon Your servant. ❖ Everyone who does right will see his face. ❖ Restore us, O LORD God of hosts; let your face shine, that we may be saved. ❖ The LORD preserves all who love him. ❖ I am indeed concerned about you. ❖ I have covered you with the shadow of My hand. ❖ God . . . comforts the downcast. ❖ I will comfort you . . . like a mother comforting her child. ❖ The LORD hath comforted his people. ❖ The eyes of the LORD are upon the righteous, and his ears are open unto their cry. ❖ The eye of the LORD is upon them that fear him, upon them that hope in his mercy. ❖ The Lord protects the simple and the childlike. ❖ I waited patiently for the LORD; and he inclined unto me, and heard my cry. ❖ You answered my prayer when I shouted for help. ❖ You are with me; your rod and your staff—they comfort me. ❖ Blessed be God, even the Father of our Lord Jesus Christ, the Father of mercies, and the God of all comfort.

PS. 4:6 NLT; PS. 31:16 NKJV; PS. 11:7 CEV; PS. 80:19 NRSV; PS. 145:20 RSV; EXOD. 3:16 NASB; ISA. 51:16 NKJV; 2 COR. 7:6 NKJV; ISA. 66:13 CEV; ISA. 49:13; PS. 34:15; PS. 33:18; PS. 116:6 TLB; PS. 40:1; PS. 31:22 CEV; PS. 23:4 NRSV; 2 COR. 1:3

It is pure and simple unbelief that is at the bottom of all our lack of comfort, and absolutely nothing else. God comforts us on every side, but we simply do not believe His words of comfort.

HANNAH WHITALL SMITH

Your arms, Lord, have no end. They encircle me, reach down and hold me, guide me on the way. Your arms, Lord, have no end, your arms of love and mercy and grace.

MMS

Am I accepting the comfort that God has promised to me?
May I bask in the light of your presence, my God.

LIFE AS IT WAS MEANT TO BE

I know, LORD, that we humans are not in control of our own lives. ❖ Make Your way straight before my face. ❖ He leads the humble in what is right, and teaches the humble his way. ❖ He leadeth me in the paths of righteousness for his name's sake. ❖ Show me Your ways, O LORD; teach me Your paths. Lead me in Your truth. ❖ I will lead them in paths that they have not known: I will make darkness light before them, and crooked things straight. ❖ You guide me with your counsel, and afterward you will take me into glory. ❖ God . . . calls you into His own kingdom and glory. ❖ Lead a life worthy of the calling to which you have been called. ❖ Walk worthy of the Lord unto all pleasing, being fruitful in every good work, and increasing in the knowledge of God. ❖ [God] "will render to each one according to his deeds": eternal life to those who by patient continuance in doing good seek for glory, honor, and immortality. ❖ I will sing unto the LORD as long as I live: I will sing praise to my God while I have my being. ❖ Goodness and mercy shall follow me all the days of my life: and I will dwell in the house of the LORD for ever.

JER. 10:23 CEV; PS. 5:8 NKJV; PS. 25:9 RSV; PS. 23:3; PS. 25:4–5 NKJV;
ISA. 42:16; PS. 73:24 NIV; 1 THESS. 2:12 NASB; EPH. 4:1 NRSV; COL. 1:10;
ROM. 2:6–7 NKJV; PS. 104:33; PS. 23:6

What we are offering the world is life as it was meant to be. . . .

Thus people become trained in the Way, increasingly taking into themselves Jesus' hopes, dreams, longings, habits, and abilities.

RICHARD FOSTER

The life of faith is a daily exploration of the constant and countless ways in which God's grace and love are experienced.

EUGENE H. PETERSON

How has God shown me his grace and love today?
How has that impacted the way I live?

OUR CONFIDENCE IS IN HIM

Be still before the LORD, and wait patiently for him; do not fret over those who prosper in their way, over those who carry out evil devices. ❖ Wait on the LORD: be of good courage, and he shall strengthen thine heart: wait, I say, on the LORD. ❖ Hope in the LORD: for with the LORD there is mercy. ❖ You are the one we trust. ❖ The LORD your God has been with you; you have lacked nothing. ❖ If we hope for what we do not see, with perseverance we wait eagerly for it. ❖ Let us hold fast the profession of our faith without wavering; (for he is faithful that promised). ❖ Always honor the LORD. Then you will truly have hope for the future. ❖ Though he slay me, yet will I trust in him. ❖ The LORD will keep you from all evil; he will keep your life. The LORD will keep your going out and your coming in from this time on and forevermore.

Ps. 37:7 NRSV; Ps. 27:14; Ps. 130:7; ISA. 26:8 CEV; DEUT. 2:7 RSV; ROM. 8:25 NASB; HEB. 10:23; PROV. 23:17–18 CEV; JOB 13:15; Ps. 121:7–8 NRSV

When it seems like nothing is happening in our lives, we should consider it a time of preparation. We're like musicians in an orchestra between movements of a symphony. We stop playing but we don't just wait. We retune our instruments. We turn the page of music. We're ready because we know at any moment the conductor may raise his baton, signaling us to play.

MMS

The *only* serious mistake we can make . . . is the mistake that Psalm 121 prevents: the mistake of supposing that God's interest in us waxes and wanes in response to our spiritual temperature.

EUGENE H. PETERSON

Am I expectantly waiting for him, trusting that he is now preparing me for what is to come?
Can I hope in him even when it seems that he's far away and not interested in what is happening to me?

SECURITY IN HIM

God is faithful, who will not allow you to be tempted beyond what you are able, but with the temptation will also make the way of escape, that you may be able to bear it. ❖ The Lord knows how to rescue godly people from their sufferings. ❖ He is your shield and your helper! He is your excellent sword! ❖ You will have confidence, because there is hope; you will be protected and take your rest in safety. ❖ Be still, and know that I am God. ❖ My help cometh from the LORD, which made heaven and earth. ❖ You are a shield around me, O LORD. ❖ When I was burdened with worries, you comforted me and made me feel secure. ❖ Surely I have calmed and quieted my soul, like a weaned child with his mother; like a weaned child is my soul within me. ❖ Return to your rest, O my soul, for the LORD has dealt bountifully with you. ❖ I will both lie down in peace, and sleep; for You alone, O LORD, make me dwell in safety. ❖ If you do what the LORD wants, he will make certain each step you take is sure. The LORD will hold your hand, and if you stumble, you still won't fall. ❖ God of angel armies protects us.

1 COR. 10:13 NKJV; 2 PETER 2:9 CEV; DEUT. 33:29 TLB; JOB 11:18 RSV;
PS. 46:10; PS. 121:2; PS. 3:3 NIV; PS. 94:19 CEV; PS. 131:2 NKJV; PS. 116:7
NASB; PS. 4:8 NKJV; PS. 37:23–24 CEV; PS. 46:11 THE MESSAGE

The promise of the psalm [121] . . . is not that we shall never stub our toes, but that no injury, no illness, no accident, no distress will have evil power over us, that is, will be able to separate us from God's purposes in us.

EUGENE H. PETERSON

The sixth petition in the Lord's Prayer is "Lead us not into temptation, but deliver us from evil." That prayer is answered every day, sometimes many times a day, in the lives of those who walk in the way of faith.

EUGENE H. PETERSON

How many times, O Lord, have you kept me from falling, sometimes, even when I wasn't aware that I had stubbed my toe?
Help me be more aware of your protection, of your deliverance.

NO RESISTANCE

God will bless you when people insult you, mistreat you, and tell all kinds of evil lies about you because of me. Be happy and excited! You will have a great reward in heaven. ❖ Even if you should suffer for righteousness' sake, you are blessed. ❖ If any of you suffers as a Christian, do not consider it a disgrace, but glorify God because you bear this name. ❖ All this they will do to you on my account, because they do not know him who sent me. ❖ They departed from the presence of the council, rejoicing that they were counted worthy to suffer shame for his name. ❖ You . . . as living stones, are being built up as a spiritual house for a holy priesthood, to offer up spiritual sacrifices acceptable to God through Jesus Christ. ❖ The ransomed of the LORD shall return, and come to Zion with songs and everlasting joy upon their heads: they shall obtain joy and gladness, and sorrow and sighing shall flee away.

MATT. 5:11–12 CEV; 1 PETER 3:14 NKJV; 1 PETER 4:16 NRSV; JOHN 15:21 RSV; ACTS 5:41; 1 PETER 2:5 NASB; ISA. 35:10

Only the man who follows the command of Jesus single-mindedly, and unresistingly lets his yoke rest upon him, finds his burden easy, and under its gentle pressure receives the power to persevere in the right way.

DIETRICH BONHOEFFER

God is greatly honored when, under trial and chastening, we have good thoughts of Him, vindicate His wisdom and justice, and recognize His love in His very rebukes.

ARTHUR W. PINK

So we feel, and even welcome, the purifying fire of God's love burning out the dross: all stubbornness, all hate, all grasping need for self-promotion. And as the self-sins are burned away, the seeds of universal life blossom and flower.

RICHARD FOSTER

Am I resisting your chastening, Lord?
Help me persevere, knowing the reward is great.

DON'T BE SURPRISED

Moses said to the people, "Do not be afraid. God has come to test you, so that the fear of God will be with you to keep you from sinning." ❖ I send you out as sheep in the midst of wolves. Therefore be wise as serpents and harmless as doves. ❖ You will be hated by all because of my name. But the one who endures to the end will be saved. ❖ Blessed are you when men hate you, and when they exclude you, and revile you, and cast out your name as evil, for the Son of Man's sake. ❖ Dear friends, don't be surprised or shocked that you are going through testing that is like walking through fire. ❖ Do not fear the reproach of men, nor be afraid of their insults. But My righteousness will be forever, and My salvation from generation to generation. ❖ For to you it has been granted for Christ's sake, not only to believe in Him, but also to suffer for His sake. ❖ But those enduring to the end shall be saved. ❖ I consider that the sufferings of this present time are not worth comparing with the glory that is to be revealed to us.

EXOD. 20:20 NIV; MATT. 10:16 NKJV; MATT. 10:22 NRSV; LUKE 6:22 NKJV; 1 PETER 4:12 CEV; ISA. 51:7–8 NKJV; PHIL. 1:29 NASB; MATT. 24:13 TLB; ROM. 8:18 RSV

When God called Abram, He said, "I will bless you and make your name great" (Gen. 12:2). That means: "I will develop your character to match your assignment."
BLACKABY AND KING

You cannot persevere unless there is a trial in your life. There can be no victories without battles; there can be no peaks without valleys. If you want the blessing, you must be prepared to carry the burden and fight the battle. . . .

God has to balance privileges with responsibilities, blessings with burdens, or else you and I will become spoiled, pampered children.
WARREN W. WIERSBE

Help me, Lord, to see the peak as well as the valley, to see the growth in the pain.
Can I say with Christ, "I'm willing to go through whatever it is that you want me to go through"?

SATAN WANTS TO BRING US DOWN

I do not pray that You should take them out of the world, but that You should keep them from the evil one. ❖ And the Lord said, "Simon, Simon! Indeed, Satan has asked for you, that he may sift you as wheat. But I have prayed for you, that your faith should not fail." ❖ Be sober, be watchful. Your adversary the devil prowls around like a roaring lion, seeking some one to devour. Resist him, firm in your faith. ❖ I was delivered out of the mouth of the lion. ❖ Do not give the devil an opportunity. ❖ Do not fear what you are about to suffer. Beware, the devil is about to throw some of you into prison, so that you may be tested. ❖ If God be for us, who can be against us? ❖ Submit yourselves therefore to God. Resist the devil, and he will flee from you. ❖ Satan tries to make himself look like an angel of light. ❖ Away with you, Satan! ❖ Put on the whole armour of God, that ye may be able to stand against the wiles of the devil. For we wrestle not against flesh and blood, but against principalities, against powers, against the rulers of the darkness of this world, against spiritual wickedness in high places. Wherefore take unto you the whole armour of God, that ye may be able to withstand in the evil day, and having done all, to stand.

JOHN 17:15 NKJV; LUKE 22:31–32 NKJV; 1 PETER 5:8–9 RSV; 2 TIM. 4:17; EPH. 4:27 NASB; REV. 2:10 NRSV; ROM. 8:31; JAMES 4:7; 2 COR. 11:14 CEV; MATT. 4:10 NKJV; EPH. 6:11–13

Satan fights us, the world opposes us, and this makes for a life of battle.
WARREN W. WIERSBE

There is no man so perfect nor so holy in this world that he sometime hath not temptations, and we may not fully be without them, for though they be for the time very grievous and painful, yet if they be resisted they be very profitable.
THOMAS À KEMPIS

The more slow that a man is in resisting, the weaker he is to resist, and the enemy is daily the stronger against him.
THOMAS À KEMPIS

Am I sluggish about resisting temptation so that Satan gains a foothold and causes my fall?
Am I on guard, fully armed and armored, ready to resist Satan's attack?

DAILY LIVING FOR HIM

Devote yourselves to prayer, being watchful and thankful. . . . Be wise in the way you act toward outsiders; make the most of every opportunity. Let your conversation be always full of grace, seasoned with salt, so that you may know how to answer everyone. ❖ So make every effort to apply the benefits of these promises to your life. Then your faith will produce a life of moral excellence. A life of moral excellence leads to knowing God better. Knowing God leads to self-control. Self-control leads to patient endurance, and patient endurance leads to godliness. Godliness leads to love for other Christians, and finally you will grow to have genuine love for everyone. The more you grow like this, the more you will become productive and useful in your knowledge of our Lord Jesus Christ. ❖ So teach us to number our days, that we may gain a heart of wisdom. ❖ Let me know how fleeting my life is.

COL. 4:2, 5–6 NIV; 2 PETER 1:5–8 NLT; PS. 90:12 NKJV; PS. 39:4 NRSV

For any way of life, any employment of our time, our talents, or our money, that is not strictly according to the will of God is as great an absurdity and failing as prayers that are not according to the will of God.

WILLIAM A. LAW

If we are to follow Christ, it must be in our common way of spending every day. . . .

If our common life is not a common course of humility, self-denial, renunciation of the world, poverty of spirit, and heavenly affection, we don't live the lives of Christians.

WILLIAM A. LAW

Let us live with urgency. Let us exploit the opportunity of life. Let us not drift. Let us live intentionally. . . . We must not trifle our lives away.

RAYMOND C. ORTLUND

Help me, Lord, to number my days. Each day is precious. Each day you have things to teach me; you have things you want me to do.

A LIFE CENTERED IN HIM

Take care to live in me, and let me live in you. For a branch can't produce fruit when severed from the vine. Nor can you be fruitful apart from me. ❖ Now set your heart and your soul to seek the LORD your God. ❖ I am devoted to you. ❖ Our fellowship is with the Father, and with his Son Jesus Christ. ❖ God, who got you started in this spiritual adventure, shares with us the life of his Son and our Master Jesus. He will never give up on you. Never forget that. ❖ Commit your works to the LORD. ❖ Train yourself in godliness. ❖ Eagerly follow the Holy Spirit and serve the Lord. Let your hope make you glad. Be patient in time of trouble and never stop praying. ❖ Godliness with contentment is great gain.

JOHN 15:4 TLB; 1 CHRON. 22:19; PS. 86:2 NRSV; 1 JOHN 1:3; 1 COR. 1:9 THE MESSAGE; PROV. 16:3 NKJV; 1 TIM. 4:7 RSV; ROM. 12:11–12 CEV; 1 TIM. 6:6

In order to be rightly oriented to God and His work, you need a God-centered life.

BLACKABY AND KING

Devotion is neither private nor public prayer, but a life given to God. He is the devout man, therefore, who considers and serves God in everything and who makes all of his life an act of devotion by doing everything in the name of God and under such rules as are conformable to His glory.

WILLIAM A. LAW

If we are to follow Christ, it must be in the way we spend each day.

WILLIAM A. LAW

Godliness is a lifelong pursuit.

DONALD S. WHITNEY

Am I pursuing godliness or am I content to go to church and call myself a Christian?

If I were devoted to God in all of my life, what would that mean? What would I have to do differently?

FRUITFUL

Now you are united with the one who was raised from the dead. As a result, you can produce good fruit, that is, good deeds for God. ❖ By this My Father is glorified, that you bear much fruit; so you will be My disciples. ❖ They are like trees planted by streams of water, which yield their fruit in its season. ❖ Bear fruit that befits repentance. ❖ The fruit of the Spirit is love, joy, peace, longsuffering, gentleness, goodness, faith, meekness, temperance: against such there is no law. ❖ By this all will know that you are My disciples, if you have love for one another. ❖ The fruit of righteousness will be peace. ❖ Happy is he who is gracious to the poor. ❖ Let your light so shine before men, that they may see your good works, and glorify your Father which is in heaven. ❖ Let Your saints shout for joy.

ROM. 7:4 NLT; JOHN 15:8 NKJV; PS. 1:3 NRSV; MATT. 3:8–9 RSV; GAL. 5:22–23; JOHN 13:35 NKJV; ISA. 32:17 NIV; PROV. 14:21 NASB; MATT. 5:16; PS. 132:9 NKJV

How often have you said to the Lord, "I yield myself to Thee for cleansing and keeping and to be made holy," but you have hesitated to add "to be used of Thee in the salvation of others." Let us acknowledge our failure here and humbly offer ourselves to the Lord for His work. Let us begin by praying for those around us, looking for opportunities to help them, and not being satisfied until we bear fruit to the glory of the Father.

ANDREW MURRAY

One China expert estimates that the revival in China represents the greatest numerical revival in the history of the church. . . . They concentrated on changing lives, not changing laws. [During government oppression of Christianity, the number of Christians has grown from 750,000 to 35 million.]

PHILIP YANCEY

Fruitless Christians accept something less than the abundant life.

JAMES S. MORRISON

Help me bear the fruit you want me to bear—nothing more, nothing less. May the abundance of your love and grace be seen in the abundance of my fruit.

HUMBLY SERVING

Moses and Aaron did as the LORD commanded them. ❖ Noah did . . . all that God commanded him. ❖ So Abram went, as the LORD had told him. ❖ [Paul] said to them: "You know . . . in what manner I always lived among you, serving the Lord with all humility, with many tears." ❖ No man, having put his hand to the plough, and looking back, is fit for the kingdom of God. ❖ Love your enemies, bless them that curse you, do good to them that hate you, and pray for them which despitefully use you, and persecute you; that ye may be the children of your Father which is in heaven. ❖ Don't be hateful and insult people just because they are hateful and insult you. Instead, treat everyone with kindness. You are God's chosen ones, and he will bless you. ❖ Comfort the fainthearted, uphold the weak, be patient with all. . . . Always pursue what is good both for yourselves and for all. ❖ I know your deeds, and your love and faith and service and perseverance. ❖ So it is right for me to be enthusiastic about all Christ Jesus has done through me in my service to God. ❖ Be humble and gentle. Be patient with each other, making allowance for each other's faults because of your love. ❖ Work with a smile on your face, always keeping in mind that no matter who happens to be giving the orders, you're really serving God.

EXOD. 7:6; GEN. 6:22 RSV; GEN. 12:4 NRSV; ACTS 20:18–19 NKJV; LUKE 9:62; MATT. 5:44–45; 1 PETER 3:9 CEV; 1 THESS. 5:14–15 NKJV; REV. 2:19 NASB; ROM. 15:17 NLT; EPH. 4:2 TLB; EPH. 6:7 THE MESSAGE

To bless people who have oppressed our spirits, emotionally deprived us, or in other ways handicapped us, is the most extraordinary work any of us will ever do.

ELIZABETH O'CONNOR

He has made us in His image and takes pleasure when we show the fruits of that image.

JERRY C. WOFFORD

I need a heart of compassion so that I can serve others joyfully, sacrificially. Am I serving the Lord wholeheartedly? Am I willing to do whatever he asks me to do?

OBEDIENT SERVICE

You shall fear the LORD your God; you shall serve Him. ❖ You must always love him and obey his laws and teachings. ❖ Has the LORD as much delight in burnt offerings and sacrifices as in obeying the voice of the LORD? Behold, to obey is better than sacrifice. ❖ He held fast to the LORD; he did not depart from following Him, but kept His commandments. ❖ Let your light so shine before men, that they may see your good works, and glorify your Father which is in heaven. ❖ They departed, and went through the towns, preaching the gospel, and healing every where. ❖ They have devoted themselves to the ministry of the saints. ❖ There are varieties of working, but it is the same God who inspires them all. ❖ What you are doing is much more than a service that supplies God's people with what they need. It is something that will make many others thank God. The way in which you have proved yourselves by this service will bring honor and praise to God. You believed the message about Christ, and you obeyed it by sharing generously with God's people and with everyone else.

DEUT. 10:20 NKJV; DEUT 11:1 CEV; 1 SAM. 15:22 NASB; 2 KINGS 18:6 NKJV; MATT. 5:16; LUKE 9:6; 1 COR. 16:15 NKJV; 1 COR. 12:6 RSV; 2 COR. 9:12–13 CEV

That weight, that clog, which seems to slow us down or even seems to prevent us from doing "Christian service," may actually be the very thing which keeps us from "good" activities so that we can do that which is God's best for our lives. If we go far with God on this earth we will usually find that we each have our own "clog" that God uses to slow us down to do his will. CHARLES HADDON SPURGEON

Our steps of obedience may be small, even going backwards at times, but the Spirit is able to change our direction and move us to service.

DOING HIS WORK

Hezekiah . . . did what was good and right and true before the LORD his God. And in every work that he began, . . . he did it with all his heart. So he prospered. ❖ Yield yourselves unto God, as those that are alive from the dead, and your members as instruments of righteousness unto God. ❖ Do not labor for the food which perishes, but for the food which endures to eternal life, which the Son of man will give to you. ❖ Do your work willingly, as though you were serving the Lord himself, and not just your earthly master. ❖ For we are God's fellow workers; you are God's field, you are God's building. ❖ From [Christ] the whole body, joined and knit together by every ligament with which it is equipped, as each part is working properly, promotes the body's growth in building itself up in love. ❖ And let the favor of the Lord our God be upon us; and do confirm for us the work of our hands; yes, confirm the work of our hands.

2 CHRON. 31:20–21 NKJV; ROM. 6:13; JOHN 6:27 RSV; COL. 3:23 CEV;
1 COR. 3:9 NKJV; EPH. 4:16 NRSV; PS. 90:17 NASB

We *can* yield our arms and legs and eyes and ears and brain to God as "instruments of righteousness."

RICHARD FOSTER

The same breath is blown into the flute, cornet, and bagpipe, but different music is produced according to the different instruments. In the same way one Spirit works in us, God's children, but different results are produced, and God is glorified through them according to each one's temperament and personality.

SADHU SUNDAR SINGH

Am I committed to doing God's work with all of my heart?
Take me, Lord Jesus; use me. All that I am is yours.

REFLECTING HIS LIGHT

Blessed are those who have learned to acclaim you, who walk in the light of your presence, O Lord. ❖ The glory of the Lord has risen upon you. ❖ Let us walk in the light of the Lord. ❖ He will teach us of his ways, and we will walk in his paths. ❖ If we walk in the light, as he is in the light, we have fellowship one with another. ❖ For you are all children of light and children of the day. ❖ I have set you to be a light for the Gentiles, that you may bring salvation to the uttermost parts of the earth. ❖ God is always fair. He will remember how you helped his people in the past and how you are still helping them. You belong to God, and he won't forget the love you have shown his people. ❖ Lord, . . . all we have accomplished is really from you. ❖ The Lord will be to you an everlasting light, and your God your glory.

Ps. 89:15 NIV; Isa. 60:1 NASB; Isa. 2:5; Isa. 2:3; 1 John 1:7; 1 Thess. 5:5 NRSV; Acts 13:47 RSV; Heb. 6:10 CEV; Isa. 26:12 NLT; Isa. 60:19 NKJV

God is like the sun and I am the moon, reflecting his light. He doesn't expect me to generate my own light. He has all the light that's needed.

MMS

Only He can guide you to invest your life in worthwhile ways. This guidance will come as you "walk" with Him and listen to Him.

BLACKABY AND KING

Have I thought about how God would have me invest my life?
Can I rest in the knowledge that what I accomplish for God's glory will be done by him through me and not by me through him?

GOD'S FELLOW WORKERS

He . . . said to them, "He who has two tunics, let him give to him who has none; and he who has food, let him do likewise." ❖ Aaron shall offer the Levites before the LORD, like a wave offering from the children of Israel, that they may perform the work of the LORD. ❖ We are labourers together with God. ❖ Be diligent to present yourself approved to God as a workman who does not need to be ashamed, handling accurately the word of truth. ❖ You have need of endurance, so that you may do the will of God and receive what is promised. ❖ Let us run with patience the race that is set before us. ❖ The eyes of the LORD range throughout the entire earth, to strengthen those whose heart is true to him.

LUKE 3:11 NKJV; NUM. 8:11 NKJV; 1 COR. 3:9; 2 TIM. 2:15 NASB; HEB. 10:36 RSV; HEB. 12:1; 2 CHRON. 16:9 NRSV

When we live as Jesus did [in love, holiness, obedience], in his power and with his presence, seekers will be drawn to us.

REBECCA MANLEY PIPPERT

Today God's eyes are still running all across America . . . the world . . . looking for someone—*anyone*—who will totally and passionately seek him, who is determined that every thought and action will be pleasing in his sight. For such a person or group, God will prove himself mighty. His power will explode on their behalf.

JIM CYMBALA

Help me to be that person, Lord, the one who is completely devoted to you and to doing your will.
Have I known his strength, his empowerment, his guidance for my work?

GOD'S WORK THROUGH US

My mother and My brothers are these who hear the word of God and do it. ❖ Why do you call me "Lord, Lord," and do not do what I tell you? I will show you what someone is like who comes to me, hears my words, and acts on them. That one is like a man building a house, who dug deeply and laid the foundation on rock. ❖ If you love Me, keep My commandments. ❖ The one who obeys me is the one who loves me; and because he loves me, my Father will love him; and I will too, and I will reveal myself to him. ❖ Be doers of the word, and not hearers only, deceiving yourselves. ❖ My friends, what good is it to say you have faith, when you don't do anything to show that you really do have faith? Can that kind of faith save you? If you know someone who doesn't have any clothes or food, you shouldn't just say, "I hope all goes well for you. I hope you will be warm and have plenty to eat." What good is it to say this, unless you do something to help? Faith that doesn't lead us to do good deeds is all alone and dead! ❖ The only thing that counts is faith expressing itself through love. ❖ We give thanks to God always for you all, making mention of you in our prayers; remembering without ceasing your work of faith, and labour of love, and patience of hope in our Lord Jesus Christ, in the sight of God and our Father.

LUKE 8:21 NKJV; LUKE 6:46–48 NRSV; JOHN 14:15 NKJV; JOHN 14:21 TLB; JAMES 1:22 RSV; JAMES 2:14–17 CEV; GAL. 5:6 NIV; 1 THESS. 1:2–3

God's work in the world is usually a joint project; he works with us as we yield ourselves to work with him.

JIM CYMBALA

I can usually sense that a leading is from the Holy Spirit when it calls me to humble myself, serve somebody, encourage somebody or give something away. Very rarely will the evil one lead us to do those kinds of things.

BILL HYBELS

Can my faith be seen in the way I love and serve others?
How has he called me to humble myself?

GOD EXPECTS ACTION

Arise and begin working, and the LORD be with you. ❖ Be strong and courageous, and act. ❖ Whatever your hand finds to do, do it with your might. ❖ You must keep whatever promises you make to the LORD. ❖ Do you not know that in a race all the runners compete, but only one receives the prize? So run that you may obtain it. Every athlete exercises self-control in all things. They do it to receive a perishable wreath, but we an imperishable. ❖ I want you to do whatever will help you serve the Lord best, with as few distractions as possible. ❖ I press toward the mark for the prize of the high calling of God in Christ Jesus. ❖ Be steadfast, immovable, always abounding in the work of the Lord, knowing that your labor is not in vain in the Lord. ❖ Be confident and do the work.

1 CHRON. 22:16 NKJV; 1 CHRON. 28:20 NASB; ECCLES. 9:10 NKJV;
DEUT. 23:23 CEV; 1 COR. 9:24–26 RSV; 1 COR. 7:35 NLT; PHIL. 3:14;
1 COR. 15:58 NKJV; 1 CHRON. 28:10 CEV

Everywhere the Word of God is against passivity and advocating action. "Fight the good fight. . . ."

R. ARTHUR MATHEWS

He who dares to call himself God's ambassador is not afforded the luxury of idle words.

MAX LUCADO

"Whatsoever ye shall bind on earth shall be bound in heaven" (Matt. 18:18). Jesus puts the initiative for action into the hands of His people and promises that when they act, Heaven will endorse.

R. ARTHUR MATHEWS

Am I giving myself fully to the work that God wants me to do?
When he is Lord of my purpose in life, I will willingly do what he has given
*   me to do.*

GROWING UP

Happy are those who do not follow the advice of the wicked, or take the path that sinners tread, or sit in the seat of scoffers; but their delight is in the law of the LORD, and on his law they meditate day and night. They are like trees planted by streams of water, which yield their fruit in its season, and their leaves do not wither. In all that they do, they prosper. ❖ They shall still bear fruit in old age; they shall be fresh and flourishing. ❖ By their fruits you will know them. ❖ Every branch that bears fruit, He prunes it, that it may bear more fruit. ❖ You used to be like people living in the dark, but now you are people of the light because you belong to the Lord. So act like people of the light and make your light shine. Be good and honest and truthful, as you try to please the Lord. ❖ Be very careful, then, how you live—not as unwise but as wise. ❖ Bear fruit that befits repentance. ❖ God's various gifts are handed out everywhere; but they all originate in God's Spirit. God's various ministries are carried out everywhere; but they all originate in God's Spirit. God's various expressions of power are in action everywhere; but God himself is behind it all.

PS. 1:1–3 NRSV; PS. 92:14 NKJV; MATT. 7:20 NKJV; JOHN 15:2 NASB;
EPH. 5:8–10 CEV; EPH. 5:15 NIV; MATT. 3:8 RSV; 1 COR. 12:4–6 THE MESSAGE

A spiritual gift is a manifestation of God at work through you. God works in and through you to bear fruit. The focus is on God and what He does through you.

BLACKABY AND KING

James shows us a person who can face trials of all kinds with rock-solid joy, a person who is plugged into a divine wisdom that sees "bitter jealousy" and "selfish ambition" for the imposters they truly are, a person who instinctively relates to all peoples on the basis of the "royal law" of love, a person who out of divine resources is able to "tame the tongue," a person who eschews "fightings and wars" because the inner well-spring of the life is so purified that from it naturally flows blessing and not cursing.

RICHARD FOSTER

Am I thoroughly equipped for the work that God has for me to do? Fill me with your Spirit, Lord Jesus, that I may be useful to you.

GOD OPPOSES THE PROUD

The apostles got into an argument about which one of them was the greatest. So Jesus told them: Foreign kings order their people around. . . . But don't be like them. The most important one of you should be like the least important, and your leader should be like a servant. ❖ For even the Son of Man did not come to be served, but to serve, and to give His life a ransom for many. ❖ Seek righteousness, seek humility. ❖ Be submissive to one another, and be clothed with humility, for "God resists the proud, but gives grace to the humble." Therefore humble yourselves under the mighty hand of God, that He may exalt you in due time. ❖ Since God chose you to be the holy people whom he loves, you must clothe yourselves with tenderhearted mercy, kindness, humility, gentleness, and patience. You must make allowance for each other's faults and forgive the person who offends you. Remember, the Lord forgave you, so you must forgive others. And the most important piece of clothing you must wear is love. Love is what binds us all together in perfect harmony.

LUKE 22:24–26 CEV; MARK 10:45 NKJV; ZEPH. 2:3 NASB; 1 PETER 5:5–6 NKJV; COL. 3:12–14 NLT

Let Christ be formed in me, and let me learn of Him all lowliness of heart, all gentleness of bearing, all modesty of speech, all helpfulness of action, and promptness in the doing of my Father's will.

JOHN BAILLIE

My unwillingness to believe that Thou hast called me to a small work and my brother to a great one: O Lord, forgive.

JOHN BAILLIE

Do I trust you with my humility, Lord? Do I believe that at the proper time you will lift me up?
Help me to be as small as you want me to be, unknown to the world but precious to you.

PATIENT IN DIFFICULTIES

Whosoever will come after me, let him deny himself, and take up his cross, and follow me. ❖ And whoever does not bear his cross and come after Me cannot be My disciple. ❖ Therefore, my beloved, be steadfast, immovable, always excelling in the work of the Lord, because you know that in the Lord your labor is not in vain. ❖ I know your works, love, service, faith, and your patience. ❖ We . . . glory in tribulations, knowing that tribulation produces perseverance; and perseverance, character; and character, hope. ❖ I am exceeding joyful in all our tribulation. ❖ When you are reviled and persecuted and lied about because you are my followers—wonderful! Be happy about it! Be very glad! for a tremendous reward awaits you up in heaven. ❖ You have need of endurance, so that when you have done the will of God, you may receive what was promised. ❖ My friends, be patient until the Lord returns. ❖ I wait for the LORD, my soul doth wait, and in his word do I hope. ❖ In repentance and rest is your salvation, in quietness and trust is your strength. ❖ Only God can save me, and I calmly wait for him.

MARK 8:34; LUKE 14:27 NKJV; 1 COR. 15:58 NRSV; REV. 2:19 NKJV; ROM. 5:3–4 NKJV; 2 COR. 7:4; MATT. 5:11–12 TLB; HEB. 10:36 NASB; JAMES 5:7 CEV; PS. 130:5; ISA. 30:15 NIV; PS. 62:1 CEV

Never allow the thought—"I can be of no use where I am"; because you certainly can be of no use where you are not.

OSWALD CHAMBERS

[Waiting] means going about our assigned tasks, confident that God will provide the meaning and the conclusions.

EUGENE H. PETERSON

Is my focus on God or on my difficult circumstances?
How do I wait—trusting God or anxious about what may happen?

SUFFERING TO GROW

I am weary with my groaning; all night I make my bed swim; I drench my couch with my tears. ❖ In the world you face persecution. But take courage; I have conquered the world! ❖ Friends, when life gets really difficult, don't jump to the conclusion that God isn't on the job. Instead, be glad that you are in the very thick of what Christ experienced. This is a spiritual refining process, with glory just around the corner. ❖ When you do good and suffer, if you take it patiently, this is commendable before God. For to this you were called, because Christ also suffered for us, leaving us an example, that you should follow His steps. ❖ While being reviled, He did not revile in return; while suffering, He uttered no threats, but kept entrusting Himself to Him who judges righteously. ❖ Therefore let those who suffer according to God's will do right and entrust their souls to a faithful Creator. ❖ May those who sow in tears reap with shouts of joy!

Ps. 6:6 NKJV; JOHN 16:33 NRSV; 1 PETER 4:12–14 THE MESSAGE; 1 PETER 2:20–21 NKJV; 1 PETER 2:23 NASB; 1 PETER 4:19 RSV; Ps. 126:5 RSV

Each thing that takes place, whether it be fortunate, unfortunate or unimportant from our particular point of view, is a caress of God's.

SIMONE WEIL

While delight is a feasting, emptiness is a fasting, and both are needed for the growth of the soul.

RICHARD FOSTER

In suffering we enter the *depths;* we are at the heart of things; we are near to where Christ was on the cross.

EUGENE H. PETERSON

Do my troubles make me wonder where God is and why he doesn't rescue me? Am I willing to suffer so that I can live and grow in Christ?

BE PERFECT

You shall be perfect, just as your Father in heaven is perfect. ❖ We proclaim him, admonishing and teaching everyone with all wisdom, so that we may present everyone perfect in Christ. To this end I labor, struggling with all his energy, which so powerfully works in me. ❖ For the one who sanctifies and those who are sanctified all have one Father. For this reason Jesus is not ashamed to call them brothers and sisters. ❖ We are sanctified through the offering of the body of Jesus Christ once for all. ❖ Our High Priest offered himself to God as one sacrifice for sins, good for all time. . . . For by that one offering he perfected forever all those whom he is making holy. ❖ Having therefore these promises, dearly beloved, let us cleanse ourselves from all filthiness of the flesh and spirit, perfecting holiness in the fear of God. ❖ For you are the temple of the living God. . . . Therefore come out from among them and be separate, says the Lord. ❖ For God has not called us for uncleanness, but in holiness. ❖ I am the LORD your God. You shall therefore consecrate yourselves, and you shall be holy; for I am holy. ❖ You are a holy people to the LORD your God.

MATT. 5:48 NKJV; COL. 1:28–29 NIV; HEB 2:11 NRSV; HEB. 10:10; HEB. 10:12, 14 NLT; 2 COR. 7:1; 2 COR. 6:16–17 NKJV; 1 THESS. 4:7 RSV; LEV. 11:44 NKJV; DEUT. 14:21 NASB

The command *Be ye perfect* is not idealistic gas. Nor is it a command to do the impossible. [God] is going to make us into creatures that can obey that command. . . . He meant what He said. Those who put themselves in His hands will become perfect, as He is perfect—perfect in love, wisdom, joy, beauty, and immortality.

C. S. LEWIS

It's not what I do that counts; it's my relationship to him. I'm not in training so that I can live a good life but so that I have a close and growing relationship with God. I discipline myself so that each day I may become more like him.

THE GOAL OF MY LIFE

Carefully keep all these commandments which I command you to do—to love the LORD your God, to walk in all His ways, and to hold fast to Him. ❖ Do what is right and good in the sight of the LORD, that it may be well with you. ❖ His heart took delight in the ways of the LORD. ❖ Grow in grace and understanding of our Master and Savior, Jesus Christ. ❖ Your faith is growing abundantly, and the love of everyone of you for one another is increasing. Therefore we ourselves boast of you . . . for your steadfastness and faith during all your persecutions and the afflictions that you are enduring. ❖ All who desire to live a godly life in Christ Jesus will be persecuted. . . . But as for you, continue in what you have learned and have firmly believed. ❖ We are to grow up in all aspects into Him, who is the head, even Christ. ❖ Because of Christ Jesus, I can take pride in my service for God. ❖ I have fought a good fight, I have finished my course, I have kept the faith.

DEUT. 11:22 NKJV; DEUT. 6:18 NKJV; 2 CHRON. 17:6 NKJV; 2 PETER 3:18 THE MESSAGE; 2 THESS. 1:3–4 NRSV; 2 TIM. 3:12, 14 RSV; EPH. 4:15 NASB; ROM. 15:17 CEV; 2 TIM. 4:7

A sense of need is a God-given thing. Thank God for the experience of disillusionment, for everything which drives us to him.

R. PAUL STEVENS

Being a Christian is like starting a journey on a complex highway system. We may feel intimidated as we round the first bend in the road; we may want to pull over and not go on. But if we continue our journey, we find that God goes with us, showing us the route to take, the bridges to cross, and where to slow down. He takes us through dark tunnels and perilous mountain passes, and as we go, we become more and more aware that he is going with us and the intimacy we experience is blessing indeed.

MMS

Lord Jesus, I commit myself to following you, to doing all that you ask me to do.

PERSEVERING THROUGH TRIALS

For to you it has been granted on behalf of Christ, not only to believe in Him, but also to suffer for His sake. ❖ We must through much tribulation enter into the kingdom of God. ❖ Jesus told the people who had faith in him, "If you keep on obeying what I have said, you truly are my disciples. You will know the truth, and the truth will set you free." ❖ Knowing God leads to self-control. Self-control leads to patient endurance, and patient endurance leads to godliness. Godliness leads to love for other Christians, and finally you will grow to have genuine love for everyone. The more you grow like this, the more you will become productive and useful in your knowledge of our Lord Jesus Christ. ❖ Keep up the good work and don't get discouraged, for you will be rewarded. ❖ Be strong and courageous! Do not tremble or be dismayed, for the LORD your God is with you wherever you go. ❖ I will look unto the LORD; I will wait for the God of my salvation: my God will hear me. ❖ These things I have spoken to you, that in Me you may have peace. In the world you will have tribulation; but be of good cheer, I have overcome the world. ❖ After you have suffered for a little while, the God of all grace, who has called you to his eternal glory in Christ, will himself restore, support, strengthen, and establish you.

PHIL. 1:29 NKJV; ACTS 14:22; JOHN 8:31–32 CEV; 2 PETER 1:6–8 NLT;
2 CHRON. 15:7 TLB; JOSH. 1:9 NASB; MICAH 7:7; JOHN 16:33 NKJV;
1 PETER 5:10 NRSV

We enforce not ourselves to follow the way that holy saints have gone before us, but when any little adversity cometh to us we be anon cast down therein and turn us over—soon to seek man's comfort.

THOMAS À KEMPIS

May we learn to mature all graces in us; fearing and trembling, watching and repenting, because Christ is coming, joyful, thankful, and careless of the future, because he is come.

JOHN HENRY NEWMAN

May I follow with endurance the way you have given me to walk, dear Lord. What have I to fear? He has overcome the world. Praise the Lord!

HE IS PREPARING ME

The weapons of our warfare are not merely human, but they have divine power to destroy strongholds. ❖ Stand firm, mature and confident in everything God wants you to do. ❖ I press on in order that I may lay hold of that for which also I was laid hold of by Christ Jesus. ❖ You have accepted Christ Jesus as your Lord. Now keep on following him. Plant your roots in Christ and let him be the foundation for your life. Be strong in your faith, just as you were taught. And be grateful. ❖ I pray that you, being rooted and established in love, may have power, together with all the saints, to grasp how wide and long and high and deep is the love of Christ. ❖ Therefore let us leave the elementary doctrine of Christ and go on to maturity. ❖ And now God is building you, as living stones, into his spiritual temple.

2 Cor. 10:4; Col. 4:12 the message; Phil. 3:12 nasb; Col. 2:6–7 cev; Eph. 3:17–18 niv; Heb. 6:1 rsv; 1 Peter 2:5 nlt

Jesus' time in the desert was a time of preparation for his ministry. For forty days he endured temptation, always saying no to it. Our preparation is for the same purpose (though it usually takes longer than forty days!). We must learn to say no to immorality, greed, pride, self-reliance—all things that Satan uses to bring people down in the midst of their ministry.

MMS

We cannot be impatient in this process [of preparation] and must realize that the period of preparation is essential to the success of our future callings. When the time is right and God is ready for us, he will begin to give us the clues that will lead us to the new platform he has prepared for us.

Sam Rima

Before God can entrust us with ministry, we must spend time in his marvelous light. Then he can move us into the spotlight of the world.

Robert Suggs

Am I getting the most out of this time of preparation so that I will be ready to do what he wants me to do in the next phase of my life? I too will press on; I too will be built up until I am useful to the Master.

VICTORIOUS IN HIM

Run in such a way that you may win. ❖ Fight the good fight of faith. ❖ Thanks be to God, who gives us the victory through our Lord Jesus Christ. ❖ God forbid that I should glory, save in the cross of our Lord Jesus Christ, by whom the world is crucified unto me, and I unto the world. ❖ Every child of God can defeat the world, and our faith is what gives us this victory. ❖ You stand firm in your faith. ❖ If you do not stand firm in faith, you shall not stand at all. ❖ Let your faith be like a shield, and you will be able to stop all the flaming arrows of the evil one. ❖ Trust in the LORD your God, and you will be established. ❖ With God's help we shall do mighty things. ❖ Overwhelming victory is ours through Christ, who loves us. And I am convinced that nothing can ever separate us from his love. ❖ Now thanks be to God who always leads us in triumph in Christ.

1 COR. 9:24 NASB; 1 TIM. 6:12; 1 COR. 15:57 NKJV; GAL. 6:14; 1 JOHN 5:4 CEV; 2 COR. 1:24 RSV; ISA. 7:9 NRSV; EPH. 6:16 CEV; 2 CHRON. 20:20 NASB; PS. 60:12 TLB; ROM. 8:37–38 NLT; 2 COR. 2:14 NKJV

When love for the Savior shall lead us to keep His holy Word—lead us to an immediate, unreserved, unhesitating obedience—lead us to say in a spirit of entire self-surrender and sacrifice, "Thy will, not mine, be done," then, farewell to doubt and darkness, to loneliness and sorrow! Then shall we mourn no more an absent Lord. Then shall we walk as seeing Him who is invisible, triumphant over every fear, victorious over every foe.

ARTHUR W. PINK

Faith is the victory! Faith is the victory!
Oh, glorious victory, that overcomes the world.
JOHN H. YATES

Am I experiencing victory in my Christian life?
Am I running to win or have I given up, assuming that my defeat is inevitable?

FILLED WITH HIS SPIRIT

If you love Me, keep My commandments. And I will pray the Father, and He will give you another Helper, that He may abide with you forever—the Spirit of truth. ❖ He who is united to the Lord becomes one spirit with him. ❖ If we love one another, God abides in us, and His love is perfected in us. ❖ The Counselor, the Holy Spirit, whom the Father will send in my name, will teach you all things. ❖ When he, the Spirit of truth, is come, he will guide you into all truth. ❖ People who don't have the Spirit of Christ in them don't belong to him. ❖ Live by the Spirit, . . . and do not gratify the desires of the flesh. ❖ Christ lives in me. ❖ Anyone who says he is a Christian should live as Christ did. ❖ If the Spirit of Him who raised Jesus from the dead dwells in you, He who raised Christ from the dead will also give life to your mortal bodies through His Spirit who dwells in you. ❖ All who are led by the Spirit of God are children of God.

JOHN 14:15–17 NKJV; 1 COR. 6:17 RSV; 1 JOHN 4:12 NASB; JOHN 14:26 NIV; JOHN 16:13; ROM. 8:9 CEV; GAL. 5:16 NRSV; GAL. 2:20 NASB; 1 JOHN 2:6 TLB; ROM. 8:11 NKJV; ROM. 8:14 NRSV

The chief thing is, not to know *what God* has said we must do, but that *God Himself* says it to us. . . . We must have the words *in us,* taken up into our will and life, reproduced in our disposition and conduct. We must have them *abiding* in us: our whole life one continued exposition of the words that are within, and filling us; the words revealing Christ within, and our life revealing Him without.

ANDREW MURRAY

What makes the Christian different from other men is the "peculiar," . . . the "extraordinary." . . . For [Jesus] the hall-mark of the Christian is the "extraordinary." . . .

What is the precise nature of the [extraordinary]? It is the life described in the beatitudes, the life of the followers of Jesus, the light which lights the world, the city set on a hill, the way of self-renunciation, of utter love, of absolute purity, truthfulness and meekness.

DIETRICH BONHOEFFER

May the power of your Spirit be seen in me today.
Do my words, does my life, reveal Christ?

HE'S HERE

Whoever confesses that Jesus is the Son of God, God abides in him, and he in God. ❖ All who keep his commandments abide in him, and he in them. And by this we know that he abides in us, by the Spirit which he has given us. ❖ You also were included in Christ when you heard the word of truth, the gospel of your salvation. Having believed, you were marked in him with a seal, the promised Holy Spirit. ❖ Do you not know that you are the temple of God and that the Spirit of God dwells in you? ❖ And you also are joined with him and with each other by the Spirit and are part of this dwelling place of God. ❖ This Spirit he poured out on us richly through Jesus Christ our Savior. ❖ Guard, through the Holy Spirit who dwells in us, the treasure which has been entrusted to you. ❖ Don't worry. My Spirit is right here with you. ❖ The Holy Spirit will teach you in that very hour what you ought to say. ❖ Because you are children, God has sent the Spirit of his Son into our hearts, crying, "Abba! Father!" ❖ Pray in the Holy Spirit. ❖ The kingdom of God is . . . righteousness and peace and joy in the Holy Spirit.

1 JOHN 4:15 NKJV; 1 JOHN 3:24 RSV; EPH. 1:13 NIV; 1 COR. 3:16 NKJV; EPH. 2:22 TLB; TITUS 3:6 NRSV; 2 TIM. 1:14 NASB; HAG. 2:5 CEV; LUKE 12:12 NKJV; GAL. 4:6 NRSV; JUDE 20 RSV; ROM. 14:17 NKJV

Wonderful, comforting thought: We and He are supernaturally interwoven and inseparable. Wherever you or I go, He goes. Whatever we think, He knows.

CHARLES R. SWINDOLL

When I go to bed at night,
your Spirit covers me with your peace.
And in the morning,
the joy of your Spirit awakens me.

MMS

It gives me joy to know that wherever I am, your Spirit is with me.
Am I experiencing the peace, joy, comfort, wisdom that Christ promised me
through his Spirit?

THE PROMISED SPIRIT

Very truly, I tell you, no one can enter the kingdom of God without being born of water and Spirit. What is born of the flesh is flesh, and what is born of the Spirit is spirit. ❖ Repent, and let every one of you be baptized in the name of Jesus Christ for the remission of sins; and you shall receive the gift of the Holy Spirit. ❖ He redeemed us in order that the blessing given to Abraham might come to the Gentiles through Christ Jesus, so that by faith we might receive the promise of the Spirit. ❖ Not by might, nor by power, but by my Spirit, says the LORD of hosts. ❖ If you then, being evil, know how to give good gifts to your children, how much more will your heavenly Father give the Holy Spirit to those who ask Him! ❖ Not only have I filled him with my Spirit, but I have given him wisdom. ❖ Our gospel came to you not only in word, but also in power and in the Holy Spirit and with full conviction. ❖ Your gentle Spirit instructed them. ❖ But when the Comforter is come, whom I will send unto you from the Father, even the Spirit of truth, which proceedeth from the Father, he shall testify of me. ❖ You shall be baptized with the Holy Spirit.

JOHN 3:5–6 NRSV; ACTS 2:38 NKJV; GAL. 3:14 NIV; ZECH. 4:6 RSV; LUKE 11:13 NKJV; EXOD. 31:3 CEV; 1 THESS. 1:5 RSV; NEH. 9:20 CEV; JOHN 15:26; ACTS 1:5 NKJV

The work of God to transfer us from the kingdom of darkness to the kingdom of light is first and foremost a work of the Holy Spirit. And it's a work of the Spirit from first to last.

NATHAN AND WILSON

Through the new birth, we've been launched on a journey in which we can expect personal visitations of the Spirit's power.

NATHAN AND WILSON

Am I aware of the Holy Spirit's power in my life?
I rejoice in you, Holy Spirit. Have your way in me!

SEEING THINGS THROUGH JESUS' EYES

This is the day the LORD has made; we will rejoice and be glad in it. ❖ May all who seek you rejoice and be glad in you; may those who love your salvation always say, "Let God be exalted!" ❖ I delight to do Your will, O my God, and Your law is within my heart. ❖ You shall put these words of mine in your heart. . . . Teach them to your children, talking about them when you are at home and when you are away, when you lie down and when you rise. ❖ These laws are not mere words—they are your life! ❖ We look not at the things which are seen, but at the things which are not seen: for the things which are seen are temporal; but the things which are not seen are eternal. ❖ You are my God. Show me what you want me to do, and let your gentle Spirit lead me in the right path. ❖ Your lovingkindness is before my eyes, and I have walked in Your truth. ❖ Grace and truth came by Jesus Christ. ❖ You will know the truth, and the truth will make you free. ❖ And their eyes were opened, and they knew him. ❖ I pray that the eyes of your heart may be enlightened, so that you may know what is the hope of His calling, what are the riches of the glory of His inheritance in the saints, and what is the surpassing greatness of His power toward us who believe.

PS. 118:24 NKJV; PS. 70:4 NIV; PS. 40:8 NKJV; DEUT. 11:18–19 NRSV; DEUT. 32:47 TLB; 2 COR. 4:18; PS. 143:10 CEV; PS. 26:3 NKJV; JOHN 1:17; JOHN 8:32 RSV; LUKE 24:31; EPH. 1:18–19 NASB

The Spirit said to me, I have chosen to reveal myself to you through words—not intellectual thoughts but spiritual words that reveal who I am. This is how I have chosen to reveal myself.

MMS

Don't evaluate your situation until you have heard from Jesus. He is the Truth of all your circumstances.

BLACKABY AND KING

Am I looking to Jesus for truth, for how to interpret the doings of the world? It's a daily challenge, to take my goals, my wants, my motivations and be sure they line up with his truth.

MY WHOLE LIFE

If you want to be my follower you must love me more than your own father and mother, wife and children, brothers and sisters—yes, more than your own life. ❖ Whoever of you does not renounce all that he has cannot be my disciple. ❖ Beware, and be on your guard against every form of greed; for not even when one has an abundance does his life consist of his possessions. ❖ The kingdom of God is within you. ❖ I know, O LORD, that a man's life is not his own; it is not for man to direct his steps. ❖ I beg you to live in a way that is worthy of the people God has chosen to be his own. ❖ We left everything to follow you. ❖ And everyone who has left houses or brothers or sisters or father or mother or wife or children or lands, for My name's sake, shall receive a hundredfold, and inherit eternal life. ❖ For those who want to save their life will lose it, and those who lose their life for my sake, and for the sake of the gospel, will save it.

LUKE 14:26 NLT; LUKE 14:33 RSV; LUKE 12:15 NASB; LUKE 17:21; JER. 10:23 NIV; EPH. 4:1 CEV; MATT. 19:27 TLB; MATT. 19:29 NKJV; MARK 8:35 NRSV

I am growing in the awareness that God wants my whole life, not just part of it. It is not enough to give just so much time and attention to God and keep the rest for myself. It is not enough to pray often and deeply and then move from there to my own projects.

HENRI J. M. NOUWEN

We must be willing to give up every dream but God's dream.

LARRY CRABB

Am I willing to let God have my whole life, to dream his dream and not my own?
You can help me to be willing, Lord. Help me, I pray.

BEING LIKE CHRIST

Now you are Christ's body, and individually members of it. ❖ And the church is his body; it is filled by Christ. ❖ It was he who gave some to be apostles, some to be prophets, some to be evangelists, and some to be pastors and teachers, to prepare God's people for works of service, so that the body of Christ may be built up until we all reach unity in the faith and in the knowledge of the Son of God and become mature, attaining to the whole measure of the fullness of Christ. ❖ May the God of peace himself make you entirely pure and devoted to God. ❖ Choose life, . . . loving the LORD your God, obeying his voice, and cleaving to him; for that means life to you and length of days. ❖ In him we live, and move, and have our being. ❖ I am the vine, you are the branches. Those who abide in me and I in them bear much fruit, because apart from me you can do nothing. ❖ God's Spirit makes us loving, happy, peaceful, patient, kind, good, faithful, gentle, and self-controlled. ❖ For the fruit of the Spirit is in all goodness and righteousness and truth.

1 COR. 12:27 NASB; EPH. 1:23 NLT; EPH. 4:11–13 NIV; 1 THESS. 5:23 TLB; DEUT. 30:19–20 RSV; ACTS 17:28; JOHN 15:5 NRSV; GAL. 5:22–23 CEV; EPH. 5:9

As images of Christ we are icons, incarnational signs that Jesus lives in this real world through real people.

R. PAUL STEVENS

But the church is the reason behind the entire human experiment, the reason there are human beings in the first place: to let creatures other than God bear the image of God.

PHILIP YANCEY

[Christ living within me] is the whole secret of being conformed to His image. If Christ is dwelling in my heart I must necessarily be Christlike. [His character] must be manifested in my daily walk and conversation.

HANNAH WHITALL SMITH

May I be completely yours, Lord — my hands serving, my eyes seeing, my feet moving at your direction.

BEING HIS REPRESENTATIVE

You are the earth's salt. ❖ You are the world's light. ❖ Let your light shine . . . in the sight of men. Let them see the good things you do and praise your Father in Heaven. ❖ I've set you up as light to all nations. You'll proclaim salvation to the four winds and seven seas! ❖ You are witnesses of these things. ❖ Take care to live in me, and let me live in you. For a branch can't produce fruit when severed from the vine. Nor can you be fruitful apart from me. ❖ By this My Father is glorified, that you bear much fruit; so you will be My disciples. ❖ But the Holy Spirit will come upon you and give you power. Then you will tell everyone about me. ❖ Your love for one another will prove to the world that you are my disciples. ❖ Go therefore and make disciples of all nations. ❖ Go into all the world and preach the gospel to all creation.

MATT. 5:13 PHILLIPS; MATT. 5:14 PHILLIPS; MATT. 5:16 PHILLIPS; ACTS 13:47 THE MESSAGE; LUKE 24:48 NKJV; JOHN 15:4 TLB; JOHN 15:8 NKJV; ACTS 1:8 CEV; JOHN 13:35 NLT; MATT. 28:19 RSV; MARK 16:15 NASB

We incarnate God in the world; what happens to us happens to him.

PHILIP YANCEY

If we abide in Him, and He in us, we can no more help bringing forth fruit than can the branches of a flourishing vine. In the very nature of things the fruit must come.

HANNAH WHITALL SMITH

How well do I represent Christ in this world? Is it obvious to the people I meet that I belong to him?
Am I flourishing with the fruit that he wants me to bear?

THE MYSTERIOUS UNION

In him you also, when you had heard the word of truth, the gospel of your salvation, and had believed in him, were marked with the seal of the promised Holy Spirit. ❖ The LORD your God has chosen you out of all the peoples on the face of the earth to be his people, his treasured possession. ❖ If Christ is in you, though the body is dead because of sin, yet the spirit is alive because of righteousness. ❖ May grace and peace be multiplied to you in the knowledge of God and of Jesus our Lord. His divine power has granted to us all things that pertain to life and godliness, through the knowledge of him who called us to his own glory and excellence, by which he has granted to us his precious and very great promises, that through these you may escape from the corruption that is in the world because of passion, and become partakers of the divine nature. ❖ Yes, dear friends, we are already God's children, and we can't even imagine what we will be like when Christ returns. But we do know that when he comes we will be like him, for we will see him as he really is.

EPH. 1:13 NRSV; DEUT. 7:6 NIV; ROM. 8:10 NASB; 2 PETER 1:2–4 RSV; 1 JOHN 3:2 NLT

But let us remember that the Spirit of God must have entire possession of us. He claims our whole heart and life. He will strengthen us in the inner man, so that we have fellowship with Christ, keep His commandments, and abide in His love.

ANDREW MURRAY

As we listen, our ear gets acute, and, like Jesus, we shall hear God all the time.

OSWALD CHAMBERS

We understand now, just as Christ is in God, and God in Christ, one together not only in will and in love, but in identity of nature and life, because they exist in each other, so we are in Christ and Christ in us, in union not only of will and love, but of life and nature too.

ANDREW MURRAY

How incredible to think that we can be like him — but that is what he said. He is pleased when we seek to reflect his character, just as an earthly father is pleased to see his son imitating him.

SEEING GOD

God is Spirit. ❖ No one has seen God at any time. ❖ You cannot see my face; for no one shall see me and live. ❖ Seek his face continually. ❖ The LORD make his face shine upon you and be gracious to you; the LORD turn his face toward you and give you peace. ❖ Make Your face shine upon Your servant. ❖ Then the LORD passed by in front of him and proclaimed, "The LORD, the LORD God, compassionate and gracious, slow to anger, and abounding in lovingkindness and truth." ❖ Jesus replied, . . ."Anyone who has seen me has seen the Father!" ❖ He is the image of the invisible God. ❖ It is he alone who has immortality and dwells in unapproachable light, whom no one has ever seen or can see; to him be honor and eternal dominion. Amen.

JOHN 4:24 NKJV; JOHN 1:18 NKJV; EXOD. 33:20 NRSV; 1 CHRON. 16:11; NUM. 6:25–26 NIV; PS. 119:135 NKJV; EXOD. 34:6 NASB; JOHN 14:9 TLB; COL. 1:15 NKJV; 1 TIM. 6:16 NRSV

Because his spiritual existence transcends form, matter, and location, we have the freedom to worship him and experience his indwelling presence wherever we are.

R. C. SPROUL

Enjoying God's immediate presence—face to face—is the Christian's highest aspiration.

R. C. SPROUL

There God, our King and Portion,
In fullness of His grace,
We then shall see forever,
And worship face to face.
BERNARD OF CLUNY

It's a mystery how we can see the invisible God, and yet he daily reveals himself to us.
We now see him face-to-face in a spiritual sense. We look forward to literally standing before him face-to-face.

SHARING IN HIS GLORY

We beheld His glory, the glory as of the only begotten of the Father, full of grace and truth. ❖ And the glory which You gave Me I have given them, that they may be one just as We are one. ❖ For those whom he foreknew he also predestined to be conformed to the image of his Son. ❖ Moses didn't realize as he came back down the mountain with the tablets that his face glowed from being in the presence of God. ❖ And all of us, with unveiled faces, seeing the glory of the Lord as though reflected in a mirror, are being transformed into the same image from one degree of glory to another; for this comes from the Lord, the Spirit. ❖ The glory of the LORD has risen upon you. . . . The LORD will rise upon you, and His glory will appear upon you. ❖ You are becoming more and more like your Creator. ❖ Now I know in part; then I shall know fully, even as I am fully known.

JOHN 1:14 NKJV; JOHN 17:22 NKJV; ROM. 8:29 RSV; EXOD. 34:29 TLB; 2 COR. 3:18 NRSV; ISA. 60:1–2 NASB; COL. 3:10 CEV; 1 COR. 13:12 NIV

While all mankind is created in God's image, only those re-created by the Son will behold the unveiled glory of the Father.

R. C. SPROUL

We want to live each hour for God, in his presence seeking his pleasure.

R. PAUL STEVENS

Presenting myself thus before God, I desire Him to form His perfect image in my soul, and make me entirely like Himself.

BROTHER LAWRENCE

How can this be? He shares his glory with me?
As I submit myself to him and have with him the intimate relationship that he desires, I begin to see the evidences of his changing my life.

INTIMACY WITH GOD

And I—in righteousness I will see your face; when I awake, I will be satisfied with seeing your likeness. ❖ I heard about you from others; now I have seen you with my own eyes. ❖ [Jacob] said, "I have seen God face to face, yet my life has been preserved." ❖ Hagar spoke of Jehovah—for it was he who appeared to her—as "the God who looked upon me," for she thought, "I saw God and lived to tell it." ❖ O LORD, You have searched me and known me . . . and are acquainted with all my ways. ❖ It is good for me to draw near to God: I have put my trust in the Lord GOD, that I may declare all thy works. ❖ Let them boast in this alone: that they truly know me and understand that I am the LORD who is just and righteous, whose love is unfailing, and that I delight in these things. I, the LORD have spoken! ❖ Blessed are the pure in heart: for they shall see God.

Ps. 17:15 NIV; JOB 42:5 CEV; GEN. 32:30 NASB; GEN. 16:13 TLB; Ps. 139:1, 3 NKJV; Ps. 73:28; JER. 9:24 NLT; MATT. 5:8

We who are in Christ have the right by the grace of God to come before the face of God.

R. C. SPROUL

You cannot obey Him unless you believe and trust Him. You cannot believe and trust Him unless you love Him. You cannot love Him unless you know Him.

BLACKABY AND KING

If I am intimate with the Lord, my heart is receptive to his urgings. I don't resist his working, his moving in me.
What an amazing privilege—to come before the face of God!

UNLIMITED INTIMACY

The friendship of the LORD is for those who fear him, and he makes known to them his covenant. ❖ I have called you friends, for all things that I heard from My Father I have made known to you. ❖ I can really know Christ and experience the mighty power that raised him from the dead. I can learn what it means to suffer with him, sharing in his death, so that, somehow, I can experience the resurrection from the dead! ❖ He is intimate with the upright. ❖ His divine power has given us everything needed for life and godliness, through the knowledge of him who called us by his own glory and goodness. Thus he has given us, through these things, his precious and very great promises, so that through them you may . . . become participants of the divine nature. ❖ For "who has known the mind of the LORD that he may instruct Him?" But we have the mind of Christ.

Ps. 25:14 RSV; JOHN 15:15 NKJV; PHIL. 3:10–11 NLT; PROV. 3:32 NASB; 2 PETER 1:3–4 NRSV; 1 COR. 2:16 NKJV

Our creaturely limitations prevent us from knowing God fully, but they do not prevent an intimacy with our heavenly Father.

R. C. SPROUL

So intimate is he with us that we are to conceive of the relationship as being face to face. We are to live at all times knowing that we are ever under his gaze and ought, therefore, to live unto his glory.

R. C. SPROUL

Those who recognize Jesus as Lord must rush to him (Mark 6:55–56), bringing every earthly concern. Our needs are met when we simply touch him, but growth and strength and maturity come from getting involved with him—letting him wrap his cloak around us. He pursues us—and we dare to touch him. Then we must pursue him until we're wrapped up in him.

MMS

Do I dare have the intimacy with God that he desires?
Pursuing intimacy with God provides limitless joy, unending blessings.

LONGING FOR INTIMACY

Seek the LORD while he may be found, call upon him while he is near. ❖ He has made from one blood every nation of men to dwell on all the face of the earth, . . . so that they should seek the Lord, in the hope that they might grope for Him and find Him, though He is not far from each one of us. ❖ If you seek Him, He will let you find Him. ❖ Then you will call upon Me and go and pray to Me, and I will listen to you. And you will seek Me and find Me, when you search for Me with all your heart. ❖ Call to me and I will answer you and tell you great and unsearchable things you do not know. ❖ You will seek the LORD your God, and you will find him if you search after him with all your heart and soul. ❖ Ask, and you will be given what you ask for. Seek, and you will find. ❖ This one will say, "I am the Lord's"; . . . and another will write on his hand, "Belonging to the LORD." ❖ Seek the LORD and his strength, seek his presence continually! Remember the wonderful works that he has done. ❖ Let the heart of them rejoice that seek the LORD.

ISA. 55:6 RSV; ACTS 17:26–27 NKJV; 1 CHRON. 28:9 NASB; JER. 29:12–13 NKJV; JER. 33:3 NIV; DEUT. 4:29 NRSV; MATT. 7:7 TLB; ISA. 44:5 NASB; PS. 105:4–5 RSV; 1 CHRON. 16:10

The purpose of Bible study should be to get to know God. The key to this goal is prayerful Bible study.

JAMES MONTGOMERY BOICE

What does intimacy with you mean, Lord? Surely if we had an intimate relationship, I would not neglect you and forget you. I would feel free to share my feelings, my love, sorrow, joy. I would always sense your indwelling Spirit and respond to your urgings. I would have your thoughts.

MMS

Intimacy with God means sharing with him on every level—emotional, intellectual, spiritual.
How I long to know you, Lord Jesus, deeply, intimately, completely.

SET APART

You . . . are among those who are called to belong to Jesus Christ. ❖ God the Father chose you long ago and knew you would become his children. And the Holy Spirit has been at work in your hearts, cleansing you with the blood of Jesus Christ and making you to please him. ❖ The blood of Christ, who through the eternal Spirit offered himself without blemish to God, [will] purify your conscience from dead works to serve the living God. ❖ By giving himself completely at the Cross, actually dying for you, Christ brought you over to God's side and put your lives together, whole and holy in his presence. ❖ Happy are those whom you choose and bring near to live in your courts. We shall be satisfied with the goodness of your house, your holy temple.

Rom. 1:6 niv; 1 Peter 1:2 tlb; Heb. 9:14 rsv; Col. 1:22 the message; Ps. 65:4 nrsv

. . . to live as pilgrims in spiritual watching, in holy fear, and heavenly aspiring after another life. . . .

I call these duties the devotion of our common life, because if they are to be practiced, they must be made parts of our common life; they can have no place anywhere else.

William A. Law

A spiritual discipline is necessary in order to move slowly from an absurd to an obedient life, from a life filled with noisy worries to a life in which there is some free inner space where we can listen to our God and follow his guidance.

Henri J. M. Nouwen

Forgive the scanty use I have made to-day of the talents Thou hast entrusted to my keeping. Cover up the poverty of my service by the fullness of Thine own divine resource. Yet grant also that, as day succeeds day, I may be so strengthened by Thy help that my service may grow less unworthy and my sins less grievous. May Christ more and more reign in my heart and purify my deeds.

John Baillie

He has chosen me! What a glorious thought!
Purify me, Lord Jesus. Make me like you.

RIGHTEOUSNESS THROUGH FAITH

The righteous man leads a blameless life. ❖ For I say to you, that unless your righteousness exceeds the righteousness of the scribes and Pharisees, you will by no means enter the kingdom of heaven. ❖ All our righteous deeds are like a filthy garment. ❖ This Good News tells us how God makes us right in his sight. This is accomplished from start to finish by faith. As the Scriptures say, "It is through faith that a righteous person has life." ❖ We are made right in God's sight when we trust in Jesus Christ to take away our sins. ❖ Not having a righteousness of my own, based on law, but that which is through faith in Christ, the righteousness from God that depends on faith. ❖ For He has clothed me with the garments of salvation, He has covered me with the robe of righteousness. ❖ But to one who without works trusts him who justifies the ungodly, such faith is reckoned as righteousness. ❖ Now you have been set free from sin, and you are God's slaves. This will make you holy and will lead you to eternal life.

PROV. 20:7 NIV; MATT. 5:20 NKJV; ISA. 64:6 NASB; ROM. 1:17 NLT; ROM. 3:22 NLT; PHIL. 3:9 RSV; ISA. 61:10 NKJV; ROM. 4:5 NRSV; ROM. 6:22 CEV

The true Christian grows in authentic righteousness.
R. C. SPROUL

Thou and Thou only, first in my heart,
High King of heaven, my Treasure Thou art.
ELEANOR HULL

How I want to do something to make myself acceptable to God! Recognizing that my puny efforts are worthless, I gladly accept what he has done for me—made me good in his sight.

HIS RIGHTEOUSNESS IS MINE

Sow for yourselves righteousness, reap the fruit of unfailing love, and break up your unplowed ground; for it is time to seek the LORD, until he comes and showers righteousness on you. ❖ Those who sow righteousness get a true reward. ❖ The righteous hold to their way, and they that have clean hands grow stronger and stronger. ❖ The LORD upholds the righteous. The LORD knows the days of the upright. ❖ But now apart from the Law the righteousness of God has been manifested, . . . even the righteousness of God through faith in Jesus Christ for all those who believe. ❖ My righteous one shall live by faith. ❖ May you always be filled with the fruit of your salvation—those good things that are produced in your life by Jesus Christ—for this will bring much glory and praise to God. ❖ You shall be perfect, just as your Father in heaven is perfect. ❖ But the path of the just is like the shining sun, that shines ever brighter unto the perfect day.

HOSEA 10:12 NIV; PROV. 11:18 NRSV; JOB 17:9 NRSV; PS. 37:17–18 NKJV; ROM. 3:21–22 NASB; HEB. 10:38 RSV; PHIL. 1:11 NLT; MATT. 5:48 NKJV; PROV. 4:18 NKJV

Holiness is a gift from God, not something I can ever claim as the result of my own doing.

HENRI J. M. NOUWEN

Self-indulgence is the enemy of gratitude, and self-discipline usually its friend and generator. That is why gluttony is a deadly sin. The early desert fathers believed that a person's appetites are linked: full stomachs and jaded palates take the edge from our hunger and thirst for righteousness. They spoil the appetite for God.

CORNELIUS PLANTINGA JR.

He has given me his righteousness. How can I not give all that I am to be what he wants me to be?
Only when I recognize that it's his righteousness can I be perfect.

GOD'S LOVE IN US

If we love one another, God abides in us, and His love is perfected in us. ❖ If anyone loves God, this one is known by Him. ❖ God is love, and he who abides in love abides in God, and God in him. ❖ Whoever keeps his word, in him truly love for God is perfected. ❖ If you obey my commands, you will remain in my love. ❖ So if I, the Master and Teacher, washed your feet, you must now wash each other's feet. ❖ I give you a new commandment, that you love one another. Just as I have loved you, you also should love one another. By this everyone will know that you are my disciples, if you have love for one another. ❖ Beloved, if God so loved us, we ought also to love one another. ❖ And God himself has said that one must love not only God but his brother too. ❖ Fervently love one another from the heart. ❖ All those who love me will do what I say. My Father will love them, and we will come to them and live with them.

1 JOHN 4:12 NASB; 1 COR. 8:3 NKJV; 1 JOHN 4:16 NKJV; 1 JOHN 2:5 RSV; JOHN 15:10 NIV; JOHN 13:14 THE MESSAGE; JOHN 13:34–35 NRSV; 1 JOHN 4:11; 1 JOHN 4:21 TLB; 1 PETER 1:22 NASB; JOHN 14:23 NLT

When you come to know God by experience, you will be convinced of His love. When you are convinced of His love, you can believe Him and trust Him. When you trust Him, you can obey Him. When you trust Him, you have no problem obeying Him. "For this is the love of God, that we keep His commandments. And His commandments are not burdensome" (1 John 5:3).

BLACKABY AND KING

He does not think God will love us because we are good, but that God will make us good because He loves us.

C. S. LEWIS

Somehow my love for God, his love for me, my obedience, and the indwelling of his Spirit all come together in making me the person he wants me to be. God loves me just because he wants to, not because I in any way deserve it.

ENJOYING GOD

You will show me the path of life; in Your presence is fullness of joy; at Your right hand are pleasures forevermore. ❖ My heart greatly rejoices. ❖ No wonder my heart is filled with joy and my tongue shouts his praises! ❖ You will be altogether joyful. ❖ I will be glad and rejoice in You. ❖ The LORD has done great things for us; we are glad. ❖ God . . . gives us richly all things to enjoy. ❖ The kingdom of God is . . . righteousness and peace and joy in the Holy Spirit. ❖ Strength and joy are in his place. ❖ I said to the LORD, "You are my Master! All the good things I have are from you." ❖ My joy knows no bounds. ❖ Without having seen him you love him; though you do not now see him you believe in him and rejoice with unutterable and exalted joy. As the outcome of your faith you obtain the salvation of your souls. ❖ I am glad and rejoice. ❖ Rejoice in the Lord alway: and again I say, Rejoice.

Ps. 16:11 NKJV; Ps. 28:7 NKJV; Acts 2:26 TLB; Deut. 16:15 RSV; Ps. 9:2 NKJV; Ps. 126:3 NASB; 1 Tim. 6:17 NKJV; Rom. 14:17 NASB; 1 Chron. 16:27 NRSV; Ps. 16:2 NLT; 2 Cor. 7:4 NIV; 1 Peter 1:8–9 RSV; Phil. 2:17 NKJV; Phil. 4:4

True happiness consists only in the enjoyment of God. His favor is life, and his lovingkindness is better than life.

ARTHUR W. PINK

May you and I be more and more drawn in, taken over, and consumed by this love from God.

RICHARD FOSTER

I cannot explain it, but there is within me a joy that cannot be extinguished, regardless of the circumstances of my life.
May I ever live, centered in you, filled with joy.

SEEING HIM

He is the image of the invisible God, the firstborn over all creation. ❖ I have now seen the One who sees me. ❖ The only one who has seen the Father is the one who has come from him. No one else has ever seen the Father. ❖ It pleased the Father that in him should all fulness dwell. ❖ And the Word became flesh and dwelt among us, full of grace and truth; we have beheld his glory, glory as of the only Son from the Father. ❖ The god of this world has blinded the minds of the unbelievers, to keep them from seeing the light of the gospel of the glory of Christ, who is the image of God. ❖ Did I not say to you, if you believe, you will see the glory of God? ❖ We do know this, that when he comes we will be like him, as a result of seeing him as he really is. ❖ Father, I desire that they also whom You gave Me may be with Me where I am, that they may behold My glory.

COL. 1:15 NKJV; GEN. 16:13 NIV; JOHN 6:46 CEV; COL. 1:19; JOHN 1:14 RSV; 2 COR. 4:4 NRSV; JOHN 11:40 NASB; 1 JOHN 3:2 TLB; JOHN 17:24 NKJV

Glory is to God what style is to an artist. . . . The style of an artist brings you as close to the sound of his voice and the light in his eye as it is possible to get this side of actually shaking hands with him.

In the words of the nineteenth Psalm, "The heavens are telling the glory of God." It is the same thing. . . .

Glory is what God looks like when for the time being all you have to look at him with is a pair of eyes.

FREDERICK BUECHNER

If we spend our time beholding the glory of the Lord, that is, letting our minds dwell upon His goodness and His love, and trying to drink in His Spirit, the inevitable result will be that we shall be, slowly perhaps, but surely, changed into the image of the Lord upon whom we are gazing.

HANNAH WHITALL SMITH

Do I long to see the artist face-to-face?

MY WHOLE HEART

Then I will give them one heart, and I will put a new spirit within them, and take the stony heart out of their flesh, and give them a heart of flesh, that they may walk in My statutes and keep My judgments and do them; and they shall be My people, and I will be their God. ❖ A new heart also will I give you, and a new spirit will I put within you. ❖ I will put My law within them, and on their heart I will write it. ❖ And I will give them an heart to know me, that I am the LORD: and they shall be my people, and I will be their God: for they shall return unto me with their whole heart. ❖ The seed on good soil stands for those with a noble and good heart, who hear the word, retain it, and by persevering produce a crop. ❖ You shall love the LORD your God with all your heart, with all your soul, and with all your mind. ❖ Your lives are a letter written in our hearts, and everyone can read it and recognize our good work among you. Clearly, you are a letter from Christ prepared by us. It is written not with pen and ink, but with the Spirit of the living God. It is carved not on stone, but on human hearts.

EZEK. 11:19–20 NKJV; EZEK. 36:26; JER. 31:33 NASB; JER. 24:7; LUKE 8:15 NIV; MATT. 22:37–38 NKJV; 2 COR. 3:2–3 NLT

We . . . must be everywhere in the spirit of devotion, with hearts always set toward Heaven, looking to God in all our actions, and doing everything as His servants, living in the world as in a holy temple of God, and always worshipping Him though not with our lips, yet with the thankfulness of our hearts, the holiness of our actions, and the pious and charitable use of all His gifts. That we must not only send up petitions and thoughts now and then to Heaven, but must go through all our worldly business with a heavenly spirit as members of Christ's mystical body, that with new hearts and new minds are to turn an earthly life into a preparation for a life of greatness and glory in the Kingdom of Heaven.

WILLIAM A. LAW

Jesus wants all of my heart. Does he have it? Am I willing to commit all of me to him?
What kind of a letter am I?

WITH ALL I AM

And now, Israel, what does the LORD your God require of you, but to fear the LORD your God, to walk in all his ways, to love him, to serve the LORD your God with all your heart and with all your soul. ❖ Cling to Him. ❖ Only fear the LORD, and serve him in truth with all your heart: for consider how great things he hath done for you. ❖ Grace to all who love our Lord Jesus Christ with an undying love. ❖ I long to know Christ and the power shown by his Resurrection. ❖ [She] stood at His feet behind Him weeping; and she began to wash His feet with her tears, and wiped them with the hair of her head; and she kissed His feet and anointed them with the fragrant oil. ❖ These women had followed him and cared for his needs. ❖ The person who loves God is the one God knows and cares for. ❖ If a person isn't loving and kind, it shows that he doesn't know God—for God is love. ❖ God is love, and he who abides in love abides in God, and God in him. ❖ Though you have never seen him, yet I know that you love him. At present you trust him without being able to see him, and even now he brings you a joy that words cannot express.

DEUT. 10:12 RSV; DEUT. 10:20 NASB; 1 SAM. 12:24; EPH. 6:24 NIV;
PHIL. 3:10 PHILLIPS; LUKE 7:38 NKJV; MARK 15:41 NIV; 1 COR. 8:3 NLT;
1 JOHN 4:8 TLB; 1 JOHN 4:16 NKJV; 1 PETER 1:8 PHILLIPS

Let all our employment be to know God; the more one knows Him, the more one desires to know Him. And as knowledge is commonly the measure of love, the deeper and more extensive our knowledge shall be, the greater will be our love; and if our love of God were great, we should love Him equally in pains and pleasures.

BROTHER LAWRENCE

If I love God with all my heart, he will be the center of my life. If I love him with all my soul, my love will be true and deep. If I love him with all of my mind, he will control my thoughts. If I love him with all of my strength, the things I do will please him.

MMS

What kind of love do I have for the Lord?
Am I withholding parts of myself from him?

GOD'S LOVE DRAWS US

See what love the Father has given us, that we should be called children of God; and that is what we are. ❖ Just as a father has compassion on his children, so the LORD has compassion on those who fear Him. ❖ His steadfast love endures for ever! ❖ We know what real love is from Christ's example in dying for us. ❖ We love him, because he first loved us. ❖ Let us draw near with a true heart in full assurance of faith. ❖ Whatever we do, it is because Christ's love controls us. ❖ Keep yourselves in the love of God, looking for the mercy of our Lord Jesus Christ unto eternal life. ❖ And I pray that Christ will be more and more at home in your hearts, living within you as you trust in him. May your roots go down deep into the soil of God's marvelous love; and may you be able to feel and understand, as all God's children should, how long, how wide, how deep, and how high his love really is; and to experience this love for yourselves, though it is so great that you will never see the end of it or fully know or understand it. And so at last you will be filled up with God himself. ❖ In heaven I have only you, and on this earth you are all I want. My body and mind may fail, but you are my strength and my choice forever.

1 JOHN 3:1 NRSV; PS. 103:13 NASB; PS. 118:1 RSV; 1 JOHN 3:16 TLB;
1 JOHN 4:19; HEB. 10:22; 2 COR. 5:14 NLT; JUDE 21; EPH. 3:17–19 TLB;
PS. 73:25–26 CEV

Thus it happens that once God's sweetness has been tasted, it draws us to the pure love of God more than our needs compel us to love him.

BERNARD OF CLAIRVAUX

The goal of authentic spirituality is a love which escapes from the closed circle of spiritual indulgence, or even self-improvement, to become absorbed in the love of God and other persons.

RICHARD LOVELACE

Help me, Lord, to love you enough.
Break down my resistance, Lord Jesus. May your love draw me completely.

THE BLESSINGS OF FOLLOWING HIM

The same Lord is Lord of all and richly blesses all who call on him. ❖ He will love you and bless you. ❖ The sheep follow him because they know his voice. ❖ My sheep hear my voice, and I know them, and they follow me. ❖ If anyone serves Me, let him follow Me; and where I am, there My servant will be also. ❖ Our fellowship is with the Father, and with his Son Jesus Christ. ❖ God is faithful, by whom you were called into the fellowship of his Son, Jesus Christ our Lord. ❖ Anyone who intends to come with me has to let me lead. You're not in the driver's seat; I am. Don't run from suffering; embrace it. Follow me and I'll show you how. ❖ Those who love me will be loved by my Father, and I will love them and reveal myself to them. ❖ The Lord loves the righteous. ❖ Those who have been ransomed by the Lord will return to Jerusalem, singing songs of everlasting joy. Sorrow and mourning will disappear, and they will be overcome with joy and gladness.

ROM. 10:12 NIV; DEUT. 7:13 NKJV; JOHN 10:4 NASB; JOHN 10:27; JOHN 12:26 NKJV; 1 JOHN 1:3; 1 COR. 1:9 RSV; MATT. 16:24 THE MESSAGE; JOHN 14:21 NRSV; PS. 146:8 NKJV; ISA. 51:11 NLT

Still He blesses those on whom He sets His love in a way that humbles them, so that all the glory may be His alone. Still He hates the sins of His people, and uses all kinds of inward and outward pains and griefs to wean their hearts from compromise and disobedience. Still He seeks the fellowship of His people, and sends them both sorrows and joys in order to detach their love from other things and attach it to Himself.

J. I. PACKER

There is only one way to love God: to take not a single step without him, and to follow with a brave heart wherever he leads.

FRANÇOIS FÉNELON

How do I love you, Lord Jesus? Recklessly, not giving a second thought to my own wants and goals? Fearlessly, not caring if I am in danger or needy or overlooked? Wholeheartedly, wanting nothing but what you want, going nowhere but where you lead? Take my heart and teach it how to love you more.

FROM THE HEART

You shall love the LORD your God with all your heart, with all your soul, and with all your strength. ❖ Show love to the LORD your God by walking in his ways and clinging to him. ❖ Jesus said, "Simon son of John, do you truly love me?" He answered, "Yes, Lord, you know that I love you." ❖ The LORD your God will circumcise your heart . . . so that you will love the LORD your God with all your heart and with all your soul. ❖ My heart greatly rejoices, and with my song I will praise Him. ❖ The heart of Asa was true to the LORD all his days. ❖ Because he has loved Me, therefore I will deliver him; I will set him securely on high, because he has known My name. ❖ Let those who love Him be like the sun when it comes out in full strength. ❖ Love others as much as you love yourself. ❖ Beloved, let us love one another: for love is of God; and every one that loveth is born of God, and knoweth God. ❖ If God so loved us, we ought also to love one another. ❖ I will love thee, O LORD, my strength. ❖ I will praise you, LORD, with all my heart.

DEUT. 6:5 NKJV; DEUT. 11:22 NLT; JOHN 21:16 NIV; DEUT. 30:6 RSV; PS. 28:7 NKJV; 1 KINGS 15:14 NRSV; PS. 91:14 NASB; JUDG. 5:31 NKJV; MATT. 22:39 CEV; 1 JOHN 4:7; 1 JOHN 4:11; PS. 18:1; PS. 9:1 CEV

Worship is not taught from the pulpit. It must be learned in the heart.

JIM ELLIOT

Love for God and love for the world cannot coexist in the same soul: the stronger drives out the weaker, and it soon appears who loves the world, and who follows Christ. The strength of people's love is shown in what they do.

RICHARD ROLLE

Increase my heart's capacity to love you, Lord.
Help me to love you completely, selflessly, purely, and increasingly.

SEEKING GOD

Nicodemus said to Him, "How can a man be born when he is old? Can he enter a second time into his mother's womb and be born?" Jesus answered, "Most assuredly, I say to you, unless one is born of water and the Spirit, he cannot enter the kingdom of God." ❖ Seek the LORD while He may be found; call upon Him while He is near. ❖ The LORD is with you, while you are with him. If you seek him, he will be found by you. ❖ Starting from scratch, he made the entire human race and made the earth hospitable, with plenty of time and space for living so we could seek after God, and not just grope around in the dark but actually find him. He doesn't play hide-and-seek with us. He's not remote; he's near. ❖ In their distress they turned to the LORD, the God of Israel, and sought him, and he was found by them. ❖ Mary . . . sat at the Lord's feet and listened to his teaching. ❖ Glory in His holy name; let the hearts of those rejoice who seek the LORD! Seek the LORD and His strength; seek His face evermore! ❖ Blessed are they that keep his testimonies, and that seek him with the whole heart. ❖ [The Lord] loves the one who pursues righteousness. ❖ He rewards those who earnestly seek him.

JOHN 3:4–5 NKJV; ISA. 55:6 NASB; 2 CHRON. 15:2 RSV; ACTS 17:26–27 THE MESSAGE; 2 CHRON. 15:4 NIV; LUKE 10:39 RSV; PS. 105:3–4 NKJV; PS. 119:2; PROV. 15:9 NRSV; HEB. 11:6 NIV

Let me seek Thee in longing; let me long for Thee in seeking; let me find Thee in love, and love Thee in finding.

ST. ANSELM

Knowing and loving God and becoming like him is the object of it all.

RONALD E. WILSON

To have found God and still to pursue Him is the soul's paradox of love. . . .

A. W. TOZER

What is the object of my life?
Am I pursuing God or am I content with what I have found?

NEVER CHANGING

Behold, God is great, and we do not know Him; nor can the number of His years be discovered. ❖ The LORD is the true God, he is the living God, and an everlasting king. ❖ The LORD is King for ever and ever. ❖ His dominion will be forever. ❖ Ever since the creation of the world his invisible nature, namely, his eternal power and deity, has been clearly perceived in the things that have been made. So they are without excuse. ❖ His ways are eternal. ❖ The Glory of Israel will not lie or change His mind. ❖ I am the LORD, I change not. ❖ The eternal God is your refuge, and underneath are the everlasting arms. ❖ Lord, you have been our dwelling place in all generations. Before the mountains were brought forth, or ever you had formed the earth and the world, from everlasting to everlasting you are God. ❖ Trust in the Lord God always, for in the Lord Jehovah is your everlasting strength. ❖ Jesus Christ the same yesterday, and to day, and for ever.

JOB 36:26 NKJV; JER. 10:10; PS. 10:16; DAN. 6:26 NASB; ROM. 1:20 RSV; HAB. 3:6 NIV; 1 SAM. 15:29 NASB; MAL. 3:6; DEUT. 33:27 NKJV; PS. 90:1–2 NRSV; ISA. 26:4 TLB; HEB. 13:8

In Exod. 19 on Mount Sinai God came in fire and smoke, making the mountain tremble violently, and a loud, long trumpet blast was heard. In Luke 15 God is the loving, compassionate, and forgiving father who runs out to meet his rebellious but now repentant son.

MMS

Because God is immutable He always acts like Himself, and because He is a unity He never suspends one of His attributes in order to exercise another.

A. W. TOZER

> I praise you Alpha and Omega,
> God at the beginning
> God at the end
> Always God.
>
> MMS

Eternal God, I worship you.

TRANSFORMED BY HIS SPIRIT

I pray that, according to the riches of his glory, he may grant that you may be strengthened in your inner being with power through his Spirit, and that Christ may dwell in your hearts through faith, as you are being rooted and grounded in love. ❖ That you may be filled with all the fullness of God. ❖ In Him you have been made complete, and He is the head over all rule and authority. ❖ Since Christ lives within you, even though your body will die because of sin, your spirit is alive because you have been made right with God. The Spirit of God, who raised Jesus from the dead, lives in you. And just as he raised Christ from the dead, he will give life to your mortal body by this same Spirit living within you. ❖ The Spirit of the LORD will come upon you in power . . . and you will be changed into a different person. ❖ For from the very beginning God decided that those who came to him—and all along he knew who would—should become like his Son.❖ But we all, with unveiled face, beholding as in a mirror the glory of the Lord, are being transformed into the same image from glory to glory, just as by the Spirit of the Lord. ❖ Our Lord Jesus Christ has power over everything, and he will make these poor bodies of ours like his own glorious body. ❖ We shall also bear the image of the heavenly.

EPH. 3:16–17 NRSV; EPH. 3:19 NKJV; COL. 2:10 NASB; ROM. 8:10–11 NLT; 1 SAM. 10:6 NIV; ROM. 8:29 TLB; 2 COR. 3:18 NKJV; PHIL. 3:20–21 CEV; 1 COR. 15:49

The maturity of a Christian experience cannot be reached in a moment, but is the result of the work of God's Holy Spirit, who, by His energizing and transforming power, causes us to grow up into Christ in all things.

HANNAH WHITALL SMITH

How silently and how mysteriously He works within us! In unexpected and spontaneous ways, He works out God's perfect and profound will.

CHARLES R. SWINDOLL

Am I willing to let him have his way in me?
Help me to live close to your Spirit, filled with your Spirit, led by your Spirit, obedient to your Spirit.

WE ADORE YOU

Sing to the LORD, bless His name; proclaim the good news of His salvation from day to day. ❖ The LORD reigns, let the earth be glad; let the distant shores rejoice. ❖ Moses made haste to bow low toward the earth and worship. ❖ All created beings in heaven and on earth . . . will bow in worship before this Jesus Christ, and call out in praise that he is the Master of all, to the glorious honor of God the Father. ❖ Worship the LORD in all his holy splendor. Let all the earth tremble before him. ❖ Worship only the Lord God. Obey only him. ❖ For the LORD is great, and greatly to be praised: he is to be feared above all gods. ❖ Lord, who will not fear and glorify your name? For you alone are holy. All nations will come and worship before you, for your judgments have been revealed. ❖ Our LORD, no other gods compare with you—Majestic and holy! Fearsome and glorious! Miracle worker! ❖ There is no God like you.

Ps. 96:2 NKJV; Ps. 97:1 NIV; Exod. 34:8 NASB; Phil. 2:10–11 THE MESSAGE; Ps. 96:9 NLT; Matt. 4:10 TLB; Ps. 96:4; Rev. 15:4 NRSV; Exod. 15:11 CEV; 2 Chron. 6:14 NIV

Whatever the cost to us in loss of friends or goods or length of days let us know Thee as Thou art, that we may adore Thee as we should.

A. W. TOZER

It may take a lifetime to learn to focus on God, to pull our gaze off the world, ourselves, our goals, and fully gaze on him and worship him.

MMS

O come let us adore him.

What would it take for me to bow in true worship and adoration before God? Am I trifling with the God of the universe?

PRAISE THE LORD!

Sing unto the LORD a new song, and his praise from the end of the earth. ❖ Glory in His holy name; let the hearts of those rejoice who seek the LORD! ❖ This will be written for the generation to come, that a people yet to be created may praise the LORD. ❖ Then we your people, the sheep of your pasture, will thank you forever and forever, praising your greatness from generation to generation. ❖ For this is what the high and lofty One says—he who lives forever, whose name is holy: "I live in a high and holy place, but also with him who is contrite and lowly in spirit." ❖ You who fear the LORD, praise Him; all you descendants of Jacob, glorify Him, and stand in awe of Him, all you descendants of Israel. ❖ Worship the LORD with reverence, and rejoice with trembling. ❖ Let me live that I may praise you. ❖ Let us be thankful and please God by worshiping him with holy fear and awe. For our God is a consuming fire. ❖ Now unto the King eternal, immortal, invisible, the only wise God, be honour and glory for ever and ever. Amen.

ISA. 42:10; PS. 105:3 NKJV; PS. 102:18 NKJV; PS. 79:13 TLB; ISA. 57:15 NIV; PS. 22:23 NASB; PS. 2:11 NASB; PS. 119:175 NRSV; HEB. 12:28–29 NLT; 1 TIM. 1:17

God's terrible grandeur is matched by his gracious nearness.
RAYMOND C. ORTLUND

The glory of God is not that of a despotic eastern tyrant, but the splendour of love before which we fall not in abject terror but lost in wonder, love and praise.
WILLIAM BARCLAY

Change my mind and heart, Lord, that I may live to praise you.
Fill me with your fullness, Lord.

MY LOVING GOD

Blessed is the nation whose God is the LORD, the people He has chosen as His own inheritance. ❖ But you will rejoice in the LORD, you will glory in the Holy One of Israel. ❖ And the LORD said to Moses, "I will do the very thing you have asked, because I am pleased with you and I know you by name." ❖ Fear not, for I have redeemed you; I have called you by your name; you are Mine. When you pass through the waters, I will be with you; and through the rivers, they shall not overflow you. . . . For I am the LORD your God, the Holy One of Israel, your Savior. ❖ He made my feet like the feet of a deer, and set me secure on the heights. ❖ You are my friend, and you are my fortress where I am safe. You are my shield. . . . Why do we humans mean anything to you, our LORD? Why do you care about us? ❖ I bring you good tidings of great joy, which shall be to all people. For unto you is born this day in the city of David a Saviour, which is Christ the Lord. ❖ [Christ] is the divine Yes—God's affirmation. For all of God's promises have been fulfilled in him.

PS. 33:12 NKJV; ISA. 41:16 NASB; EXOD. 33:17 NIV; ISA. 43:1–3 NKJV;
PS. 18:33 NRSV; PS. 144:2–3 CEV; LUKE 2:10–11; 2 COR. 1:19–20 NLT

God is round about us in Christ on every hand, with His many-sided and all-sufficient grace. All we need to do is to open our hearts.

O. HALLESBY

I love you, Lord, not doubtingly, but with absolute certainty. Your Word beat upon my heart until I fell in love with you, and now the universe and everything in it tells me to love you, and tells the same thing to us all, so that we are without excuse.

AUGUSTINE

Is there a choice, an option? How can I choose other than to love him with all that I am?

Am I finally convinced that my greatest blessing, my greatest joy is in trusting him?

GOD'S TRUE WORD

The judgments of the LORD are true and righteous altogether. ❖ For the word of the LORD is right; and all his works are done in truth. ❖ The entirety of Your word is truth, and every one of Your righteous judgments endures forever. ❖ Every word of God proves true. ❖ For whatever was written in earlier times was written for our instruction, that through perseverance and the encouragement of the Scriptures we might have hope. ❖ Remember that Christ came as a servant to the Jews to show that God is true to the promises he made to their ancestors. And he came so the Gentiles might also give glory to God for his mercies to them. ❖ For in him every one of God's promises is a "Yes." For this reason it is through him that we say the "Amen," to the glory of God. ❖ [Jesus] closed the book and handed it back to the attendant and sat down, while everyone in the synagogue gazed at him intently. Then he added, "These Scriptures came true today!" ❖ They believed the scripture, and the word which Jesus had said. ❖ They must keep hold of the deep truths of the faith with a clear conscience. ❖ Sanctify them by Your truth. Your word is truth.

Ps. 19:9; Ps. 33:4; Ps. 119:160 NKJV; PROV. 30:5 RSV; ROM. 15:4 NASB; ROM. 15:8–9 NLT; 2 COR. 1:20 NRSV; LUKE 4:20–21 TLB; JOHN 2:22; 1 TIM. 3:9 NIV; JOHN 17:17 NKJV

The Bible is not a guidebook to a theological museum. It is a road map showing us the way into neglected or even forgotten glories of the living God.

RAYMOND C. ORTLUND

But the foundation of Christian faith [is not in the church or even in the Bible] but the living God himself and his Word that is both ever new and ever the same.

DONALD G. BLOESCH

I thank you for your Word, Almighty God. It is truth and it is life.
Do I believe your Word? Do I trust it to guide me all my days?

THE AUTHORITY OF GOD'S WORD

The secret things belong to the LORD our God, but those things which are revealed belong to us and to our children forever, that we may do all the words of this law. ❖ But know this first of all, that no prophecy of Scripture is a matter of one's own interpretation, for no prophecy was ever made by an act of human will, but men moved by the Holy Spirit spoke from God. ❖ When you received the word of God which you heard from us, you accepted it not as the word of men but as what it really is, the word of God, which is at work in you believers. ❖ God's commission . . . was given to me for you, to make the word of God fully known, the mystery that has been hidden throughout the ages and generations but has now been revealed to his saints. ❖ The grass withers, and its flower falls away, but the word of the LORD endures forever. ❖ I assure you, until heaven and earth disappear, even the smallest detail of God's law will remain until its purpose is achieved.

DEUT. 29:29 NKJV; 2 PETER 1:20–21 NASB; 1 THESS. 2:13 RSV; COL. 1:25–26 NRSV; 1 PETER 1:24–25 NKJV; MATT. 5:18 NLT

We don't have loose-leaf Bibles. We can't just open the binding and take out what we don't want to do or believe.

ROBERT SUGGS

The Bible is the Law-Word of the Sovereign King, not merely the advice of a good friend. It reveals the extent of God's sovereignty and the required response of man.

R. C. SPROUL

Am I willing to rest my whole weight on the authority of God's Word? Help me, Lord, to take all of your Word seriously, to take it to heart.

HIS WORD IS TRUSTWORTHY

He must hold firmly to the trustworthy message as it has been taught, so that he can encourage others by sound doctrine and refute those who oppose it. ❖ For the commandment is a lamp; and the law is light. ❖ Your word is a lamp to my feet and a light to my path. ❖ Moses brought our people together in the desert, and the angel spoke to him on Mount Sinai. There he was given these life-giving words to pass on to us. ❖ When Moses had finished speaking all these words to all Israel, he said to them, "Take to your heart all the words with which I am warning you today, which you shall command your sons to observe carefully, even all the words of this law. For it is not an idle word for you; indeed it is your life." ❖ The words of the LORD are pure words: as silver tried in a furnace of earth, purified seven times. ❖ All his precepts are trustworthy. ❖ Your testimonies, which You have commanded, are righteous and very faithful. ❖ These words are faithful and true.

TITUS 1:9 NIV; PROV. 6:23; PS. 119:105 NKJV; ACTS 7:38 CEV; DEUT. 32:45–47 NASB; PS. 12:6; PS. 111:7 RSV; PS. 119:138 NKJV; REV. 22:6 NKJV

True success is promised to those who meditate on God's Word, who think deeply on Scripture, not just at one time each day, but at moments throughout the day and night. They meditate so much that Scripture saturates their conversation.

DONALD S. WHITNEY

The reason many of us do not ardently believe in the gospel is that we have never given it a rigorous testing, thrown our hard questions at it, faced it with our most prickly doubts.

EUGENE H. PETERSON

Give me understanding, dear Lord. I long to know and abide by your truth. Help me to commit myself to serious study of your Word.

STUDY GOD'S WORD

This book of the law shall not depart out of your mouth, but you shall meditate on it day and night, that you may be careful to do according to all that is written in it; for then you shall make your way prosperous, and then you shall have good success. ❖ God gave his Law to Jacob's descendants, the people of Israel. And he told our ancestors to teach their children, so that each new generation would know his Law and tell it to the next. Then they would trust God and obey his teachings, without forgetting anything God had done. ❖ And these words which I command you today shall be in your heart. You shall teach them diligently to your children, and shall talk of them when you sit in your house, when you walk by the way, when you lie down, and when you rise up. . . . You shall write them on the doorposts of your house and on your gates. ❖ People need more than bread for their life; they must feed on every word of God. ❖ Blessed is he who reads and those who hear the words of this prophecy, and keep those things which are written in it; for the time is near.

JOSH. 1:8 RSV; PS. 78:5–7 CEV; DEUT. 6:6–7, 9 NKJV; MATT. 4:4 NLT; REV. 1:3 NKJV

Regardless of how busy we become with all things Christian, we must remember that the most transforming practice available to us is the disciplined intake of Scripture.

DONALD S. WHITNEY

Those who know the Word of God are those who have his teaching in their hearts.

DONALD G. BLOESCH

The purpose of a prayerful study of God's Word is to get to know and to possess God himself.

JAMES MONTGOMERY BOICE

What priority do I give to studying the Word of God?
Is it part of me, impacting all that I do and say?

DISCIPLINED STUDY

Read and explain the Scriptures to the church. ❖ All the people were attentive to the book of the law. ❖ And all the people went their way to . . . rejoice greatly, because they understood the words that were declared to them. ❖ Day by day, from the first day until the last day, [Ezra] read from the Book of the Law of God. ❖ They stood where they were and read from the Book of the Law of the LORD their God for a quarter of the day, and spent another quarter in confession and in worshiping the LORD their God. ❖ For Ezra had prepared his heart to seek the law of the LORD, and to do it, and to teach in Israel statutes and judgments. ❖ [The Bereans] gladly accepted the message. Day after day they studied the Scriptures to see if these things were true. ❖ I will delight myself in Your statutes; I will not forget Your word. ❖ I have treasured in my bosom the words of his mouth. ❖ For I delight in the law of God in my inmost self. ❖ The Law of the LORD makes them happy, and they think about it day and night.

1 TIM. 4:13 TLB; NEH. 8:3 NASB; NEH. 8:12 NKJV; NEH. 8:18 NKJV; NEH. 9:3 NIV; EZRA 7:10; ACTS 17:11 CEV; PS. 119:16 NKJV; JOB 23:12 RSV; ROM. 7:22 NRSV; PS. 1:2 CEV

Here, then, is the real problem of our negligence. We fail in our duty to study God's Word not so much because it is difficult to understand, not so much because it is dull and boring, but because it is work. Our problem is not a lack of intelligence or a lack of passion. Our problem is that we are lazy.

R. C. SPROUL

A man can no more take in a supply of grace for the future than he can eat enough for the next six months, or take sufficient air into his lungs at one time to sustain life for a week. We must draw upon God's boundless store of grace from day to day as we need it.

D. L. MOODY

Am I disciplined in my study of God's Word or do I neglect it because it is work?

Help me realize, O God, that I need to hear your Word, I need to read your Word, I need to study your Word, and I need to allow your Word to become part of me.

THE POWER OF THE WORD

The sacred writings . . . are able to instruct you for salvation through faith in Christ Jesus. All scripture is inspired by God and is useful for teaching, for reproof, for correction, and for training in righteousness, so that everyone who belongs to God may be proficient, equipped for every good work. ❖ You have been born again not of seed which is perishable but imperishable, that is, through the living and abiding word of God. ❖ For the word of God is full of living power. It is sharper than the sharpest knife, cutting deep into our innermost thoughts and desires. It exposes us for what we really are. ❖ Now to Him who is able to establish you according to my gospel and the preaching of Jesus Christ, according to the revelation of the mystery kept secret since the world began but now has been made manifest, and by the prophetic Scriptures has been made known to all nations, according to the commandment of the everlasting God, for obedience to the faith—to God, alone wise, be glory through Jesus Christ forever. Amen.

2 TIM. 3:15–17 NRSV; 1 PETER 1:23 NASB; HEB. 4:12 NLT; ROM. 16:25–27 NKJV

The instrument of our sanctification is the Word of God. The Spirit of God brings to our minds the precepts and doctrines of truth, and applies them with power. . . . The truth is our sanctifier. If we do not hear or read it, we will not grow in sanctification.

CHARLES HADDON SPURGEON

[Scripture's] worthiness as a theological guide and norm does not become clear until it is acclaimed as the sword of the Spirit (Eph. 6:17), the divinely chosen instrument by which the powers of sin and death are overthrown in the lives of those who believe.

DONALD G. BLOESCH

Does the Word have power in my life?
Have I felt it entering my heart like a sword? Have I been taught and corrected by it?

YOUR WORD WITHIN

I will give them one heart, and I will put a new spirit within you . . . that they may walk in my statutes, and keep mine ordinances, and do them: and they shall be my people, and I will be their God. ❖ All the people wept, when they heard the words of the law. ❖ "Does not my word burn like fire?" asks the LORD. "Is it not like a mighty hammer that smashes rock to pieces?" ❖ The law of the LORD is perfect, restoring the soul. ❖ God's laws are perfect. They protect us, make us wise, and give us joy and light. ❖ The words that I speak to you are spirit, and they are life. ❖ I will take pleasure in your laws and remember your words. ❖ If you abide in me, and my words abide in you, ask whatever you will, and it shall be done for you. ❖ You shine as lights in the world, holding fast the word of life. ❖ We speak of these things in words not taught by human wisdom but taught by the Spirit, interpreting spiritual things to those who are spiritual. ❖ He opened their understanding, that they might comprehend the Scriptures.

EZEK. 11:19–20; NEH. 8:9; JER. 23:29 NLT; PS. 19:7 NASB; PS. 19:8 TLB; JOHN 6:63 NKJV; PS. 119:16 CEV; JOHN 15:7 RSV; PHIL. 2:15–16 NKJV; 1 COR. 2:13 NRSV; LUKE 24:45 NKJV

Interpretations of the Word of God can be handed down by the church from one generation to another, but none of us can actually know the Word of God until God personally reveals himself to us. When God speaks we will know it, for his word is "living and active, sharper than any two-edged sword" (Heb. 4:12).

DONALD G. BLOESCH

Let the Bible have proper place; and grant that as I read I may be alive to the stirrings of the Holy Spirit in my soul.

JOHN BAILLIE

Does your Word touch me, does it move me, does it burn me? When I read it, does my heart know that it is from you?
May your Word be my teacher, my guide. May it lead me into truth and life.

A PRECIOUS GIFT

You, Lord, are good, and ready to forgive, and abundant in mercy to all those who call upon You. Give ear, O LORD, to my prayer; and attend to the voice of my supplications. ❖ We don't even know what we should pray for, nor how we should pray. But the Holy Spirit prays for us with groanings that cannot be expressed in words. And the Father who knows all hearts knows what the Spirit is saying, for the Spirit pleads for us believers in harmony with God's own will. ❖ With all prayer and petition pray at all times in the Spirit. ❖ Call upon Me in the day of trouble; I will deliver you. ❖ Then you will call upon me and come and pray to me, and I will hear you. ❖ Watch and pray, that ye enter not into temptation. ❖ Be anxious for nothing, but in everything by prayer and supplication, with thanksgiving, let your requests be made known to God. ❖ God's there, listening for all who pray, for all who pray and mean it. He does what's best for those who fear him—hears them call out, and saves them.

Ps. 86:5–6 NKJV; Rom. 8:26–27 NLT; Eph. 6:18 NASB; Ps. 50:15 NKJV; Jer. 29:12 RSV; Matt. 26:41; Phil. 4:6–7 NKJV; Ps. 145:18–19 THE MESSAGE

True prayer is not in the time, in the will, or in the power of the person praying. Rather, it is a gift of God that resides in his Spirit. It is not ours, but it is given to us. Therefore, it is ours to wait upon the Spirit, to wait for the Spirit to move and breathe in us, and to give us the ability to call upon the Father and give us the power of prevailing with the Father, in the name and through the life of the Son.

ISAAC PENINGTON

I bless Thee, O most holy God . . . that I, a weak and erring mortal, should have this ready access to the heart of Him who moves the stars.

JOHN BAILLIE

When I pray, you, Creator of the universe, listen to me. When I am crushed and don't know what to say, your Holy Spirit says it for me. When I need help, you, Almighty One, meet my need. What could be more wonderful than this?

AN EXPRESSION OF WORSHIP

She never left the temple, serving night and day with fastings and prayers. ❖ [Solomon] stood on the platform before the entire assembly, and then he knelt down and lifted his hands toward heaven. He prayed, "O LORD, God of Israel, there is no God like you in all of heaven and earth. You keep your promises and show unfailing love to all who obey you and are eager to do your will." ❖ Lift up your hands in the sanctuary, and bless the LORD. ❖ O come, let us worship and bow down: let us kneel before the LORD our maker. ❖ The prayer of the upright is His delight. ❖ The four living creatures and the twenty-four elders fell down before the Lamb, each holding a harp, and with golden bowls full of incense, which are the prayers of the saints. ❖ And when the time for the burning of incense came, all the assembled worshipers were praying outside. ❖ Let my prayer be set before You as incense, the lifting up of my hands as the evening sacrifice. ❖ I will bless you as long as I live, lifting up my hands to you in prayer.

LUKE 2:37 NASB; 2 CHRON. 6:13–14 NLT; PS. 134:2; PS. 95:6; PROV. 15:8 NKJV; REV. 5:8 RSV; LUKE 1:10 NIV; PS. 141:2 NKJV; PS. 63:4 TLB

We must pray not first of all because it feels good or helps, but because God loves us and wants our attention.

HENRI J. M. NOUWEN

God has designed prayer as a means of intimate and joyous fellowship between God and man.

O. HALLESBY

Have I thought that prayer was just a way of having my needs met?
Have I realized that God desires my coming to him in prayer, that he desires fellowship with me?

CONFORMED TO HIS WILL

I bring you the Good News and offer you up as a fragrant sacrifice to God so that you might be pure and pleasing to him by the Holy Spirit. ❖ It is God's will that you should be sanctified. ❖ Truly, I say to you, unless you turn and become like children, you will never enter the kingdom of heaven. Whoever humbles himself like this child, he is the greatest in the kingdom of heaven. ❖ Amend your ways and your deeds. ❖ Turn to Me with all your heart, with fasting, with weeping, and with mourning. ❖ They will return to the LORD, and he will listen to their supplications and heal them. ❖ Create in me a clean heart, O God; and renew a right spirit within me. ❖ He cleansed their lives through faith. ❖ For we who live are always delivered to death for Jesus' sake, that the life of Jesus also may be manifested in our mortal flesh. ❖ Though our outer nature is wasting away, our inner nature is being renewed day by day.

ROM. 15:16 NLT; 1 THESS. 4:3 NIV; MATT. 18:3–4 RSV; JER. 7:3 NASB; JOEL 2:12 NKJV; ISA. 19:22 NRSV; PS. 51:10; ACTS 15:9 TLB; 2 COR. 4:11 NKJV; 2 COR. 4:16 NRSV

Most think of prayer as necessary simply to petition God to make his will known. But while prayer is important in this respect, its primary purpose in guidance would not be for gaining a knowledge of God's will but rather for gaining the willingness to do it.

M. BLAINE SMITH

Prayer is not a question of altering things externally, but of working wonders in a man's disposition. When you pray, things remain the same, but you begin to be different.

OSWALD CHAMBERS

In my heart I desire to be like you, O God.
Am I being renewed in his image day by day?

THE PRAYER OF THE HUMBLE

He went a little farther and fell on His face, and prayed, saying, "O My Father, if it is possible, let this cup pass from Me; nevertheless, not as I will, but as You will." ❖ Jesus said to them, "My food is to do the will of Him who sent Me, and to accomplish His work." ❖ I seek not my own will but the will of him who sent me. ❖ Humble yourselves in the sight of the Lord, and he shall lift you up. ❖ I am not worthy of the least of all the steadfast love and all the faithfulness that you have shown to your servant, for with only my staff I crossed this Jordan; and now I have become two companies. ❖ May I never boast except in the cross of our Lord Jesus Christ, through which the world has been crucified to me, and I to the world. ❖ I will worship toward Your holy temple, and praise Your name for Your lovingkindness and Your truth; for You have magnified Your word above all Your name. In the day when I cried out, You answered me, and made me bold with strength in my soul.

MATT. 26:39 NKJV; JOHN 4:34 NASB; JOHN 5:30 RSV; JAMES 4:10; GEN. 32:10 NRSV; GAL. 6:14 NIV; PS. 138:2–3 NKJV

It is *through prayer* that Jesus successfully overcomes the dichotomy between his will and God's. And how he prays is most significant. He begins by confessing his true desires to God: "My father, if it is possible, let this cup pass from me." . . . In effect, by praying in this way Jesus was asking God to grant him the willingness to yield to the Father's will above his own. The essence of Jesus' prayer, then, was "God, grant me the strength to do your will."

M. BLAINE SMITH

Even with finite human minds we are enabled to pray in accord with the will of God, because the Spirit takes humble, obedient prayer to God and conforms it to God's will.

BRYAN CHAPELL

I praise you, Lord Jesus, for your example of humility. Help me to follow you. I praise you, Holy Spirit, for making my prayer acceptable.

PRAYERS OF A HUMBLE HEART

And when you pray, you shall not be like the hypocrites. For they love to pray standing in the synagogues and on the corners of the streets, that they may be seen by men. Assuredly, I say to you, they have their reward. But you, when you pray, go into your room, and when you have shut your door, pray to your Father who is in the secret place; and your Father who sees in secret will reward you openly. ❖ Do not be hasty in word or impulsive in thought to bring up a matter in the presence of God. For God is in heaven and you are on the earth; therefore let your words be few. ❖ When you pray, don't babble on and on as people of other religions do. They think their prayers are answered only by repeating their words again and again. Don't be like them, because your Father knows exactly what you need even before you ask him! ❖ So we fasted and petitioned our God for this, and he listened to our entreaty. ❖ And when they had appointed elders for them in every church, with prayer and fasting they committed them to the Lord in whom they believed. ❖ If my people will humble themselves and pray, and search for me, and turn from their wicked ways, I will hear them from heaven and forgive their sins and heal their land.

MATT. 6:5–6 NKJV; ECCLES. 5:2 NASB; MATT. 6:7–8 NLT; EZRA 8:23 NRSV; ACTS 14:23 RSV; 2 CHRON. 7:14 TLB

In all petitional prayer, the one who really prays must be ready to yield.

DOUGLAS V. STEERE

When we humbly confess the limitations of our vision while obediently offering the desires of our hearts, the Holy Spirit molds our prayers into petitions that please God and satisfy our deepest needs.

BRYAN CHAPELL

I praise you, Lord, that I can come before you in prayer with the confidence that you will hear me. Teach me, though, to come before you humbly, with an attitude of submission, of yielding.

UNHINDERED PRAYER

Hear the plea of your servant and of your people Israel, when they pray toward this place; may you hear from heaven your dwelling place; hear and forgive. ❖ The tax-gatherer, standing some distance away, was even unwilling to lift up his eyes to heaven, but was beating his breast, saying, "God, be merciful to me, the sinner!" ❖ Beloved, if our heart does not condemn us, we have confidence toward God. And whatever we ask we receive from Him, because we keep His commandments and do those things that are pleasing in His sight. And this is His commandment: that we should believe on the name of His Son Jesus Christ and love one another. ❖ Love your enemies, bless them that curse you. ❖ Husbands, . . . be considerate as you live with your wives, and treat them with respect . . . so that nothing will hinder your prayers. ❖ The prayer of a person living right with God is something powerful to be reckoned with. Elijah, for instance, human just like us, prayed hard that it wouldn't rain, and it didn't—not a drop for three and a half years. Then he prayed that it would rain, and it did. The showers came and everything started growing again. ❖ The LORD . . . hears the prayer of the righteous.

2 CHRON. 6:21 NRSV; LUKE 18:13 NASB; 1 JOHN 3:21–23 NKJV; MATT. 5:44;
1 PETER 3:7 NIV; JAMES 5:16–18 THE MESSAGE; PROV. 15:29 RSV

Prayer is . . . a condition of mind, an attitude of heart, which God recognizes as prayer whether it manifests itself in quiet thinking, in sighing or in audible words.
O. HALLESBY

For why do men lift their hands when they pray? Is it not that their hearts may be raised at the same time to God?
JOHN CALVIN

Does God hear my prayers?
Dear Lord Jesus, I come to you, asking you to reveal anything in me that separates us, any sin that hinders my prayer.

ANSWERS TO PRAYER

Whatever you ask in My name, that I will do, that the Father may be glorified in the Son. If you ask anything in My name, I will do it. ❖ Call to Me, and I will answer you. ❖ Before they call, I will answer; and while they are yet speaking, I will hear. ❖ It is for you, O LORD, that I wait; it is you, O Lord my God, who will answer. ❖ From inside the fish, Jonah prayed to the LORD his God: When I was in trouble, LORD, I prayed to you, and you listened to me. From deep in the world of the dead, I begged for your help, and you answered my prayer. ❖ As soon as he hears, he will answer you. ❖ I love the LORD, because he has heard my voice and my supplications. Because he inclined his ear to me, therefore I will call on him as long as I live. ❖ I am the LORD their God and I will answer them. ❖ The righteous cry out, and the LORD hears, and delivers them out of all their troubles.

JOHN 14:13–14 NKJV; JER. 33:3 NASB; ISA. 65:24; PS. 38:15 NRSV; JON. 2:1–2 CEV; ISA. 30:19 NIV; PS. 116:1–2 NRSV; ZECH. 10:6 RSV; PS. 34:17 NKJV

In times of decision making, people often seek God in ways they have not before. But they want to obtain from God a red or green light—a quick vending-machine answer—when God is out to nurture us and form our character. We want God to give us an answer : "Go" or "Stay." But we're more likely to hear *how* we should go or stay—with compassion or integrity in thoughts and actions.

JAN JOHNSON

If God doesn't seem to be giving you what you ask, maybe he's giving you something else.

FREDERICK BUECHNER

Do I pray with the expectation that God hears and will answer me?
Do I recognize his answers when they come?

PART OF EVERY DAY

He Himself often withdrew into the wilderness and prayed. ❖ And when he had sent them away, he departed into a mountain to pray. ❖ He took Peter and John and James, and went up into a mountain to pray. ❖ And he told them a parable, to the effect that they ought always to pray and not lose heart. ❖ Pray without ceasing. ❖ Devote yourselves to prayer, keeping alert in it with an attitude of thanksgiving. ❖ Be earnest and disciplined in your prayers. ❖ Be patient in trouble, and prayerful always. ❖ By common consent all these men, together with the women who had followed Jesus, Mary his mother, as well as his brothers, devoted themselves to prayer. ❖ And they continued stedfastly in the apostles' doctrine and fellowship, and in breaking of bread, and in prayers. ❖ We will give ourselves continually to prayer, and to the ministry of the word. ❖ There on the beach we knelt to pray.

LUKE 5:16 NKJV; MARK 6:46; LUKE 9:28; LUKE 18:1 RSV; 1 THESS. 5:17; COL. 4:2 NASB; 1 PETER 4:7 NLT; ROM. 12:12 TLB; ACTS 1:14 PHILLIPS; ACTS 2:42; ACTS 6:4; ACTS 21:5 NIV

The only way to pray is to pray; and the way to pray well is to pray much. If one has no time for this, then one must at least pray regularly. But the less one prays, the worse it goes. And if circumstances do not permit even regularity, then one must put up with the fact that when one does try to pray, one can't pray—and our prayer will probably consist of telling this to God.

HENRI J. M. NOUWEN

The scope of prayer is as wide as the world and as full as the hours in our day. God wants us to bombard the heavenlies with our prayers.

TONY EVANS

Is my life full of prayer or do I find it hard to fit prayer into my busy schedule? Do I daily see answers to my prayers?

MY FIRST AND LAST THOUGHT

In the morning, a great while before day, he rose and went out to a lonely place, and there he prayed. ❖ In the morning, O LORD, you hear my voice; in the morning I lay my requests before you and wait in expectation. ❖ Morning by morning he wakens me and opens my understanding to his will. The Sovereign LORD has spoken to me, and I have listened. ❖ I give myself to prayer. ❖ The LORD will command His lovingkindness in the daytime; and His song will be with me in the night, a prayer to the God of my life. ❖ When I remember You on my bed, I meditate on You in the night watches. Because You have been my help, therefore in the shadow of Your wings I will rejoice. ❖ [Jesus] went out into a mountain to pray, and continued all night in prayer to God. ❖ I can lie down and sleep soundly because you, LORD, will keep me safe.

MARK 1:35 RSV; PS. 5:3 NIV; ISA. 50:4–5 NLT; PS. 109:4 NKJV; PS. 42:8 NASB;
PS. 63:6–7 NKJV; LUKE 6:12; PS. 4:8 CEV

There is a way of ordering our mental life on more than one level at once. On one level we may be thinking, discussing, seeing, calculating, meeting all the demands of external affairs. But deep within, behind the scenes, at a profounder level, we may also be in prayer and adoration, song and worship and a gentle receptiveness to divine breathings. . . . Walk and talk and work and laugh with your friends. But behind the scenes, keep up the life of simple prayer and inward worship. Let inward prayer be your last act before you fall asleep and the first act when you awake.

THOMAS KELLY

Eternal Father of my soul, let my first thought today be of Thee, let my first impulse be to worship Thee, let my first speech be Thy name, let my first action be to kneel before Thee in prayer.

JOHN BAILLIE

How often, O Lord, have I determined that I will think of you through the day and find at the end of the day that you were little on my mind? Draw my thoughts to you, my God. Make my mind restless until it focuses on you. Give my heart a longing that only communion with you can satisfy.

THE PRAYER OF THE HELPLESS

I cry aloud to God. ❖ I cry out with my whole heart; hear me, O LORD! ❖ Listen to my cry for help, my King and my God, for to you I pray. ❖ Please listen to my prayer and my cry for help, as I lift my hands toward your holy temple. ❖ The real widow, left alone, has set her hope on God and continues in supplications and prayers night and day. ❖ Out of the depths I cry to you, O LORD. Lord, hear my voice! Let your ears be attentive to the voice of my supplications! ❖ Now this is the confidence that we have in Him, that if we ask anything according to His will, He hears us. And if we know that He hears us, whatever we ask, we know that we have the petitions that we have asked of Him. ❖ They shall call on my name, and I will hear them. ❖ And in the time of their trouble, when they cried to You, You heard from heaven; and according to Your abundant mercies You gave them deliverers who saved them from the hand of their enemies. ❖ Go back to Hezekiah, the leader of my people, and tell him that the Lord God of his ancestor David has heard his prayer and seen his tears. I will heal him. ❖ Ask, and you will receive, that your joy may be made full.

PS. 77:1 RSV; PS. 119:145 NKJV; PS. 5:2 NIV; PS. 28:2 CEV; 1 TIM. 5:5 NRSV; PS. 130:1–2 NRSV; 1 JOHN 5:14–15 NKJV; ZECH. 13:9; NEH. 9:27 NKJV; 2 KINGS 20:5 TLB; JOHN 16:24 NASB

Prayer and helplessness are inseparable. Only he who is helpless can truly pray.
O. HALLESBY

I have so much to do today, I'll need an extra hour of prayer just to prepare.
MARTIN LUTHER

Do I feel helpless enough to pray?
Do I believe that he hears me and if he hears me, he will answer me?

MY PART

Call to Me, and I will answer you, and show you great and mighty things, which you do not know. ❖ The Spirit Himself bears witness with our spirit that we are children of God. ❖ Morning by morning he wakens me and opens my understanding to his will. ❖ Whether you turn to the right or to the left, your ears will hear a voice behind you, saying, "This is the way; walk in it." ❖ My sheep hear my voice, and I know them, and they follow me. ❖ We are the people of His pasture, and the sheep of His hand. Today, if you will hear His voice: Do not harden your hearts. ❖ Do whatever he tells you. ❖ He who has ears to hear, let him hear. ❖ Samuel said, "Speak, for your servant is listening." ❖ I was in the Spirit on the Lord's day, and heard behind me a great voice, as of a trumpet, saying, I am Alpha and Omega, the first and the last: and, What thou seest, write in a book. ❖ As it is written: "Eye has not seen, nor ear heard, nor have entered into the heart of man the things which God has prepared for those who love Him." But God has revealed them to us through His Spirit. ❖ Blessed are your eyes, for they see: and your ears, for they hear.

JER. 33:3 NKJV; ROM. 8:16 NASB; ISA. 50:4 NLT; ISA. 30:21 NIV; JOHN 10:27; PS. 95:7–8 NKJV; DEUT. 30:20 CEV; MATT. 11:15 RSV; 1 SAM. 3:10 NRSV; REV. 1:10–11; 1 COR. 2:9–10 NKJV; MATT. 13:16

The core of all prayer is indeed listening, obediently standing in the presence of God.

HENRI J. M. NOUWEN

Prayer is not getting God to conform to us. Prayer is conforming ourselves to God.

TONY EVANS

Indeed, wisdom and discernment are among the natural results of a prayer-filled life.

RICHARD FOSTER

In prayer, do I do all the talking? I must wait and listen to what God wants to say to me.

Do I recognize his voice? I must get to know him well enough that if he speaks to me, even after my prayer time is over, I will know it is him.

PRAYERS OF FAITH

If any of you is lacking in wisdom, ask God, who gives to all generously and ungrudgingly, and it will be given you. But ask in faith, never doubting. ❖ Jesus answered and said to them, "Have faith in God. . . . Therefore I say to you, whatever things you ask when you pray, believe that you receive them, and you will have them." ❖ And all things you ask in prayer, believing, you shall receive. ❖ One day Jesus told his disciples a story to illustrate their need for constant prayer and to show them that they must keep praying until the answer comes. ❖ I pray to GOD—my life a prayer—and wait for what he'll say and do. ❖ The LORD will hear when I call unto him. ❖ But truly God has listened; he has given heed to the voice of my prayer. ❖ I wait confidently for God to save me, and my God will certainly hear me. ❖ For the eyes of the Lord are on the righteous and his ears are attentive to their prayer.

JAMES 1:5–6 NRSV; MARK 11:22, 24 NKJV; MATT. 21:22 NASB; LUKE 18:1 TLB; PS. 130:5 THE MESSAGE; PS. 4:3; PS. 66:19 RSV; MICAH 7:7 NLT; 1 PETER 3:12 NIV

A prayer to God asked with whatever reservation in respect of consequences devolving upon the prayer's not being answered, cannot be called the prayer of faith.

JIM ELLIOT

The most difficult prayer, and the prayer which, therefore, costs us the most striving, is persevering prayer, the prayer which faints not, but continues steadfastly until the answer comes.

O. HALLESBY

Jesus teaches us to pray in faith and he also teaches us to persevere in prayer. Those two directives are not contradictions. If what we are praying for fits into God's will, we can pray in faith. It may not be time for the answer, though, so we must continue to pray until it comes. The continuing in prayer is not for God—he longs to give us what we want and need. It's for us. It helps us remember the importance of the need and it helps us trust that God is working until it is finally answered.

MMS

Am I willing to persevere in prayer, though I am impatient for the answer?

PRAYER FOR OTHERS

Then the priests the Levites arose and blessed the people: and their voice was heard, and their prayer came up to his holy dwelling place, even unto heaven. ❖ I urge . . . that requests, prayers, intercession and thanksgiving be made for everyone. ❖ Then after fasting and praying they laid their hands on them and sent them off. ❖ I do not cease to give thanks for you as I remember you in my prayers. ❖ We pray always for you. ❖ Without ceasing I make mention of you always in my prayers. ❖ We give thanks to God and the Father of our Lord Jesus Christ, praying always for you, since we heard of your faith in Christ Jesus, and of the love which ye have to all the saints. ❖ Stay alert and keep praying for God's people. Pray that I will be given the message to speak and that I may fearlessly explain the mystery about the good news. ❖ Pray for us also, that God may open to us a door for the word, to declare the mystery of Christ, on account of which I am in prison, that I may make it clear, as I ought to speak. ❖ We trust that He will still deliver us, you also helping together in prayer for us, that thanks may be given by many persons on our behalf for the gift granted to us through many.

2 CHRON. 30:27; 1 TIM. 2:1 NIV; ACTS 13:3 RSV; EPH. 1:16 NRSV; 2 THESS. 1:11; ROM. 1:9; COL. 1:3–4; EPH. 6:18–19 CEV; COL. 4:3–4 RSV; 2 COR. 1:10–11 NKJV

Intercessory prayer is hard work. It is hard to hold people in our hearts and then to take them to God in our praying hearts. . . . But consider what intercessory prayer does in our journey out of ourselves toward God and his purposes with other people.

R. PAUL STEVENS

Our lives should be, according to our Lord's plans, quiet but steadily flowing streams of blessing, which through our prayers and intercessions should reach our whole environment.

O. HALLESBY

Do I remember to pray for the needs of others? Do I hold them in my heart? Do I thank God for what he is doing in the lives of others and how he's using them for his glory?

POWER IN PRAYER

And being let go [from prison], they went to their own companions and reported all that the chief priests and elders had said to them. So when they heard that, they raised their voice to God with one accord and said: "Lord, You are God, who made heaven and earth. . . . For truly against Your holy Servant Jesus, whom You anointed, both Herod and Pontius Pilate, with the Gentiles and the people of Israel, were gathered together to do whatever Your hand and Your purpose determined before to be done. Now, Lord, look on their threats, and grant to Your servants that with all boldness they may speak Your word. . . ." And when they had prayed, the place where they were assembled together was shaken; and they were all filled with the Holy Spirit, and they spoke the word of God with boldness. ❖ [Hannah] prayed to the LORD and wept in anguish. . . ."O LORD of hosts, if You will indeed . . . remember me, and not forget Your maidservant, but will give Your maidservant a male child, then I will give him to the LORD all the days of his life." . . . So it came to pass in the process of time that Hannah conceived and bore a son, and called his name Samuel, saying, "Because I have asked for him from the LORD." ❖ The eyes of the Lord watch over those who do right, and his ears are open to their prayers. ❖ Then you will call, and the LORD will answer; you will cry, and He will say, "Here I am."

ACTS 4:23–31 NKJV; 1 SAM. 1:10–11, 20 NKJV; 1 PETER 3:12 NLT;
ISA. 58:9 NASB

The work of praying is prerequisite to all other work in the kingdom of God, for the simple reason that it is by prayer that we couple the powers of heaven to our helplessness, the powers which can turn water into wine and remove mountains in our own life and in the lives of others, the powers which can awaken those who sleep in sin and raise up the dead, the powers which can capture strongholds and make the impossible possible.

O. HALLESBY

When I come to God in prayer, do I really believe that he can do the impossible? that he will do it for me?

PAYING ATTENTION TO HIM

But you have God-blessed eyes—eyes that see! And God-blessed ears—ears that hear! ❖ Therefore everyone who hears these words of Mine, and acts upon them, may be compared to a wise man, who built his house upon the rock. ❖ Seek the counsel of the LORD. ❖ Seek the things that are above, where Christ is, seated at the right hand of God. Set your minds on things that are above, not on things that are on earth. ❖ Let the words of Christ, in all their richness, live in your hearts and make you wise. Use his words to teach and counsel each other. ❖ And the peace of God, which passes all understanding, will keep your hearts and your minds in Christ Jesus. ❖ Make use of the Light while there is still time; then you will become light bearers. ❖ Blessed is the man who trusts in the LORD, whose trust is the LORD. ❖ If you keep in mind what I have told you, the Lord will help you understand completely. ❖ You must never stop looking at the perfect law that sets you free. God will bless you in everything you do, if you listen and obey, and don't just hear and forget.

MATT. 13:16 THE MESSAGE; MATT. 7:24 NASB; 2 CHRON. 18:4 NIV; COL. 3:1–2 NRSV; COL. 3:16 NLT; PHIL. 4:7 RSV; JOHN 12:36 TLB; JER. 17:7 RSV; 2 TIM. 2:7 CEV; JAMES 1:25 CEV

Every time we hear the Word of God and refuse to respond, something happens to our hearing. A kind of deafness sets in, and we become progressively unable to hear it at all. . . . As Christians, we have to cultivate a keen sense of hearing, so that we don't just tune out the things we don't want to hear.

R. C. SPROUL

If you set your heart to pay attention to God, who is indeed present, depend upon this: *God will invade even the unlikely moments of life.*

JAN JOHNSON

Do I read God's Word, pray, hear his Word preached, and still forget what he says?

I want to be in tune with your Spirit, Lord. Help me to listen. Help me to hear.

A HEART OF OBEDIENCE

Circumcise yourselves to the LORD, circumcise your hearts. ❖ Circumcision is that of the heart, in the spirit, and not in the letter; whose praise is not of men, but of God. ❖ Then Mary said, "Here am I, the servant of the Lord; let it be with me according to your word." ❖ When Joseph awoke, he did as the angel commanded and brought Mary home to be his wife. ❖ And he left everything behind, and rose and began to follow Him. ❖ Then He said to the man, "Stretch out your hand." And he stretched it out, and it was restored as whole as the other. ❖ And Asa did that which was good and right in the eyes of the LORD his God. ❖ Fear the LORD, and serve him in sincerity and in truth. . . . as for me and my house, we will serve the LORD. ❖ We show our love for God by obeying his commandments. ❖ We will walk in the name of the LORD our God for ever and ever.

JER. 4:4 NIV; ROM. 2:29; LUKE 1:38 NRSV; MATT. 1:24 TLB; LUKE 5:28 NASB; MATT. 12:13 NKJV; 2 CHRON. 14:2; JOSH. 24:14–15; 1 JOHN 5:3 CEV; MICAH 4:5–6

While Christ bore our guilt which is heavy, it is laid upon us to bear his yoke which is light (Matt. 11:29, 30).

DONALD G. BLOESCH

Our response to God's command must be the response of love not obligation. Love turns the burden into no burden at all.

ROBERT SUGGS

O Lord, may I be directed what to do and what to leave undone; and then may I humbly trust that a blessing will be with me in my various engagements.

ELIZABETH FRY

Is it my intention to always respond to God in obedience?
In all things, Lord, may you direct me that I may be pleasing to you.

RESPONDING TO HIS LOVE

I have loved you with an everlasting love; therefore I have drawn you with lovingkindness. ❖ I led them with cords of compassion, with the bands of love. ❖ You are my portion, O LORD. ❖ Let your people rejoice in your kind deeds. ❖ Grace be with all who have an undying love for our Lord Jesus Christ. ❖ They had sworn with all their heart, and had sought him with their whole desire, and he was found by them. ❖ We know how much God loves us, and we have put our trust in him. God is love, and all who live in love live in God, and God lives in them. And as we live in God, our love grows more perfect. ❖ Therefore if there is any consolation in Christ, if any comfort of love, if any fellowship of the Spirit, if any affection and mercy, fulfill my joy by being like-minded, having the same love, being of one accord, of one mind. ❖ And the Lord direct your hearts into the love of God, and into the patient waiting for Christ.

JER. 31:3 NASB; HOSEA 11:4 RSV; PS. 119:57 NKJV; 2 CHRON. 6:41 TLB; EPH. 6:24 NRSV; 2 CHRON. 15:15 RSV; 1 JOHN 4:16–17 NLT; PHIL. 2:1–2 NKJV; 2 THESS. 3:5

From the outset John makes it clear that our love is not an *originating* love but a *responding* love. "We love because he first loved us" (1 John 4:19).

RICHARD FOSTER

I love you, Lord, not doubtingly, but with absolute certainty. Your Word beat upon my heart until I fell in love with you, and now the universe and everything in it tells me to love you, and tells the same thing to us all, so that we are without excuse.

AUGUSTINE

How can I experience your great love and then give back to you my little, feeble expressions of affection?
I long to love you more, dear Lord Jesus, with all that I am, with every part of me.

IN HIS HANDS

LORD, you have assigned me my portion and my cup; you have made my lot secure. ❖ Does He not see my ways, and count all my steps? ❖ I did not shrink from declaring to you the whole purpose of God. ❖ He prays constantly and earnestly for you, that you may become mature Christians, and may fulfill God's will for you. ❖ In all my prayers, I ask God to make it possible for me to visit you. ❖ I will return again unto you, if God will. ❖ You ought to say, "If the Lord wills, we shall live and we shall do this or that." ❖ As long as he sought the LORD, God made him to prosper. ❖ Because of what Christ has done, we have become gifts to God that he delights in, for as part of God's sovereign plan we were chosen from the beginning to be his, and all things happen just as he decided long ago. ❖ Not everyone who says to Me, "Lord, Lord," shall enter the kingdom of heaven, but he who does the will of My Father in heaven. ❖ And now, may the God of peace, who brought again from the dead our Lord Jesus, equip you with all you need for doing his will.

PS. 16:5 NIV; JOB 31:4 NKJV; ACTS 20:27 NASB; COL. 4:12 PHILLIPS; ROM. 1:10 CEV; ACTS 18:21; JAMES 4:15 RSV; 2 CHRON. 26:5; EPH. 1:11 TLB; MATT. 7:21 NKJV; HEB. 13:20–21 NLT

We do not belong to ourselves, nor should we operate independently of the Spirit of God. Now that we have been converted, we are the Lord's, and as our Master, He has every right to use us in whatever way He chooses. In living out the Christian life, we have one major objective: to "glorify God in [our] body."

CHARLES R. SWINDOLL

Give me the spirit, I pray Thee, to keep myself in continual training for the punctual fulfillment of Thy most holy will.

JOHN BAILLIE

Is it the deepest desire of my heart to follow God wherever he leads me? Keep me humble before you, Lord, waiting on you for your direction.

HE LETS ME KNOW

If you keep on obeying what I have said, you truly are my disciples. You will know the truth, and the truth will set you free. ❖ Just tell me what to do and I will do it, Lord. As long as I live I'll wholeheartedly obey. ❖ There is a God in heaven who reveals mysteries. ❖ He uncovers the deeps out of darkness, and brings deep darkness to light. ❖ It is just as the Scriptures say, "What God has planned for people who love him is more than eyes have seen or ears have heard. It has never even entered our minds!" God's Spirit has shown you everything. ❖ But there is a spirit in man, and the breath of the Almighty gives him understanding. Great men are not always wise, nor do the aged always understand justice. ❖ Jesus said, "I thank you, Father, Lord of heaven and earth, because you have hidden these things from the wise and the intelligent and have revealed them to infants." ❖ May your Will be done here on earth, just as it is in heaven. ❖ For behold, He who forms mountains, and creates the wind, Who declares to man what his thought is . . . the LORD God of hosts is His name.

JOHN 8:31–32 CEV; PS. 119:34 TLB; DAN. 2:28 NASB; JOB 12:22 RSV;
1 COR. 2:9–10 CEV; JOB 32:8–9 NKJV; MATT. 11:25 NRSV; MATT. 6:10 NLT;
AMOS 4:13 NKJV

It has pleased God to reveal Himself and to declare His will unto the Church.
WESTMINSTER CONFESSION

The geography and the details of His plan will be different for each one of us, of course, but the Spirit's sovereign working is far beyond what the human mind can ever imagine [Isa. 55:8–9].

CHARLES R. SWINDOLL

When Jesus taught us to pray to God, he said we should pray "Thy will be done," not "my will be done." Because God has the heart of a heavenly father, this is no risk. We need not fear the will of him who loves us enough to sacrifice his own Son on our behalf.

BRYAN CHAPELL

How amazing, all wise God, that you would want me to know your thoughts, your will.
Open my heart, I pray, to the mysteries of your truth.

SETTING PRIORITIES

Seek first the kingdom of God and His righteousness. ❖ Love the Lord your God with all your heart, soul, and mind. ❖ Love your neighbor as much as you love yourself. ❖ Be diligent to present yourself approved to God as a workman who does not need to be ashamed, handling accurately the word of truth. ❖ Study this Book of the Law continually. Meditate on it day and night. ❖ These words which I command you today shall be in your heart. You shall teach them diligently to your children. ❖ Keep His commandments, listen to His voice, serve Him, and cling to Him. ❖ Keep away from worthless and useless talk. ❖ Take every thought captive to obey Christ. ❖ Never stop praying. ❖ Abhor what is evil. Cling to what is good. ❖ Glorify God in your body. ❖ Contribute to the needs of the saints; extend hospitality to strangers. ❖ Let your light so shine before men, that they may see your good works, and glorify your Father which is in heaven. ❖ Grow in grace, and in the knowledge of our Lord and Saviour Jesus Christ. ❖ Commit your way to the LORD.

MATT. 6:33 NKJV; MATT. 22:37 TLB; MATT. 22:39 TLB; 2 TIM. 2:15 NASB; JOSH. 1:8 NLT; DEUT. 6:6–7 NKJV; DEUT. 13:4 NASB; 2 TIM. 2:16 CEV; 2 COR. 10:5 RSV; 1 THESS. 5:17 CEV; ROM. 12:9 NKJV; 1 COR. 6:20; ROM. 12:13 NRSV; MATT. 5:16; 2 PETER 3:18; PS. 37:5 NKJV

We may wish that God would tell us exactly what to do, where to go, and how to choose. Yet Jesus only requires that we make sure our heart is good, our motives are pure, and our basic direction is right, pointing toward the "true north" of the kingdom of God. . . . In the end what matters most is that we seek first God's kingdom and righteousness.

GERALD L. SITTSER

Spiritual growth is hard work. We are to "press on toward the goal" and "run the race with endurance," to "put to death the deeds of the body" and "pick up our cross." Spiritual progress is made when we make those hard daily choices to be filled with the Spirit and to say no to the flesh.

DOUG BANISTER

Is the way I spend my time pleasing to the Lord?
How do I need to reprioritize my life?

WITH A DESIRE TO PLEASE HIM

Do you really love life? Do you want to be happy? Then stop saying cruel things and quit telling lies. Give up your evil ways and do right, as you find and follow the road that leads to peace. ❖ I have chosen the way of faithfulness, I set your ordinances before me. ❖ Stand therefore, having girded your waist with truth, having put on the breastplate of righteousness, and having shod your feet with the preparation of the gospel of peace. ❖ You must quit being angry, hateful, and evil. You must no longer say insulting or cruel things about others. And stop lying to each other. You have given up your old way of life with its habits. ❖ Pursue righteousness, faith, love, peace with those who call on the Lord out of a pure heart. ❖ My heart is steadfast, O God; I will sing, I will sing praises, even with my soul. ❖ Their hearts are firm, secure in the LORD.

1 PETER 3:10–11 CEV; PS. 119:30 NRSV; EPH. 6:14–15 NKJV; COL. 3:8–9 CEV;
2 TIM. 2:22 NKJV; PS. 108:1 NASB; PS. 112:7 NRSV

That is the perpetual process in human life. Yielding to God, light falls upon the pathway, and creates love. Love suggests obedience. The will, impulsed by love, yields to light. The experience that follows obedience increases love and light, and thus there is perpetual progress, growth, development in the grace that makes men grow in favour with God and man.

G. CAMPBELL MORGAN

That is the source of Jeremiah's living persistence, his creative constancy. He was up before the sun, listening to God's word. Rising early, he was quiet and attentive before his Lord. Long before the yelling started, the mocking, the complaining, there was this centering, discovering, exploring time with God.

EUGENE H. PETERSON

Do I spend enough time with God to center on, discover, explore the things important to him?
What keeps me from moving forward in faith and trusting and living for him?

IN HIM IS JOY

The jailer brought them into his house and set a meal before them; he was filled with joy because he had come to believe in God—he and his whole family. ❖ And they departed from the presence of the council, rejoicing that they were counted worthy to suffer shame for his name. ❖ But let all those rejoice who put their trust in You. ❖ Let the righteous be glad; let them rejoice before God: yea, let them exceedingly rejoice. ❖ He has shown me the path to life, and he makes me glad by being near me. ❖ You have given me greater joy than those who have abundant harvests of grain and wine. ❖ The important thing for us as Christians is not what we eat or drink but stirring up goodness and peace and joy from the Holy Spirit. ❖ Rejoice in the Lord always; again I will say, Rejoice. ❖ My heart is glad, and my soul rejoices. ❖ I have trusted in Your mercy; my heart shall rejoice in Your salvation. I will sing to the LORD, because He has dealt bountifully with me. ❖ I will rejoice greatly in the LORD, my soul will exult in my God; for He has clothed me with garments of salvation, He has wrapped me with a robe of righteousness. ❖ Make a joyful noise unto God, all ye lands: sing forth the honour of his name: make his praise glorious.

ACTS 16:34 NIV; ACTS 5:41; PS. 5:11 NKJV; PS. 68:3; ACTS 2:28 CEV; PS. 4:7 NLT; ROM. 14:17 TLB; PHIL. 4:4 RSV; PS. 16:9 NRSV; PS. 13:5–6 NKJV; ISA. 61:10 NASB; PS. 66:1–2

The main thing is not work for the Lord; it is not suffering in the name of the Lord; it is not witnessing to the Lord; it is not teaching Sunday School for the Lord; it is not being responsible for the sake of the Lord in the community; it is not keeping the Ten Commandments; not loving your neighbor; not observing the golden rule. "The chief end of man is to glorify God and enjoy him forever." Or, in the vocabulary of Psalm 134, "Bless the LORD." All the movements of discipleship arrive at a place where joy is experienced. Every step of assent toward God develops the capacity to enjoy. Not only is there, increasingly, more to be enjoyed, there is steadily the acquired ability to enjoy it.

EUGENE H. PETERSON

Thank you, Lord God, for the joy you give. In you I am glad every moment of the day. In you my rejoicing will increase.
May it soon be true, Lord Jesus, that I find joy in nothing but you.

CELEBRATE YOUR FREEDOM!

Now the Lord is the Spirit, and where the Spirit of the Lord is, there is freedom. ❖ There is therefore now no condemnation to those who are in Christ Jesus, who do not walk according to the flesh, but according to the Spirit. For the law of the Spirit of life in Christ Jesus has made me free from the law of sin and death. ❖ You will know the truth, and the truth will set you free. . . . If the Son gives you freedom, you are free! ❖ "We must celebrate with a feast, for this son of mine was dead and has returned to life. He was lost and is found." So the party began. ❖ It was for freedom that Christ set us free; therefore keep standing firm and do not be subject again to a yoke of slavery. ❖ For you were called to freedom, brothers and sisters. ❖ You are free, but still you are God's servants, and you must not use your freedom as an excuse for doing wrong. ❖ I will walk about in freedom, for I have sought out your precepts. ❖ They will celebrate and sing about your matchless mercy and your power to save. ❖ A cheerful heart has a continual feast. ❖ Make a joyful shout to the LORD, all you lands! Serve the LORD with gladness; come before His presence with singing.

2 COR. 3:17 RSV; ROM. 8:1–2 NKJV; JOHN 8:32, 36 CEV; LUKE 15:23–24 TLB; GAL. 5:1 NASB; GAL. 5:13 NRSV; 1 PETER 2:16 CEV; PS. 119:45 NIV; PS. 145:7 CEV; PROV. 15:15 NASB; PS. 100:1–2 NKJV

Some of us seem so anxious about avoiding hell that we forget to celebrate our journey toward heaven.

PHILIP YANCEY

A lot of Christians are going to get to heaven and find out that God offered so much more than they experienced.

STEVE BROWN

Am I living in freedom in Christ? Am I celebrating?
Help me, Holy Spirit, to live life to the fullest in you.

OUR RESPONSIBILITY

Go therefore and make disciples of all the nations, baptizing them in the name of the Father and of the Son and of the Holy Spirit, teaching them to observe all things that I have commanded you; and lo, I am with you always, even to the end of the age. ❖ And daily in the temple, and in every house, they ceased not to teach and preach Jesus Christ. ❖ Peter and John returned to Jerusalem, preaching the gospel in many Samaritan villages. ❖ And with great power the apostles were giving witness to the resurrection of the Lord Jesus. ❖ We bring you the good news. ❖ Don't be ashamed to speak for our Lord. ❖ Let your light shine before others, so that they may see your good works and give glory to your Father in heaven. ❖ Then I, the King, shall say to those at my right, "Come, blessed of my Father, into the Kingdom prepared for you from the founding of the world." ❖ Then I will turn to those on my left and say, "Away with you, you cursed ones, into the eternal fire prepared for the devil and his demons." ❖ And these shall go away into everlasting punishment: but the righteous into life eternal. ❖ For what is our hope, or joy, or crown of rejoicing? Is it not even you in the presence of our Lord Jesus Christ at His coming? For you are our glory and joy.

MATT. 28:19–20 NKJV; ACTS 5:42; ACTS 8:25 NIV; ACTS 4:33 NASB; ACTS 13:32 RSV; 2 TIM. 1:8 CEV; MATT. 5:16 NRSV; MATT. 25:34 TLB; MATT. 25:41 TLB; MATT. 25:46; 1 THESS. 2:19–20 NKJV

The largest and deepest reference of the Gospel is not to the world or its social problems, but to Eternity and its social obligations.

P. T. FORSYTH

Hell is the recognition of what we have missed.

HELMUT THIELICKE

Am I aware of my responsibility to spread the good news of the gospel? Am I accepting my responsibility?

LOVING OTHERS

Let us love one another, for love is from God; and everyone who loves is born of God and knows God. ❖ If we love other Christians, it proves that we have been delivered from hell and given eternal life. ❖ Live a life filled with love for others, following the example of Christ. ❖ Beloved, if God so loved us, we ought also to love one another. ❖ And the Lord's servant must not be quarrelsome but kindly to every one, an apt teacher, forbearing. ❖ Love each other as brothers and sisters and honor others more than you do yourself. ❖ Do nothing out of selfish ambition or vain conceit, but in humility consider others better than yourselves. ❖ May the Lord make your love for each other and for everyone else grow by leaps and bounds. ❖ You yourselves have been taught by God to love one another. . . . We urge you, beloved, to do so more and more. ❖ Love one another with a pure heart fervently. ❖ All that matters is your faith that makes you love others.

1 JOHN 4:7 NASB; 1 JOHN 3:14 TLB; EPH 5:2 NLT; 1 JOHN 4:11; 2 TIM. 2:24 RSV; ROM. 12:10 CEV; PHIL. 2:3 NIV; 1 THESS. 3:12 CEV; 1 THESS. 4:9–10 NRSV; 1 PETER 1:22; GAL. 5:6 CEV

A gospel that taught no responsibility for your neighbor could not be accepted as the true gospel.

SPENCER PERKINS

Most of the church's ministry takes place not when the church is gathered, but when it is scattered.

BOWMAN AND HALL

Do I love others enough to feel responsible to them?
Am I following Christ's example of boundless, selfless love?

BE A COMFORTER

Remember those who are in prison, as though you were in prison with them; those who are being tortured, as though you yourselves were being tortured. ❖ I was naked and you clothed me, I was sick and you visited me, I was in prison and you came to me. ❖ Whenever you did it for any of my people, no matter how unimportant they seemed, you did it for me. ❖ Love is patient, love is kind. ❖ Is this not the fast that I have chosen: To loose the bonds of wickedness, to undo the heavy burdens, to let the oppressed go free, and that you break every yoke? Is it not to share your bread with the hungry, and that you bring to your house the poor who are cast out? ❖ [God] comforts us in all our tribulation, that we may be able to comfort those who are in any trouble, with the comfort with which we ourselves are comforted by God. ❖ Pleasant words are as an honeycomb, sweet to the soul, and health to the bones. ❖ Ruth said, "Do not urge me to leave you or turn back from following you; for where you go, I will go, and where you lodge, I will lodge. Your people shall be my people, and your God, my God." ❖ She loves you more than seven sons . . . would love you. ❖ We did everything for you that parents would do for their own children. We begged, encouraged, and urged each of you to live in a way that would honor God.

> HEB. 13:3 NRSV; MATT. 25:36 RSV; MATT. 25:40 CEV; 1 COR. 13:4 NASB; ISA. 58:6–7 NKJV; 2 COR. 1:4 NKJV; PROV. 16:24; RUTH 1:16 NASB; RUTH 4:15 CEV; 1 THESS. 2:11–12 CEV

God does not comfort us to make us comfortable, but to make us comforters.

J. H. JOWETT

Dear Father of mankind, make me the human channel, so far as in me lies, through which Thy divine love and pity may reach the hearts and lives of a few of those who are nearest to me. Amen.

JOHN BAILLIE

Do I take advantage of opportunities to comfort others?
Am I so busy with my own life that I don't notice when others need my
*   comfort—the comfort that God has given me and expects me to share?*

BLESSING OTHERS

Now thanks be to God who always leads us in triumph in Christ, and through us diffuses the fragrance of His knowledge in every place. ❖ Be careful how you behave among your unsaved neighbors; for then, even if they are suspicious of you and talk against you, they will end up praising God for your good works when Christ returns. ❖ Do not repay evil for evil or abuse for abuse; but, on the contrary, repay with a blessing. It is for this that you were called—that you might inherit a blessing. ❖ I desire you to insist on these things, so that those who have believed in God may be careful to apply themselves to good deeds. ❖ Always be ready to give a defense to everyone who asks you a reason for the hope that is in you, with meekness and fear. ❖ Let your speech always be with grace, seasoned, as it were, with salt, so that you may know how you should respond to each person. ❖ You are to live clean, innocent lives as children of God in a dark world full of crooked and perverse people. Let your lives shine brightly before them. ❖ For we are what he has made us, created in Christ Jesus for good works, which God prepared beforehand to be our way of life.

2 Cor. 2:14 nkjv; 1 Peter 2:12 tlb; 1 Peter 3:9 nrsv; Titus 3:8 rsv; 1 Peter 3:15 nkjv; Col. 4:6 nasb; Phil. 2:15 nlt; Eph. 2:10 nrsv

When we live as Jesus did [in love, holiness, obedience], in his power and with his presence, seekers will be drawn to us.

Rebecca Manley Pippert

Our lives should be, according to our Lord's plans, quiet but steadily flowing streams of blessing, which through our prayers and intercessions should reach our whole environment.

O. Hallesby

Do others like to have me around? Do I encourage, honor, bless them? Am I careful to ignore insults and to bless the insulter instead?

SERVANTS

For the ministry of this service is not only fully supplying the needs of the saints, but is also overflowing through many thanksgivings to God. ❖ You are serving the Lord Christ. ❖ I have freely and happily become a servant of any and all so that I can win them to Christ. ❖ For we preach not ourselves, but Christ Jesus the Lord; and ourselves your servants for Jesus' sake. ❖ My friends, you were chosen to be free. So don't use your freedom as an excuse to do anything you want. Use it as an opportunity to serve each other with love. ❖ Like good stewards of the manifold grace of God, serve one another with whatever gift each of you has received. ❖ Be subject to one another out of reverence for Christ. ❖ Do not forget to do good and to share, for with such sacrifices God is well pleased. ❖ Serve wholeheartedly, as if you were serving the Lord, not men. ❖ God is always fair. He will remember how you helped his people in the past and how you are still helping them. You belong to God, and he won't forget the love you have shown his people. ❖ If you give even a cup of cold water to one of the least of my followers, you will surely be rewarded. ❖ Whoever desires to become great among you, let him be your servant. And whoever desires to be first among you, let him be your slave—just as the Son of Man did not come to be served, but to serve, and to give His life a ransom for many.

2 COR. 9:12 NASB; COL. 3:24 RSV; 1 COR. 9:19 TLB; 2 COR. 4:5; GAL. 5:13 CEV; 1 PETER 4:10 NRSV; EPH. 5:21 RSV; HEB. 13:16 NKJV; EPH. 6:7 NIV; HEB. 6:10 CEV; MATT. 10:42 NLT; MATT. 20:26–28 NKJV

We are called to love, to serve, to identify need and to respond. . . . The Christian must be the one who loves, cares and listens first. We all can take initiative, whether quietly or openly.

REBECCA MANLEY PIPPERT

If the attitude of servanthood is learned, by attending to God as Lord, then serving others will develop as a very natural way of life.

EUGENE H. PETERSON

Do I live to serve others as Christ did?
Be Lord of my life, dear Jesus, so that my first inclination will be to care for the needs of others. May they see you in me.

JUSTICE

Do you mighty people talk only to oppose justice? Don't you ever judge fairly? You are always planning evil. ❖ Now the LORD saw, and it was displeasing in His sight that there was no justice. ❖ "What do you mean by crushing my people, by grinding the face of the poor?" says the Lord GOD of hosts. ❖ He expected them to yield a crop of justice but found bloodshed instead. He expected righteousness, but the cries of deep oppression met his ears. ❖ You people are in for trouble! You have made cruel and unfair laws. ❖ [You] deprive the innocent of their rights! ❖ [You] have neglected the weightier matters of the law: justice and mercy and faith. ❖ Let justice roll on like a river, righteousness like a never-failing stream!

Ps. 58:1–2 CEV; ISA. 59:15 NASB; ISA. 3:15 RSV; ISA. 5:7 TLB; ISA 10:1–2 CEV; ISA. 5:23 NRSV; MATT. 23:23 NRSV; AMOS 5:24 NIV

We cannot speak of love and at the same time be part of institutional structures that perpetuate injustice.

RICHARD FOSTER

The contribution of the civil rights movement to the black man's struggle for justice and equality is one that is undeniably great. And this is so, because those who led the movement were committed men and women. They were committed to the cause. And to the struggle.

But how sad that so few individuals equally committed to Jesus Christ ever became a part of that movement. For what all that political activity needed—and lacked—was spiritual input. Even now, I do not understand why so many evangelicals find a sense of commitment to civil rights and to Jesus Christ an "either-or" proposition.

JOHN PERKINS

When it is within my power to encourage justice, do I keep silent?
When I should respond in righteousness, do I turn away?

WHO IS MY NEIGHBOR?

They judge not with justice the cause of the fatherless, to make it prosper, and they do not defend the rights of the needy. ❖ All who are cruel and arrogant will be gone forever. Those who live by crime will disappear, together with everyone who tells lies in court and keeps innocent people from getting a fair trial. ❖ You completely forget about justice and the love of God. ❖ Let none of you imagine evil against his brother in your heart. ❖ There will be no mercy to those who have shown no mercy. But if you have been merciful, then God's mercy toward you will win out over his judgment against you. ❖ He has told you, O man, what is good; and what does the LORD require of you but to do justice, to love kindness, and to walk humbly with your God? ❖ Defend the poor and fatherless; do justice to the afflicted and needy. Deliver the poor and needy; free them from the hand of the wicked. ❖ Love your neighbors as much as you love yourself. . . . Who are my neighbors? ❖ The rich and the poor have a common bond, the LORD is the maker of them all.

JER. 5:28 RSV; ISA. 29:20–21 CEV; LUKE 11:42 TLB; ZECH. 7:10; JAMES 2:13 TLB; MICAH 6:8 NASB; PS. 82:3–4 NKJV; LUKE 10:27, 29 CEV; PROV. 22:2 NASB

Nowadays legalism has changed its focus. In a thoroughly secular culture, the church is likely to show ungrace through a spirit of moral superiority or a fierce attitude toward opponents in the "culture wars."

PHILIP YANCEY

The Gospel is in reality a world-changing message, but it has been reduced to a world-resisting message by an overemphasis on individual salvation to the neglect of community responsibility.

CARL HENRY

Am I able to consider that person who is so unlike me as my neighbor?
Almighty God, teach me mercy. Teach me to love without distinction the person of a different race, a different political party, a different culture, a different generation, a different religion.

FORGIVE EACH OTHER

Be gentle and ready to forgive; never hold grudges. Remember, the Lord forgave you, so you must forgive others. ❖ Always be humble and gentle. Patiently put up with each other and love each other. ❖ Forgive us our sins, just as we have forgiven those who have sinned against us. ❖ For if you forgive others their trespasses, your heavenly Father will also forgive you; but if you do not forgive others, neither will your Father forgive your trespasses. ❖ [Love] is not arrogant or rude. Love does not insist on its own way; it is not irritable or resentful. ❖ Be kind to one another, tenderhearted, forgiving one another, just as God in Christ forgave you. ❖ Above all things have fervent love for one another, for "love will cover a multitude of sins." ❖ Finally, all of you, have unity of spirit, sympathy, love for one another, a tender heart, and a humble mind.

COL. 3:13 TLB; EPH. 4:2 CEV; MATT. 6:12 NLT; MATT. 6:14–15 NRSV; 1 COR. 13:5 RSV; EPH. 4:32 NKJV; 1 PETER 4:8 NKJV; 1 PETER 3:8 NRSV

If you want to love people, you've got to understand them. Sometimes a lion will bite its trainer and people will ask, "Why don't you kill it?" The trainer will say, "Because *I* made the mistake." The animal was just doing what came natural. It's strange that people understand that about animals but not about human beings. You've just got to forgive them.

GEORGE FOREMAN

Study always that thou be patient in suffering of other men's defaults, for thou hast many things in thyself that others do suffer of thee, and if thou cannot make thyself to be as thou wouldst, how mayest thou then look to have another to be ordered in all things after thy will?

THOMAS À KEMPIS

"To love a person," said Dostoevsky, "means to see him as God intended him to be."

PHILIP YANCEY

Do I expect friends and family to be without sin, while I am indulgent of my own?
Help me to learn from you, dear Lord, how to forgive.

REAL LOVE

You can tell God's children from the devil's children, because those who belong to the devil refuse to do right or to love each other. From the beginning you were told that we must love each other. . . . Our love for each other proves that we have gone from death to life. But if you don't love each other, you are still under the power of death. ❖ He who does not love does not know God, for God is love. ❖ If instead of showing love among yourselves you are always critical and catty, watch out! Beware of ruining each other. ❖ Those who do not love a brother or sister whom they have seen, cannot love God whom they have not seen. The commandment we have from him is this: those who love God must love their brothers and sisters also. ❖ He who says he abides in Him ought himself also to walk just as He walked. ❖ But the one who hates his brother is in the darkness and walks in the darkness, and does not know where he is going because the darkness has blinded his eyes. ❖ But if we really are living in the same light in which he eternally exists, then we have true fellowship with each other, and the blood which he shed for us keeps us clean from any and every sin.

1 JOHN 3:10–11, 14 CEV; 1 JOHN 4:7–8 NKJV; GAL. 5:15 TLB; 1 JOHN 4:20–21 NRSV; 1 JOHN 2:6 NKJV; 1 JOHN 2:11 NASB; 1 JOHN 1:7 PHILLIPS

I see the confusion of politics and religion as one of the greatest barriers to grace. C. S. Lewis observed that almost all crimes of Christian history have come about when religion is confused with politics. Politics, which always runs by the rules of ungrace, allures us to trade away grace for power, a temptation the church has often been unable to resist.

PHILIP YANCEY

Let us hope and pray that the vast intelligence, imagination, humor, and courage of Americans will not fail us. Either we learn a new language of empathy and compassion, or the fire this time will consume us all.

CORNEL WEST

Take from me, Lord, anything that is incompatible with being your child. I want nothing to hinder my relationship with Jesus; therefore, I will make every effort to keep nothing from hindering my relationship with others.

A COMMAND

"You must love the Lord your God with all your heart, all your soul, and all your mind." This is the first and greatest commandment. A second is equally important: "Love your neighbor as yourself." All the other commandments and all the demands of the prophets are based on these two commandments. ❖ The entire law is summed up in a single command: "Love your neighbor as yourself." ❖ A new commandment I give to you, that you love one another; as I have loved you, that you also love one another. ❖ Choose good instead of evil! See that justice is done. ❖ I command you, you shall open wide your hand to your brother, to the needy and to the poor, in the land. ❖ Don't just pretend that you love others: really love them. ❖ God wants us to have faith in his Son Jesus Christ and to love each other. This is also what Jesus taught us to do. ❖ The goal of our instruction is love from a pure heart and a good conscience and a sincere faith. ❖ This is love, that we walk according to His commandments.

MATT. 22:37–40 NLT; GAL. 5:14 NIV; JOHN 13:34 NKJV; AMOS 5:15 CEV;
DEUT. 15:11 RSV; ROM. 12:9 TLB; 1 JOHN 3:23 CEV; 1 TIM. 1:5 NASB;
2 JOHN 6 NKJV

Every volunteer in [Martin Luther] King's organization pledged to follow eight principles, including these: meditate daily on the teachings and life of Jesus, walk and talk in the manner of love, and observe with both friend and foe the ordinary rules of courtesy.

PHILIP YANCEY

Because social justice is a divine mandate, liturgical life can never be divorced from it.

RICHARD FOSTER

Am I actually putting into practice what I believe to be your command—to love others?
It's easy to agree to your command and think that in my agreement I am loving, when in fact my actions show that I don't agree at all.

WE NEED EACH OTHER

You are better off to have a friend than to be all alone. . . . If you fall, your friend can help you up. ❖ Let mutual love continue. ❖ Love each other with genuine affection, and take delight in honoring each other. ❖ Rejoice with those who rejoice, and weep with those who weep. Be of the same mind toward one another. Do not set your mind on high things, but associate with the humble. Do not be wise in your own opinion. ❖ If you see your enemy trying to get his donkey onto its feet beneath a heavy load, you must not go on by but must help him. ❖ And let us not be weary in well doing: for in due season we shall reap, if we faint not. As we have therefore opportunity, let us do good unto all men, especially unto them who are of the household of faith. ❖ At this time your abundance may be a supply for their want, that their abundance also may be a supply for your want: that there may be equality. ❖ Let us consider how to stimulate one another to love and good deeds, . . . encouraging one another. ❖ The love of every one of you for one another is increasing. ❖ Share what you have with others. God takes particular pleasure in acts of worship—a different kind of "sacrifice"—that take place in kitchen and workplace and on the streets. ❖ You shall be a blessing.

> ECCL. 4:9–10 CEV; HEB. 13:1 NRSV; ROM. 12:10 NLT; ROM. 12:15–16 NKJV; EXOD. 23:5 TLB; GAL. 6:9–10; 2 COR. 8:14; HEB. 10:24–25 NASB; 2 THESS. 1:3 RSV; HEB. 13:16 THE MESSAGE; ZECH. 8:13 NKJV

Whenever we develop significant friendships with those who are not like us culturally, we become broader, wiser persons.

RICHARD FOSTER

Christian brotherhood is not an ideal which we must realize; it is rather a reality created by God in Christ in which we may participate.

DIETRICH BONHOEFFER

Do I treasure all of my brothers and sisters, regardless of their ethnic background or position in society?

REMEMBER HIS MERCY

"The waters surrounded me, even to my soul; the deep closed around me; weeds were wrapped around my head. I went down to the moorings of the mountains; the earth with its bars closed behind me forever; yet You have brought up my life from the pit, O Lord, my God. When my soul fainted within me, I remembered the Lord; and my prayer went up to You, into Your holy temple." . . . So the Lord spoke to the fish, and it vomited Jonah onto dry land. ❖ But this I call to mind, and therefore I have hope: The steadfast love of the Lord never ceases, his mercies never come to an end; they are new every morning; great is thy faithfulness. "The Lord is my portion," says my soul, "therefore I will hope in him." ❖ Speak to the Israelites, and tell them to make fringes on the corners of their garments throughout their generations and to put a blue cord on the fringe at each corner. You have the fringe so that, when you see it, you will remember all the commandments of the Lord and do them, and not follow the lust of your own heart and your own eyes. So you shall remember and do all my commandments, and you shall be holy to your God. ❖ You will praise me for the wonderful things I have done. ❖ You must not forget.

Jonah 2:5–7, 10 nkjv; Lam. 3:21–24 rsv; Num. 15:38–40 nrsv; Joel 2:26 cev; Deut. 25:19 nasb

After Jonah, you could never trust God not to be merciful again.
Robert Frost

When Jesus was on the cross, he was thinking about me. If he had been thinking about himself and the agony he was going through, he would have called the angels to rescue him. But he was thinking about me, my need of a Savior, and my helplessness. His thoughts about me kept him on the cross until it was finished.
MMS

How many times have I been like Jonah, disobedient, running from God, and he in his mercy brought me back to him?
How little I think of the great sacrifice that made our reconciliation possible!

GOD SHOWS HIMSELF

For we did not follow cleverly devised myths when we made known to you the power and coming of our Lord Jesus Christ, but we were eyewitnesses of his majesty. . . . He received honor and glory from God the Father and the voice was borne to him by the Majestic Glory, "This is my beloved Son, with whom I am well pleased." ❖ And [Jesus] was transfigured before them: and his face did shine as the sun, and his raiment was white as the light. ❖ Then Jesus cried out and said, "He who believes in Me, believes not in Me but in Him who sent Me. And he who sees Me sees Him who sent Me." ❖ I and the Father are one. ❖ The Father is in me, and I in him. ❖ The words I say are not my own but are from my Father who lives in me. And he does his work through me. ❖ For in Christ all the fullness of the Deity lives in bodily form. ❖ I am the First and the Last. I am He who lives, and was dead, and behold, I am alive forevermore. ❖ I am the first, and I am the last; and beside me there is no God.

2 PETER 1:16–17 RSV; MATT. 17:2; JOHN 12:44–45 NKJV; JOHN 10:30 NASB; JOHN 10:38; JOHN 14:10 TLB; COL. 2:9 NIV; REV. 1:17–18 NKJV; ISA. 44:6

In Christ and by Christ, God effects complete self-disclosure, although He shows Himself not to reason but to faith and love. Faith is an organ of knowledge, and love an organ of experience. God came to us in the incarnation; in atonement He reconciled us to Himself, and by faith and love we enter and lay hold on Him.

A. W. TOZER

From A to Z (Rev. 1:8), Jesus was the divine alphabet spelling out God in such a way that even the most elementary of us could grasp His essence. This Word, John reveals to us, was *with* God, face-to-face, in eternity past. Yet in some mysterious way, this Word was not only with God but *was* God. Jesus was not simply the revealer of God but God Himself revealed.

CHARLES R. SWINDOLL

I long to know you better, Lord Jesus. May my faith and love increase. Thank you, Everlasting Father, Prince of Peace, for wanting me to know you intimately.

HIS DAILY PRESENCE

He will come to us like the rain, like the spring rain watering the earth.
❖ I have set the LORD always before me: because he is at my right hand,
I shall not be moved. ❖ We were burdened beyond measure, above
strength, so that we despaired even of life. . . . Yes, we had the sentence
of death in ourselves, that we should not trust in ourselves but in God
who raises the dead. ❖ Listen from heaven and forgive the sins of your
people, and teach them what is right; and send rain upon this land that
you have given to your people as their own property. ❖ If we live in the
Spirit, let us also walk in the Spirit. ❖ You hold me by my right hand.
You will guide me with Your counsel, and afterward receive me to glory.
❖ You have made known to me the ways of life; you will make me full
of gladness with your presence. ❖ [You] set me before Your face forever.
❖ Having therefore these promises, dearly beloved, let us cleanse
ourselves from all filthiness of the flesh and spirit, perfecting holiness
in the fear of God. ❖ We pray this so that the name of our Lord Jesus
may be glorified in you, and you in him, according to the grace of our
God and the Lord Jesus Christ.

HOSEA 6:3 NASB; PS. 16:8; 2 COR. 1:8–9 NKJV; 2 CHRON. 6:27 TLB;
GAL. 5:25; PS. 73:23–24 NKJV; ACTS 2:28 NRSV; PS. 41:12 NKJV; 2 COR. 7:1;
2 THESS. 1:12 NIV

Souls who can recognize God in the most trivial, the most grievous and the most
mortifying things that happen to them in their lives, honour everything equally
with delight and rejoicing, and welcome with open arms what others dread and
avoid.

JEAN-PIERRE DE CAUSSADE

God's goal in interfering with our lives to bring about such change is very simple:
He wants us to discover our real identities.

MATTSON AND MILLER

*Do I welcome difficult times, knowing that through them God is perfecting
me?*
Have I discovered my real identity?

FACE-TO-FACE

As for me, I shall behold your face in righteousness; when I awake I shall be satisfied, beholding your likeness. ❖ In my flesh shall I see God. ❖ Pursue peace with all people, and holiness, without which no one will see the Lord. ❖ The throne of God and of the Lamb shall be in [the city]; and his servants shall serve him: and they shall see his face. ❖ I saw also the Lord sitting upon a throne, high and lifted up, and his train filled the temple. ❖ He said, "I am the God of your father, the God of Abraham, the God of Isaac, and the God of Jacob." And Moses hid his face, for he was afraid to look at God. ❖ With [Moses] I speak mouth to mouth, even openly, and not in dark sayings, and he beholds the form of the LORD. ❖ And [Moses] said, "Please, show me Your glory." Then He said, "I will make all My goodness pass before you, and I will proclaim the name of the LORD before you." . . . But He said, "You cannot see My face; for no man shall see Me, and live." ❖ Blessed are the pure in heart: for they shall see God.

Ps. 17:15 NRSV; JOB 19:26; HEB. 12:14 NKJV; REV. 22:3–4; ISA. 6:1; EXOD. 3:6 RSV; NUM. 12:8 NASB; EXOD. 33:18–20 NKJV; MATT. 5:8

God is also invisible to you; his revealed Word truly reflects his mind and heart, but not in a way adequate to the reality. When Christ comes again, however, we shall know the divine mind and heart as fully and directly as ours are known now.

J. I. PACKER

Yet the goal of every Christian is to be allowed to see what was denied to Moses. We want to see him face-to-face. We want to bask in the radiant glory of his divine countenance.

R. C. SPROUL

How glorious it will be to stand in your presence, to see you face-to-face! Am I preparing for that great day when I will behold his face?

HE'S COMING BACK

This same Jesus, which is taken up from you into heaven, shall so come in like manner as ye have seen him go into heaven. ❖ You too, be ready; for the Son of Man is coming at an hour that you do not expect. ❖ Take heed, watch and pray; for you do not know when the time is. ❖ For the Son of man is to come with his angels in the glory of his Father. ❖ You also must be patient. Strengthen your hearts, for the coming of the Lord is near. ❖ They shall see the Son of man coming in the clouds of heaven with power and great glory. ❖ Look, he is coming with the clouds, and every eye will see him, even those who pierced him; and all the peoples of the earth will mourn because of him. So shall it be! ❖ You have every grace and blessing; every spiritual gift and power for doing his will are yours during this time of waiting for the return of our Lord Jesus Christ. ❖ Watch for his return!

ACTS 1:11; LUKE 12:40 NASB; MARK 13:33 NKJV; MATT. 16:27 RSV; JAMES 5:8 NRSV; MATT. 24:30; REV. 1:7 NIV; 1 COR. 1:7 TLB; MARK 13:37 NLT

He went up to heaven unopposed; no high priests, nor scribes, nor Pharisees, nor even one of the rabble opposed his ascension; it were ridiculous to suppose that they could; and when he comes a second time none will stand against him. His adversaries shall perish; as the fat of rams shall they melt away in his presence. When he cometh he shall break rebellious nations with a rod of iron, for his force shall be irresistible in that day.

CHARLES H. SPURGEON

. . . the doctrine of the second coming of Christ can bring warning to the lost and encouragement to persevere to the found.

JILL BRISCOE

I'll be back!

How amazing! How awesome! How exciting!
Come, Lord Jesus!